RESEARCH IN THE SOCIOLOGY OF HEALTH CARE

Volume 5 • 1987

INTERNATIONAL COMPARISONS OF HEALTH SERVICES

RESEARCH IN THE SOCIOLOGY OF HEALTH CARE

A Research Annual

INTERNATIONAL COMPARISONS OF HEALTH SERVICES

Editor: JULIUS A. ROTH
    Department of Sociology
    University of California, Davis

VOLUME 5 • 1987

 JAI PRESS INC.

Greenwich, Connecticut   *London, England*

CONTENTS

LIST OF CONTRIBUTORS

Hans A. Baer

Department of Sociology and
    Anthropology
University of Arkansas
Little Rock

Wolfgang Ertler

Austrian Federal Institute for Public
    Health
Vienna

Deborah Frederick

Department of Behavioral Sciences
University of Michigan
Dearborn

Ruth Breece Pickard

Health Care Financing
    Administration
Office of Research and
    Demonstrations
Baltimore

Marilyn M. Rosenthal

Department of Behavioral Sciences
University of Michigan
Dearborn

Lisbeth Sachs

Department of Communication
    Studies
Linköping University
Sweden

Hannes Schmidl

Austrian Federal Institute for Public
    Health
Vienna

Ingeborg P. Spruit   Institute of Social Medicine
                                        Leiden University
                                        The Netherlands

Johannes M. Treytl   Austrian Federal Institute for Public
                                            Health
                                        Vienna

Helmut Wintersberger   European Centre for Social Welfare
                                            Training and Research
                                        Vienna

INTRODUCTION

The papers in this volume are intended to demonstrate differences in the provisions of health services in different countries or in the same country for different nationality groups. Three of the papers are written by European authors and three by American authors. They all make comparisons between a given medical situation in the United States and in foreign countries, from one country to another (or others), or one nationality group to another. No particular aspects of health services were selected for the theme of this volume, so the breadth of focus varies considerably. A comparison of health service systems in seven countries with different socioeconomic settings is made in the Ertler et al. paper. The patterns of physician distribution in four countries are examined in the Rosenthal paper. The Baer paper provides a historical analysis of the development of osteopathy in the United Kingdom and the United States. The Pickard paper examines the position of "mid-level" practitioners in the Soviet Union and in the United States. The two "internal" papers—Spruit in the Netherlands,

Sachs in Sweden—compare the way in which Third World guestworkers fare in relation to the native population in various aspects of health care.

Each of the authors provides some explanations for the differences they found; these, in turn, make possible projections into the future. In this sense, these papers represent an advance over most comparative statements in the international health services sphere.

In addition to weaving explanations into the presentation of their discussion, all the authors provide systematic lists of an explanatory scheme at some point, usually near the end of each paper. For example:

- *Osteopathy* (Baer)—Reasons this occupation is more medicalized in the United States than in the United Kingdom.
- *Physician distribution* (Rosenthal and Frederick)—Factors associated with the reduction of maldistribution.
- *Immigrant populations* (Spruit; Sachs)—Reasons for problems of Western medical providers dealing with Third World immigrants.
- *Mid-level practitioners* (Pickard)—Reasons for different directions of feldshers and physicians' assistants in terms of the organizational conditions in each country.
- *Characteristics of medical services and the likelihood of change under various socioeconomic conditions* (Ertler et al.)

	Industrial	Developing
Capitalist		
Socialist		

Although this opening statement describes what I regard as the main thrust of these papers, the authors also make some other useful points. When appropriate, they grapple with difficulties of measurement and definition; for example, when does the distribution of physicians become "maldistribution" in the countries investigated? They point out, not only differences, but also basic similarities of circumstances and behavior between regions and peoples; for example, the ways in which the response to medical services is the same for Swedish women and for Turkish women in Sweden. And when comparing different styles of therapy and the delivery of services, they point out that various belief systems are supported by the fact than *anything* will work most of the time.

Julius A. Roth
Series Editor

THE SOCIAL DIMENSIONS OF HEALTH AND HEALTH CARE:
AN INTERNATIONAL COMPARISON

Wolfgang Ertler, Hannes Schmidl,
Johannes M. Treytl and Helmut Wintersberger

A comparative analysis of health systems often concentrates exclusively on comparing health indicators on an international scale. In this article, considerable attention is devoted to the general socioeconomic and political context influencing health and health policy. We recognize that, at least in developed countries, there is some margin for autonomous health policy which is, however, limited by socioeconomic and political restraints [22]. The relations between health and the societal context will be analyzed and demonstrated in several national studies of three developing countries (Cuba, Nicaragua and Bangladesh), three Western industrialized countries (Austria, the United Kingdom and Italy) and one socialist country (German Democratic Republic).

Research in the Sociology of Health Care, Volume 5, pages 1-62.
Copyright © 1987 by JAI Press Inc.
All rights of reproduction in any form reserved.
ISBN: 0-89232-597-6

I. COMPARATIVE ANALYSIS OF HEALTH CARE SYSTEMS

The definition and evaluation of the health care system depends first of all on the underlying concept of health and disease. The situation of a national health system and its perspective may be better assessed by comparing it with the respective situation and trends in other countries. However, to avoid premature and wrong conclusions, an international study requires adequate consideration of external determinants of the health system, its historical, economic, social and political context, as described in the second section of this paper. Two of the several typologies of health systems are described in the last section in terms of their respective societal context.

A. A Conceptualization of Health and Disease

Roughly, three different concepts of health and disease may be distinguished [2].

1. *Health as the mere absence of disease in individuals.* This rather restricted notion of disease corresponds to a similarly restricted view of the health care system which strongly emphasizes the curative intervention of the medical system of the physician as well as financial benefits from the social insurance system (e.g., sick pay, invalidity pension).
2. *Disease as an epidemiological problem.* According to this concept, health policy focuses on monitoring the distribution of diseases in society, determining potential risk factors and taking action in the form of vaccination and other measures of medical prevention, as well as planning and distribution of medical resources (physicians, hospitals, etc.).
3. *Health and disease in a socio-historical view.* This concept is linked to the Marxist idea of social formation; each stage of economic and social development generates a specific configuration for the emergence of diseases and produces specific ways and methods to cope with them. This approach places emphasis on occupational disease and nonspecific diseases influenced by the organization of labor and production, as well as on preventive measures going beyond mere medical prevention (e.g., labor and social policies, education, housing, transportation, environmental protection). In this sociohistorical view of disease, health promotion becomes a predominantly political issue.

B. Health and Health Care

It is not meaningful to ask in general terms which of the above concepts of health and disease is the best, as this depends on the respective application. The first approach is the most limited and may therefore be very useful for restricted purposes (e.g., in the daily practice of curative intervention). The second concept has a wider scope but is still limited (it may be useful for health authorities). The sociohistorical notion, finally, leads to a very general and complex view. It should be applied only if generality and complexity are aimed at. However, physicians, health administrators and politicians should always be able to apply this concept whenever they arrive at the limits of the other approaches. This necessity is disregarded in most (although not all) Western European countries where training and education of medical doctors is based exclusively on the individual and curative approaches.

The World Health Organization (WHO) definition of health, which also includes the social dimension, is rather close to the sociohistorical concept. Nevertheless, it has been interpreted and applied by governments—if at all—more in the context of the epidemiological view. The WHO/UNICEF Conference on Primary Health Care (Alma-Ata, 1978) explicitly stressed the predominantly social and political nature of health and health care.

In a multinational comparison, the sociohistorical concept goes beyond the traditional approach restricted to comparisons of the legal and institutional frameworks and/or quantitative health indicators. The production and management of diseases are to be considered in their respective economic, social and political contexts. Not only must the different systems of medical care be compared but also the different societal frameworks and the relations between the medical care system on the one hand and their societal context on the other.

For a characterization of the social context we propose the following groups of indicators:

Natural Indicators

Natural indicators (e.g., geographical, ecological factors) create different conditions for the generation and distribution of diseases. The epidemiological spectrum of tropical countries is quite different from that of countries with a moderate climate. We do not assert that all the differences can be explained by natural factors. There is, however, a variety of risks and diseases in tropical countries which may have natural explanations. This makes it necessary to orient medical research and assistance in such countries toward the specific risks and diseases affecting the population.

Historical and Sociocultural Factors

These comprise a rather heterogeneous set of factors, such as mode and content of socialization and life-styles (nutrition, drugs), value systems in general (attitudes toward life and death as well as toward work), and in particular the traditions in health care (popular medicine, etc.).

State and Development of Productive Forces

The technological and economic development of a country—usually expressed in productivity indicators or per capita GNP—determines the health of a population as well as a society's potential for managing diseases. Improved living standards (food and housing conditions) in industrialized countries have generally led to an increase of life-expectancy and other health indicators. On the other hand, improved living standards and changes in the work and general environment have created new health risks which to some extent question the positive development toward better health achieved during the last hundred years. The impact of economic and technological developments on the health care system is also contradictory. In principle, scientific-technological progress also means medical progress, and some previously incurable diseases have become curable. Yet belief in the unlimited capabilities of modern medicine through scientific-technological and pharmaceutical progress has led to some mistaken political decisions.

Relations of Production

Contrary to the productive forces which can be described by quantitative indicators, the relations of production are of a qualitative nature. In line with the Marxist approach of classifying relations of production according to predominant property relations in society, we distinguish between pre-capitalist, capitalist and socialist relations of production. In our view, it is difficult to establish a direct link between the relations of production and the morbidity/mortality profile of society. On the one hand the morbidity/mortality profile has changed fundamentally from the early to the mature stage of capitalism (due to the development of productive forces); on the other hand there are no marked structural differences between the morbidity/mortality profiles of developed capitalist and socialist countries. However, we shall show that there is a strong connection between relations of production and the types of health care systems.

Ideological Superstructure, Potential of Reform and Innovation

The above indicators were appropriate for describing the state of a social or a health care system and allowing a static comparison of the two systems. In contrast, the ideological dimension, the potential of reform and innovation stresses dynamic developments and changes of the system. Changes may be caused by external events such as wars and other catastrophes (e.g., the introduction of the national health service in the United Kingdom after World War II or the extension of the social welfare system in Cyprus after the Turkish invasion). Changes may also be the outcome of internal conflicts, pressures or struggles. For example, the labor movement in most capitalist countries had been struggling against the most brutal forms of health deprivation at the workplace and for the introduction of more egalitarian medical care. In many countries this struggle has brought forth compensatory social reforms (like the introduction of labor inspection and social insurance by Bismarck in Germany). In other cases such changes and reforms were not just of the compensatory type, implemented by

bourgeois governments, but clearly showed the handwriting of the labor movement: The social reforms of the Austro-Marxists in the so-called Red Vienna of
the 1920s and 1930s are an example of a highly developed workers' culture and a
unique social housing program which emphasized the preventive nature of social
policies. Another example is the "Workers' Medicine" movement of the 1970s
in Italy, in which the trade unions launched a campaign against diseases directly
or indirectly connected with the modern capitalist production. The new aspect of
this approach was the rejection of traditional methods of delegation (to labor
inspectors, company doctors or the management) and the promotion of direct
workers' control of the working environment, work organization, work safety
and health.

However, such strategies are only viable if the working class has achieved a
certain degree of political and cultural maturity and hegemony. The concept of
hegemony was already used by Lenin, but it was the merit of the Italian philoso-
pher Antonio Gramsci to adapt it to the needs of Western European countries.
Hegemony is cultural and political leadership. Usually the ruling class is also the
hegemonic class (e.g., bourgeois dominance corresponds to bourgeois hegemony). There are, however, cases where dominance and hegemony are separated.
This was the case in "Red Vienna" surrounded by a bourgeois conservative
Austria in the 1920s and 1930s, and this has also been the case with Italy at least
during some periods of its postwar history.

National Independence/Colonial or Semicolonial Dependence

Another dimension, particularly important for developing countries, is national independence. It is a major question whether a country's government has
sufficient control over its domestic affairs, whether it can independently determine its health policy and programs, or whether such efforts are eroded by open
or subtle interference by other governments or transnational corporations.

C. Typologies of Health Care Systems

In the foregoing section we reduced the complex configuration of socioeconomic and sociopolitical systems to a few parameters. In this part we will have to
streamline the complexity of health care systems. This is an easier task because
several typologies of health care systems have already been developed in medical
sociology.

Mark Field [19] offers a typology consisting of five prototypes of health care
systems. The five systems (see Table 1) are described with internal indicators
(such as the status of physicians, the role of professional associations, ownership
of facilities, etc.). The socioeconomic context is not considered. However, Field
postulates an automatic convergence of health care systems toward a socialist
health system.

Table 1. Field's Five Prototypes of Health Care Systems

Health System	Type 1 Private	Type 2 Pluralistic	Type 3 Insurance/ Social Security	Type 4 National Health Service	Type 5 Socialized
General Definition	Health care as item of personal consumption	Health care as predominantly a consumer good or service	Health care as an insured/guaranteed consumer good or service	Health care as a state supported consumer good or service	Health care as a state provided public service
Position of the Physician	Solo entrepreneur	Solo entrepreneur and member of variety of groups/ organizations	Solo entrepreneur and member of medical organizations	Solo entrepreneur and member of medical organizations	State employee and member of medical organizations
Role of Professional Associations	Powerful	Very strong	Strong	Fairly strong	Weak or nonexistent
Ownership of Facilities	Private	Private and public	Private and public	Mostly public	Entirely public
Economic Transfers	Direct	Direct and indirect	Mostly Indirect	Indirect	Entirely indirect
Prototypes	United States; Western Europe; Russia in 19th Century	United States in 19th Century	Sweden; France; Japan in 20th Century	Great Britain in 20th Century	Soviet Russia in 20th Century

Source: F. Field, "Comparative Health Systems: Differentiation and Convergence," paper submitted to the National Center for Health Services Research, Cambridge, MA, 1976.

Milton Terris [57] distinguishes three prototypes:

1. *Public assistance:* This system is found predominantly in Third World countries and covers about 50% of the world population. The majority of the population in these countries gets medical assistance from public hospitals or health centers. These institutions generally lack resources, which means that medical assistance for the majority of the population is generally insufficient.

2. *Health insurance:* This system is found in capitalist, industrialized countries (mainly in North America, Western Europe, Japan, Australia, etc.). Here physicians offer their services as small-scale entrepreneurs. The income of physicians as well as major parts of the income of other health services come from contributions to health insurance funds. Insurance usually covers dependent workers and employees as well as their families; also, in many countries self-employed persons as well as farmers and their families are covered by health insurance schemes. In some countries almost the whole population is protected by such a scheme (in Austria, 99 percent of the total population).

3. *National health service:* This prototype goes back to the famous reform of the Soviet health system initiated in the 1930s by Nikolai Semashko, the first People's Commissar for Health. After World War II this system was realized in some Eastern European and Asian countries, and was also implemented in Cuba after the victory of the revolution. About one-third of the world's population lives under this system. Semashko formulated the principles for a national health service in the following way:

- unitarian and comprehensive organization of health services;
- participation of the entire population in health measures; and
- emphasis on prevention.

Since then, the national health service of socialist countries has been characterized by two tendencies:
- extension of out-patient care into the districts and mainly into the factories and offices, and
- regional organization of health services (sectorization).

The typologies of Field and Terris are not contradictory per se. Field's types 1 and 2 correspond to Terris' type 1. The apparent contradiction between the terms "private system" used by Field and "public assistance" from Terris demonstrates the different viewpoints from which the two authors observe the problem: Field considers medical care of the middle and upper classes provided by private physicians (therefore "private system"), whereas Terris has in mind medical care for the majority of the population, provided by the public institutions (therefore "public assistance"). As for type 3 in Field's typology or system 2 in Terris' scheme, we believe it to be problematic not to distinguish between private health insurance and social health insurance. Introduction and extension of social health insurance requires specific socioeconomic and sociopolitical conditions (e.g., industrialization, strengthening of the labor movement); it leads, moreover, to a specific configuration of interest groups in the health system (as described in the later section on Austria). Field's type 5 corresponds to type 3 in Terris' typology, whereas Field's type 4 (e.g., the British National Health Service) is considered by Terris as a transition form. The main difference between the two conceptions, however, is not the different number of health system prototypes. It is the automatic convergence toward a socialist health system postulated by Field, an opinion clearly rejected by Terris as well as by the authors of this article.

Our hypothesis is that the development of the health system, its transition from one type to a "higher" type, depends on the socioeconomic and sociopolitical context. We shall try to confirm this hypothesis by selecting a few countries and discussing the development of their health systems as well as the basic features of their socioeconomic and sociopolitical systems.

For this task we shall use the two typologies introduced in this section. As for the social, economic and political context, we shall exclude the natural conditions (which influence more the morbidity profile rather than the health system). We cannot discuss in detail the historical development and the national peculiarities of each country. Applying the concept of productive forces we can distinguish roughly between industrialized and developing countries. In the discussion of developing countries, the concept of national dependence/ independence will play a major role. Two Latin American countries (Cuba, a socialist country, and Nicaragua, a country in transition) will be compared with other developing countries, in particular Bangladesh. From the industrialized world we shall select four countries: a socialist one, the German Democratic Republic, which after World War II introduced a health system more or less similar to the Soviet one; and three capitalist countries with differing histories—the United Kingdom, Austria and Italy. The United Kingdom was the first Western country to introduce a national health service after World War II. The Austrian health system is based on the principle of social health insurance. In Italy the system based on social health insurance was recently replaced by a national health service. It is obvious that in comparing the experiences of industrialized countries, two sets of indicators will be used predominantly: relations of production and potential for innovation and reform.

II. IMPERIALISM, LIBERATION AND HEALTH

All who think reading statistical yearbooks is a boring exercise are advised to look at some of the recent health statistics published by the WHO [66]. Table 2 shows some health indicators by continent and WHO region: Life expectancy at birth is 72 years for Europe (without the USSR), but only 48 years for the WHO African region (corresponding more or less to "Black Africa"). But statistics do not sufficiently reflect the situation in the very poorest countries of Africa (e.g., Angola: life expectancy 42 years/infant mortality 155 p.m.; Ethiopia: 40/146; Burundi: 42/122; Mali: 43/154; Niger: 43/146; Somalia: 44/146; Upper-Volta: 39/214) or of Asia (Afghanistan: 37/205; Bangladesh: 46/136) [21]. Differences between North and Latin America are not quite so marked but still considerable: Life expectancy is 74 years in the United States and in Canada, but between 53 and 65 years in most Latin American countries (with the exception of Chile: 67; Argentina: 70; Costa Rica and Panama: 70; and Cuba: 73).

These figures demonstrate—better than any academic or political argument—the correlation between underdevelopment, neocolonial dependency and disease and early death of large parts of the population in countries of the Third World. This is one of the most embarrassing phenomena in the North-South comparison, highlighted by Fidel Castro in the second declaration of Havana [11]:

> On this continent [Latin America] four persons per minute, two million persons per year are dying because of hunger and curable diseases; and at the same time 4,000 dollars per minute, 2 million dollars per year are flowing from Latin America to the U.S.A. For every thousand dollars one dead person back home. Thousand dollars for each death, four times a minute, this is the price of imperialism.

Awareness of this connection between health and imperialism has induced a variety of medical doctors in developing countries to give up the medical profession in the strict sense and to continue the struggle against hunger, disease and death in the framework of the anti-imperialist movement as a struggle for independence, human rights and human dignity for the people of the Third World. Che Guevara and Salvador Allende are two famous examples.

It also seems that with the Alma-Ata Conference the WHO has lost its belief that Western development models—replacement of colonial dependence by more subtle forms of neocolonial dependencies—would slowly overcome the health differences between the haves and the have-nots in health. Since then, the WHO has officially endorsed new strategies to guide health policy in developing countries.

A. From a Developing Country to a Welfare State: The Cuban Example

Demographic Data

The Caribbean island of Cuba has an area of approximately 114,500 km^2 and a population of 9.7 million inhabitants; or 85 inhabitants/km^2, with an annual growth rate of 1.4. Two-thirds of the population are living in urbanized areas.

To avoid misunderstanding, it has to be clarified that Cuba is still a developing

Table 2. 1. Population, Area, Density and Selected Health Indicators for the World, Around 1980
1. Population, Superficie, Densité et Quelques Indicateurs de Santé Pour le Monde, Vers 1980

	Estimated population Population estimée (millions)	Area Superficie (km²) ('000)	Density Densité (p. km²)	Birth rate p. 1 000 population Taux de natalité p. 1 000 habitants	Death rate p. 1 000 population Taux de mortalité p. 1 000 habitants	Natural increase p. 1 000 population Accrois-sement naturel p. 1 000 habitants	Infant mortality p. 1 000 liveborn* Mortalité infantile p. 1 000 nés vivants*	Expectation of life at birth Espérance de vie à la naissance	Physicians per 10 000 population Médecins pour 10 000 habitants (1979)[a]	Hospital beds per 10 000 population Lits d'hôpitaux pour 10 000 habitants (1978)[a]
WORLD TOTAL . . . . TOTAL MONDIAL	**4 431**	**135 906**	**32**	**28**	**11**	**17**	**85**	**62**	**9**	**38**
Africa—Afrique	470	30 320	16	46	16	30	122	50	2	19
America—Amérique	611	42 083	15	26	9	17	53	68	13	45
Asia (excl. USSR) . . . . Asie (sans URSS)	2 578	27 655	89	29	11	18	91	60	4	20
Europe (excl. USSR— sans URSS)	484	4 936	98	14	11	3	17	72	20	96

10

Oceania—Océanie	23	8 510	3	22	9	13	40	70	14	104
USSR—URSS	265	22 402	12	18	9	9	27	70	b36	122

WHO REGIONS
RÉGIONS DE L'OMS

African Region / Région africaine	356	20 000	18	47	17	30	124	48	1	19
Region of the Americas / Régions des Amériques	611	42 000	15	26	9	17	53	68	13	45
South-East Asian Region / Région de l'Asie du Sud-Est	1 053	8 000	132	35	14	21	115	51	3	10
European Region / Région européenne	834	33 000	25	18	10	8	43	70	24	97
Eastern Mediterranean Region / Région de la Méditerranée orientale	268	13 000	21	42	14	28	117	53	5	14
Western Pacific Region / Région du Pacifique occidental	1 309	20 000	65	21	7	14	48	68	5	30

Source: WHO 1982 Référence (66)

a Excluding Bhutan, Democratic People's Republic of Korea and Sikkim—Non compris le Bhoutan, la République populaire démocratique de Corée et le Sikkim.
b Including dentists—Y compris les dentistes.

country and not a welfare state in the usual sense of the word, used to characterize some of the Western industrialized countries. Cuba is still poor but the welfare of the population has increased steadily and considerably since the victory of the revolution.

Struggle against repression, exploitation, hunger, illiteracy, disease and death were declared goals of the Cuban revolution. In 1953, when the leader of the revolutionaries, Fidel Castro, was captured by Batista's troops, he used the opportunity of a public trial to describe in his famous speech "History will absolve me" the cycle of poverty and health deprivation of an average Cuban family, particularly in rural areas: The father working only four months a year, the children insufficiently nourished and dressed and often affected by parasitic and infectious diseases, poor families seldom admitted to the public hospitals without the recommendation of a "big shot." "Society is full of compassion if a child is kidnapped or murdered, but criminally indifferent to the mass murder of thousands of children who die because there is no money to buy medicine" [62].

The controversial societal model introduced in Cuba after the revolution of 1959 is not discussed here. We will focus on the Cuban health system and the results achieved by the new health structures which are generally recognized. Before the revolution, the epidemiological situation of the country was typical for a Third World country: Diseases caused by poverty, deprivation and underdevelopment (parasitic and infectious diseases) dominated the country's morbidity and mortality profile. Infant and mother mortality was high; life expectancy was low (55 years). Health care institutions were concentrated in the capital of Havana and—to a high degree—reserved to the oligarchy and upper classes of Cuban society. The masses of campesinos, small farmers and workers were totally deprived of medical assistance or admitted only in exceptional circumstances.

The Cuban Health Service [62]

Immediately after the revolution, new structures of health care were created. The main goals at that time were:

- Extension of medical care to rural areas (construction of district hospitals and rural health centers as well as obligatory assignment of doctors to rural areas for one or two years);
- Reduction of parasitic and infectious diseases, such as malaria, poliomyelitis, tuberculosis, gastroenteritis;
- Improvement of maternity and infant care (reduction of infant and mother mortality);
- Increase of the number of medical doctors and other health professionals (before the revolution, in Cuba there were 6,000 medical doctors, i.e., 1:1,000; 50 percent of them left the country during or immediately after the revolution).

All these difficult tasks were performed in a surprisingly short time, in spite of all kinds of military and economic pressures exercised by the U.S. government.

The new Cuban health service is under the direction of the Ministry of Public Health.

The crucial element of the new Cuban health service is the polyclinic with its peripheral health posts. The type of health personnel depends on the demographic situation of a district, but minimum services are comprised of pediatrics, gynecology and obstetrics, internal medicine, dermatology, otorhinolaryngology, dentistry, neurology and psychiatry. In remote rural areas the polyclinic, principally an outpatient unit, may also have some beds for emergency inpatient care (rural hospital).

The outpatient sector was also expanded. Cuba has a two-level hospital system, similar to that of most developed countries: regional hospitals (for standard care), and provincial hospitals offering in addition more specialized, complicated and expensive forms of medical diagnosis and treatment. The most expensive and sophisticated diagnostic or therapeutic methods are offered only in the capital or—if necessary—free of charge abroad (mostly in the Soviet Union).

Health personnel numbers have increased rapidly. In 1981, there were 15,247 physicians in Cuba, i.e., 1 per 641 inhabitants; in addition, the Cuban health service employed 27,062 medical assistants and 27,558 technical and administrative staff members.

These efforts, which are extraordinary for a Third World country, are reflected in the improvement of health standards in the people of Cuba. Since the revolution, life expectancy has risen from 55 to 72 years, infant mortality has gone down from 60:1,000 to 22:1,000; the same holds for the mortality rate for mothers which was reduced from 12:1,000 to 4.4:1,000. A variety of infectious diseases of endemic character in Third World countries were completely eradicated (for example, malaria or poliomyelitis) or are now more or less under control (e.g., gastroenteritis and tuberculosis). The following section is a short description of the successful battle against malaria.

The Battle Against Malaria

Before the revolution in Cuba, malaria was an endemic disease. In November 1973, the WHO declared Cuba the first Latin American territory free of malaria. According to Ramón Martinez, director of the anti-malaria campaign in Cuba, the program was started with epidemiological investigations between May 1959 and February 1960 to obtain data of the malaria-affected territory of 37,500 km^2 with 1,874,000 inhabitants or 28.4 percent of the total population of Cuba at that time. In the second half of the 1960s, epidemiological centers were created in this area to register and report each case of malaria fever. Between 1962 and 1967, the area was sprayed with DDT twice a year; after 1965, the area to be sprayed could be reduced significantly.

The anti-malaria program was initiated and directed by the Ministry of Public

Health, but it operated as an autonomous program, with personnel recruited from the Department of Health Education of the Ministry of Health. The program was supported decisively by mass organizations such as the Committees for the Defence of the Revolution, the Federation of Cuban Women and the National Association of Farmers.

Post-revolutionary Trends of Bureaucratization and Professionalization

As already mentioned, it is not the purpose of this chapter to evaluate the Cuban social system on the whole. However, it must be recognized that an assessment of Cuban health policies cannot be entirely separated from existing general political prejudices, from enthusiastic admiration (from a position of sympathy to Cuba) to disregard or rejection (from a principally negative attitude toward Cuba). Consequently it is useful to include the views of a critical author who cannot be subsumed in either group. David Werner [62], famous for his health projects with Mexican campesinos, visited Cuba in 1978. In his report on this mission he recognizes the success of revolutionary Cuban health policies but criticizes several aspects of it, for example:

- Rigid medical hierarchies and dependence of the population on experts (medical doctors);
- Inadequate training and responsibility of paramedical staff;
- Inadequate health education of the population;
- High centralization of the overall health system;
- Low cost/benefit ratio of the "top-heavy" Cuban health system.

Werner makes the mistake of comparing two experiences, namely the Cuban health policy and his own projects with Mexican campesinos, without clarifying that these two represent completely different paradigms of medical assistance. The Cuban paradigm does not question the principle of the traditional Western medical paradigm. As a socialist-oriented country, Cuba took over many organizational structures from the Soviet system of comprehensive health care for the whole population. Werner, like many people in Western industrialized countries (including the authors of this article), regards the traditional medical paradigm from a critical distance and tries to develop rudimentary lay-care and self-help in deprived Mexican districts, where medical assistance is totally or almost completely nonexistent ("donde no hay doctor").

Under the given circumstances, both approaches are valid. Cuba used the basis of the military and political victory of the revolution and far-reaching socioeconomic transformation to create a national health service aimed at prevention as well as curative treatment of diseases and covering the whole country and the total population. In a surprisingly short time the Cuban government succeeded in bringing the health standard of the Cuban population to a level which is not too far from the standards of developed industrialized countries. This is an exceptional achievement which so far has not been repeated by any other country.

Under this paradigm medical professionalism plays an important role in the curative sector. Community participation is stimulated mainly in the preventive sector. Mothers are informed in detail how to protect their children from gastroenteritis, a very common disease in earlier Cuba as in other Third World countries. However, no recommendations are given for self-treatment but the parents are urged to bring their children immediately to the doctor when they suffer from diarrhea. Werner believes that this is unnecessary and that parents should instead be taught to give their children enough liquid to prevent them from dying. Such instructions may indeed be life-saving in many cases where no doctor is available (for geographical or financial reasons). But is it not problematic to promote self-treatment and self-medication in countries where a sufficient network of polyclinics is operating all over the country?

The role of the paramedical staff may be restricted in Cuba. However, this is not a typically Cuban problem, and the Cuban health administration is aware of it. Efforts have been made recently to restimulate cooperation between physicians and paraprofessionals as well as the participation of the people. Bureaucratic and centralistic trends in the health system are also not limited to Cuba. However, the real "faux pas," in our opinion, is Werner's argument of a "low cost/benefit ratio of the top-heavy Cuban health system." Considering the deprivation of about half of the world's population this argument is, in our view, inconsistent and politically dangerous.

B. Revolution is Health: The New Health Care System in Nicaragua

Demographic Data [14, 32, 33] *and Historical Review* [49]

According to official figures, Nicaragua's area comprises approximately 130,000 km^2. The population is 2.8 million, with a density of 21.7 per km^2. About half of the population lives in rural areas. The annual growth rate of the population is 3.3 percent. The Literacy Crusade of 1980 helped reduce the illiteracy rate from 59.3 percent (80 percent in rural areas and up to 100 percent among women in certain areas) to 12.9 percent. The public administration consists of 16 departments, which are becoming increasingly identical to the administrative units of the public health service.

A short look at the development of the health service in Nicaragua since the turn of the century is intended to show the problems facing Nicaragua's population after their victory over the Somoza dictatorship in July 1979.

Late colonial period: health service based on charity. Around 1900 there was practically no public health service. The economically weak parts of the population were dependent on the scarce aid from religious orders. The leisure classes had access to private doctors in the urban centers.

Semi-colonial period: slow participation of the public institutions in the health service.   In the 1940s welfare commissions were created both on the local and the national level (*Juntas Locales y Nacionales de Asistencia y Previsión Social*) to administer the scarce means provided for the poor. The honorary heads of these commissions were members of the bourgeoisie. For the vast majority of the Nicaraguan population this did not mean any considerable improvement of the health service.

Beginning of industrialization: introduction of a social security system for a minority [40].   The Nicaraguan Institute for Social Security (*Instituto Nicaragüense de Seguridad Social*—INSS) was founded in 1957. Sole beneficiaries were employees indispensable for the development of the economy who, on account of their qualifications, could not be replaced in case of illness. By 1978 the INSS was available for 16 percent of the economically active population, or 8.4 percent of the total population. An analysis of insured people by economic sectors clearly shows the aims pursued by this social insurance:

Structure of the population covered by the INSS (1978)

Primary sector (agriculture)	2.7 percent
Secondary sector (industry)	28.0 percent
Tertiary sector (services)	66.0 percent
No data or inactive	3.3 percent

At that time, about two-thirds of all employees worked in agriculture and industry, and less than one-third in the service sector.

Pre-revolutionary phase: health service as an instrument of compensation and power.   In the 1970s, the Somoza dictatorship desperately tried to retain its dwindling international reputation and to stop the growing resistance of the Nicaraguan population, by superficial reforms of the health system. Loans by the Interamerican Development Bank (BID) were used to established health centers and health posts all over the country; in most cases, however, these were not used and fell into disrepair because the young Nicaraguan physicians who had to do a mandatory year of social practice normally found ways to avoid assignment to these posts.

Although the program for community health action in rural areas (*Programa Rural de Acción Communitaria en Salud*—PRACS), carried out by Somoza's Ministry of Health in cooperation with the North American Agency for International Development (AID), from 1976 onwards had a progressive touch, its aim was not to improve the state of health but to safeguard power. Significantly, the program was carried out in communes of the department *Esteli*, where the revolutionary forces were becoming increasingly stronger and purely repressive measures were no longer successful. But people realized quickly that the aim of the program was not the removal of existing grievances but rather a better administration of poverty. Distrust and rejection were complete among those concerned when they learned that the communal health groups were to be put under the command of people loyal to Somoza [48].

In the official point of view, the intensively pursued birth control campaign was to bring about a reduction of infant mortality by lowering the birth rates. The unofficial aim, however, was to reduce the number of dissatisfied—and therefore oppositional—groups mostly in the militant regions in the north of the country. An Austrian team of physicians that cared for Nicaraguan refugees in Honduras from December 1978 to July 1979 found repeatedly that women who had undergone an abortion in Nicaragua were sterilized on this occasion without being told [58].

The clearest symbol of the exploitation of the Nicaraguan people can be seen in the Somoza-owned company *"Plasmaferesis de Nicaragua"* which bought blood from the poorest people in order to export plasma [9].

The heritage of the Somoza dictatorship. The situation of the Nicaraguan people after their victory over the Somoza dictatorship in July 1979, following 50 years of suppression, was dreadful in the health sector as well: 50,000 dead, 100,000 injured, 45,000 orphans; a population drained by malnutrition, insufficient water supply, catastrophic hygienic conditions and inhumane working conditions (or unemployment); a population afflicted by epidemic diseases such as diarrhea, parasites, pneumonia, tuberculosis, malaria and rheumatism; hospitals where people had taken shelter from the attacks of the National Guard mostly destroyed by bombs and grenades. The few remaining supply units such as health centers and health posts were mostly inoperable since a considerable number of doctors and officials of the health administration had been close to the overthrown regime and left the country in the course of the liberation war.

Principles of the New Health System [59]

On August 8, 1979, hardly three weeks after the victory of the liberation movement, the Government Junta of the National Reconstruction issued a decree to create a Uniform National Health System (*Sistema Nacional Unico de Salud*— SNUS) [38]. This system is based on the following considerations:

• Everybody has a right to health. The introduction of a social security system according to Western patterns (joint responsibility) would mean that about 50 percent of Nicaragua's population are excluded from health care. Because of low incomes or unemployment they would not be able to pay the insurance premiums. Therefore it is the responsibility of the state to guarantee the right to health for everybody by taking appropriate measures [34].

• Health services must be offered free of charge in order to be accessible by everyone. A minimum fee at the first consultation is designed to prevent abuse. Needy persons may be exempted from this fee.

• Individual interest groups must not be allowed to try to gain advantage from the health system. This demand as well as the scarce resources of personnel, material and finances make it necessary to pool all professional groups and institutions into one effective and economical care system. The Ministry of Health is responsible for central planning of this uniform national health system.

• Health sector planning is a definite component of overall national planning. Although given priority, it still suffers from the consequences of several decades of exploitation and lack of development. This means that the health service to be established must primarily take into account the basic needs of the population. Children, mothers, workers and farmers enjoy priority.

• Each individual service is an integral part of the overall care. No matter whether it is a measure of prevention, curative medicine, rehabilitation, health education, environmental hygiene or environmental protection, they are all subject to one aim: the creation of living conditions to enable the full development of the individual in society.

This comprehensive task can only be fulfilled by close cooperation of all health care professionals.

An important factor for the decentralized implementation of the centrally developed care system is the particiption of the population. The structure of the unified national health system could not be imposed and consolidated without the help of mass organizations such as the trade unions of the workers and farmers, the women's, youth and children's organizations and the defense committees.

The principles of the Nicaraguan health system are largely based on the declaration of Alma-Ata of 1978 [65]. The World Health Organization has recognized this fact by defining Nicaragua as a pilot country—the first in Latin America.

Administration of the Health Service

The Nicaraguan health system is organized on three levels: central (*Nivel Central*), regional (*Nivel Regional*) and local (*Nivel de Areas de Salud*).

The central level, which is directly subordinated to the Ministry of Health, comprises the national hospitals, the Central Bureau of Preventive Medicine, the national training centers, as well as other national institutions.

Activities on the regional level are coordinated by the regional offices of the Ministry of Health. Institutions on this level consist of the regional hospitals, regional bureaux of preventive medicine, regional training centers, as well as other regional institutions. Nicaragua is divided into health regions that are not always identical with the political administration districts. One region has up to 200,000 people.

The third or local level is considered the most important one. A "health area" has about 20,000 to 30,000 inhabitants. Its focal point is the health center, which is supplied with 20 to 30 beds if the nearest regional hospital is too far away. All health activities at this level are started from and related to the health center. Health care concentrates mainly on prevention, such as vaccination, mother-child programs, programs to combat malaria, tuberculosis, occupational and venereal disease, as well as measures in the field of environmental hygiene. The health center staff is responsible for finding an appropriate solution for the health problems in their respective area within the framework of established standards.

The health area is divided into sectors of 3,000 to 5,000 inhabitants. These sectors are supplied either by health posts or by mobile units. The health posts are staffed with paramedics who cooperate closely with the health brigadists.

The health brigadists constitute the closest link to the population within the supply chain of the new health system. They take care of up to 500 inhabitants each. Their role is modelled after similar functions in health services of Third World countries, e.g., the Chinese barefoot doctors. The health brigadists have both curative and preventive medical tasks. In addition, they keep records about their activities and make health statistics. In the curative sector their training enables them to administer medicine in cases of certain diseases such as gastroenteritis, cold, fever, anaemia, fungus infection, malaria and tuberculosis. In the preventive sector they have knowledge of prenatal and mother-child care, blood and saliva sampling and vaccination. They are trained to hold first aid courses and to conduct "health talks" (*Charlas de Salud*) on topics such as nutrition, oral rehydration measures (fluid intake in case of severe diarrhea), personal and environmental hygiene, construction of toilets, disposal of garbage and sewage, etc. The health brigadists should come from the community in which they are working, to ensure that they are familiar with the local problems. They are selected on the local level by health councils (see Table 3) upon consultation with the mass organizations and the health authorities. They work on a voluntary basis in addition to their main profession, without extra payment [29].

The people's involvement in the solution of the health problems must not be limited to participation in health programs and health campaigns. It must be understood as a procedure to lead to a conscious cooperation of the organized people in problem posing, planning, implementation, monitoring and evaluation of health services and programs. Without the participation of the mass organizations the Ministry of Health would not be able to actually solve the health problems in this country.

In order to create a link between the mass organizations and the national health administration, People's Health Commissions were established on a national level and in individual departments. Their counterparts at the community level are the People's Health Councils. The People's Health Commissions and the People's Health Councils represent the people vis-à-vis the public administra-

Table 3. Diagram Showing the Functioning of People's Health Commissions and People's Health Councils

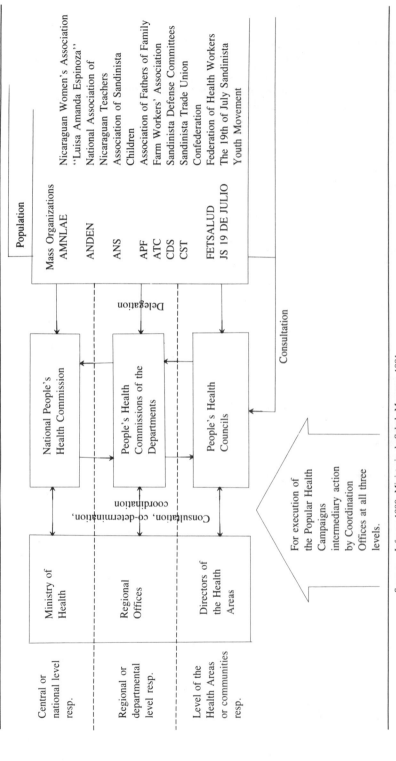

Central or national level resp.	Ministry of Health	→	National People's Health Commission	←	Mass Organizations AMNLAE	Nicaraguan Women's Association "Luisa Amanda Espinoza"
					ANDEN	National Association of Nicaraguan Teachers
					ANS	Association of Sandinista Children
Regional or departmental level resp.	Regional Offices	→	People's Health Commissions of the Departments	←	APF	Association of Fathers of Family
					ATC	Farm Workers' Association
					CDS	Sandinista Defense Committees
					CST	Sandinista Trade Union Confederation
Level of the Health Areas or communities resp.	Directors of the Health Areas	→	People's Health Councils	←	FETSALUD	Federation of Health Workers
					JS 19 DE JULIO	The 19th of July Sandinista Youth Movement

Population

Delegation

Consultation

Consultation, co-determination, coordination

For execution of the Popular Health Campaigns intermediary action by Coordination Offices at all three levels.

Sources: Informe 1980. Ministerio de Salud, Managua 1981.
Jornadas Populares de Salud. Ministerio de Salud, Managua 1981.

tion. Their members are appointed by the mass organizations. All projects in the field of health care are discussed at this level and—a most important aspect—the intended measures are adapted to the specific needs of individual regions and communities. The institutions have a dual role in that on the one hand they share the decision-making process and responsibility with central planning, whereas on the other hand they are firmly integrated among those concerned who thus are given an opportunity to criticize and correct.

In short, the aim of the structural organization of the Nicaraguan health system is to ensure access to the health institutions for all Nicaraguans, no matter whether they live in rural or urban areas, based on the principles of participative democracy. It must be admitted that at present this principle is still wishful thinking rather than reality. In the decades of Somoza's dictatorship the Nicaraguan people learned to exercise passive resistance and to refuse participation in programs of the regime. At the same time, they developed a deep distrust of all external influences. This ingrained attitude cannot be discarded overnight. Communication, participation and co-determination have to be learned slowly.

Health Programs

Health planners in Nicaragua faced such a number of problems in all fields (organization, training of personnel, infrastructure, financing, etc.) that they were forced to set priorities and to develop programs mainly in the field of basic supplies in order to cope with the most serious shortcomings as soon as possible. Right from the beginning they attached particular importance to health protection for mothers and children as well as for farmers and workers. The following examples are intended to illustrate the procedure.

In 1979, 121 out of 1,000 live-born children died during the first year of life. In 1982, this figure had been reduced to 70–80. This clear drop in infant mortality was achieved by the creation of nationwide "units for oral rehydration" (*Unidades de Rehidratación Oral*—UROs), i e. special children's wards to combat the loss of fluid caused by severe diarrhea. Diarrhea, which leads to progressive dehydration of the body, has always been the main cause of death of Nicaraguan children up to the fourth year of life. In extreme cases the children have to be hospitalized and hydration must be provided by intravenous infusion. The UROs make it possible to treat dehydrated children in the early stages of the disease. As a result, hospital mortality rates—caused by secondary intestinal infections—also declined by 75 percent [26].

Great efforts have also been made to fight malnutrition of children. Sixty-eight percent of all Nicaraguan children under the age of four suffered from malnutrition because of insufficient supply of proteins and calories. In order to improve the situation on a general and nationwide basis, the government increased the production of basic foods. Measures against speculation and food hoarding have also achieved some positive results. The three main staples—corn, rice and beans—are subsidized in order to guarantee supply to all families [2].

The Ministry of Health, together with the Ministry of Education, initiated an information campaign about the advantages of breast-feeding in order to combat intestinal infections of children caused by the improper use of powdered milk. At the same time advertisements for powdered milk were prohibited [39]. In 1982, the first mother's milk bank was founded at the children's hospital of Managua.

Unlike many other developing countries which sacrifice the health and security of their workers to rapid industrialization, the Nicaraguan government attaches particular importance to the health protection of the workers. A national committee founded for this purpose deals with problems such as control of insecticide imports and their correct application, determination of maximum permissible values for heat, vibration and noise, and standards for lead and mercury processing factories.

The Department of Workers' Security of the Ministry of Health developed programs for the industrial and agricultural sectors to improve working conditions and to avoid occupational accidents. These measures include supervision of lead content of fuels, examination of poisonous insecticides, lung examinations for miners, and prevention of typical risks for agricultural laborers. The department is also training inspectors and assistants responsible for the prevention of accidents.

Community Health Campaigns (Jornadas Populares de Salud)

Health campaigns constitute one of the most important instruments to improve the state of health of the population. They are a joint project of the mass organizations and the Ministry of Health, planned by the Ministry of Health and the National People's Health Commission (*Comisión Popular Nacional de Salud*) representing the mass organizations. Implementation is by the National Coordination Board (*Coordinación Nactional*) which is staffed both by the Ministry of Health and the National People's Health Commission. It is entrusted with organization, training, information, administration and finances. An Advisory Council (*Consejo Nacional de Apoyo y Asesoría*) formed by the ministries, universities, professional organizations, etc. is to contribute to the efficiency of planning and implementation. Health campaigns aim to get the whole population to take part actively in health programs, to make the people aware of health problems and to strengthen the confidence into one's own power by the experience of joint success. The means of national mobilization is used in particular for problems of special importance for the people's health. The health campaigns carried out since 1981—some of them repeated annually—had the following objectives: vaccination against poliomyelitis; environmental hygiene; vaccination against rabies; anti-malaria campaign; vaccination agaist measles, triple shots against diphtheria, whooping cough and tetanus; and first aid.

In order to carry out a campaign, a great number of specially trained assistants are needed. Based on the successful literacy campaign of 1980, a strategy was

Table 4.   Training Concept for the Popular Health Campaigns

Level	Number of Trainers	Selection of Candidates, Organizations and Institutions Involved	Number of Students per Trainer	Total Number Instructed
National level	10	Candidates proposed by the mass organizations and already trained health educators	12	120 educators
Regional level	120	Health Commissions of the Departments, teachers, health workers, mass organizations	10	1,200 multiplicators
Community level	1,200	People's Health Councils, production units, mass organizations	20	24,000 brigadist
Villages, valleys, town sectors	24,000	The entire population		

Source: Jornadas Populares de Salud. Ministerio de Salud. Managua 1981

identified to train the required number of assistants for their specific tasks within a very short time (see Table 4). This multiplication method was introduced within the framework of Popular Health Campaigns in February 1981 by training 80 candidates suggested by the mass organizations and 40 persons with relevant professional experience as health educators (*Educatores Populares de Salud*) on a national level. The curriculum included: vaccinations, blood sampling, compiling census data and health statistics, as well as administrative matters. These 120 educators passed their knowledge on to 1,200 multiplicators at a regional level, who in turn imparted it to 24,000 brigadists (who are not necessarily identical with the health brigadists described above), at a community level. Trainees and brigadists were provided with manuals. The candidates were recruited from the People's Health Commissions and the People's Health Councils, from teachers and health workers, production units and mass organizations. The health campaigns get massive support from the mass media and the mass organizations. Information brochures with illustrated stories (*folletos populares*), animating the population in a humorous way, are a popular aspect of these campaigns.

In this way, structures were created which not only serve to implement health campaigns but also permit permanent health education (*Programa Permanente de Educación Popular de Salud*). The individual begins to think about his own understanding of health. He learns to establish a connection between his disease and his social status. He has the experience that as a member of the community he has good chances to fight successfully the causes of malnutrition, life-threatening diarrhea, tuberculosis, malaria, tetanus, and so on, and thus to improve his living conditions considerably.

Effects of the Political Situation on Health Service [47]

Originally the "Year of Literacy" (1980) was to be followed by the "Year of Health." But increasing attacks by the Anti-Sandinistas and the aggravating economic situation forced the Government of National Reconstruction to set new priorities, so 1981 had to be proclaimed the "Year of Defense and Production." None of the aims of the uniform national health system were abandoned, but the chance to concentrate on the nationwide development and implementation of the health system for the period of one year, with the close participation of the population, had to be foregone. Instead, health care had to give way increasingly to aspects of defense and economy. Military aspects had to be integrated into the planning of health institutions, both with regard to their equipment and their situation. The first aid campaigns had to be adjusted to civil defense, and the improvement of personnel and structural shortcomings was delayed because of a scarcity of means. In particular, bottlenecks in the supply of medicine were the results of a lack of foreign exchange.

The development of the new health system is enormously impeded by the attacks of heavily armed counter-revolutionary units operating from the neighboring countries of Honduras and Costa Rica. Many health workers have been murdered or seriously wounded (partly by torture), and health posts and health centers have been looted and destroyed. Several of them had to be closed down because of the imminent threat to the staff. In some cases construction of health institutions was not started whereas others were not completed. The murder of two foreign physicians by counter-revolutionaries led to the partial withdrawal of foreign experts from exposed areas.

Nicaragua tries to master this difficult situation by using mobile health units and specially trained health brigades, composed of Nicaraguan doctors, nurses, paramedics and epidemiologists. Furthermore, the capacity and scope of health care units situated in safe areas have been extended.

Results

In spite of the destruction and difficulties caused by the non-declared war against Nicaragua, significant successes have been achieved in the field of health care in the few years since Somoza's overthrow [10, 37].

Apart from a drastic reduction of infant mortality (see also the section describing the units for oral rehydration; about 200,000 children are treated there annually), great progress has been achieved in combating infectious diseases: In 1982, not one case of dengue fever was found, malaria cases were reduced by 80 percent, and diphtheria was diagnosed in only two cases. The community health campaigns were the main factor of this positive development. In 1930, 1.7 million vaccinations were given against polio, tuberculosis, measles, diphtheria, whooping cough and tetanus; in 1981, the number was 2.5 million, and in 1982, 3.5 million. Tuberculosis immunization in 1982 reached 81 percent of children under the age of one, tuberculous meningitis could be eliminated completely from the hospitals.

In 1982, 26 acute hospitals, 5 hospitals for the chronically ill, 15 health centers with beds, 83 health centers without beds and 366 health posts were available to the people of Nicaragua. The number of hospital beds has risen to 4,700; 344 health care facilities have been established since the liberation.

Hospital deliveries rose from 42,000 in 1977 to 58,000 in 1982, and the number of surgical operations increased from 36,000 to 55,000 within the same period. In 1977, 13 of 100 hospital inpatients died, in 1981 the figure dropped to 6.

Outlying rural areas, where hardly any health workers could be found during Somoza's time, are now provided with health professionals. For example, in Zelaya Norte, a border region subject to counter-revolutionary attacks, the number of outpatient consultations per capita grew from 1.9 in 1981 to 3.7 in 1982. Altogether, consultations increased from 2.4 million in 1977 to more than 6 million in 1982, 60 percent of them in health centers and health posts.

Training of health workers is promoted in all areas. Thus the number of medical students has doubled.

State expenditure for health care was less than 180 córdobas per capita under Somoza, but rose to more than 500 córdobas per capita in 1983. The budget item of "health" rose to 16 percent of the overall budget and thus is far above the Latin American average (1.5 percent). In 1983, 1,400 million córdobas were allocated for health care, the highest figure in the history of Nicaragua.

C. Bangladesh: New Regulations for the Pharmaceutical Supply

Demographic Data and Historical Development

Bangladesh has an area of 144,000 km^2 and about 90 million inhabitants, 90 percent of them living in rural areas. They live in a total of 68,000 villages, most of which can be reached only by foot or, during and after the monsoon period, by boat. Three-quarters of the population are illiterate. The annual population growth is 3 percent.

By the end of 1971, the liberation struggle of the Bengalese people had brought political independence from Pakistan and the chance for self-determination. At the beginning of 1972, an extensive reform program was started under the government of Mujibur Rahman: nationalization of bank and insurance systems, foreign trade and parts of the industry, and implementation of a land reform. But the destabilization measures of the United States and their allies in Bangladesh and abroad were successful, contrary to Cuba and Nicaragua, which have proved sufficient power of resistance up to now. With his rigorous measures against progressive forces, Mujibur Rahman contributed to his own downfall. He was murdered during the overthrow in August 1975. The military took over, and their strongman, Major-General Zia ur Rahman, had himself elected president in 1978, but soon withdrew his promise of liberalization and democratization. The multiple party system remained a mere farce. Feudal power structures continued to exist. The second five-year plan announced in 1979, whose priorities were food, education and family planning, very soon came to a standstill. Zia ur Rahman died at the end of May 1981 in the course of an unsuccessful coup by leftist military units. Vice-President Abdus Sattar became his interim successor. A state of emergency was imposed on the country for several months and all civil rights were suspended. The presidential elections in November 1981 brought victory to Sattar and his ruling National Party. The opposition Awami League, which follows the tradition of Majibur Rahman, and their candidate Kamal Hussain, accused them of falsifying the election results.

Since Sattar did not comply with the request for a constitutional role of the military in the government, which had been put forward before the elections by the chief of the army, General Hossain Mohammad Eshad, the army took over in May 1982. Eshad imposed martial law, declared himself Supreme Administrator of Martial Law, dissolved Parliament and revoked the constitution. According to Eshad, the coup had been justified and necessary in order to protect the country from a serious crisis, to safeguard the nation and to restore law and order. He promised free elections to reinstate the democratic process as well as the appointment of a civilian president. The real reasons for the serious crisis he referred to were to be found in maladministration, corruption and speculation, above all in the neglect of agricultural production and the failure to carry out the land reform. This already difficult situation was aggravated by a series of droughts and floods.

Bangladesh's economy drifted into total foreign dependence. The foreign trade deficit already amounted to 1.5 billion dollars. More than half of the national budget had to be financed by international funds. The International Monetary Fund (IMF) threatened to suspend payment of credits already granted in case the government did not stop subsidizing basic staples—a doubtful measure to save a country in which 80 percent of the total population and 45 percent of the children suffer from malnutrition.

In March 1982, A. M. Chowdhury, a former judge, was appointed president of Bangladesh. A staff of advisors selected by the military took over government functions. According to the ideas of the IMF, the private sector should be strengthened, non-profitable national enterprises, (e.g., banks and insurance) should be denationalized, and imports of consumer goods which can be produced in the country should be prohibited. Nevertheless, provisions had to be made for importing 1.3 million tons of grain in 1982/83 in order to prevent a supply crisis.

From September 1982 onward, Bangladesh experienced the most serious cholera epidemic of the past two decades. By March 1983 the number of victims had risen to 15,000.

Health Care [61]

The health institutions and the number of personnel had suffered considerably in the course of the struggle for liberation. Although new possibilities to train doctors were created and a compulsory year of practice in rural health centers was introduced, there still are hardly any doctors to be found in the villages. According to statistics there is one doctor for every 30,000 inhabitants in rural areas. Training was based on Western curative medicine, concentrating on hospital treatment, and its result was that most doctors remained in hospitals and private practices in the cities. The number of nurses in Bangladesh has traditionally been even lower than that of doctors. Their training also concentrates on hospital treatment. Relief is expected from the paramedical professional groups such as sanitary inspectors, medical assistants and family welfare workers. The sanitary inspectors are mainly responsible for preventive medical measures, such as the prevention of epidemics, environmental sanitation and food hygiene, as well as family planning. They are appointed at a district level. Their training takes one and one-half years. The medical assistants are to ensure the provision of primary health care in rural areas. Their tasks include diagnosis and treatment of frequent diseases, obstetrics, family planning, small operations and measures of preventive medicine. They are trained over a period of three years. The family welfare workers, directly trained and instructed by the sanitary inspectors and medical assistants, are employed for field activities: mother and child health care, vaccinations, blood examinations, administration of certain drugs, and family planning. They are to visit each household once a month. The most important health care unit is the health center for inpatient and outpatient treatment as well as preventive medicine. As regards inpatient treatment, one hospital bed is available for 6,000 inhabitants. In spite of all efforts, two-thirds of the population in Bangladesh have no access to medical care.

The Conflict over the Pharmaceutical System [36]

In June 1982, the military government of Bangladesh enacted new drug regulations for the immediate prohibition of 237 drugs. Another 1,500 drugs were considered "superfluous" and were to be phased out by the end of the year, either because they were too expensive or because their therapeutic effect was doubtful. The goal of this measure was a reduction to 250 drugs in compliance with a WHO-compiled list of "essential drugs" to guarantee basic medical supply of the population. In addition, the import of pharmaceutical products was to be restricted considerably. According to the new law, foreign companies may no longer produce drugs in Bangladesh that are already offered by domestic companies. Sales are to be restricted to those manufacturers who are producing in the country itself.

The committee of experts appointed by the government and entrusted with the preparation of new guidelines for the production, sale and use of drugs gave the following reasons for the defects on the pharmaceutical sector:

- Insufficient legal regulations and lack of implementation;
- Exploitation of consumers, one-third of whose expense for medicine was wasted on ineffective, unnecessary and sometimes harmful drugs;
- Domination of multinational corporations, controlling 80 percent of the pharmaceutical market in Bangladesh;
- Waste of the national budget by the import of finished pharmaceutical products, which made up 20 percent of the total expenses for drugs.

The following reform measures were suggested in the field of health policy:

- Safeguarding of quality of essential drugs;
- Guaranteed access of all to these drugs;
- Price control;
- Removal of ineffective and harmful drugs from the market;
- Promotion of local production;
- Prevention of squandering abuse;
- Improvement of quality of hospitals and drugstores.

Of the 250 essential drugs, 150 are considered basic drugs, which satisfy most therapeutical needs. Twelve of them can be administered by the family welfare workers, another 33 are used in health centers and 105 in hospitals. The remaining 100 drugs are reserved for the treatment of rare diseases by specialists.

The motivation for these measures can be found in the political situation (appeasement) but also has its roots in the precarious economic situation of the country as outlined above. Considerable savings of foreign exchange are possible as a result of these measures. Developing countries spend about 30 percent of their health budget for imported drugs. The time for enactment was well chosen: In May 1982, the WHO members had unanimously adopted a resolution calling for accompanying measures in order to realize a more reasonable supply of drugs. The industrialized nations and pharmaceutical corporations showed understanding and offered their help.

Before the introduction of the new regulation, there were 4,140 drugs on the market in Bangladesh, representing approximately 100 million dollars per year. Eighty percent of the pharmaceutical market was controlled by eight multinational corporations: Fisons, Glaxo, ICI (the United Kingdom); Höchst (F.R.G.); May & Baker (France); Organon (Netherlands); Pfizer and Squibb (the United States). It did not take long before these companies launched their counter-attack. All good intentions and promises were forgotten; commercial interests dominated. The companies threatened to discontinue their overall pharmaceutical production in Bangladesh in case the government implemented its new drug policy. A spokesman of the U.S. State Department declared that the government of Bangladesh had been encouraged to postpone enactment of the new regulations and to examine the possible adverse effects on the medical supply—a doubtful demand if one considers that 70 percent of the drugs banned from Bangladesh are considered dangerous and/or ineffective by American and European health authorities. The pressure exercised by the embassies of the United States, the Federal Republic of Germany, the Netherlands and the United Kingdom finally led to the formation of a revision committee. In August 1982, 41 drugs were excluded from the ban and the deadline for the removal of certain drugs from the market was extended. However, the request of ICI, May & Baker and Organon to be granted permission for re-exporting some drugs banned from Bangladesh did not meet with success. (The pharmaceutical companies had intended to relabel the drugs and transfer them to Saudi Arabia and South Africa.) The head of the drug control board refused approval, giving the following reason: "What is bad for our children is also bad for others."

In spite of these difficulties the new regulation of the drug system in Bangladesh has already shown favorable effects. The critical awareness of the population with regard to drugs is growing noticeably. The patients inquire which drugs are prohibited, and the doctors are gradually changing their attitudes from confidence in quantity to trust in quality. This means a first step toward the "demedicalization" of medicine required by the WHO already in 1977. On the other hand, there has been some success in the establishment of a national pharmaceutical production adjusted to the WHO list of essential drugs. Nevertheless, the conflict is still continuing.

III. HEALTH CARE IN THE INDUSTRIALIZED WORLD

A. Austria: Stability and Immobility of a Welfare State

The Social Nature of Health Care

Important sectors of the Austrian social and health care system have been public in Austria since the nineteenth century. Earlier hospitals, open to everybody, were run mostly by foundations or religious communities; yet, this limited supply of hospitals did not come close to the actual needs of the population. This situation became particularly obvious at the transition from feudalism to capitalism when masses of socially uprooted people began to settle in the cities and industrial centers and when the caring for the sick could no longer be fulfilled by the families.

When the poor state of health of the males reaching the age for military service could not be denied any longer and the enlisting commissions had to exempt an ever increasing number of recruits, the Taaffe Government decided to introduce the first social insurance laws in 1887. This move corresponded to the social policy implemented in Germany at that time. Accident and health insurance for workers was soon introduced, starting a trend in health care which has been maintained until today with its principles of autonomy, territorial sectorization, and internal segmentation into different insurance branches. There is also a "producer-pays" principle according to which the funding is shared between employers and workers, except for (occupational) accident insurance where funds come exclusively from employers.

In the course of time, the insurance coverage was extended to more and more groups of the population and the supply of services grew in number.

The quantitative dimension of the health care system has increased enormously. Particularly in the last few decades the expenditures have risen immensely, nowadays totalling about 10 percent of the gross national income. In the following distribution of expenditures for 1979, the private budget (including private insurance) and the public budget (comprising the whole range of the social insurance branches) were considered separately: the private budget spent on health care amounted to 29.7 percent, and the public budget spent 70.3 percent. All together, these expenditures represented 9.53 percent of the gross national income. For the most part, policy in Austria is following a steady course. Important structural changes will not take place in the Austrian health care system unless slumps on the labor market and long-term stagnation impose a dramatic change on both productive forces and the conditions of production [53].

What are the concrete decision-making institutions in health care policy and what are their interests? These can be classified as follows [23]:

General interests of capital disposal. The industrialists and top management of medium and large-sized national and foreign firms in Austria and their pressure groups must be taken into account. They are represented by the Union of Austrian Industrialists and political lobbies such as the trade association which is closely linked to the OEVP (*Oesterreichische Volkspartei*, the conservative party of this country). This group is interested in the preservation of the working capacity and of mass loyalty, under the condition that the costs of the health care system do not add to their financial burden or contribute to the loss of profits, and that this situation does not jeopardize the accumulation of capital.

Interests of the medical supply industry. This group is comprised of all firms producing consumer goods (pharmaceutical, food-producing and textile industries) as well as capital goods (electrical, furnishing and building industries). Each of these groups is aiming at an expansion of the medical sector in Austria which would mean an increase of their sales.

Interests of private insurance companies. They, too, are interested in an expansion of their market share. This, however, bears the danger of undermining the legally warranted health insurance system in Austria and strengthens the trend away from standard medical care open to the whole population.

Class interests of physicians and pharmacists. This group is important not only because its fees are a vital factor in the health system but also because it plays a key role in the health services. Physicians and pharmacists are well-organized in their respective professional chambers; they try to keep up their monopoly and thus the level of their fees.

Interests of the social bureaucracy. It is difficult to define this bundle of interests because a great number of external factors interfere with the health administration, such as the trade unions that try to extend or at least maintain the social security system, or the pharma-industry promoting the sector of the medical supply industry.

Interests of the paramedical staff. The financial, professional and health interests of hospital nurses, medical-technical assistants, etc. will have to be taken into account in the reform plans.

Interests of workers' representatives. In the field of occupational medicine, the Austrian trade union federation is inspired by highly professional models which are, to a great extent, separated from the real situation of workers and employees. Occupational medicine is mainly presented in a scientific and, at the same time, non-political form. Its traditional connection with the emancipatory targets of the workers' movement is not being questioned.

Health care interests of the population. For the time being these are scarcely articulated, with the exception of the physicians' professional organization which tries to channel these interests. However, a reform aiming at a long-term success would have to consider these interests. Associations like the *"Kritische Medizin"* (Critical Medicine) or the *"Demokratische Psychiatrie"* (Democratic Psychiatry) founded a few years ago can be considered as first attempts in this field.

The Social Health Insurance

The Austrian health insurance system is compulsory and is based on professional categories. The nine provinces each have a regional sick fund providing service and care for all workers and employees, pensioners and their relatives, as well as pupils and students who otherwise would be unprotected.

The financing system is based on a contribution paid in equal shares by the employer and the worker/employee or pensioner according to his gross income, up to a certain level of income. This means that the contribution to the social insurance diminishes relative to the increasing income, which limits the possibilities of a vertical re-distribution. The level of contribution is fixed by law.

The same is true for the compulsory duties of the health insurance authorities. The consequence is that the autonomy of the individual authorities is limited to the negotiation of agreements with professional associations (of medical doctors, etc.) and the conclusion of contracts with individual physicians, as well as various control measures with respect to their contract partners and the insured persons. All insurance branches are members of a central top organization, the *"Hauptverband der oesterreichischen Sozialversicherungstraeger,"* attending to common interests and having a sort of balancing function. Seventy-five percent of all people paying a contribution have insurance with the regional sick funds. Other important health insurance institutions are the funds for civil servants, the farmers' sick funds and the insurance organizations for self-employed in the trade field.

All together, 99 percent of the Austrian population has health insurance. The social insurance is based on the principle of solidarity and includes regulations for those excluded from social insurance according to the principle of subsidiarity. Social help is regulated by state and not by federal laws. Consequently, the individual services vary from province to province. In addition, the state as well as local authorities organize social services such as health visitors, mobile nurses, medical emergencies and care for the elderly.

Ambulatory Care

The Austrian ambulatory health system is dominated by physicians with individual practices. Their interests determine the policy of their professional representation, the *"Oesterreichische Aerztekammer"* (Austrian physicians' chamber), of which every practitioner is required by law to be a member. This explains why there is only one such chamber. At the end of 1981 a total of 18,949 practitioners were registered, 4,261 of them still in training (after graduation each doctor has to serve a term in a hospital; during this period he/she is not allowed to open a practice). In 1981, 6,006 of the physicians who had completed their training were general practitioners; 8,682 were specialists. For the primary health care, those physicians are important who are on contract with the regional sick funds, and at that time, there were 3,486 practitioners and 3,558 specialists included. Disparities are considerable if one compares rural and urban areas, or underdeveloped and flourishing regions [16]. However, the contribution of the sick funds to public assistance is of crucial importance. The distribution of physicians on contract with the funds is much more balanced than the distribution of physicians in general. The specialized sector of ambulatory care has developed since World War II. Within the last thirty years, the number of practitioners has been augmented by 63 percent; the greatest increase is to be found in the field of specialists.

The free access to Austrian universities, the demographic developments, an increased desire to study and an undeniable prestige of the medical profession have resulted in an increase in the number of medical students, so a massive growth in the number of physicians is to be expected by 1995. The management of this increase in physicians will be one of the challenges of the next 15 years.

The alternative to the hospital sector is the locally established doctor working alone, with just the help of a receptionist for administrative tasks. Legislation has made it very difficult to create group practices. The spirit of competition, highly developed among physicians, is another factor. Thus, cooperative forms of medical assistance outside of hospitals are almost unknown in Austria. However, it is possible for a patient to go directly to a hospital asking for ambulatory services. Although this sort of care is legally limited to specific cases (emergencies), patients are usually admitted. The number of ambulatory cases has increased considerably in the last few years and is becoming a competitive factor in medical care. In this context the increased number of locally established doctors must be taken into account. The practitioner is usually the first person to be consulted in the medical field and prefers to refer his patients to the hospital ambulatory service, as this makes him sure that his patients will return to see him for future treatment. If he refers his patients to an independently practicing colleague, he might be afraid that the colleague could take over the treatment.

Hospitals

In 1979, 315 hospitals with a capacity of 79,951 beds were in operation, and there were 5,253 beds in clinics for chronically sick people. Of this total of 85,204 beds, 80.4 percent belong to public insurance branches, and the rest are privately run. Many private clinics run by religious societies having concluded contracts with the public insurance branches are open to the general public. On the other hand, every public hospital may legally reserve one quarter of its beds for private patients. The resulting income is divided between the managing institution and the physicians, especially the leading hospital doctors. The share of income due to private patients—mostly financed by private extra-insurance— amounts to 10–15 percent [8]. In 1981, 9,650 physicians were working in Austrian hospitals according to four categories: young physicians still in training but fulfilling all demands of medical assistance, trained physicians, employed physicians and so-called consulting specialists. The consulting specialists do not work permanently in hospitals but treat patients in their specialty when this need is expressed by the hospital. In 1981, 7,718 physicians were employed in general hospitals, 4,084 of them still in training, 3,211 as employed physicians and 423 as consulting specialists.

The intensity of treatment in hospitals has increased considerably. In 1970, there were 681 employees for 1,000 beds, compared to 734 in 1974 and 895 in 1979. Personnel costs amount to 70 percent of the hospital costs. However, it must be noted that more patients are being treated for a shorter period of time, as the average length of stay in hospital has decreased (in 1980 an average of 13 days in the case of acute illness). The higher intensity of diagnostic and thera-peutic services also increases the demands on the personnel.

A special problem of the Austrian hospitals is the shared financing system between health insurance branches, and federal, state and local authorities. This splitting as well as the principle that the costs of hospitals are to be covered by public sources irrespective of their efficiency, hinders the systematic develop-ment of the infirmary system as well as impedes the restructuring of the financing system itself. The decision on how to spend funds depends too much on local authorities and leading hospital doctors.

In spite of increasing costs, reform plans concerning the financing system usually end up making the weakest partner responsible for the extra charges. This practice has led to the fact that small and medium sized local hospitals are no longer in a position to finance their clinics. The share of the overall costs paid by the sick funds is under 50 percent. One must expect that reform plans will only be implemented under the pressure of massive financing difficulties. One has to stress that in this situation a highly mechanized hospital is being fostered, pro-moting a medicine with extreme curative orientations and totally excluding the patient from any decision-making process or participation.

Prevention and Rehabilitation

From 1970 onwards, the program of the first socialist government promoted a series of measures in the field of prevention. Their success was uneven.

The "mother-child-passport" bases the payment of state maternity benefits on a number of medical examinations of the pregnant woman and of the mother and child during the first two years following the birth. This measure had a vital impact on infant mortality which dropped to 25.2 percent in 1972, 15.0 percent in 1978 and 12.6 percent in 1981. This decrease cannot only be attributed to the "mother-child-passport" because general improvements of the hygienic condi-tions and increased prosperity also play an important role in this context.

Free check-up services were introduced in 1973 with the aim of providing a total screening free of charge to every Austrian over age 19. However, only a few physicians were prepared to offer their services on a voluntary basis, and only a few patients were interested in this new program. In 1979 a doctor with check-up facilities and working under contract with the official health insurance conducted an average of 2.2 check-ups per month, and 2.3 percent of eligible persons benefited from this service [52]. The lack of interest on the part of physicians as well as of the population was responsible for this failure. On the other hand, the sick funds themselves as granters of these services are not very interested in propagating these check-ups out of fear that this program might limit funds only available until now to the ambulatory, clinical and admin-istrative sector. This illustrates the attitude of the sick funds which, though dominated by the trade unions, promote curative structures of a traditional type and neglect the prevention aspect.

On the contrary, the growth of the rehabilitation sector seems to be a successful achievement of the Austrian social insurance system. A number of spa hotels and special clinics serve to continue the treatment with the aim of a total vocational rehabilitation. This principle of rehabilitation has been stressed during the 1970s and even extended as to comprise "physical, psychic and emotional capacities." Physical efficiency remains nevertheless the main criterion for the granting of rehabilitation services. Problems arise as a consequence of the exclusion of the population from potential local rehabilitation clinics and their services. One example is modern isotope facilities in a countryside rehabilitation center. These facilities are seldom used by the patients of the center, and the population of the surrounding area in need of such services has to travel to distant clinics for treatment.

Problems of the Austrian Health System [1]

Obviously, the main problem increasingly seems to be a lack of integration in the different fields of the social and health system. The increasing complexity in the curative field, the development of sub-specialization, the coordination of care services, as well as the necessity of comprehensive assistance in the psychosocial field in close connection with the health system demand a closer cooperation of different professions and levels of service. The splitting up of services and the lack of a prevailing power entail an increase of the costs involved. This lack of integration not only results in overlapping of services, multiple examinations and divergent regional developments, but also in more complex administrative work. Moreover, within the given structures sensible planning is almost impossible. The reduction of administrative complexity is one of the essential conditions for a better integration in Austria where, for instance, 24 sick funds and several pension and accident insurances act in some fields not only autonomously but even in a contradictory manner.

Neither patients nor the personnel—above all in non-medical spheres—have a say in the matter. Clinics are still dominated by a strict hierarchy and administration; nursing and medical services/personnel are more or less completely isolated from each other. Integrative forms of care hardly exist in hospitals. They are nonexistent in the ambulatory sector as well as between the ambulatory and hospital sector.

An advantage of the splitting of social and health systems is the fact that now and then new forms of care are being fostered because of the initiatives of individual communities, physicians, politicians, and institutions. This does not mean, however, that the usual unplanned confusion does not exist any more. The Viennese attempt to decentralize the care of the mentally ill and to supplement it by ambulatory forms has been quite successful so far. This allowed reduction in the hospital sector for mental care. These relative successes make the overall disadvantage of the system obvious. On the whole, the psychosocial care stagnates. Individual achievements serve as an alibi. They are restricted to certain

areas and disappear when the promoting institutions lose interest or have to deal
with other problems. The important field of health education is lagging behind;
the study of housing, working and environmental conditions is always neglected.
The right to self-responsibility has not induced the individual to participate.
From a conservative or technocratic angle, the concept of self-responsibility is
often reduced to the concept of self-payment. The lack of health education goes
hand in hand with the near absence of primary prevention. Prevention going
beyond inoculation is a favorite topic of Sunday speeches but this has practically
no impact. Occupational medicine has gained value during the last few years and
was adapted to European Economic Community standards. Nevertheless it is still
dominated by the physicians employed by the firms. The employees' representatives have hardly any possibility of taking part in the decision-making process
and forms of direct participation of employees/workers do not exist.

   Globally, one can affirm that in Austria there exists no more than a minimal
potential for reforms in the health care system. The social security institutions
and their activities are firmly based on the comprehensive and basic consensus of
all the politically relevant powers. Under the pressure of increasing financing
problems, no reforms are to be expected. There will be smaller curtailments of
services, but their scope will be limited. The trade unions influence social insurance to a great extent and because of their dominant role in the Austrian system
of social partnership, they could play a leading role in the launching of reforms;
but they argue that the health sector comes in third position after job and income
security. Considering the increasing unemployment rates and the stagnating
economy, one cannot expect a quantitative extension of the health sector.
Qualitative improvements will not be implemented because of the bureaucratic
rigidity of the institutions and the general lack of responsibility for the development of the health sector. This perspective corresponds on the whole to the
political apathy of the majority of Austrians.

B. Nationalization vs. Privatization:
Health Care in the United Kingdom

From Public Assistance to the National Health Service (NHS)

   With the establishment of the NHS in 1948, the United Kingdom raised its
medical care to a level "which in most capitalist countries only the educational
system achieved" [12]. Before 1948 the health care system was founded on three
pillars: hospitals, ambulatory care, and local health councils having the character
of welfare institutions [51]. Private and public hospitals carried out inpatient
treatment. Ambulatory medical care was performed by physicians partly privately paid and partly paid through the National Health Insurance. But only half
of the British population was insured by this institution that was founded in 1911.
The third level of care was provided by the local health councils in the commu-

nities. They were responsible for medical care and prevention measures. Thus, before 1948 medical and social medical care seems to have been still firmly rooted in the Elizabethan Poor Law and Welfare Concept. Even long after 1948, public hospitals bore the stigma of welfare institutions.

The introduction of the NHS partly eliminated the class-oriented tripartite curative sector. Only the third level of the health care system, the one assigned to local authorities, remained unchanged in its structure. With the introduction of the NHS two basic principles of socialist health care policy were put into practice: first, an equal opportunity for access to the services was implemented; then, the financing of the NHS out of taxes was secured. Only a minimal part of the costs had to be paid by the patient. The political guarantee of the right of every citizen to health care led to the nationalization of nearly all hospitals. Specialists working there became employees of the state. General practitioners were registered as free contract partners of the NHS and paid according to the number of citizens registered in a patients' list, i.e., they were paid independently of the services actually performed. In the mid-1960s doctors received additional payment for special services (vaccination, family planning) and for the registration of special patient groups (pregnant women, elderly people).

The National Health Service Act (1948) was the result of close cooperation of physicians' organizations with the Ministry of Health. The particular aim of the physicians had been to protect practitioners, especially those working in hospitals, from community interference. Subsequently, the proponents of the NHS made efforts to promote the unification of health care through centralization and horizontal integration.

The reform of 1974 brought about essential alterations. The organizational separation of hospitals, practitioners and public assistance was replaced by a structure of complete integration combining all these sectors into one comprehensive organization. The NHS remained faithful to this principle although another reform enacted in 1982 shifted some of the stresses. This reform was mainly implemented to improve management through far-reaching centralization eliminating the "Area Health Authorities" created in 1974 and replacing them by 192 "District Health Authorities." Another important factor of the 1982 reform was the promotion of the private sector through a simplification of the privately organized care structures [30].

Present Structure and Financing of the NHS

The NHS comprises four separate sections: England (46.5 million inhabitants), Wales (2.8 million), Scotland (5.2 million) and Northern Ireland (1.5 million). The differences lie mainly in administrative details. The total amount of financial means of the NHS provided by the Treasury was distributed among the four sections as follows: 80 percent to England, 12 percent to Scotland, 5 percent to Wales and 3 percent to Northern Ireland.

Usually in descriptions reference is made to the English NHS, as will also be the case in this article.

The present administrative structure consists of the Department of Health and Social Security, 14 Regional Health Authorities, and 192 District Health Authorities. Districts are often structured into "sectors" which may be geographical parts of a district or functional parts, (for instance, a psychiatric sector). The Unit Administrator is in charge of larger care systems, such as general hospitals.

The NHS is financed by three sources. The greatest part comes from general taxes (in 1981/82 they represented 87 percent). About 10 percent come from contributions, which date back to the regulations of the former social insurance system of 1911 and which have been taken over in the NHS law. Finally, 2.8 percent originate from extra payments made by patients for prescription charges as well as individual services of dentists and eye doctors. In 1981/82 the total sum amounted to £11.1 billion, about 6 percent of the gross national product (see Table 5).

So far, private structures have played a less important role in English health care, although the government promotes its development. At present 5 percent of the population is privately insured. NHS physicians may practice privately in or outside NHS institutions. From 1975 onwards the share of privately complementary insured persons has increased visibly. From 1976 to 1979 the Labour government created the basis for an increase in private hospitals by a stricter distinction between private and public hospitals. The attempt to reduce the number of private beds in the NHS area has been problematic so far. The following Conservative government fostered the private sector by granting tax concessions, improving the opportunities to open a practice, and promoting "freedom of choice" in the health care.

The cost structure of the NHS defeats the theory that a socialized medicine is characterized by waste and extremely high costs. With its health costs constituting a relatively low share of its gross national product, the United Kingdom is at any rate at the bottom of a list of industrialized countries. The main reason for the low costs lie in the system of budgeting and payment. Countries whose care systems are based on a theoretically unlimited expenditure induced by demand have higher costs, whereas systems with budgeting controls in most cases keep their expenses within the predetermined limits. The fee system of individual services for physicians augments the costs whereas a general scheme of payment lowers the expenses. This may be seen in the low income rate of physicians compared to the average income of workers in the United Kingdom. In 1974, this rate was 2.7 in the United Kingdom compared to 7.0 in France, 6.1 in the FRG and 4.4 for a sample of 14 industrialized countries [26].

The Structure of Services and Personnel

The rigid separation of ambulatory and stationary sectors is typical for many health care systems, especially for those organized on the principles of social security; this separation is abolished in the NHS in favor of more integrated forms of care.

The general practitioner is the first person involved in all health care activities (with the exception of emergencies and special treatment) and thus represents the first important structural element of the system. Ninety-seven percent of the population are registered with such a family doctor. In England about 22,000 general practitioners are working, for the whole of the United Kingdom the number amounts to 28,000.

About 17 percent of the practitioners are working in health care centers within primary health care teams, together with social workers, nurses, health visitors and midwives. Right now, already more than 3,000 physicians work in 900 health care centers. Since 1971 the number of health care centers has risen enormously.

An even greater number of physicians work in group practices and one can say without exaggeration that cooperative health care forms outnumber by far the conventional individual practice.

Special care is carried out by more than 10,000 consultants. About twice as many so-called young doctors (comprising "registrars" and "senior registrars") still undergo their training to become consultants. All these doctors work in hospitals. The consultants work either full or part time (in case they have attained the permission to run a private practice).

The number of doctors has increased since the introduction of the NHS. The number of new medical students is fixed by the government and by now amounts to about 4,000 every year. In the last decade the number of new doctors in Great Britain and Northern Ireland amounted every year to 1,100, while the yearly increase of all doctors was 650. Thus, one can speak of a yearly decrease of 450 doctors. Yet, this decrease is more than compensated by a yearly net increase of doctors from overseas [13] who have found work mainly in unpopular branches such as psychiatric care and elderly care.

In 1980/81 local health services and hospitals fully employed about 800,000 (full time equivalents). The main groups are 38,000 practitioners and dentists (4.75 percent of all the personnel), 367,000 hospital nurses (45.8 percent), 18,000 ambulatory personnel (2.25 percent) and 106,000 administrative employees (13.25 percent). One-third of the 2,600 hospitals were built partly or completely before 1900. Eighty-five new and bigger hospital projects are being planned. On the whole these clinics offer 474,000 beds and the intensity of service is increasing. From 1974 onwards most of local care services has been integrated into the administration of the health districts. The district care official is thus responsible for the home nurses. More than 12,000 home nurses care for patients at their home. About 7,000 health visitors medically advise young mothers and elderly people.

The scope of prevention and public health was integrated in 1974 in the NHS. The physicians employed as community medicine doctors manage the health teams as well as tasks such as health care in schools or inoculation campaigns.

Table 5. NHS Overview, 1981/82 (as of September 1981, in £ millions)

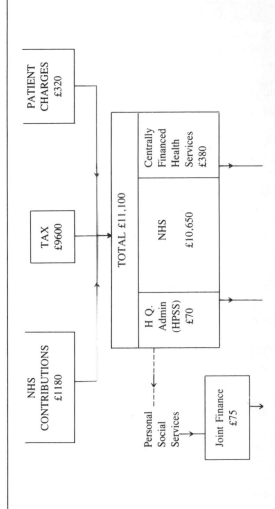

HOSPITAL AND COMMUNITY HEALTH SERVICES
£8250

Current		Capital £630
Medical and Paramedical Support Services	Hotel and General Support Services	
Direct Treatment Services and Supplies		
£3600	£945	£3000

OUTPUT: e.g.

4	m Acute Inpatient cases
28	m Acute Outpatient attendances
13	m Accident & Emergency attendances
1.6 m	Psychiatric outpatient attendances
3.7 m	Health Visitor cases
3.2 m	District Nurse cases

FAMILY PRACTITIONER SERVICES
£2400

Medical £690	Dental £470	Optical £130	Drugs £1110
22,000 GPs 21,000 other staff	12,500 Dentists	8,000 Opticians and Omps	9,000 Pharmacists

180	m GP Consultations
30	m GP Home visits
30	m Courses of dental treatment
300	m Prescriptions
8.5 m	Sight Tests

Source: I. A. Gilbert, "Seeking greater efficiency in the British National Health Service," ISSA (4th) *Improving Cost Effectiveness in Health Care*, Studies and Research No. 19, Geneva 1983; 88

Only a few social services have remained with the local authorities, such as home assistance and housing facilities for the elderly and the mentally ill.

Problems of the British Health Service

The integration of health and care services has been improved by the 1974 reform. Nevertheless, integration is weakened by the fact that occupational medicine was left under the jurisdiction of the Ministry of Labor and therefore organizationally separated from the NHS. The social services which remained within the communities, such as domestic social work, are of great importance for the efficiency of the public health system, so that their financial and organizational separation from the NHS also weakens the integration of services.

The main problem of the NHS is related to the development of British economics since 1974. Beginning with the oil crisis, the situation deteriorated with the devaluation of the British pound in 1976. Since the share of personnel costs in the NHS amounts to 70 percent of the budget, the main effect of the shortage of financial means fell on the employees. The consequences were massive income cuts and acute labor conflicts, because of the low pay and the low social status of the employees in the health system. In 1982 labor conflicts broke out when the government offered a 4 percent wage increase, later extended to 6 percent, compared to the 12 percent inflation rate. The porters, cleaners and catering workers employed in health care systems—a total of 200,000 persons— had such low basic income that they received additional family income supplements usually reserved for persons with an income under the poverty line [30]. Labor conflicts and income cuts in the NHS lead to high levels of personnel turnover and thus contribute to driving qualified personnel to the private health sector.

As there were also cuts in the income of physicians working for the NHS, some concern was expressed as to the low social prestige of all workers (medical and non-medical) in the NHS. The reaction to this danger was the reshuffling of professional structures; practitioners founded a "Royal College" comparable to other professional bodies controlling the access to specialists' careers and thus fostering the formation of elites in the respective disciplines.

The fundamental objective of the NHS, expressed in the Beveridge Report, is threefold, promoting "positive health," interpreted as prevention, "curative medicine" against disease and disability, as well as "rehabilitative and profession-related treatment" as medical and extramedical duties. Obviously, only the second of these aims (curative medicine) plays an important role within the health sector, whereas prevention and rehabilitation have to be limited to a smaller scale and do not enjoy high prestige. Within the NHS the primacy of curative medicine and moreover the priority of clinical medicine is promoted by the centralization and expansion of the hospital system [24].

The history of the NHS defeats the theory that professional autonomy and governmental control cannot be combined. In the course of the development of the NHS, professional power has obviously been increased. The rationalization of the health system has not resulted in the repression of a technically and pharmaceutically intensive hospital medicine in favor of prevention targets. On the contrary, the clinical sphere claims an even higher share of financial means. But on the other hand, new forms of practice are encouraged by the structure of the NHS. Cooperative forms of ambulatory services have increased during the last ten years. Another positive factor is the development of patients' participation groups where laymen cooperate with professionals from the health centers. Because of the collective administration of key sectors of the health centers within the NHS, planning is a high priority compared to other health systems. The reforms of the past few years show the extraordinary importance of improving planning facilities and management and information systems [46].

Recently a Royal Commission described the aims of the NHS in the following way: to encourage the individual and to help him/her to keep his/her health; to contribute to equal rights with regard to consultation of health care facilities; to contribute to high quality care; to contribute to equal availability of facilities and services; to contribute to the free use of these services; and to satisfy the reasonable demands of its users as well as local demands on a national service institution. It seems that these ambitious aims may be more easily achieved in the NHS than in any other Western health services.

C. Pros and Cons: Administration of Health and Health Care in the German Democratic Republic

Historical Foundations

The Second World War left behind not only a ravaged Germany but also a divided one. The German Democratic Republic was founded in 1949 in the area of the Soviet-occupied zone, originally without the recognition of Western states. Due to this difficult situation of isolation, deep-going societal changes had to be implemented rapidly in order to justify trust in socialism or prevent an increase of existing distrust. For this task, the GDR had to rely on the assistance of the Soviet Union.

Obviously, the medical care system was also in a catastrophic state. Many health facilities were destroyed. Physicians, like those in other "liberal" professions, had been overrepresented in, or at least close to. fascist organizations of Hitler's Germany. Consequently, many of them did not want to work in a socialist health system and made off to West Germany. On the other hand, the political leadership of the GDR was glad to forego their assistance in building a socialist health care system. But even those physicians still remaining were skeptical. A part of them saw their West German colleagues had better chances for making profit, which induced them to leave the GDR in order to work in the

FRG. This "flight of physicians" could be more or less stopped only by building the Wall in 1961.

On this basis, a central administration for health care was created immediately after the end of the War in agreement with the Soviet Military Administration (SMAD). The SMAD used its experience in building the Soviet health care system as a guideline so that there are still some similarities in the principles of both health systems:

- Uniformity in the organization of health services;
- Participation of the population in the realization of health protection;
- Prophylactic measures . . . the basis for the overall health care in the country [55].

Right from the beginning in 1946 the Socialist Unity Party (*Sozialistische Einheitspartei Deutschlands*) laid the foundations of a progressive public health program comprising the principles of a comprehensive health care system. These principles were rapidly implemented:

a. legislation protecting the labor force and the right to work;
b. establishment of a uniform social insurance system permitting the expansion of the insurance obligation to all workers;
c. promotion of medical care, establishment and development of hospitals, outpatients' and dental departments;
d. priority to prophylaxis (pregnant and nursing women, children) and establishment of social and medical dispensary care;
e. extension of medical and pharmaceutical laboratories;
f. restructuring of medical study with special emphasis on social sciences;
g. modification in the principles of social welfare; federation of all private welfare institutions to committees of national solidarity [54].

All these changes were implemented in the framework of a national health service, homogeneously organized on the basis of provinces, regions and districts. Thus the majority of medical workers became national employees. As already stated, many qualified doctors emigrated to the FRG, so the need for good doctors was acute. In 1958 the Socialist Unity Party tried to improve the situation with the publication of a memorandum for physicians:

a. further education was organized to change the capitalist thinking and behavior of physicians;
b. new medical publications were created;
c. the scientific exchange of experiences with experts from the USSR and other socialist countries was organized to correct prejudices of GDR physicians with regard to the advantages of a national health system;

   d. finally, a new income scheme was introduced for medical workers, secur-
       ing their existence and guaranteeing a permanent improvement of their
       living standard and professional status.

Beyond that, a commission of physicians was instituted to plan the development of public health and medical science. In the beginning, few physicians
engaged in these activities, but later more of them participated because they saw
that they could implement their own ideas. Eight hundred members of various
medical professions worked on this plan which was later discussed publicly by
factory workers. This created good contacts between physicians and workers and
laid the foundation for an alliance between these two groups [35]
   This plan also took into account physicians with a private practice. In a decree
of the German economic commission dated February 23, 1949, the doctors'
rights to a private practice was regulated: existing practices could usually go on,
but sometimes the permission was only given when the physicians also worked in
the national health service. Physicians engaged in fascist organizations during
the Second World War had to close their practice or did not receive permission to
open one.
   Since 1956 there has been a uniform insurance system with two branches in
the GDR:

   1. The social insurance for workers and employees which cares for 90 per-
       cent of the population and is organized and financially associated with the
       Free German Federation of Labor (*Freier Deutscher Gewerkschaftsbund*);
   2. The social insurance is part of the national insurance, for members of
       socialist production, farming or handicraft cooperatives, for self-em-
       ployed and other groups.

The budget of the social insurance branches is established in the national budget.
The budget of the social insurance for workers and employees is financed by the
insured persons, the factories and the state. In 1980, the national expenditures for
medical care amounted to about 6 percent of the national income.

Outpatient Care

The first outpatient department was established in 1946. In 1950 there were
already 184 outpatient departments and 575 ambulatory care facilities. They
increased in number until the present. On the other hand, the number of private
practices continuously decreased (see Table 6).
   To improve the medical care by specialists in rural areas a net of ambulatory
care facilities was established, with a general practitioner or a specialist for
internal diseases, a dental surgeon and a pediatrician. Beyond that the facilities
had to perform activities in the field of hygiene information and further education
of medical workers. Thus the isolated work of private physicians was abolished

Table 6.   Outpatient Care in the GDR, 1950–1980

	1950	1960	1970	1980
Outpatient departments	184	399	452	561
Ambulatory care facilities	575	766	828	969
National doctor's practices	—	298	1,301	1,645
Private doctor's practices	—	2,253	1,888	863
National nursing stations	2,620	4,493	4,716	5,279

Source: Das Gesundheitswesen in der DDR, Berlin, 1981.

in rural areas in favor of collective facilities. As in many other countries, there are still many vacancies in collective rural practices as physicians prefer to work in cities [18].

Inpatient Care

The number of hospitals and beds decreased from 1950 to 1980. At the same time, the number of hospital patients increased while their average stay in hospital decreased (see Table 7).

Principles of an Integrated and Uniform Public Health

The separate description of outpatient and inpatient care could produce the wrong impression that these two elements of health exist without being integrated. This is not the case. The old 1954 hospital regulation provided the establishment of close functional and personal links between the outpatient departments and the hospital. Of course, the implementation was not easy to perform. The personal linking between hospital and outpatient departments was impossible to realize. The functional linking existed only in the following way: the central outpatient department and a hospital in a given district care for a defined number of people, work together and in cooperation with other services (dispensaries, emergency services, special clinics) but are separated from an organizational point of view.

Table 7.   Inpatient Care in the GDR, 1950–1980

	1950	1960	1970	1980
Number of hospitals	1,063	822	626	549
Number of beds per 1,000 of the population	10.2	11.9	11.1	10.3
Number of patients in hospitals per 1,000 of the population	—	1,178	1,356	1,409
Average days of stay in hospitals	—	29.3	23.3	19.1

Source: Gesundheitswesen in der DDR, Berlin, 1981.

The new 1979 hospital regulation emphasized the principles of integration and unity of public health: With the linking of inpatient and outpatient care the hospital performs the unity of prophylaxis, diagnosis, therapy and "metaphylaxis" which is understood as part of rehabilitation. According to a common GDR definition, it is the complex of all medical and social follow-up measures which aim at supporting and improving the effects of curative treatment. As a center of medical care for citizens of a territory it warrants continuous medical help [25].

The new hospital regulation determines the foundations of medical care, groups and achievements of hospitals and last but not least the management of hospitals. The strong emphasis on hierarchical principles is to be noted. The hierarchy in GDR hospitals is often criticized by Western health managers. The new hospital regulation stipulated nine levels in management functions. Of course, the medical director is subjected to control twice a year he is accountable, for instance, for the implementation of the plan, the collective agreement (to be compulsorily concluded between the medical director and the federation of labor with the participation of all workers).

Two elements of this regulation can be criticized [43]: the long waiting periods in outpatient care and the behavior of the nursing staff vis-à-vis the patient in hospitals (lack of human warmth and attention).

Development of Personnel in Public Health

Contrary to Western industrial countries, there is still a shortage of qualified workers in the GDR. This situation is more marked in the health and social system than in the production of goods. The percentage of workers without professional training in the health and social system (31 percent) is higher than the percentage of workers without professional education in the whole nation (23 percent).

But it must be stressed that in the GDR the number of personnel in health and social care has doubled in the last 25 years, above all in outpatient care. From 1974 to 1977 the staff in outpatient care rose by 20 percent, while in inpatient care this percentage increased only by 7 percent. The nursing staff increased also. In 1980 the physician/nurse ratio was 1 to 2. (See Table 8)

Table 8. Development of Number of Physicians and Nursing Staff from 1949 to 1980 in the GDR

	1949	1973	1976	1980
Physicians	13,222	29,275	32,097	33,894
Dental surgeons	7,100	7,558	8,108	9,709
Nursing staff	—	62,600	71,400	74,000
Nursing staff for sucklings/children	—	12,700	13,400	6,000

Source: Das Gesundheitswesen in der DDR, Berlin, 1981.

Three types of medical care typical for the public health in the GDR will be described next: dispensary care, occupational medical care, and care of handicapped children and youths.

Dispensary Care

This type of care represents a comprehensive health care comprising the examination of the healthy population, therapy, rehabilitation and also permanent observation of chronic and sick people. Prophylaxis, diagnosis, therapy, rehabilitation and "metaphylaxis" should be performed in an integrated way. Dispensary care begins before birth and ends with death. This guarantees a comprehensive and continuous medical care for the entire population [17].

Occupational Medical Care

The theoretical framework of dispensary care allows medical attention to be concentrated on specific groups of the population. This concerns first of all workers with their specific risks.

The prevention and therapy of occupational diseases is a very important task of public health in the GDR. The occupational diseases are considered to be important, not only from a humanitarian point of view but also for economic reasons. However, there is a principle according to which every case of occupational disease expresses a criticism of the working conditions, of occupational health services and of prevention [6]. Occupational care comprises two main groups:

a. In all factories, all the workers with health risks should be registered. Comprehensive health care should be accessible to all healthy and sick people.
b. Occupational medical attention should be directed to chronically sick people, disabled and rehabilitated workers.

The importance of occupational medical care in the GDR can be seen from the fact that, in 1980, 2,731 specialists for occupational diseases were working full time. This number must also be seen in comparison with Western European countries where occupational medicine is a profitable additional income for doctors under contract with the national health system.

Beyond that, there are centers and advisory boards for labor hygiene. About 800 physicians were trained to become specialists in labor hygiene. This fact shows clearly that occupational medicine is not an appendix of curative medicine and that prophylaxis is not merely a slogan in the GDR.

Care of Handicapped Children and Youths

Occupational medicine aims at a higher productivity at work. The care of handicapped children is not based on this motivation. For that reason, interests and needs dominating the health and social system of a country become evident.

A complete registration of, and therapy for, the handicapped can be guaranteed because of the legal obligation to report physically and mentally handicapped children. In 1980, 153,821 children with mental diseases and 378,278 children with physical handicaps were registered. The principle of dispensary care guarantees systematic care of these cases.

Of course, not only handicapped children are cared for, but also healthy children from birth on. This has helped to drastically reduce the infant mortality rate from 131.4 per 1000 in 1946 to 12.1 per 1000 in 1980.

D. Health and Social Struggle: The Italian Case

Before 1978 the Italian health system was based on the principle of social health insurance characterized by structural and functional shortcomings typical of countries with a similar health care system: namely, a lack of preventive strategies, a fragmentation of services and funding institutions, etc. The specifics of the Italian situation were the following:

1. The existence of marked economic and regional disparities were reflected in both the epidemiologic situation and the distribution of health services; the epidemiologic situation in the South was characterized by the emergence of diseases typical of underdeveloped areas (infant mortality, typhus, cholera, etc.), whereas the density of health services was much higher in the North [4].

2. The Italian capital was openly following a strategy of profit maximization at the cost of the health of the working class; labor intensification without corresponding capital investment led to a tremendous increase of occupational accidents and diseases [5].

3. The pharmaceutical industry, in particular, imposed its marketing strategies sometimes in clear contradiction to the health needs of the population [41]. An extreme example was the belated introduction of oral immunization against poliomyelitis in Italy to protect a company producing the previously used vaccine "Salk"; the price for this four-year delay: 1,000 dead and 1,800 paralyzed children [50].

4. On the other hand, there was a strong and conscious working class which, after the Second World War and more specifically in the late 1960s, opened a lively debate on health politics and on the protection of workers in companies and finally started a "battle for health." This debate was channelled through parties and labor unions [63].

5. More distinctly than in other countries, there emerged at that time a radical democratic intelligentsia of medical doctors and other professional groups. They developed, partly autonomously, partly in alliance with the working class, a public debate on health and health strategies. As an illustration of this tendency, we note the movement of democratic psychiatry which finally obtained the complete abolition of traditional psychiatric institutions [3] or the

implementation of the "workers' medicine" paradigm by the Italian trade unions in cooperation with progressive intellectuals.

The Battle for Health

The battle for health initiated and performed by the organizations of the Italian working class (above all the labor unions and the communist party) had its most important formal reference point in Article 32 of the Constitution, which requires the state "to protect health as a basic right of the individual and in the interest of the community." The first step was the creation of a Ministry of Health in 1958, a reflection of an earlier recommendation of the Allied Forces expressed in 1945. Then, in 1959 the socialist-communist labor union CGIL asked the government to establish a national health service. In 1965, the Italian communist party introduced a bill proposing the establishment of a national health service. At the same time the planning bureaucracy and the central left government launched a health reform project. In 1970/71 the first strikes for a comprehensive reform of the Italian health system took place. Then the socialist Minister of Health prepared another bill aiming at the institution of a national health service; however, the Christian-Democrat Prime Minister did not approve it. In 1973 the conference of the regional councillors of health joined those demanding a comprehensive restructuring of the health care system. The five-year plan for 1971–1975 as well as long-term plan "project 80" proposed the establishment of a national health service. In 1973 the communist party presented a revised bill in parliament, again proposing the establishment of a national health service and containing details of its functioning [7, 56, 64].

Finally, in 1978, in a specific stage of Italian politics, characterized by the political formula of national solidarity which meant the inclusion of the communist party in the parliamentary majority, the national health service was finally approved by the government and the parliament. This was a victory after a long-lasting battle of the Italian working class aiming at a comprehensive restructuring of the Italian health system. However, this victory came in a period when the economic situation deteriorated dramatically in Italy. This circumstance was used by the traditional enemies of the reform to jeopardize its implementation. According to Giovanni Berlinguer [15] this obstruction strategy is comprised of four different aspects: delays in implementation; falsification; financial cuts; and clear tendencies of counter-reform. Before the 1983 elections, the propaganda of the Catholic party and its allies showed more or less open intention to sabotage the reform. However, during these elections, this party experienced its heaviest defeat since the Second World War. The coming years therefore will show whether the health reform, "the most significant social reform in Italy since the defeat of fascism" [15], will find an interpretation corresponding to the original intention of the Italian parliament as well as a coherent implementation at the national, regional and local levels.

Workers' Health and Workers' Medicine

At the beginning of the 1970s a new model of prevention of industrial pathology was launched and implemented by the trade unions under the title "Workers' Medicine" [20]. This social experiment led to remarkable changes of institutions (as the unions themselves), of professional images (e.g , in occupational medicine), as well as of industrial relations (at enterprise and national level), and it involved more people than had ever been involved in labor experiments, such as autonomous and semi-autonomous groups. Originally, the new approach was developed in the late 1960s by FIAT workers and leftist intellectuals. In 1969, this principle was published for the first time by the Italian Metal Workers' Federation (FLM). In the brochure "l'ambiente del lavoro" prepared for the Federation's training course, the work environment is defined as the universe of production conditions under which labor and capital invested are being transformed into goods, income (profit and wages) and health disturbances. The factors causing these disturbances can be roughly divided into four groups: (a) factors such as temperature, humidity, lighting, draughts and noise; (b) factors typical for factories such as powders, smoke, radiation; (c) factors connected with hard physical work; and (d) factors pertaining to mental load, such as monotony, repetitiveness, high responsibility, stress, and night-shift work. The health disturbances caused by these factors are mainly accidents, occupational diseases and nonspecific diseases.

Prevention has to concentrate on the place where diseases and accidents are generated and where they can be analyzed and controlled in an easier way: the work environment is such a place. However, there is only one group that has an immediate interest in safeguarding the health of the workers: namely, the workers themselves. Therefore, the Italian trade unions formulated the principle of nondelegation of safeguarding health to other groups or institutions (entrepreneurs, factory inspectors and company doctors). These other groups might also be interested, but always in an intermediate and restricted sense (e.g., increase of productivity, application of law and other regulations). As a main agent of primary prevention and participation, the Italian trade unions did not identify the single worker but the homogeneous group of workers, homogeneous with respect to health risks resulting from the work environment. The homogeneous group, therefore, is nothing else than a product of work organization (it may be a department, an assembly line, a conveyor belt, a group of piece workers). The health risk connected with work is a very clear concept for this group: it is experienced in terms of frequency of minor diseases within the group; absenteeism (frequency and duration of sickness leave); frequency and kind of accidents; staff fluctuations.

In addition to the traditional instruments of (objective) measurement (thermometer, audiometer, etc.), the subjective methods of consensual validation of a given working situation by a homogeneous group were introduced, thus assigning to the workers' experience a major role in the research process and in the management of the preventive system. The title under which this model was disseminated was *"Medicina dei lavoratori"* (workers' medicine) to be distinguished from *"Medicina del lavoro"* (occupational medicine).

The homogeneous group which was mainly described as an epidemiologic entity and the result of work organization was subsequently embedded and integrated in the organizational structure of the Italian trade unions. Each homogeneous group elects a delegate who has to represent the interests of the group. The factory council, which is the assembly of all delegates, is recognized as the representative body of the workers both from the trade unions and the management side.

Safeguarding health and safety in factories is not to be seen as completely separated from health care policy in general. It is not by accident that at the same time the new model was introduced in factories, the battle for the establishment of a national health service was going on in Italy.

It has to be stressed that the national health service contains many elements which facilitate workers' participation in safety and health programs at the factory level. In addition, the unions have created their own network of centers dealing with occupational risks in various regions and districts as well as a national research and documentation center on health risks. It publishes a bimonthly journal (*Medicina dei Lavoratori*) reporting the recent development in occupational medicine at the national and international level as well as the Italian workers' and unions' experiences in respect to work health and safety.

At the beginning, experts in occupational medicine were rather skeptical in view of these initiatives. But in the meantime the contribution made by workers and unions is being accepted by experts. Many of them evaluate these experiences in a very positive way, for instance, the Director of the medical service in the Pirelli Company, Professor Sassi, or the Director of the Institute of Occupational Medicine of the Milan University, Professor Grieco [27], who refers to it as an actual "cultural revolution."

IV. QUALITATIVE SYNOPSIS

A. Developing Countries

The inclusion of Cuba, Nicaragua and Bangladesh in a comparative study reuires some explanation. A variety of aspects indicate that a comparison of the very countries may be a fruitful exercise.

All three countries emerged from liberation wars after World War II. Cuba had a new beginning in 1959, Bangladesh in 1971 and Nicaragua in 1979. The peoples of the three countries had experienced centuries of repression and exploitation. The implications for the health of the population were disastrous. The strategies adopted by the governments of the three countries in order to gain control of the major health problems therefore have many common features. However, they go different ways in implementation.

Depending on the internal power relations, health policy may become a mere instrument of pacification or development. As the selected cases show, liberation, dependence and self-determination do not necessarily lead to "socialist ways." Seen from outside, reforms may be similar, whereas their motivations and goals are controversial. In one case, popular participation means involvement of the population at the decision-making and responsiblity level, in another case it may mean self-limitation and deprivation of the poor population. On the other hand, even under a military dictatorship, popular involvement may be used to further democratic and progressive developments.

Similarities between the countries exist with respect to size and climatic conditions, but there are great differences with respect to population density: Nicaragua 21.7/km², Cuba 84.4/km² and Bangladesh 622.7/km².

In spite of the differences between developing countries on the one hand and the rather arbitrary selection of countries on the other, some paradigms of health care in developing countries may be elaborated.

Popular Medicine

Popular medicine ranges from superstition to empirically confirmed knowledge which does not necessarily imply the existence of a scientific epidemiologic-etiological model. As important as it may be to conserve certain positive elements of popular medicine, it would not be responsible to secure health care of the population on the mere basis of traditional popular medicine.

Western Development Strategies

Such strategies are implicitly mentioned in this article as elaborated methods of health care for the oligarchy and upper classes and as development programs for improving medical care for other classes. These programs are often financed by Western industrialized countries as well as by international organizations. They are based on the professional and technical know-how of the Western world and are often inadequate in respect to the actual needs of the population in developing countries. As a consequence, the cost-benefit ratio may be rather low. And because of the relatively high costs, such programs are mostly not intended to cover the whole country but only to improve health care in limited and selected areas. Sometimes the programs are connected with contradictory expectations reflecting the interest of Western countries to secure neocolonial dependencies through social participation programs.

Alternative Basic Health Care

This approach may be referred to Ivan Illich's "expropriation of health" [31] based on his experiences in Mexico; however, due to an increasingly critical attitude with respect to a more and more medicalized, centralized, professionalized medicine in developed countries, this approach has found considerable attention in Western industrialized countries. In Werner's [62] Mexican experiences with medical care of campesinos we see good examples of rudimentary forms of alternative medical care mainly aiming at the establishment of life-saving forms of self-help in deprived areas or among deprived population groups. This is no doubt a valid approach, at least as valid as the Western developed strategies. However, this approach is very restricted because self-help does not emerge automatically in these circumstances but has to be initiated externally.

The Cuban Paradigm of a National Health Service

The Cuban case is presented in its own section. As was shown, after the victory of a national and subsequently socialist revolution, Cuba has established a health system comparable to the standards of Western and Eastern European countries. The Cuban achievements are convincing: the epidemiologic and health care standards are similar to standards in industrialized countries. Therefore, the Cuban system has become an internationally recognized paradigm. Cuban health workers are active in various developing countries all over the world, in Latin America and in other regions, At present, Nicaragua is developing its health and education strategies following the Cuban example. It may therefore be problematic to mention Cuba as a developing country with respect to its health care system. However, one has to bear in mind that specific political prerequisites have enabled the Cuban government to distribute resources according to its own judgment, thus implementing a health policy without open or hidden interference of other governments or of multinational corporations. These conditions cannot easily be reproduced because the control and exploitation of the Third World is directly connected to the hegemony of Western industrialized countries.

The World Health Organization's Paradigm of "Primary Health Care"

The concept of primary health care was jointly launched by WHO and UNICEF during the famous Alma-Ata Conference in 1978 [65]. The background paper submitted to the Conference stressed that the current situation is characterized by ''a widening gap between the health 'haves' in the affluent countries and the health 'have-nots' in the developing world.''
Primary health care is defined in the following way:

> Primary health care is essential health care based on practical, scientifically sound and socially acceptable methods and technology made universally accessible to individuals and families in the community through their full participation and at a cost that the community and the country can afford to maintain at every stage of their development in the spirit of self-reliance and self-determination. It forms an integral part both of the country's health system, of which it is the central function and main focus, and of the overall social and economic

development of the community. It is the first level of contact of individuals, the family and the community with the national health system bringing health care as close as possible to where people live and work, and constitutes the first element of a continuing health care.

Hannu Vuori [60] interprets this definition in the following ways as:

- a philosophy, emphasizing the basic principles of social justice and equality, individual responsibility, international solidarity and a broader concept of health;
- a strategy to develop the health care system along the following key issues: accessibility, relevance, functional integration, community participation, cost-effectiveness, intersectoral collaboration, redistribution of resources, legislative reforms, re-orientation of health personnel, improved planning and management, utilization of appropriate technology.
  It is also a strategy for social development in general with particular regard to policy sectors as housing, education, employment, etc.
- the lowest and most accessible level of care;
- a set of activities comprising health education and prevention, nutrition, safe water and basic sanitation, etc.

The primary health care paradigm was formulated with particular (not exclusive) regard to the developing countries. It subsumes in itself a variety of positive elements of the other paradigms mentioned before. In several countries primary health care programs were initiated under the auspices of the World Health Organization (e.g., the program of pharmaceutical control in Bangladesh). It is, however, too early to make a conclusive evaluation of these programs.

B. Industrialized Countries

In the comparison of health systems several problems arise as far as industrialized countries are concerned. Resulting from a historical process, health systems are nationally quite different. General conclusions about organization and structure of different systems have to take into account the unique qualities of each. We started from the assumption that the health care system of a particular country is determined by: the relations of production, the economic development, the stage of the class conflicts in and about the health care system, and both the political and economic links of the health care system with other social sectors. This assumption will be confirmed in the following qualitative synopsis of the health systems of the four industrialized countries described in this article.

It is obviously of central concern whether health care is organized privately or publicly and whether it is paid for privately or via health insurance or via taxes. Further relevant points are the level of decision (centralized or decentralized), the role of health workers and clients in the decision-making process, as well as the regional distribution of health care institutions. In this respect the following differences and similarities emerge from the comparison of the four health care systems:

1.   State intervention in the health care systems exists in all the four countries, however, there are large variations in the scope of this intervention. The role of the state is strongest in socialist countries (GDR), rather strong in capitalist countries with a national health service, and weaker in countries with a social-insurance-based health system (Austria).

2.   The coverage of the population is total in socialist countries as well as in capitalist countries with a national health service. It has become almost total in some countries with a social-insurance-based system (in Austria almost 99 percent of the population is covered by social health insurance).

3.   In capitalist countries there prevail mainly private property relations in pharmaceutical and medical industry (at national or multinational levels).

4.   Tendencies of centralization and bureaucratization prevail in all investigated countries (GDR, Austria, United Kingdom, as well as Italy before the reform). The Italian example, however, contradicts the widespread assumption that a national health service necessarily furthers these tendencies. On the contrary, the institution of the national health system promoted decentralization and popular participation.

5.   As far as regional distribution of health care institutions is concerned, there exists a gap between urban and rural areas.

Concerning the function of the health system, it seems relevant whether emphasis is placed on preventive or curative aspects. As far as preventive measures are concerned, we distinguish between individual secondary prevention and primary preventive measures. In this context the quality of occupational health care is an important parameter. Beyond that, the functional integration of the various sectors of the health system, including the psychosocial sector and the integration of groups of social concern (handicapped, elderly and mentally ill people) is of interest.

From the comparison we draw the conclusion that primary prevention is inadequate in all four countries. In political decision-making, economic arguments (with short-term effects) dominate social, health and ecological arguments (sometimes concentrating on long-term results, e.g., chronic diseases). Besides that, in capitalist countries there are additional obstacles and resistances against primary prevention originating from the necessities of capital reproduction at enterprise level. Therefore, the systems of occupational medicine are generally better organized in socialist countries, such as the GDR, than in capitalist countries. Comprehensive care of groups of social concern can only be performed when doctors cooperate with other social and health workers, and this is more likely to occur in a country with an integrated health service, such as in the United Kingdom, than in another system.

Different social groups have different interests in the health system: the patients want to secure their personal existence and survival; other groups (practicing doctors, pharmaceutical and medical firms, private hospitals and insurance companies) pursue their own economic interests. There is also the general interest of capital which consists of the reproduction of the human labor force, whereas the state and the public sector aims at creating consensus through its health and welfare policies but at the same time restricting its expenditures for health and welfare services. Although private capital has more or less disappeared in the GDR, the reproduction of the human labor force is still an important function of the health care system there. Corporate interests of medical doctors may still exist to a certain extent.

Everywhere the influence of the mid-1970s economic crisis has generated incisive effects on the health care systems. Austerity measures, reprivatization, co-payment by the patients—all these are measures which have been proposed and implemented, at least in capitalist countries. Potential for resistance against these tendencies are represented particularly by the workers and the trade union movement. Generally, at times of economic crisis, health care ranges as third priority behind state intervention in support of the economic system and the labor market.

The synopsis of the various health care systems allows us to formulate the following ten theses:

1.   Only a socialist society creates the prerequisites necessary for the establishment of a comprehensive public health care system. In capitalist countries, pressure coming from the working class can lead to a partial socialization of the health system (as in the United Kingdom or in Italy). However, this development is a steady one but characterized by moments of stagnation or regression and tends to exclude "unproductive" sectors (restricted possibilities of rehabilitation for elderly and insufficient integration of disabled persons).

2.   Both social systems have in common the difficulties of convincing the intelligentsia of the advantages of the public health care system. The majority of medical doctors represents a rather conservative element in society and therefore is clearly against the establishment of such a system.

3.   Economically higher developed European countries tend to assign a higher portion of the national income to health care expenditures. This tendency may be reversed in times of economic crisis when the health care system becomes the target of austerity measures and service reductions.

4.   The structures of the health system are rather immobile. The health care sector in developed capitalist countries, such as the United Kingdom and Austria, comparable from the point of view of size and importance with the agri-

cultural sector, is dominated by big and well-established pressure groups: doctors, the pharmaceutical industry, etc. These groups do not allow changes which could jeopardize their profits. The social bureaucracy (social insurance and/or health departments) is not powerful enough to successfully oppose the particular profit and capital interest of those groups.

5.   Preventive measures fail generally, and particularly in capitalist countries, because of the existing and antagonistic interests (e.g., the restriction of the maximum speed limit on highways in Austria is prevented by the transnational petrol companies). There is not a sufficient response to the challenge of the new threats to man's health (ecological crisis). On the other hand the positive impact of curative health care is more and more questioned in highly developed industrialized countries. Ever-rising expenditures for health care (in particular for hospitals) do not find a sufficient reflection in improving health indicators (rising life expectancy).

6.   The number of mental diseases is increasing. Their medical treatment takes place either in badly equipped psychiatric hospitals or outside the traditional care system and mainly on a private basis. This holds true also for the alternative forms of health care such as homeopathy, acupuncture and new methods of cancer treatment.

7.   The bureaucratic and professional dominance as well as confidence in technical/medical progress are the main trends in health care in industrialized countries. New initiatives (e.g. self-help groups) emerge outside the traditional health system. If there are lasting and successful experiences, they may later be subsumed under the traditional system. Because of the rather rigid organization of health care in socialist countries, alternative models may encounter more obstacles and resistance there than in comparable capitalist countries.

8.   In capitalist countries with a public health care system or a very broad social security system, the private sector never retreats completely from health care. A class-oriented society obviously demands a class-oriented medical system (e.g., two classes of hospital beds in Austria).

9.   Short-term political changes may represent a big threat for a national health service directly controlled by the government (austerity policy in the United Kingdom and Italy). Social security systems might be in a slightly better position insofar as their financial means come directly from contributions.

10.   Health planning is easier to implement in comprehensively organized care systems (as in the GDR or the United Kingdom), whereas in a fragmented system (like in Austria) planning measures can only concern parts of the system.

C. Conclusions

It is almost impossible to compare the health systems of developing countries and industrialized countries. The situations are too different. The Cuban example shows that it is possible to improve considerably the health standards of the population in developing countries and to gradually overcome the gap between the "health haves" and the "health have-nots". The most frequent diseases in Third World countries are well known and they could easily be eradicated if the concerned government would dedicate a sufficient amount of money to health care and distribute resources equitably to all classes in a given society, and if the industrialized countries would assist the poorest countries in their fight against hunger, malnutrition, illiteracy and disease. For each stage of development there exists a catalogue of measures which could help drastically reduce morbidity and mortality rates.

Therefore, it is rather clear what is to be done, the open question being "how to do it?" under the present circumstances of a world characterized by the existence of two ideological hemispheres fighting for influence in the Third World, as well as by political instability in those countries due partly to internal structural problems and partly to all kinds of outside interventions (general, economic, political and military interests and in particular the marketing interests of multinational companies).

In industrialized countries most infectious diseases are under control, hunger has disappeared, and the level of education has risen. Even in societies with marked social inequalities, the lower strata of the population have achieved a living standard which is much higher than that of the majority of the world population. However, because of different social organizations of production and reproduction, new diseases have emerged and now dominate the morbidity/mortality profile of industrialized countries (cardiovascular diseases, cancer, psychosomatic diseases, etc.). And it seems as if medical science and medical practice do not have a coherent answer to this challenge. The main question to be answered by the medical professional as well as the health politician and administrator is therefore: "What to do?" This evaluation of positive and negative experiences of various countries may contain at least some ideas about ways and directions to be followed or to be avoided.

In both developing and developed countries, a major question is the identification of social actors in health policy. Health policy, like any other policy, is more than a set of good ideas. It needs for its implementation and the bringing about of reforms a minimum of consensus and collaboration as well as a stable constellation of alliances of the various groups operating in the field: doctors, paraprofessionals, administrators and, last but not least, the clients—the people themselves.

REFERENCES

1. Autorenkollektiv, *Systemanalyse des Gesundheitswesens in Oesterreich*, 2 Baende, Melk, 1978.
2. Barraclough, S., *Food systems and society*. The case of Nicaragua. Progress report. UNRISD, Geneva, 1981 (photocopied manuscript).
3. Basaglia, F., *Die negierte Institution*. Frankfurt, 1971.

4. Berlinguer, G., Scarpa, S., *La riforma sanitaria*, Roma, 1974.
5. Berlinguer, G., *La salute nelle fabriche*, Bari, 1969.
6. Braeunlich, A., Konetzke, G., Entwicklungstendenzen, Bekämpfung und Begutachtung von Berufskrankheiten in der DDR, in: *Zeitschrift fuer die gesamte Hygiene 25* (1979), H.9, pp. 675–680.
7. Buiatti, E., Gededes, M., Maciocco, G., *Manuale di sanità pubblica*, Roma, 1981.
8. Bundesministerium fuer Gesundheit und Umweltschutz und Oesterreichisches Statistisches Zentralamt, *Bericht über das Gesundheitswesen in Oesterreich im Jahr 1979*, Wien, 1981.
9. Cardenal, F., Testimony before an Investigation Committee of the US Congress, 8–9 June 1976, in: Informationsbuero Nicaragua (ed.): *Nicaragua—ein Volk in Familienbesitz*, Reinbek bei Hamburg, 1979, p. 22.
10. Carta Informativa. Logros y Realizaciones 1979–1983. *Junta de Gobierno de Reconstrucción Nacional*. Managua, 1983, pp. 1–6.
11. Castro, F., *Second Declaration of Havana*, p. 18.
12. Chester, T., *The British National Health Service*, translated paper, 1976.
13. Cuyler, A., Gesundheitssysteme der Welt: England, in: *Medita 6*, 1981, pp. 21–28.
14. *Datos basicos sobre Nicaragua, FSLN*, Managua, 1980.
15. Delogu, S., *L'impatto dell'attuale crisi del sistema capitalistico internazionale sui servizi sanitari: il caso Italia*.
16. Ertler, W., et al., *Ärztliche Versorgung in Oesterreich* (Teil 1), OeBIG, Wien 1983, pp. 50ff.
17. Ewert, G., Hornei, R., Theoretischer Ansatz für eine perspektivisch orientierte Dispensairbetreuung, in: *Zeitschrift für die gesamte Hygiene 19* (1973) Nr. 6, pp-448–455.
18. Ewert, G., oral communication.
19. Field, F., *Comparative Health Systems: differentiation and convergence*, Paper submitted to the National Center for Health Services Research, Health Resources Administration, Public Health Service, Cambridge, Mass., 1976.
20. FIM- FIOM—UILM, 1969.
21. Fischer Weltalmanach. Frankfurt, 1984.
22. Fleissner, P., Karner, W., Wintersberger, H., Grundsätzliche Überlegungen zu einer komparativen Analyse von Gesundheitssystemen am Beispiel Italiens, Großbritanniens und der Deutschen Demokratischen Republik, in: *Gesundheit im gesellschaftlichen Konflikt*, W. Schoenbaeck (ed.), Muenchen-Wien-Baltimore, 1980.
23. Fleissner, P., *Gesundheitsinformationssysteme*, OeBIG, Wien 1981 (unpublished manuscript).
24. Gerhardt, U., 30 Jahre nationaler Gesundheitsdienst, in: *Oesterreichische Zeitschrift fuer Soziologie*, Wien, 3/4 (1977), pp. 16–28.
25. *Gesetzblatt der Deutschen Demokratischen Republik*. Berlin, 15. Februar 1980, Sonderdruck Nr. 1032. Rahmen-Krankenhausordnung (RKO vom 14. November 1979, p. 2).
26. Gilbert, I., Seeking greater efficiency in the British National Health Service, in: *ISSA, Improving cost effectiveness in health care*, Studies and Research No 19, Geneva, 1983, pp. 86–91.
27. Grieco, oral statement at a meeting on workers' medicine organized by the National Research Council, Italy, 1982.
28. Heisler, W., Der nationale Gesundheitsdienst Großbritanniens, in: *Krankenhaus Umschau* 2/1979, pp. 90–93.
29. Horejs, I., and Kovatsch, G., *Propuesta de una estructura de la formación basica de los Brigadistes Lideres de Salud*. (BLS). El Rama, 1983 (photocopied manuscript).
30. Iliffe, S., *The economic and political crises in the British National Health Services* (paper presented at the International Conference on Health Policies in Western Europe, Frankfurt, 1982).
31. Illich, I., *Medical Nemesis*, Reinbek bei Hamburg, 1975.
32. Incer, J., *Geografía Basica de Nicaragua*, Managua, 1977.

33. *Indicadores Socio-Economicos 1970–1980*. Instituto Nacional de Estadística y Censos, Managua, 1981.
34. *Informe sobre cuatro anos de revolución (1979–19 de Julio 1983)*. Instituto Nicaragüense de Seguridad Social y Bienestar. Managua, 1983.
35. Kuehn, K., (ed.), *Ärzte an der Seite der Arbeiterklasse*. Beitraege zur Geschichte der Bündnisse der deutschen Arbeiterklasse mit der medizinischen Intelligenz, VEB-Verlag, Volk und Gesundheit, Berlin, 1973.
36. Lachkovics, E., Bangladesh -wenn sich die Armen wehren . . . in: *Entwicklungspolitische Nachrichten*, 2/1983, pp. 10–12.
37. La salud avanza en Nicaragua. Logros de salud en 1982, in: *El Nuevo Diario*, 13/1/1983, pp. 5–8.
38. Ley del sistema nacional de salud, in: *Decretes—Leyes para Gobierno de un pais a traves de una Junta de Gobierno de Reconstrucción Nacional*. Managua, 1979, pp. 39–41.
39. *Ley de Promocion de Lactancia Materna, in: Leyes de la República de Nicaragua*. Volumen V. Ministerio de Justicia, Managua, 1982, pp. 291–293.
40. Marcias Gomez, E., Algunas consideraciones sobre la Seguridad Social en Nicaragua, in: *Revista Centroamericana de Ciencias de la Salud* 5(1979)12, pp. 149–165.
41. Marri, G., Pan e veleno, in: *Rinascita*, No 43/1976.
42. Marri, G., *L'ambiente di lavoro anni '70*. Roma, 1975.
43. Mueller-Dietz, H., Die Rahmen-Krankenhausordnung der DDR vom November 1979, in: *Die Berliner Ärztekammer 18* (1981) Nr. 4, pp. 163–170.
44. Navarro, V., Work, Ideology and Science, the case of medicine, in: *Health and Work Under Capitalism*, Navarro, Beaman (eds.), New York 1977.
45. Oddone, I., Marri, G., *L'ambiente di Lavoro*, Roma, 1977.
46. Pritchard, P., *Patient Participation in General Practice*, unpublished manuscript, 1982.
47. Repercusion de la agresion en la situation de salud del pais, in: *El Nuevo Diario*, 9.8/1983.
48. Revolution ist Gesundheit. Das neue Gesundheitswesen in Nicaragua. *Medico International*, Frankfurt/Main, 1981, pp. 11–12.
49. Salud: politicas, logros y limitaciones. *Ministerio de Salud. Managua 1980*. second revised edition, pp. 18–20.
50. Scarpa, S., Chiti, L., *Di farmaci si muore*. Roma, 1975.
51. Schicke, R., Der organisatorische Wandel der Gesundheitsdienste in England seit Begirn dieses Jahrhunderts, in: *Gesundheitswesen* 25(1973) pp. 500–508.
52. Schindl, K., Gesundenuntersuchungen, in: *Review Nr. 1*, 1981, p. 37 f.
53. Schoenbaeck, W., Markt versus Staat im Gesundheitswesen, in: Schoebaeck, W., *Gesundheit im gesellschaftlichen Konflikt*, Muenchen-Wien-Baltimore, 1980, p. 313.
54. Schueler, H., Die Entwicklung des Gesundheitswesens in *der Deutschen Demokratischen Republik, in: Sozialismus und Gesundheit*. Probleme der Gesundheit und der physischen Entwicklung des Menschen, Medizin und Gesellschaft Band 6, VEB Fischer Verlag Jena, 1979.
55. Semashko, N., *People's Commissar for Health in the USSR from 1918–1920*. Co-founder of the soviet national health system.
56. Spandonaro, M., Approvato dalla Camera il disegno di legge di riforma sanitaria, in: *Medicina dei Lavoratori*, 3–4/1978.
57. Terris, M., *The Functions and Structures of Health Departments in a National Health Service: Experience in other countries*. Paper presented at the annual meeting of the American Public Health Association, Los Angeles, 1978.
58. Treytl, J., the author took part in the organization and implementation of the Austrian aid program.
59. Voigt, H., *Das Gesundheitswesen im neuen Nicaragua*. Abteilung für Politische Soziologie und Entwicklungsforschung der Universität Linz, Linz, 1982.

60. Vuori, H., Research in Primary Health Care, in: *Eurosocial Reports No. 21*, Wien 1982, p. 30.

61. Vutuc, Ch., Medizinische Versorgung in Entwicklungsländern: Darstellung der Problematik am Beispiel von Bangladesh, in: Öffentliches Gesundheitswesen 40 (1978) pp. 71–78.

62. Werner, D., Lateinamerika, *Analysen und Berichte 4. Internationale Strategien und Praxis der Befreiung*, Veronika Bennholdt-Thomsen (ed.), et al., Berlin, 1980.

63. Wintersberger, H., Arbeitermedizin in Italien, *Ein Beitrag zur Komparativen Analyse der Entstehungs-und Bewältigungbedingungen von Krankheiten im entwickelten Kapitalismus*, Wissenschaftszentrum Berlin, Wien, 1981.

64. Wintersberger, H., Arbeitermedizin in Italien -und in der BRD? In: *Unsere tägliche Gesundheit*, 1981, pp. 218–234.

65. World Health Organization, *Primary Health Care*, Alma Ata, Geneva 1978.

66. World Health Organization, *World Health Statistics*, vital statistics and causes of death, Geneva, 1982.

THE DIVERGENT EVOLUTION OF OSTEOPATHY IN AMERICA AND BRITAIN

Hans A. Baer

This paper will discuss the divergent evolution of an alternative health system, namely osteopathy, in the United States and Britain. It will be argued that this divergence must be accounted for in large measure by differences in the sociopolitical contexts of these two countries as well as their respective plural medical systems. While much of the attention that has been given to medical pluralism has focused on Asian and African societies, there is a growing recognition that industrial societies are also characterized by a wide array of alternatives to allopathic or cosmopolitan medicine. For example, Charles Leslie [32:9] notes that:

> Even in the United States, the medical system is composed of physicians, dentists, druggists, clinical psychologists, chiropractors, social workers, health food experts, masseurs, yoga teachers, spirit teachers, Chinese herbalists, and so on. The health concepts of a Puerto Rican

Research in the Sociology of Health Care, Volume 5, pages 63-99.
ISBN: 0-89232-597-6

worker in New York City, the curers he consults, and the therapies he receives, differ from those of a Chinese laundryman or a Jewish clerk. Their concepts and the practitioners they consult differ in turn from those of middle-class believers in Christian Science or in logical positivism.

Just as in the case of the United States, Britain's plural medical system includes an array of alternative health practitioners, including not only osteopaths but also chiropractors, naturopaths, and homeopaths.

Since several scholars, including myself, have discussed the development of osteopathy in the United States in some detail, this paper will only present a brief review of this subject [1, 3, 19, 38]. Instead my main concern in this essay will be in the development of osteopathy in Britain. Whereas osteopathy has become osteopathic medicine and osteopaths have become osteopathic physicians in the United States, in many ways osteopathy in Britain and in other parts of Europe resembles what it looked like in the United States perhaps sixty or seventy years ago. Whereas osteopathic physicians (DOs) in the United States have full practice rights in all fifty states (since 1974), osteopaths in Britain, much like chiropractors in the United States (and also Britain) are generally restricted to "nonmedical" techniques of health care such as spinal manipulation. Conversely, it will be shown that in adapting to a different sociopolitical context, osteopathy in Britain has undergone changes of its own, not to speak of various lines of development.

Also like chiropractic in the United States, osteopathy in Britain has been characterized by intense factionalism. Osteopathic factionalism in Britain is even more complex in that there appear to be at least five different camps of osteopaths. Brian Inglis [24:97], a sympathetic observer of "unorthodox medicine," describes British osteopaths as having a "caste system" of their own:

> There are osteopaths and osteopaths. In the eyes of the law—and of many doctors—they are all equal; but in their own eyes, some are more equal than others. The differences are not so much of technique, though they also exist, as of status. The rivalry is not on a horizontal plane, between different groups advocating different theories or methods; it is vertical—a caste system of a kind only the British could evolve, with a well-established pecking order.

Although many comparative studies of allopathic or cosmopolitan medicine have been conducted, little attention has been paid to the development of alternative health systems in different sociopolitical settings. One notable exception to this observation is Julius Roth's [46] examination of "natural medicine" or *Naturheilkunde* in the United States and West Germany. "In Germany 'natural' approaches to health and healing have a long history: They have been experienced by large segments of the population and are not the minor fringe movement that they have been in the United States until recently" [46:79]. Most practitioners of *Naturheilkunde,* homeopathy, and anthroposophy are also members of the allopathic medical profession. While these practitioners constitute a relatively small proportion of the medical profession, many of them hold respectable positions in *Kurorte* (cure places), *Bäder* (baths), and sanatoria as well as private practices, hospitals, or the teaching staffs of medical schools. Furthermore, these various alternative health systems enjoy the legal support of some state governments. While a certain degree of tension does indeed exist between allopathic medicine and "outsider medicine" in West Germany, Roth [46:87–88] describes the relationship between the two as a truce. In attempting to account for the differential status of natural medicine and other unorthodox healing methods in the United States and West Germany, he points to their respective structural positions relative to allopathic medicine. Whereas the natural health approach has developed almost entirely outside of allopathic medicine in the United States, in West Germany it is an integral "part of the same overriding professional structure" [46:92]. Elsewhere, Unschuld [54] demonstrates that the status of homeopathy, anthroposophy and botanical medicine in West and East Germany, particularly with respect to their use of alternative drug therapy, has been shaped by the larger sociopolitical systems in those two countries. Whereas the government in the centrally planned political economy of East Germany has placed relatively strong restrictions on alternative drug therapy, the more laissez-faire market of West Germany has resulted in the government there tending to avoid an explicit preference for any specific therapy system. Following along the general lines suggested by the work of both Roth and Unschuld, I will analyze the divergent evolution of osteopathy in terms of certain factors within the larger sociopolitical environments that this occurred.

I. A BRIEF REVIEW OF THE DEVELOPMENT OF OSTEOPATHY IN THE UNITED STATES

Osteopathy emerged in the 1860s and the 1870s as a reaction to what its founder Andrew Taylor Still perceived to be the excesses of regular or allopathic medicine. Along with several other nineteenth-century medical sects, including chiropractic, it challenged the emphasis that allopathic medicine placed on the use of drugs, bleeding and surgery. Based upon his anatomical investigations of the human body, Still came to believe that many, if not all, diseases were due to the faulty articulation of the various parts of the musculosketal system particularly the spinal vertebra and their associated musculature. Such dislocations produce disordered nerve connections which in turn act to impair the proper circulation of the blood and other body fluids. In his practice, Still began to rely more and more upon manipulation as a form of therapy and came to oppose the use of drugs, vaccines, serums, and, except for special circumstances, surgery.

It was not long before American osteopathy began to accommodate itself to the practices of regular medicine. According to Reed [44], by the early 1930s the curriculum of osteopathic colleges closely resembled that of regular medical schools. With time, most of the specialties of regular medicine became part of the osteopathic profession in the United States. DOs began to refer to themselves as osteopathic physicians rather than osteopaths and to their practice as osteopathic medicine rather than osteopathy. Only a small but at times vocal minority of American osteopaths emphasize the centrality of osteopathic manipulation therapy (OMT) in the treatment of health problems.

Until recently, organized medicine in the United States waged a vigorous campaign against osteopathy and particularly chiropractic. In addition to having branded osteopaths "cultists," the medical profession employed a variety of tactics to destroy or restrict their practice, including opposition to the licensure of DOs, denial of membership for DOs in local medical societies, the prohibition of professional interaction between MDs and DOs, and support for limited licensure laws which prohibited the use of various drugs and surgery by DOs. During World War II, the American Medical Association (AMA) successfully blocked the appointment of DOs as medical officers. Despite the fact that the United States Congress authorized the appointment of DOs as military officers, organized medicine's dominance of military hospitals delayed such appointments until 1966 [6:415]. The AMA also opposed governmental financial support of osteopathy, such as aid for osteopathic colleges.

Despite the various attempts on the part of organized medicine to weaken the osteopathic profession, the fact that DOs had gradually gained full practice rights in most states and constituted a large proportion of general practitioners in certain states made it clear that osteopathy was not being eliminated. Beginning in the early 1950s, organized medicine began to shift its policy to one of cooptation. The climax of this strategy occurred in 1961 when the California Medical Association and the California Osteopathic Association merged. As a result of this merger, 86 percent of the DOs in California (about 2,000 in number) became MDs, the California College of Osteopathic Physicians and Surgeons became the University of California College of Medicine, Irvine, and most of the osteopathic hospitals in the state were converted into allopathic hospitals. About the same time of the merger, the AMA decreed that each state medical society could determine whether or not to accept DOs as professional equals. "The test should be: Does the individual doctor of osteopathy practice osteopathy or does he in fact practice a method of healing founded on a scientific basis?" [25:774]. Despite the vehement reaction of the American Osteopathic Association (AOA) to the California merger, merger proposals between the two professions were discussed by the AMA at the national level in June 1967 for the first time. The House of Delegates authorized the trustees to negotiate for merger of osteopathic and allopathic colleges [6].

Regardless of how rank-and-file members of the osteopathic profession may have viewed the California merger, the general reaction of its leadership in the AOA was one of strong disapproval and alarm. Despite some other attempts at mergers, such as those in the states of Pennsylvania and Washington, the osteopathic profession successfully prevented the loss of other state societies to organized medicine [41]. With the loss of most DOs in California to organized medicine, the leadership of the osteopathic profession fell upon the Michigan group.

The most concrete indicator of a process of organizational rejuvenation in the American osteopathic profession is the tremendous increase in the number of osteopathic schools that has occurred since 1969. In 1969, the first osteopathic school to have been established since 1916 was established as a private college in Pontiac, Michigan [55]. When the osteopathic profession in Michigan realized that it could not support an osteopathic college on its own, it turned to support from the state legislature. Partly because DOs, particularly since World II, have provided much of the primary care in Michigan, the state legislature approved the annexation in January 1970 of the osteopathic college to the Michigan State University. In contrast to all previously established osteopathic colleges, the College of Osteopathic Medicine at Michigan State became the first state-sponsored osteopathic college in the history of the profession. In addition, nine other osteopathic colleges have been established in the past decade, and there are plans to establish an osteopathic school at Arizona State University.

II. THE DEVELOPMENT OF OSTEOPATHY IN BRITAIN

Since its early development, American osteopathy has had strong connections with Great Britain. Although the connections between bonesetting, an ancient art of healing, and osteopathy are obscure, Gevitz [19:15–16] has suggested that the latter was in large measure inspired by the former. Bonesetters worked in a relatively unrestricted environment in preindustrial England and could be found in America since the colonial period. It is noteworthy to add that Andrew Taylor Still advertised himself as the "lightening bone setter" during the 1880s. During the early years of osteopathy, several men from Great Britain studied this new philosophy of healing at its mecca in Kirksville, Missouri. Shortly after Still opened the American School of Osteopathy in 1892, he met William Smith (1862–1912), a Scottish physician who had earned his graduate licentiate in medicine and surgery at the University of Edinburgh [21:37]. Smith became so enthralled by Still's theories that he became the first lecturer in anatomy at the new school.

Undoubtedly the most important figure linking osteopathy between the two sides of the Atlantic was John Martin Littlejohn (1865–1947). A native of Glasgow, Scotland, Littlejohn was a renaissance man of sorts. He apparently received training in the arts, theology, Oriental languages, political economy, and physiology and anatomy [5]. Although Littlejohn received most of his higher education from the University of Glasgow, he earned a Ph.D. from Columbia University in 1894. From 1894 to 1898, he served as the president of Amity College at College Springs, Iowa. Littlejohn's poor health, particularly involving neck and throat complications, forced him to resign his position but led him to visit Andrew Still in Kirksville for treatment several times. After being cured, Littlejohn enrolled as a student at the American School of Osteopathy and, shortly thereafter, was appointed its Dean of Faculty and Professor of Physiology. After receiving his DO degree in 1900, he founded, with his brothers, James and John, the American College of Osteopathic Medicine and Surgery, the forerunner of the Chicago College of Osteopathic Medicine. Littlejohn continued his education by earning an MD degree from the Dunham homeopathic college in Chicago. Littlejohn left the United States in 1913 in order to permanently settle in London, although it is not clear whether the differences that he had with the leadership of the AOA were a critical factor in his decision to do so.

In 1898, Littlejohn introduced osteopathy in Britain by reading a paper on it before the Society of Science and Arts in London [21:8]. Dr. F. J. Horn was the first person to practice osteopathy in Britain when he opened an office in London in 1902. His example was followed by several other American-trained osteopaths, including Dr. Willard Walker, who established an osteopathic practice in Scotland, and Drs. Jay Dunham and Harvey Foote, who started practices in Ireland. As early as 1903, Horn discussed with Littlejohn the possibility of establishing an osteopathic school in England [20:9]. While Still emphasized the importance of anatomy in osteopathic training, Littlejohn regarded physiology as being of greater significance. Whereas many osteopaths at the time rejected the use of drugs, anesthetics, and antiseptics, Littlejohn, while urging the use of these substances in moderate amounts, felt that their use was an integral part of osteopathy as a complete philosophy of medicine. The ironic twist is that osteopaths in Britan exhibit an approach to healing much more faithful to the principles espoused by Still than those of osteopathic medicine in its present form in the United States.

Apparently there was a sufficient number of American-trained osteopaths in Britain for some of them to convene in 1910 or 1911 in Manchester in order to establish the British Osetopathic Society, later renamed the British Osteopathic Association [35]. The British Osteopathic Association (BOA) applied for registration under the Companies Act as a scientific society. The British medical establishment, however, voiced its opposition to this request through the General Medical Council and the petition was refused by the Board of Trade. John Martin Littlejohn, with the assistance of F. J. Horn, established in 1915 the British School of Osteopathy (BSO), later incorporated in 1917. Although one share of stock in the BSO was originally controlled by the BOA, further collaboration between the two groups broke down when the latter insisted that it own the school. With the exception of occasional cooperative arrangements when faced by external threats, the rivalry between these two osteopathic factions or camps has continued up to the present day.

In 1920, William Looker, who had practiced osteopathy in Pennsylvania for many years, returned to England and established a practice in Manchester [35]. The following year, he founded the Manchester School of Osteopathy (known as the "Looker School"). This institution was later moved to London but ceased operations when its founder died in 1926.

The members of the Looker School banded together to form the Incorporated Association of Osteopathy, Limited, in 1925. The association later became the Osteopathic Association of Great Britain. Members of the Looker School allied themselves with the British School of Osteopathy, and were given a series of twelve lectures at monthly intervals by the faculty of the school. Those who passed were granted the School's diploma. This same privilege was extended to a few graduates of the old British College of Chiropractors [4:107].

Despite the differences between the BOA and BSO factions, they managed to unite on what they both perceived to be a common threat, namely the ability of independent or "free-lance" osteopaths to practice under common law. Since under British common law, anyone may practice as an osteopath, chiropractor, or naturopath (regardless of previous training), various individuals—some of whom apparently served as apprentices for other osteopaths or took short courses in osteopathy—began to practice osteopathy or at least some form of spinal manipulation, much to the chagrin of the BOA and BSO osteopahs. In order to counter the competition of what they felt were unqualified manipulators, organizationally-based osteopaths believed that the best form of professional protection preventing the practice of the former would be the establishment of a legal register somewhat analogous to the one dictating entree into the allopathic profession. An early effort, spearheaded by the Osteopathic Defence League, along these lines met with failure when its petition was rejected in 1925 by the Ministry of Health [35:58–61]. Bills to establish a government-sanctioned register for osteopaths were read before the House of Commons in 1931, 1933, and 1934 [24, 35].

When these attempts failed, a request to the House of Lords for consideration of a registry bill was granted. The Select Committee of the House of Lords met on twelve occasions between March 14 and April 12, 1935. The supporters of the bill, which read that "an unqualified and incompetent quack and charlatan would be debarred from practicing osteopathy," included the British Osteopathic Association, the Incorporated Association of Osteopaths, the Osteopathic Defence League, and the British School of Osteopathy [quoted in 35:59]. Opponents of the bill included the British Medical Association, the General Medical Council, a number of universities and medical schools, the Royal College of Surgeons of England, and the Royal College of Physicians of London as well as the Chartered Society of Massage and Medical Gymnastics, the Nature Cure Association, and the British Chiropractors' Association. Wilfred Streeter, counsel for the supporters of the bill, argued before the Select Committee that "The practice of osteopathy, though widespread in the United States of America and Canada, is carried on in the United Kingdom by not more than two or three thousand practitioners of whom only one hundred and seventy can claim to be 'qualified' '' [quoted in 35:99]. Another source reported a slightly higher number of "qualified" osteopaths in Britain, 96 of whom were graduates of the BSO and 83 of whom were graduates of American osteopathic colleges [10].

Because of a number of factors, including the opposition of organized medicine and the differences between the BOA and BSO on educational standards, the parliamentary bill to regulate osteopathy in Great Britain failed to pass [21:45–46, 47:42]. Instead the investigating committee of the House of Lords recommended that the concerned osteopathic bodies establish a voluntary register of their own. A consequence of this was the establishment by the General Council and Register of Osteopaths, Ltd. of a register which permits an osteopath to place the letters MRO (Member of the Register of Osteopaths) after the letters DO (Diploma in Osteopathy). The Register of Osteopaths requires completion of four years of training at the BSO or an American osteopathic college or one year of training at the London College of Osteopathy. As the size of the BSO camp became larger than the BOA, however, many members of the latter chose to disaffiliate themselves from the Register.

In addition to the voluntary register, another consequence of the hearings of the Select Committee was the establishment of the London College of Osteopathy. After a long formative period, the College was finally opened in 1946 as a postgraduate institution providing training in osteopathy to regular medical practitioners. Over the years, enrollment at the College has been small, as is indicated by Beal's [4] report that it had graduated only ten students and had an enrollment of three students at the time of its fourth year of operation. A later report indicates that the college limited its enrollment for each year of its two-year curriculum (consisting of nine months full-time study and an additional nine months part-time clinical work) to seven [40]. Physicians not only from Britain but also from various countries on the Continent have studied at the College. The school ceased operations in 1975 but was reestablished in 1978 as the London College of Osteopathic Medicine (LCOM) [43]. The College attempts to enroll only students who intend to specialize in osteopathic manipulative therapy (OMT). In 1983, five students, four Britons and a New Zealander, were enrolled in the LCOM's 13-month course. According to Inglis [24:98], graduates of the school "think of themselves as, and call themselves, 'Dr.' [and] tend to feel more comfortable with doctors, from whom the great majority of their patients are referred, than with the British-trained osteopaths who are not doctors."

Since World War II, the development of at least two more factions has added to the complexity of the osteopathic scene in Britain. Both of these factions tend to be much more eclectic in their approaches to health care than osteopaths affiliated with the older organizations and have their own schools and voluntary registers. In fact, the first of these factions, the British Naturopathic and Osteopathic Association (BNOA) was initially a naturopathic group which over time added spinal manipulation to its regimen. The British Naturopathic Association, which was renamed the BNOA in 1961, "was formed in 1945 from a merger of the Nature Cure Association of Great Britain (then nearly 30 years old) and the British Association of Naturopaths (then 20 years old)" [9:6]. The BNOA operates the British College of Naturopathy and Osteopathy, which is housed in "Frazer House" in London The school's four-year curriculum results in the graduate being awarded the Diploma in Naturopathy (ND) as well as the Diploma in Osteopathy (DO). When the BSO faction opposed the inclusion of the BNOA manipulators under its register, the latter formed its own register, allowing its members to place the letters MBNOA (Member of the British Naturopathic and Osteopathic Association) after their names and degrees [24:100].

The Society of Osteopaths, the newest faction on the osteopathic scene in Britain, emerged as a result of a conflict within the BNOA. Although in large part many of its original members were former members of the BNOA or, in some instances, practitioners who maintained dual membership in the SO and BNOA, some were individuals who for a variety of reasons decided to resign from the OAGB. This faction apears to be eclectic in its approach to health care, translating into an openness to more controversial osteopathic techniques, such as cranial and visceral manipulation, but also naturopathy, herbalism, acupuncture, and homeopathy.

The Maidstone Osteopathic Clinic and Institute of Applied Technique was founded in 1954 in the Maidstone section of Kent, a suburb of London, by John Wernham and T. Edward Hall, both graduates of the BSO [21]. While the exact reasons that Wernham and Hall broke with the BSO are not clear, they apparently wished to preserve the holistic osteopathic concept of John Littlejohn, the founder of the BSO.

In order to complete the story of the emergence of the Society of Osteopaths, we must briefly consider the development of osteopathy on the Continent. The origins of osteopathy on the other side of the English Channel remain obscure but apparently many French and Belgian physiotherapists, who are independent practitioners (unlike the situation in Britain where physiotherapists work as auxiliaries or under the supervision of regular medical practitioners), have been converting themselves into osteopaths over the past several decades. The Ecole Francaise d'Ostéopathie was established in 1951 in Paris, at least in part, to assist in this conversion process [42]. While it is illegal for anyone, except a regular medical practitioner, to perform spinal manipulation in France and Belgium, law enforcement agencies have generally looked the other way, arresting osteopaths only in incidents where allopathic physicians complained about such infractions. It seems that the operation of an illegal osteopathic school in Paris was a bit too much for the French medical establishment and the French School of Osteopathy was forced to close. It moved its location in 1965 to the premises of the BCNO in London. When tensions developed between the BCNO administration and the faculty of the French school, the latter reestablished itself as the Ecole Européene

d'Ostéopathie (EEO) and became the teaching unit of the Maidstone Osteopathic
Clinic.

Initially, the EEO offered courses for French and Belgian physiotherapists in
French-speaking classes, but later expanded its program to include English-
speaking students. The creation of the English-speaking program, called the
European School of Osteopathy (ESO), occurred as a result of a request by a
large portion of the BCNO faculty and student body who felt disgruntled with the
manner in which osteopathy was being taught at their institution. In 1974, the
ESO was administratively separated from the Maidstone Clinic, but was housed
next door and maintained a close relationship with the clinic. In 1979, the ESO
moved to new premises in Maidstone but its students continued to receive
clinical training at the Maidstone Clinic. As a result of disagreements concerning
the types of manipulative techniques to be used at the clinic that developed
between the former's director and the ESO, the latter established its own clinic
on its premises in the summer of 1981. Because facilities at the ESO became
extremely crowded, the school constructed a new clinic and additional classroom
space. At the present time, the ESO offers two programs of study leading to the
DO (European). One is a six-year part-time tutorial course (conducted in French)
for French and Belgian state-registered physiotherapists. These practitioners continue their practices on the continent but periodically commute to England for
classes. The second program is a four-year, full-time course conducted in English. The ESO does not accept regular medical practitioners or medical students
into its programs, unless they choose to give up the practice or study of allopathic
medicine. Graduates of ESO are eligible to become members of the Society of
Osteopaths.

Excluding the Osteopathic Medical Association, a now almost defunct group
of regular medical practitioners who have received training in OMT at the
LCOM, there are five or six distinct camps of osteopaths in Britain. As is
indicated in Table 1, four of these camps are centered around the various osteopathic associations and their affiliated educational institutions. A fifth camp
consists of the unregistered or "free-lance" osteopaths. It appears that over the
years in response to the voluntary registers of the organized osteopaths and in
order to gain a degree of legitimacy of their own, some of the free-lance osteopaths established several associations and registers of their own, often centered around various part-time schools, and in essence formed what may be
regarded as a sixth osteopathic camp. Since these groups often consist of a loose
assemblage of practitioners with various degrees of training in manipulative
therapy as well as other natural therapies, it seems most appropriate to classify
them as the "quasi-organized" osteopaths. In many cases, practitioners in this
category may hold membership in two or more quasi-associations. A few osteopaths who hold membership in the more established associations also maintain membership in one or more of the quasi-associations.

At the top of the osteopathic pecking order are members of the British Os-

Table 1. Osteopathic Organizations in Great Britain in 1983*

Osteopathic Association	Date Established	Number of Actively-Practicing, Registered Members in Britain	Affiliated School	Enrollment of School
British Osteopathic Association	1911	69	London College of Osteopathic Medicine	5
Osteopathic Association of Great Britain	1925	296	British School of Osteopathy	304
British Naturopathic and Osteopathic Association	1945	155	British College of Naturopathy and Osteopathy	100
Society of Osteopaths	1971	115	European School of Osteopathy**	100

Notes:
*Information obtained by the author from associations and schools.
**Figure excludes approximately 160 students in part-time course.

teopathic Association, the only osteopathic group in Britain that is officially recognized by the American Osteopathic Association. It must be pointed out, however, that the AOA recognition of the BOA is partial in that only graduates of American osteopathic schools may be members of the AOA. Medically qualified graduates of the LCOM are not eligible for "associate" membership in the AOA, much to the consternation of the leadership of the BOA which is urging the AOA to change this policy. Ironically, since World War II, the number of American-trained DOs in the BOA has steadily declined whereas the number of members who are LCOM graduates has gradually but steadily increased. In contrast to 1936 when the BOA had 79 DOs in Great Britain, in 1983 it had only 19 DOs but 50 LCOM graduates. Since the flow of American-trained DOs (both British and American) has virtually ceased, the BOA has evolved increasingly into an organization that is isolated from American osteopathy as well as the rest of British osteopathy. In contrast, many medically qualified graduates of the LCOM, while perhaps maintaining membership in the BOA, are finding a niche with their allopathic colleagues in the British Association of Manipulative Medicine.

Next in the osteopathic hierarchy are the members of the Osteopathic Association of Great Britain, who for the most part are graduates of the British School of Osteopathy. Somewhere below them one finds members of the British Naturopathic and Osteopathic Association and the Society of Osteopaths. Since members of the SO are reputedly more interested in manipulative techniques and are presently being incorporated into the Register of Osteopaths, it may be that in osteopathic circles the SO has a higher status, despite its johnny-come-lately arrival, than the BNOA. While members of the BOA regard themselves the social equals of allopathic physicians, most of the organizationally-affiliated osteopaths view themselves as superior to the chiropractors and far superior to the quasi-organized and free-lance osteopaths.

As indicated in Table 1, compared to American osteopathic medicine, which now has well over 20,000 actively-practicing physicians, organized osteopathy in Britain is quite small but does show some sign of modest growth. Although Wilfred Streeter contended before the House of Lords in 1935 there was possibly two or three thousand "unqualified" practitioners of osteopathy in Britain, his estimate was probably exaggerated. In 1983, about 800 individuals were listed as osteopaths in all of the Yellow Pages telephone directories in the United Kingdom. More than half of this number indicated affiliation with one or more of the four main osteopathic associations in the country. The free-lance and quasi-organized osteopaths have acquired their training in a variety of ways, including apprenticeships under some of the remaining bonesetters, self-instruction from books on manipulation, and attendance at "diploma mills" and a variety of part-time programs. According to Kowalski [30:21], "for a fee you may purchase a 'D.O.' degree from the Nebraska College of Osteopathy; for a 'D.C.' degree the name changes to the Nebraska College of Chiropractic." The Northern Institute of Massage provides courses in massage, chiropody, manipulative therapy, and health and beauty therapy and offers membership in the London and Counties Society of Physiologists. The College of Osteopaths conducts a part-time course which convenes one weekend each month over a period of five years and permits its graduates to add the letters MCO after their DO. Graduates of the Andrew Still College of Osteopathy and Natural Therapeutics in Surrey as well as other practitioners of osteopathy are eligible for membership in the British and European Osteopathic Association. Other quasi-osteopathic associations include the Faculty of Osteopaths, the Foster Clinic and Osteopathic Guild, the Natural Therapeutic and Osteopathic Society, and the Cranial Osteopathic Association. No less than in the 1930s, when the organizationally-affiliated osteopaths attempted to obtain a government-sanctioned register, the free-lance osteopaths (and the quasi-organized osteopaths) still constitute the nemesis of those osteopaths seeking professional respectability.

III. THE POLITICS OF MANIPULATION

The politics of manipulation are very complex in that it presently involves several categories of healers: osteopaths, osteopathic physicians, chiropractors, naturopaths, some physiotherapists, and regular medical practitioners trained in manual medicine. Osteopaths as well as other alternative health practitioners presently have no official relationship with the General Medical Council, the legal body which supervises the standards and training criteria for regular medical practitioners in Great Britain. For many years, the Council ruled that "doctors must not refer patients to, or work in conjunction with, any medically unqualified practitioner, other than one who was licensed as an auxillary'' [24:33]. However, the Council recently lifted this ban and now permits regular medical practitioners to refer patients to osteopaths and other "natural healers." Furthermore, the Department of Health and Social Security (DHSS) now permits organizationally-affiliated osteopaths to issue certificates to patients incapable of working because of musculoskeletal disorders and who wish to claim National Insurance Incapacity benefits [27].

Considering the time that spinal manipulation requires, it would seem that the logical candidates within the auspices of regular medicine for the administration of this modality would be physiotherapists. The General Medical Council sponsors a register of physiotherapists which means that physiotherapists serve as medical auxiliaries who can only obtain their patients by referral from a regular medical practitioner [24:114]. Furthermore, registered physiotherapists may not provide manipulative therapy unless it is approved by a regular physician. For the most part, however, regular medical practitioners, including orthopedists, and physiotherapists in Britain have neglected manipulative techniques. In fact, the Chartered Society of Physiotherapy in 1973 "explicitly excluded manipulation in its revised curriculum" [47:184].

The tendency on the part of regular physicians and physiotherapists to neglect manipulative therapy also occurs in the United States and other countries. Nevertheless, there has been a trend among some regular physicians, both in the United States and in Europe, to become trained in spinal manipulation. In 1980, there were 216 physicians, including some DOs, listed as members of the North American Association of Manual Medicine. Membership in the British Association of Manipulative Medicine (BAMM) is reported to fluctuate between 200 and 300 [24:80]. Many regular medical practitioners interested in manipulative therapy are also affiliated with the International Federation of Manual Medicine, which has had annual congresses since 1973. While the manual medicine people at first excluded osteopathic physicians from their ranks, they recently have allowed DOs trained in American osteopathic colleges to join their associations. Several years ago, the BAMM extended honorary membership to all American-trained DOs in the BOA. Furthermore, many graduates of the LCCM are very active members of the BAMM. The irony of all these developments is that some DOs are now teaching manipulation to members of the manual medicine movement, both in the United States and Europe. However, many osteopaths feel that it is impossible to teach a skill as complicated and delicate as manipulation in a few weekend courses. In addition, if the manual medicine movement successfully incorporates manipulation into allopathic medicine, many osteopaths fear that their form of manual medicine will become superfluous in the eyes of not only clients, but also of certain strategic elites within the corporate and governmental sectors who in recent years have been giving increasing recognition to alternative health systems.

Despite the fact that most regular physicians as well as physiotherapists have neglected and continue to neglect manipulative therapy as a modality for treating musculoskeletal problems, a few of them recognize its merits. One of these individuals, James Cyriax, has been conducting a virtual one-man campaign for several decades to get regular medical practitioners and physiotherapists to accept this viewpoint. He has admonished his colleagues not to leave the application of spinal manipulation in the hands of what he regards to be "unqualified" practitioners, namely the osteopaths and chiropractors. Cyriax feels that the four years of instruction that organizationally-affiliated osteopaths receive is a "huge waste of time and money" and instead argues that spinal manipulation may be adequately taught in less than a year [47:94]. In recognition of the fact that most of his medical colleagues would find manipulative therapy too time-consuming, he recommends that it be administered by physiotherapists and has called for the establishment of an Institute of Orthopaedic Medicine, which would serve as a "centre of non-cultist teaching" on manipulation [47:94]. Cyriax claims that he has taught some one thousand physiotherapiss himself in manipulative therapy during his 57 years as a consultant at St. Andrew's Hospital in London. Although it would seem that Cyriax might have much in common with members of the manual medicine movement, Inglis [24:80] notes that "His dogmatism has alienated him from many members of the organization formed by doctors in the subject: the British Association of Manipulative Medicine."

During the past decade or so, there has been a growing tendency, despite the strong objection of organized medicine, on the part of political and economic elites in many countries (including China and those in the Third World) to legitimize as well as subsidize various alternatives to allopathic or cosmopolitan medicine. Governmental bodies in the United States and Britain have been showing an increasing interest in the techniques used by both osteopaths and chiropractors in dealing with musculoskeletal problems.

In the case of osteopathic medicine in the United States, one finds that DOs have full practice rights in all fifty states and that legislatures in seven states since 1970 have voted to financially support public osteopathic schools. In addition, the federal government has considerably stepped up its financial support of research in osteopathic colleges.

As is noted in the following remarks by Wardwell [59:241], chiropractic, although not to nearly the same extent as osteopathy, is also achieving increasing professional recognition and financial support from strategic elites in American society:

> The turning point in chiropractic's long struggle for acceptance as part of the American health care establishment came in 1974, with four significant occurrences: (1) the last state (Louisiana) voted to license chiropractors, (2) the U.S. Office of Education gave the Chiropractic Commission on Education power to accredit chiropractic colleges, (3) Congress voted to reimburse chiropractors' fees under the Medicare program, and (4) Congress instructed the National Institutes of Health to allocate $2 million to study the scientific basis of chiroprac-

tic. . . . In 1975 the AMA eliminated two bodies which for many decades spent most of their resources and efforts trying to eliminate or at least "contain" chiropractic. Chiropractors are also reimbursed by Workmen's Compensation in all states, by Medicaid, and by most private insurance companies, including Blue Cross-Blue Shield. . . .

Although the number of osteopaths in Britain is much smaller both proportionally and in absolute terms than in the United States, it appears that the government there is taking note of osteopathy as well as other "natural therapeutic" systems. On May 17, 1973, a committee of the House of Commons invited representatives from various natural therapeutic associations, including the Acupuncture Association, the British Chiropractors' Association, the British Naturopathic and Osteopathic Association, the Incorporated Society of Registered Naturopaths, the National Institute of Medical Herbalists, the Osteopathic Association of Great Britain, the Radionic Association, the Society of Osteopaths, the Research Society for Naturopathy, and the General Council and Register of Osteopaths, for a meeting on the general status of alternative health systems in the country [21]. Representatives from all of these organizations, except for the General Council and Register of Osteopaths, were present at the parliamentary committee meeting. Although representatives of the General Council and Register of Osteopaths were not interested in the proposed joint representation of the invited associations, they were willing to be included in benefits that might be obtained from future legislation resulting from such representation. Also the Department of Health and Social Security has approached various osteopathic bodies in an attempt to carry out a study of the methods other than those generally used by orthopedists and orthopedic surgeons in treating back pain [18]. Even more recently, the Guy's Health District appointed Peter Blasgrave, President Emeritus of the Society of Osteopaths, for a one-year research project in the Department of Rheumatology at Guy's Hospital [28]. This was the first appointment of an osteopath under the British National Health Service.

Some efforts are being made for cooperation among the various osteopathic bodies in Britain and on the Continent. During the past few years, a strong drive toward some sort of political unity has emerged among the three nonmedical or lay organized osteopathic camps. The most significant part of this effort was the decision by the General Council and Register of Osteopaths in late 1982 to extend eligibility for application to the Register of Osteopaths to members of the Society of Osteopaths and graduates of the ESO. Most members of the SO have been accepted into the Register or are in the process of being considered for membership. Although the SO will be maintained as a separate organization from the OAGB, members of the former will now use the initials MRO and are explicitly prohibited from using the initials MSO any longer.

Negotiations between GCRO and BNOA are presently being conducted with the aim of incorporating BNOA members into the Register. Partly because of deep historical strains between the ESO faction and the BNOA, these negotiations are considerably more delicate than those that brought SO members into the Register. The leadership of the BNOA feels that its members who hold a DO (the vast majority) should be incorporated en masse rather than on the basis of individual application as has been the case for members of the SO. Also, in order to retain their identity as naturopaths, the general membership of the BNOA voted that, in the event that its members would become eligible for the register, the BNOA could revert its name back to its earlier designation as the British Naturopathic Association and maintain a separate register of naturopaths. This measure would also guarantee those few members who did not hold a DO continuing membership in a register.

The ultimate objective in unifying members of the OAGB, the SO and the BNOA under one common register is to present a "united front" to the British government in the drive for statutory recognition of osteopathy. Representatives of the osteopathic profession have been repeatedly told by government health officials and Members of Parliament that they will have to be politically unified if organized osteopathy is to have any hope of obtaining statutory recognition. If unity is achieved, the various osteopathic associations are expected to continue to function as postgraduate extensions of their associated schools. In the event that the GCRO seeks recognition from Parliament for its members, it can be expected that the quasi-organized osteopaths as well as perhaps the free-lance osteopaths will oppose any proposed legislation that would exclude them.

On the international level, the Society of Osteopaths maintains strong ties with its sister organizations in France and Belgium. The three groups as well as a loose assortment of osteopaths in other European countries have been convening annually at the Congress of European Osteopathy which met for the first time in the fall of 1978 [29]. As a response to various moves by the European Economic Community to pass regulations requiring the licensing of natural healers, the SO combined forces with its sister organizations in the establishment of the European Economic Community Committee for Osteopathy. The SO has expressed a strong commitment to strengthening the ties between itself and "other osteopathic professional bodies and those of other 'natural therapies'" [27]. It was, along with its sister organizations, a leading, if not the primary force in the International Federation of Practitioners of Natural Therapeutics (IFPNT), an organization which was involved in lobbying for the recognition of natural healers in the European Economic Communitity (EEC) and the World Health Organization. The BNOA was also a member of the IFPNT. The leadership role played by the SO in the IFPNT ended in 1979, partly because of fiscal problems. The West German *Heilpraktikers* (natural healers) offered financial assistance to the organization and were instrumental in establishing a reconstituted body, called the International Federation of Healers, headquartered in Düsseldorf. Although they were not affiliated with the new federation, the SO and her sister organizations continue to lobby for favorable EEC legislation for natural healers.

Despite the absence of the GCRO and the OAGB in the broader political activities of the SO and, to a lesser extent, the BNOA, collaborative relationships among major lay osteopathic bodies in Britain have dramatically increased during the past several years. This has been marked by a considerable amount of inter-visiting on the part of the members of these associations at each other's conferences, symposia, and postgraduate courses. For example, a few years ago, members of the SO were invited to attend a postgraduate conference at the BSO and a Principal Emeritus of the BSO presented a lecture at the annual conference of the SO. Student organizations at the BSO, ESO, and the BCNO have also been engaged in a similar pattern of social intercourse. Although a few members of the BOA are also present at the meetings of the lay osteopaths, most BOA members prefer to maintain stronger ties with their counterparts in either American ostepathy or the British manual medicine movement.

Although organizationally-affiliated osteopaths in Britain see themselves as holding true to the principle first promulgated by Andrew T. Still, they have not, with the exception of those connected with the BOA and the LCOM, been able to obtain the official sanction of the American Osteopathic Association. Although various American osteopathic physicians have over the years been in contact with these unrecognized osteopathic groups in Britain, the attitude of the AOA toward them can perhaps be best described as one of "benign neglect." In reality, the following comments from an editorial in the *Journal of the American Osteopathic Association* by George Northrup [39:37–38], a prominent American osteopathic physician, probably reflects the view that most osteopathic physicians in the United States have of osteopaths in other parts of the world:

> England, Austrilia, and New Zealand have institutions which grant degrees in "Osteopathy". . .
>
> The few graduates of American colleges of osteopathic medicine practicing in these countries are now grossly outnumbered by graduates of institutions purporting to be "osteopathic" and granting degrees in "osteopathy". . .
>
> Qualified osteopathic physicians, graduates of colleges of osteopathic medicine approved by the AOA, deserve the support and encouragement of the AOA wherever they practice. If osteopathic medicine is to gain the recognition in foreign countries, it must be based on high standards of osteopathic/medical educational attainment and on legislation which supports the full practice rights of osteopathic physicians. . .

Undoubtedly these remarks were not appreciated by the organizationally-affiliated osteopaths in the countries toward which they were directed. In large part, what Northrup was criticizing about osteopathy outside the United States is the fact that it has not evolved into osteopathic medicine.

IV. PARALLELS BETWEEN BRITISH OSTEOPATHY AND AMERICAN CHIROPRACTIC

The price that osteopathy in Britain has had to pay for evolving along a different trajectory than in the United States is that it has remained a "marginal profession." Wardwell [56:340] first coined this term in referring to the status of chiropractic in the United States.

The role of the chiropractor is structurally comparable to that of the Negro, for it is marginal to the well institutionalized role of the doctor. Physicians are fully accepted as doctors, of course; but chiropractors have attained little acceptance. In fact, the "official" position of the American Medical Association is that chiropractors are not doctors at all, but quacks—i.e., imposters in the doctor's role. The public is less harsh in its evaluation, but there is no question that the role of the chiropractors is a marginal one.

As I suggested earlier, there are some striking parallels between British osteopathy and American chiropractic. We have already seen that osteopathy in Britain is characterized by considerable factionalism, being divided into five or more camps. One or two of these camps, the BOA and the Osteopathic Medical Association, consisting of American-trained osteopathic physicians and regular medical practitioners with training in OMT, hold themselves relatively aloof of the other camps. These practitioners identify very closely with either their counterparts in the United States or their colleagues in regular medicine. The remaining factions, with the exception of perhaps the free-lance osteopaths, are involved in a constant struggle for some sort of legitimization from the medical establishment, the AOA, the British government, or the European Economic Community.

The factionalism of the various osteopathic bodies follows not only historical lines but also different philosophies of healing. In large measure, this translates into different views of the degree that osteopaths should or should not combine other therapeutic modalities with spinal manipulation. This also parallels the case of chiropractic in the United States. At the national level, American chiropractic is often described as a division between the "straights" (represented by the International Chiropractic Association) and the "mixers" (represented by the American Chiropractic Association). Lin [33] termed this dual division as one between the "traditionalists" and the "expansionists." Whereas the straights or traditionalists advocate a "hands only" approach to chiropractic, the mixers or expansionists include various other modalities, usually naturopathy, nutrition, and physical therapy but in some instances minor surgery, obstetrics, and psychotherapy. When the Universal Chiropractors Association (UCA), which was established in 1906, decided to admit mixers in 1912, several years of internal strife followed, culminating in 1925 with the resignation from the organization of B. J. Palmer, the son of D. D. Palmer, the founder of chiropractic. The following year, he established what later became the International Chiropractic Association (ICA). The American Chiropractic Association (ACA), which was established as a mixer organization, merged with the UCA in 1930 to become the National Chiropractic Association (NCA), and was renamed the American Chiropractic Association in 1963. There is indication that at least some American chiropractors wish to follow an evolution analogous to that undergone by American osteopaths in their transformation into osteopathic physicians. According the Lin [33], some expansionist chiropractors want to be perceived as "chiropractic physicians" and perceive chiropractic per se as a specialty within medicine.

There tends to be a general notion among various scholars that the mixers appear to be winning the battle for dominance in chiropractic [5, 20]. In reality, although American chiropractic organizationally consists of two divisions, this dual scheme accepted by many academics masks a much more complex situation. As Wardwell [60:217] observes, there appear to be many shades of straights and mixers:

> Despite the continued existence of two competing national organizations, the terms "straights" and "mixers" designate the ends of a continuum rather than two discrete groups of chiropractors, most of whom fall somewhere in the middle between the two poles. And this has probably always been true of the profession; rhetoric has belied the facts. Many Palmer graduates mix spinal manipulation to some degree with physical therapy modalities and nutritional guidance; very few chiropractic mixers actually incorporate into their practices such nonchiropractic modes of treatment as obstetrics, herbal remedies, or (that anathema of straights) high colonic irrigations. The central tendency is for chiropractors to employ manual manipulation of vertebrae, plus to a small degree physical therapy devices and nutritional counseling. The vast majority of chiropractic treatment is for neuromusculo-skeletal conditions, with perhaps 10 to 15 percent for organic conditions. Whether chiropractors are straight or mixers seems unrelated to how often they treat organic conditions.

It is interesting, however, to note the emergence of a "superstraight" faction in American chiropractic as a reaction to the growing collaboration between the ACA and the ICA on educational policies [60:229–230].

Like the "chiropractic physicians" in the United States, but probably even more so, osteopaths affiliated with the BOA regard themselves as physicians, despite the fact that in Britain they lack the full practice rights that all of their American counterparts now hold. It appears that they practice osteopathic medicine in a manner similar to that followed by earlier American DOs who, prior to the 1960s or the early 1970s, possessed only limited practice rights under the licensing laws of certain states. According to one of my informants, an American DO who practiced for several years in Britain, most BOA-affiliated osteopaths during the 1950s employed primarily OMT but others developed strategies for extending their range of health care. Some of them in essence were "mixers," employing nutritional, vitamin, and dietary therapies, hydrotherapy, electrotherapy, colonic irrigation, and physical therapy devices. Although osteopaths are not legally permitted to prescribe certain drugs, such as codeine, some osteopaths had arrangements with pharmacists or chemists by which they could obtain drugs or antibiotics that were directly unavailable to them. One female osteopath became known as an ear, nose, and throat specialist; however, she did not perform any operations.

Despite its being held at a distance by the AOA and the osteopaths with medical training, the BSO faction has in a sense become the standard bearer of osteopathic orthodoxy. Essentially this group constitutes the "straight" camp of British osteopathy in that its members tend to utilize primarily traditional spinal manipulative techniques, although some members have been learning cranial manipulation during the past several years. Osteopaths with a more eclectic orientation often refer to them as "orthopedic" osteopaths who purportedly function largely as specialists in the area of spinal mechanics. There has been a concerted effort on the part of OAGB osteopaths to make British osteopathy more "scientific" than in the past—an emphasis which is revealed by the highly technical content of most of the articles published in their *British Osteopathic Journal*. This tendency to restrict osteopathy to spinal mechanical problems rather than to one that sees a strong relationship between musculoskeletal complications and other somatic and organic disorders is probably strongly related to a concerted effort to make osteopathy more acceptable to the British medical establishment. The assertion by Richard H. Tyler [53:54], a chiropractor who visited the BSO, that the BSO osteopath is "straighter" than the chiropractic "straight," however, is probably an oversimplified view of reality. In the past decade or so, many BSO graduates as well as current BSO students have come to view ostepathy, at least in theory, as a broad approach to health care and as part of the larger holistic health movement. According to a prominent member of the OAGB, many of the older BSO osteopaths (those that completed their training prior to the 1950s) also view themselves as generalists. Essentially, the curriculum of the BSO remains conservative, as can be seen by its refusal up until the present time to teach cranial manipulation to undergraduate students, although this technique is taught at the school to postgraduates. Because of pressure from both certain faculty members and many students, however, the administration recently established a committee to investigate the possibility of teaching cranial manipulation at the undergraduate level.

As was hinted earlier, the BNOA and the SO may be regarded to be the "mixer" groups of British osteopathy. In addition to stressing extensive training in naturopathy and osteopathy, the four-year curriculum of the British College of Naturopathy and Osteopathy includes courses in psychology, psychotherapy, ophthalmology, dermatology, gynecology, pediatrics, geriatrics and tropical medicine [9]. In a sense, the BNOA is divided into osteopathic naturopaths and naturopathic osteopaths. The former tend to view osteopathy as part of naturopathy whereas the latter maintain that naturopathic principles are part and parcel of osteopathy. Although the BCNO administration has moved the curriculum of the school increasingly over the years toward osteopathy, some faculty members and some, if not many, students feel that the naturopathic side should be given greater emphasis. One BCNO student told me, with no overt disagreement from some of his fellow students, that the BCNO could increase its enrollment appreciably, particularly since it is the only full-time, four-year naturopathic school in Britain, if it emphasized naturopathy rather than merely attempted to compete with several other osteopathic schools.

The European School of Osteopathy, in addition to standard courses in the basic sciences and osteopathic principles and techniques, offers training in cranial manipulation and psychotherapy. Although the ESO does not offer courses in other natural therapies as a standard point of its curriculum, it does encourage faculty members, students, and outside speakers to give presentations on home-opathy, herbalism, acupuncture, Alexander technique, yoga, etc. The ESO teaches its students that osteopathy is a form of health care that extends far beyond the simple treatment of specific musculoskeletal problems. Despite this emphasis on osteopathy as a comprehensive form of alternative medicine, most British osteopaths, including ones affiliated with the SO, admit that most of their patients seek their services primarily for the treatment of musculoskeletal prob-lems, particularly low back pain. Consequently, many British osteopaths lament that the public has a rather limited view of their role.

V. SOME FACTORS ACCOUNTING FOR THE DIVERGENT EVOLUTION OF OSTEOPATHY IN THE UNITED STATES AND GREAT BRITAIN

Thus far in this paper, we have seen that osteopathy as an alternative health system has undergone appreciably different trajectories in the United States and Great Britain. In the United States, it has evolved into a complete school of medicine with full practice rights in all fifty states. Some social scientists have even argued that American osteopathy is essentially indistinguishable from reg-ular medicine [16, 17, 52]. Conversely, British osteopathy has undergone a development, or, perhaps better stated, a series of developments which sharply distinguish it from its American parent. Indeed, the status of British osteopathy closely resembles that of chiropractic in various countries, including the United States and even Great Britain.

In attempting to account for the divergent evolution of osteopathy in America and Britain, I will focus on four factors: (1) the existence or nonexistence of licensing regulations for various types of health practitioners; (2) the relative presence of regular physicians in osteopathy; (3) the organization of medical care; and (4) the relative size of chiropractic. This is not to imply that these are the only factors contributing to this divergent evolution of an alternative health system. In order to more completely address this issue, considerably more re-search is needed on the relationship of osteopathy to both regular medicine and the larger political economy of health care.

A. Licensing Regulations

Licensing regulations or the lack thereof appear to have played a crucial role in the development of osteopathy in not only the United States and Britain but also in other countries such as France, Belgium, Canada, Australia, and New Zealand [36, 45]. The history of the licensing of health practitioners of different types has been a tumultuous and variegated one in America. By the end of the eighteenth century, regular physicians persuaded legislatures in many states to pass medical licensing in order to restrict or prohibit the practices of herbal healers [11]. The Popular Health Movement resulted in the repeal of these laws in almost all states during the Jacksonian period (1828–1836) because they were regarded as elitist. Under the pressure of the regular medical societies, however, state legislatures beginning in the 1870s established and sometimes reestablished medical examining boards. By 1893, 18 states required that applicants pass an examination and another 17 states demanded a diploma from a medical school that had been declared "in good standing" in order to obtain a medical license [51:43]. Although nonregular physicians participated in some ways in medical licensing in at least 33 of the 45 states that had enacted licensing laws by 1900, the boards administering these were dominated by the allopathic medical profession.

It should be noted, however, that separate licensing boards in some states gave homeopaths, osteopaths, and chiropractors more autonomy than in those states where the allopaths monopolized or dominated the boards. Some states also passed "drugless practitioner acts" authorizing licensure for a wide range of "nonmedical" practitioners. As early as 1910, osteopaths had acquired separate licensing boards in 17 states [12].

In most states, the licensing of osteopathic physicians continues to be monopolized or dominated by members of the regular medical profession. In nine states, boards consisting exclusively of MDs or MDs and one or two laypersons, are responsible for the granting of full practice rights to osteopathic physicians [26]. The licensing of DOs for full practice rights is administered by composite boards in 25 states and in the District of Columbia. Most composite boards include only one DO but those in Colorado, Georgia, Iowa, Missouri, New York, and Oregon include two DOs and the one in Kansas has three DOs. The licensing of DOs for full practice rights is administered by osteopathic examining boards in only 16 states. DOs have been able to exert considerably more control over requirements determining their ability to practice in states where they have been granted their own licensing boards than in states where they have either consisted of a distinct minority on a composite board or have been denied a seat on a MD board. Consequently, American osteopathy has tended to be the strongest in states, such as California, Michigan and Pennsylvania, where it has its own boards as opposed to states, such as New York, Wisconsin, and Indiana, where DOs are licensed by composite boards or boards monopolized by MDs.

Larson [31] argues that the licensing of physicians was a major form by which the allopathic profession restricted competition from osteopaths, chiropractors, and other types of health professionals. The demands of the allopathic-dominated boards played an important role in the osteopathic schools adjusting their curricula in order that their graduates could pass the licensing examinations. As Gevitz [19:69–70] documents in the following passage, such changes in the course work of the osteopathic schools occurred as early as in the first decade of the turn of the century:

In defending their schools, a number of faculty members and administrators argued that there should be some classroom discussion of chemicals and biologicals so that students could intelligently decide the merits of their use for themselves. Furthermore, it appeared to them that even more instruction in these modalities would have to be given, whether they liked it or not, if their graduates were to secure greater legal privileges insofar as surgery and obstetrics were concerned. In Illinois, for example, the medical act allowed for the granting of two types of license, one for a physician and surgeon and the other for a drugless practitioner. To be eligible for the first, candidates had to be graduated from schools approved by the state board of health, which required the inclusion of a complete course in *materia medica*. Supporters of the Chicago school first tried to change the law, but repeatedly failed. Consequently, in 1909 the college attempted to comply by adding "osteopathic *materia medica*" to the curriculum. . .

A similar situation occurred in California with different outcome. Since 1906 D.O.'s could secure full physicians and surgeons certification if they passed the same test required of the M.D.'s. However, in 1913 the law was amended to stipulate that anyone wishing to take the examination must be a graduate of a college giving a minimum number of hours in specified subjects including pharmacology. The Los Angeles School, therefore, made the necessary changes and thus became approved by the composite California Medical Board.

Although Andrew Still, now 87 years of age, responded to the increasing trend to teach *materia medica* in osteopathic schools by warning his colleagues at the AOA convention in 1915 that "the enemy has broken through the picket," the osteopathic profession in time disregarded the alarm of its eminent founder [quoted in 7:442].

Beginning in the 1920s, "Unable to convince the legislatures to eliminate independent osteopathic boards, the M.D.'s adopted the strategy of lobbying for a common test in the basic sciences that was to be taken prior to an actual licensing examination" [19:82]. The immediate result of this strategy was a relatively low pass rate among osteopathic students relative to that of allopathic students (i.e., 88.3 percent for MDs and 54.5 percent for DOs in 1930). Over the next decade or so, the pass rates among the osteopathic students improved to the point that they compared favorably to those of the allopathic students. Since the basic science examinations focused on subjects typical of the curricula of the regular medical schools, they undoubtedly contributed to the growing tendency to de-emphasize instruction in OMT and related areas in the osteopathic schools.

Another factor, in large part stimulated by restrictions of the regular medical profession of entrance into its schools, contributing to the movement of American osteopathy toward regular medicine has been the large proportion of osteopathic students who have viewed their education as a "back door into medicine." In his study of osteopathic students at four of the then existing osteopathic schools, New [38] found that most of them had entered osteopathic medicine as a second choice to regular medicine or by accident. Out of the 103 students he interviewed, only 34 had not applied to an allopathic school. More recently, Sharma and Dressel [48] administered a questionnaire to 61 of the 64 graduates of the 1975 class at the College of Osteopathic Medicine of the Michigan State University and found that 75 percent of them had applied to at least one allopathic school. On the other hand, only 15 percent of the students had been accepted at one or more allopathic schools.

In contrast to the United States, licensing requirements for health practitioners in Great Britain are minimal if not essentially nonexistent. While registration by regular medical practitioners with the General Medical Council confers some legal rights, such as being permitted to sign death certificates and prescribe dangerous drugs, under common law a physician does not need a license to order to practice medicine [14:429, 50:369]. In theory, this absence of licensing regulations eliminates many of the concerns that osteopathy as well as other alternative health systems, such as chiropractic, face in the United States. On the other hand, this arrangement poses a double-edged sword for at least the organizationally-affiliated osteopaths in Britain who have for years attempted to overcome the stigma of being members of a marginal profession and cope with the competition that they perceive from those practitioners who also practice some form of spinal manipulation.

As was noted earlier, the organizationally-affiliated osteopaths made several unsuccessful attempts in the early decades of this century to have the government establish a legally-binding register for practitioners claiming to be proficient in osteopathy. At best, what the organizationally-affiliated osteopaths were able to obtain in their drive to eliminate the virtually unrestricted practice of the free-lance osteopaths was a voluntary register. While certain letters behind an osteopath's name may impress some patients or prospective patients, they mean little—if anything—to the medical establishment or the National Health Service and there is therefore a certain hollowness to their use. Despite the fact that British osteopathic schools have not been forced to conform to the curricula of the allopathic schools so that their students are able to pass basic science or licensing examinations, they have chosen to do so to some degree in order to achieve some measure of legitimacy and respectability. The BSO, the BCNO, and the ESO all include a fairly extensive coverage of the basic sciences (biology, anatomy, physiology, pathology, etc.) in their respective curricula. In reality, however, standard medical courses are much less emphasized in British osteopathic schools than in American osteopathic schools. It is quite clear that these schools place a much greater emphasis on osteopathic principles, diagnosis, and techniques than their American counterparts.

B. The Medical Presence Within Osteopathy

A second factor which may have contributed to the divergent evolution of osteopathy is the degree of medical presence in its respective developments in the United States and Britain. In noting that Andrew T. Still and some of his early disciples were initially medical men, whereas David D. Palmer and his followers were medical outsiders, Wardwell [58] follows a similar line of reasoning in attempting to explain the divergent evolution of osteopathy and chiropractic in this country. It is his contention that "Chiropractors . . . have always been outsiders to the medical profession. More than osteopaths, who were considered to be irregulars and sectarian by orthodox medicine, chiropractors have been totally rejected as incompetent quacks or as hopeless cultists" [58:9]. Wardwell [58:13] even suggests that "Probably the stigma associated with chiropractors has also to some degree encouraged osteopaths to forsake manipulation for allopathic medicine."

In contrast to chiropractic, which at least initially viewed itself as a radical departure both philosophically and therapeutically from regular medicine, Still regarded osteopathy as a reform movement within medicine. Prior to originating osteopathy, Still functioned as essentially a regular physician, although, like many other physicians of the time, he received most of his medical training under the apprenticeship system (with his father as the mentor). Still also briefly in 1860 attended the Kansas City School of Physicians and Surgeons. He planned to first formally present his new osteopathic concept at Baker University in Kansas (an allopathic school that his father and brothers had helped to establish), but was denied permission to do so. As was noted earlier, another regular physician, William Smith, was the first lecturer in anatomy at the American School of Osteopathy which Still had started. That Smith, with his impeccable credentials in medicine from a prestigious European university, provided early American osteopathy with a certain needed aura of legitimacy is made evident from a student's remark that " 'Bill' furnished the 'front.' He 'looked good' to the people and inspired confidence in infant osteopathy" [quoted in 19:20]. The early faculty of the American School of Osteopathy included several individuals with MD degrees from both allopathic and homeopathic colleges. Among those enrolled in the early osteopathic schools in this country were regular physicians who desired to learn OMT as an adjunct to their own practices. In many instances, these individuals "were pressed into teaching some subjects in lieu of part or the whole of their tuition fee" because the colleges did not have sufficient numbers of instructors [19:44].

A rather unusual lineage between osteopathy and allopathy was the short-lived Columbian School of Osteopathy. This institution was started by Marcus Ward, who, after being cured of asthma by Still, became a major stockholder and a vice-president of the American School [19:46–47]. When personal differences developed between Ward and his healer, the former left Kirksville, obtained an MD degree from the University of Cincinnati in 1897, and returned to Kirksville to establish his own school. Ward not only claimed to be the "co-founder of osteopathy" but also asserted that he was the originator of "True Osteopathy"—a combination of OMT, surgery, and *materia medica*. After completion of the DO degree, students at the Columbian School could matriculate for an additional year in order to receive an MD degree. Although this institution closed in 1901, it is symbolic of the strong tendency toward incorporating allopathic medicine that existed during the early years of American osteopathy.

As a result of the relatively small number of osteopathic surgeons, the lack of surgical training facilities in osteopathic institutions, and restrictive state licensing laws that existed particularly prior to 1920, osteopathic students who wished to become surgeons were often encouraged by their professors to obtain an MD degree once they had graduated [19:62–63]. Ironically, one of the individuals who embarked upon such a course of action was George A. Still, the grandnephew of the founder of osteopathy. Despite the attempt by the AMA to prohibit MDs from teaching in osteopathic schools, their faculties have generally included at least a few regular physicians with no apparent interest in osteopathy per se. While it is difficult to assess the impact that such instructors had on osteopathic students, it seems likely that their presence was one more reason why American osteopathy evolved into osteopathic medicine. Furthermore, in more recent years, many graduates of osteopathic schools have gone on to do their residencies or receive postgraduate training in allopathic settings.

In contrast to American osteopathy, British osteopathy for the most part has developed outside the confines of regular medicine. Except for a few regular medical practitioners with postgraduate training in OMT, there appears to have been almost a total absence of regular physicians in British osteopathic institutions. While it is true that John Martin Littlejohn, the founder of the British School of Osteopathy, had obtained an MD degree after having become a DO, the former was earned at a homeopathic college rather than an allopathic college. With the exception of recent members of the BOA, it does not appear that many individuals with training in allopathic medicine have been found within the ranks of British osteopathy.

At the fourth sitting of the House of Lords Select Committee on Osteopathy in 1935, it was reported that 5 or 6 of the 71 members of the BOA were also listed on the Medical Register [10]. Since nearly all of the BOA osteopaths at this time were graduates of American osteopathic schools (which had by now developed curricula very similar to those found in allopathic schools), it should be no surprise that the BOA was already contemplating the possibility of establishing a college not only to train osteopaths but also to provide courses for medical students and regular medical practitioners interested in OMT. As was already noted, of the various osteopathic factions in Britain, it is the BOA camp that most closely resembles American osteopathy. Whereas the BOA osteopaths, like their colleagues in America, had come to define themselves as physicians, the BSO was willing to grant a Diploma in Osteopathy to chiropractors upon completion of a year-long course consisting of twelve lectures. Although organized chiropractic opposed the joint effort of the BOA and BSO factions to persuade the British government to establish a register for osteopaths, it seems that to a large degree the BSO people had more in common with the chiropractors at this time than with the aspiring osteopathic physicians affiliated with the BOA who hoped to eventually obtain full practice rights.

C. Organization of Medical Care

Although the United States and Britain are both advanced capitalist societies, they exhibit striking differences in their provision of health care. In contrast to the American system where most health services are organized and financed by private parties, these services have been almost totally nationalized in Britain since 1948. Although general practitioners in the British system are not direct employees of the government, most of their income is derived from the National Health Service. Another significant difference between the organization of medical care in these two countries is in the distribution of types of physicians. One of the consequences of the growth of capital-intensive or technological medicine in the United States has been a diminishing percentage of primary care physicians and a rapidly growing percentage of specialists. Whereas in 1931 there were 90 general practitioners per 100,000 people in the United States, by 1962 there were only 37 per 100,000 people [23]. While the declining percentage of primary care physicians in this country has somewhat leveled out in the last decade or so, largely because of concerted efforts to reverse the trend toward specialization, the great majority of regular physicians are found in one of the specialties. Despite the fact that the proportion of the total National Health Service spending on hospitals has steadily increased while that on general medicine has decreased, the role of the general practitioner as the first point of patient contact has been maintained if not reinforced under the British system as is made apparent in the following remarks:

> The structure of NHS primary care, with relatively stable lists of patient and pay based on annual contract (actually, a modified salary) rather than on fee-for-service, encouraged what are now universally recognized as the essential features of primary care as a specialty, which justify, dignify, and make necessary the role of the general practitioner. . . . None of these features is universally or completely met, but a pattern of thought has quite clearly emerged and become ideologically dominant in British general practice which accepts these features as the aim and the definition of primary care as we wish to see it. [22:360]

In his now classic comparative study of the health care systems of three Western countries, Anderson [2:125] presented data, listed in Table 2, comparing the distribution of types of physicians in the two countries of interest to us here. Furthermore, at the same time that the proportion of active general practitioners in Britain has remained about fifty percent, the number of physicians per population there is now nearly the same as in the United States [49].

In attempting to deal with the maldistribution of physicians brought about by capital-intensive medicine, corporate and governmental elites in the United States have resorted to a variety of strategies. These have included the development of family practice as a specialty and nurse practitioner and physician assistant training programs. As I have noted elsewhere, another strategy to

Table 2.   Distribution of Physicians by Type of
Primary Activity

	United States		England	
Patient Care				
General Practice	23%		48%	
Specialties	70%		50%	
Medical		21		14
Surgical		27		20
Other		22		16
Administration	7%		2%	
	100%		100%	

Source: Anderson, 1972.

alleviate this problem has been financial support from the federal government and state legislatures for the training of osteopathic physicians [3]. When MDs vacated positions in general practice in order to seek more prestigious and financially rewarding jobs in the specialties, osteopathic physicians often filled their positions. This pattern became particularly pronounced during World War II when many MDs took medical positions in the military, which the allopathic profession had managed to deny DOs. Because the osteopathic profession developed its hospital system relatively late and had limited funds for its schools, it was far slower in specializing than regular medicine. "In 1967–68, 29 percent of traditional physicians and 90 percent of osteopaths were in general practice. By 1978 only 18 percent of the allopaths were in general practice" [1:191]. As Albrecht and Levy [1] argue, the evolution of American osteopathy from a marginal profession to a full profession was related to its ability to adapt to the medical marketplace.

Although the tendency to resort to DOs as an alternative to MDs in the area of primary care has resulted in an organizational rejuvenation of osteopathy, it has been part of the process by which the profession has come to closely resemble regular medicine. On the other hand, the increasing respectability of osteopathic medicine has also helped to legitimize scientific research on spinal manipulation. Whether the osteopathic profession will attempt to exploit this trend in order to distinguish itself from allopathic medicine or even reclaim its "birthright" remains to be seen.

Since the practice rights of British osteopaths are considerably more limited than those of osteopathic physicians in the United States, the two groups occupy very different niches in the delivery of health care. A study of 5,310 patients selected at random from a sample of practitioners listed in the 1974–75 Directory of the OAGB shows the following breakdown in percentages of the site of patient presenting complaints: 52% low back, 20% neck, 13% thorax, 7% head, 7%

lower extremity joint, 5% upper extremity joint, and 2% visceral [13]. Although this finding does not state what these patients were actually treated for, it strongly suggests that at least OAGB osteopaths treat a larger percentage of individuals with musculoskeletal problems. My conversations with osteopaths affiliated with other groups in Britain suggests a roughly similar pattern. Nevertheless, it seems that some people rely on osteopaths as alternatives to the allopathic general practitioner and even the hospital consultant.

While Britain does not face the same acute shortage of primary care physicians as does the United States, it is experiencing many of the same contradictions, including rising health expenditures, as other capitalist countries. It is not clear why the British government has shown some interest in recent years in "natural therapeutics," but Navarro [37:53] suggests that this interest may be the beginnings of one strategy by which to cope with a growing "health crisis":

> Specifically in terms of the NHS, the enormous increase in expenditures in the health sector—from 455 million pounds to approximately 2,500 pounds within 25 years—had created a good deal of alarm, leading to a demand for slowing down, cutting back, and generally trimming the fat in the NHS, and it was this concern that produced the call for further strengthening the centralized direction of the NHS and its management structure, as well as an exploration of alternatives to the care provided by costly hospital-oriented medicine.

If indeed the NHS attempts to incorporate osteopaths and other alternative health practitioners into its health care delivery system, it is difficult to determine how the latter groups will react to such a move. While such a process would provide a much-desired legitimacy for many of them, there might be some resistance to it since some of these practitioners enjoy rather lucrative practices and are free to literally charge what the market will bear. Despite the fact that these practitioners could probably still maintain a private clientele under a new arrangement, they would also be required to accept a somewhat lower fee based on the capitation system of the NHS.

D. The Relative Size of Chiropractic

Another factor affecting the differential evolution of osteopathy in the United States and Britain is the relative size of chiropractic in these two settings. Before discussing this issue, some discussion of the relationship of the two to each other seems appropriate. Although osteopathy was "discovered" prior to chiropractic (the former in Missouri and the latter in the adjacent state of Iowa) and despite the assertion of some, such as Gevitz [19:58], that the latter is "osteopathy under a different name," Wardwell [57:55] argues that the historical relationship between the two is a much more complex one:

> Osteopathy and chiropractic were not new discoveries by Andrew Taylor Still and Daniel David Palmer respectively. On the contrary, there was a long tradition of irregular practi-

tioners, mainly "bonesetters," who treated patients by putting bones that were "out" back in place by manipulation. Elizabeth Lomax's conclusion that one can only regard osteopathy and chiropractic as legitimate offspring of contemporary thought explains such metaphysical expression as innate intelligence and also where osteopathy and chiropractic derive some of their therapeutic theories and techniques.

American osteopathy has existed in a middle ground between allopathic medicine and chiropractic for some time. Since both osteopathy and chiropractic developed techniques of spinal manipulation (based on somewhat different theories), these two systems competed, at least in their early years, for essentially the same types of patients. While initially this competition was not a serious one, it quickly developed into one as chiropractic expanded at an amazingly phenomenal rate. According to one source, at the turn of the century, there were 1,136 osteopaths as opposed to fewer than 100 chiropractors in America [52]. About three decades later, Reed [44] reported that some 7,650 osteopathic physicians in the country were significantly outnumbered by some 16,000 chiropractors. That chiropractic posed a serious threat to the osteopathic profession is made evident by the fact that the latter joined its foe, the regular physicians, in a vigorous campaign to prevent the enactment of laws granting chiropractors the legal right to practice their healing techniques [19:59–60]. Nevertheless, in 1913, Kansas and Arkansas passed the first chiropractic bills, which required an 18-month course of instruction at a "duly chartered college," and by 1922, 20 other states had similar statutes. According to Gevitz [19:59–60].

At this time, the number of D.C.'s (Doctors of Chiropractic) legally and illegally in practice probably exceeded the number of legitimate osteopaths in the country. Thus, while the D.O.'s through the AOA had made considerable progress in obtaining some professional recognition, insofar as certain measures of organization, autonomy, socioeconomic organization, and education were concerned, they nevertheless could not prevent the rise of others capitalizing upon the therapeutic modality that was the central feature of their own system.

It appears that the increasing competition for patients with musculoskeletal problems that osteopaths faced from chiropractors in the decades following the turn of the century was one of the social forces that propelled American osteopathy toward its evolution into osteopathic medicine. As they developed in different directions, with osteopathy becoming more and more like regular medicine and chiropractic remaining a distinct alternative to it, the direct competition between osteopathy and chiropractic became less pronounced. A recent study found that out of the 188 individuals who responded to a questionnaire which was sent to 308 osteopathic general practitioners, 39 percent indicated that they do not use OMT at all in their practice [34]. In contrast, spinal manipulation continues to be the primary modality employed by chiropractors. Whereas osteopathic physicians filled the positions in primary care vacated by the MDs, it appears that to a large extent chiropractors have filled the vacuum in the area of spinal manipulation left by the osteopaths in their conversion into osteopathic physicians.

Chiropractic has continued to maintain an edge over osteopathic medicine in terms of the number of active practitioners. In 1976, there reportedly were some 18,000 active chiropractors and 15,572 active DOs in the United States [59:232–233]. In October, 1980, the total enrollment at the 17 chiropractic colleges in the United States was reported to be 9521 [60:230–231]. In contrast, the total enrollment for the twelve accredited American osteopathic colleges during the 1977/78 academic year was reported to be 3,916 [26]. Although the latter enrollment figure does not include the number of students at three osteopathic colleges to be accredited in Maine, California, and Florida, it indicates that the chiropractic profession will grow at a faster rate than the osteopathic profession for some time to come.

Conversely, relative to the United States, British chiropractic remains a very tiny enterprise. According to one in-house source, "Osteopathy is better known in the UK than Chiropractic. Britain is the only country where Osteopaths outnumber Chiropractors; in most countries Chiropractic is more widely known and recognized" [8:14]. This same source cites estimates that, as opposed to 13,060 people per chiropractor in the United States, there are 635,542 people per "qualified" chiropractor in England and Wales and 871,500 people per "qualified" chiropractor in Scotland [8:11]. Largely because of its small size, it appears that British chiropractic is even a more marginal profession than British osteopathy or, for that matter, American chiropractic.

Just as is the case for osteopathy, anyone in Britain may advertise himself as a chiropractor. In response to this problem, a small group of chiropractors established the British Chiropractors' Association (BCA) and an associated register in 1925. The 1983 register of the association lists 150 regular members and 8 "associate" members in the United Kingdom as well as 30 "associate" members in several other countries. Although the BCA is a member of the European Chiropractic Union (headquartered in Oslo, Norway) and has formal ties with chiropractic associations in Canada, Hong Kong, New Zealand, and Zimbabwe, it has no formal ties with the two American chiropractic associations. Although data on the number of free-lance chiropractors practicing in Britain are unavailable, it does not appear that this figure exceeds that of the BCA membership. It should be noted, however, that a few American-trained chiropractors in Britain have chosen not to affiliate with the BCA. At the present time, BCA members are particularly concerned about potential competition by graduates from the McTimoney Chiropractic School, which offers a three-year, part-time course in Oxford. Most free-lance practitioners of manipulative therapy have chosen to identify themselves as osteopaths rather than chiropractors due to the former's somewhat higher status in Britain.

A major factor contributing to the slow growth of British chiropractic was the absence for many decades of a chiropractic school in Europe. It was not until

1965 that a small private foundation consisting of six British, Swiss, and Belgian chiropractors started the Anglo-European College of Chiropractic in Bourne- mouth, England. In 1980, the European Chiropractic Union assumed control of the governing structure of the school. Of some 150 students at the institution, about half are reportedly British nationals [8:8]. Prior to 1965, chiropractors working in Britain were generally graduates of American and Canadian chi- ropractic schools. Although the establishment of a chiropractic college will en- sure the growth of organized chiropractic in Britain, it is almost certain that it will remain a more marginal profession than osteopathy in that nation for some time to come.

Osteopathy has not faced the same direct competition from chiropractic in Britain, primarily because of the latter's small size, as it has in the United States, particularly during the 1910s and 1920s. Instead, the main competition for pa- tients with musculoskeletal complications that organized osteopathy in Britain has encountered has come from the free-lance and quasi-organized osteopaths, some of whom also advertise themselves as chiropractors. Although some of the American-trained osteopaths affiliated with the BOA have come to resemble regular physicians in their mode of practice, most organizationally-affiliated osteopaths in Britain have not encountered a sufficiently serious threat from the BCA chiropractors, the osteopathically-oriented regular medical practitioners, and even the free-lance and quasi-organized osteopaths/chiropractors, to shed their strong emphasis on OMT.

VI. SUMMARY AND CONCLUSIONS

The comparative study of osteopathy presented in this paper reveals that this alternative health system has undergone a divergent evolution in the United States and Britain. Although American osteopathy (perhaps better named os- teopathic medicine) remains organizationally separate from organized medicine, it is not clear to what extent it remains a distinct alternative to allopathic medi- cine. It must be noted, however, that there exists a small but vocal minority within American osteopathic medicine that emphasizes the centrality of the os- teopathic concept in the treatment not only of musculoskeletal problems but also other complications. Many of these DOs are affiliated with the American Acade- my of Osteopathy, an organization which is viewed by many osteopathic physi- cians as a quasi-certifying body for those who place great stress upon manip- ulative techniques. Some if not many members of this minority feel comfortable with the label of "osteopath" in referring to themselves and are opposed to the involvement of some DOs in the manual medicine movement. They contend that merely teaching various manipulative techniques to regular physicians will not only dilute the osteopathic concept but will serve to even further erode the distinction between osteopathy and allopathic medicine. Within the ranks of this minority one finds several individuals who are engaged in active intercourse with osteopathic groups in Britain and on the Continent. Since American osteopathy is more research-oriented than its European counterparts, some American DOs are sharing their findings with their colleagues across the Atlantic. Furthermore, a few American DOs occasionally offer courses in new techniques of manipulation to European osteopaths.

In contrast to American osteopathic medicine, British osteopathy continues to place a much stronger emphasis on Osteopathic Manipulation Therapy. British osteopathy has undergone internal developments of its own, resulting in several osteopathic camps with their own associations and educational institutions. Osteopathic physicians and regular medical practitioners with postgraduate training in osteopathy in large part function as specialists in the treatment of musculoskeletal problems. Osteopaths affiliated with the lay groups, the British Naturopathic and Osteopathic Association, the Society of Osteopaths, and the Osteopathic Association of Great Britain, exhibit many of the characteristics of early American osteopathy but also of chiropractic today.

In some ways, the differences between osteopathy and chiropractic are more in name and theory than in practice. This is partly reflected by the tendency on the part of some free-lance and quasi-organized osteopaths in Britain to also identify themselves as chiropractors. In fact, in one Anglophile country, Australia, some practitioners have attempted to institutionlize a merger of osteopathy and chiropractic (in a manner perhaps not too different from that found in the BNOA). This merger is made evident by the names of two professional organizations, namely the Australian Chiropractors, Osteopaths, and Naturopathic Physicians Association and a group called Chiropractic and Osteopathic Incorporated [45:261]. According to Wardwell [58:8], "Differences between osteopathic and chiropractic manipulative treatment appear to be more of who applies the technique than differences in technique itself. The distinction between chiropractors and naturopaths is even more blurred because often they were trained at the same schools and sometimes studied both fields simultaneously." Although British osteopaths and chiropractors often claim that the former rely primarily on low velocity, long lever techniques whereas the latter on high velocity, specific thrust techniques, most admit that there has been a great deal of exchange of techniques between the two categories of practitioners.

In attempting to explain the divergent evolution of osteopathy in the United States, I have taken into consideration the larger sociopolitical contexts and the plural medical systems within which these separate developments occurred. It was argued that at least four factors, namely the existence or nonexistence of licensing regulations, the degree of medical presence in osteopathy, the organization of medical care, and the relative size of chiropractic, contributed to this divergent evolution. While it is difficult to predict the directions that osteopathy will take in the two countries of concern in this paper, it seems appropriate to conclude by considering the possibilities. Despite the fact that American osteopathy has undergone a tremendous organizational growth in the past decade or so, it is uncertain whether or not this will be translated into a rejuvenation and a refinement of the osteopathic concept—the birthright of osteopathy so to speak. Eventual merger with organized medicine along the lines of the California merger of the early 1960s still remains a possibility. Gevitz [19:146] notes that "At the present time, the number of D.O.'s who are actively in favor of a merger with the AMA appears to be comparatively small, however, there are a greater number who, while wishing to keep the profession autonomous, are in favor of their schools changing the degree awarded to an M.D. and wish to be allowed to list themselves in that manner." Furthermore, a significant minority within organized medicine is still committed to a strategy of coopting DOs. A resolution urging state medical societies to sponsor legislation permitting DOs to identify themselves as MDs was narrowly defeated in the AMA House of Delegates in 1974 [19:146–147]. As I have suggested elsewhere, however, the futures of both osteopathic medicine and regular medicine in the United States depend on changes in the larger political economy of health care [3]. The fact that American osteopathy has become an integral part of capital-intensive medicine may mean that its subsequent development is in large part beyond the control of its practitioners.

The status of British osteopathy is considerably more marginal than that of its American parent. Although some British osteopaths seem to have evolved into osteopathic physicians and some British regular medical practitioners have come to incorporate OMT into their regimen of treatment, most British osteopaths continue to view their approach to health care as a distinct alternative to allopathic medicine. Whereas there remains a strong possibility that American osteopathic medicine will eventually merge in one way or another with regular medicine, such a possibility, with the exception of the BOA, appears to be remote at the present time in the case of British osteopathy. Osteopathy, whether or not it obtains statutory recognition and becomes included under the National Health Service, is likely to enjoy a pattern of at least modest growth in Britain. Much of this growth will come from the recent expansion of the British School of Osteopathy from an enrollment in its former premises of under 100 students to an anticipated enrollment of over 400 in its new premises near Trafalgar Square. Since most osteopaths are presently concentrated in Greater London and the Home Counties, they often observe that the profession's greatest potential for growth exists in other parts of Britain. Ultimately, however, it must be noted that the future evolution of osteopathy in Britain as well as the United States will be shaped by factors in the larger sociopolitical environments within which it exists.

ACKNOWLEDGMENTS

The idea for the research upon which this article is based began to emerge while I was a NIMH post-doctoral fellow in the Medical Anthropology Program at Michigan State University during the 1979–80. Fred Mitchell, Jr., John Upledger, Myron Beal and Alice Raynesford of the Michigan State University College of Osteopathic Medicine first acquainted me with the status of osteopathy in Britain and on the Continent. An educational grant from the National Osteopathic Foundation made it possible for me to conduct archival research and visit the various osteopathic institutions and their representatives in Great Britain during the summer of 1983. Many individuals—practitioners, administrators, faculty, students and staff associated with the Society of Osteopaths, the British Osteopathic Association, the Osteopathic Association of Great Britain, the British naturopathic and Osteopathic Association, the British Chiropractors' Association, the European School of Osteopathy, the British School of Osteopathy, the London College of Osteopathic Medicine, the British College of Naturopathy and Osteopathy, the Anglo-European College of Chiropractic, and the Institute for Complementary Medicine—generously gave of their time and made their resources available to me. I am especially indebted to George E. Aitkin, Margery and Bob Bloomfield, Colin Dove, Ian P. Drysdale, Tom Dummer, Clarence L. Johnson, Dennis J. Kieley, Harold S. Klug, Sir Norman Lindop, Audrey Smith, and John Wernham for sharing their perceptions of the British osteopathic scene with me.

REFERENCES

1. Albrecht, Gary L., and Judith A. Levy, "The Professionalization of Osteopathy: Adaptation in the Medical Marketplace." Pp. 161–206 in Julius A. Roth (ed.), *Research in the Sociology of Health Care: Changing Structure of Health Service Occupations*, Volume 3. Greenwich, CT: JAI Press, 1982.
2. Anderson, Odin W., *Health Care: Can There Be Equity? The United States, Sweden, and England*. New York: John Wiley & Sons, 1972.
3. Baer, Hans A., "The Organizational Rejuvenation of Osteopathy: A Reflection of the Decline of Professional Dominance in Medicine." *Social Science and Medicine: An International Journal* 15A:701–711, 1981.
4. Beal, Myron C., "The London College of Osteopathy." Pp. 107–108 in American Academy of Applied Osteopathy, *1950 Yearbook of Selected Osteopathic Papers*, 1950.
5. Berchtold, Theodore A., *To Teach, To Heal, To Serve: The Story of the Chicago College of Osteopathic Medicine*. Chicago: Chicago College of Osteopathic Medicine, 1975.
6. Blackstone, Erwin A., "The AMA and the Osteopaths: A Study of the Power of Organized Medicine." *The Antitrust Bulletin* 2:405–440, 1977.
7. Booth, E. R., *History of Osteopathy and Modern Medical Practice*. Cincinnati: Caxton 1924.
8. *The British Chiropractic Handbook*. Chelmsford, Essex: The British Chiropractors' Association and the Chiropractic Advancement Association, n.d.
9. *The British College of Naturopathy and Osteopathy*. London: British College of Naturopathy and Osteopathy, n.d.
10. *British Medical Journal*, "Osteopath's Bill: Select Committee." March 23, 1935.
11. Brown, E. Richard, *Rockefeller Medicine Men: Medicine and Capitalis in America*. Berkeley: University of California Press, 1979.
12. Burrow, James G., *AMA—Voice of American Medicine*. Baltimore: John Hopkins University Press, 1963.
13. Burton, A. Kim, "Characteristic of Patients," *A Work Study of the Osteopathic Association of Great Britain*, n.d.
14. Camp, Francis E. (ed.), *Granwohl's Legal Medicine* (third edition). Bristol, England: John Wright & Sons, 1976.
15. *Chiropractic in California: A Report by the Stanford Research Institute*. Los Angeles: The Haynes Foundation, 1960.

16. Coe, Rodney M., *Sociology of Medicine*. New York: McGraw-Hill, 1970.
17. Denton, John A., *Medical Sociology*. Boston: Houghton Mifflin, 1978.
18. Editorial, *Journal of the Society of Osteopaths* Spring, No. 4, 1978.
19. Gevitz, Norman, "The D.O.'s: A Social History of Osteopathic Medicine." Ph.D. dissertation, University of Chicago, 1981.
20. Gibbons, Russell W., "Chiropractic in America: The Historical Conflicts of Cultism and Science." *Journal of Popular Culture* 10:720–731, 1977.
21. Hall, T. Edward, and John Wernham, *The Contribution of John Martin Littlejohn to Osteopathy*. Maidstone, England: Maidstone Osteopathic Clinic, 1974.
22. Hart, J. Tudor, "Primary Care in the Industrial Areas of Britain: Evolution and Current Problems." *International Journal of Health Services* 2:349–365, 1972.
23. Huntley, R. R., "Primary Medical Care in the United States: Present Status and Future Prospects." *International Journal of Health Care* 2:195–206, 1972.
24. Inglis. Brian, *The Book of the Back*. New York: Hearst, 1978.
25. *Journal of the American Medical Association,* "Osteopathy: Special Report of the Judicial Council of the AMA House of Delegates." September 16, 177 (11):774–776, 1961.
26. *Journal of the American Osteopathic Association, 1978 Almanac*. Chicago: American Osteopathic Association, 1978.
27. *Journal of the Society of Osteopaths* Autumn, No. 1, 1976.
28. *Journal of the Society of Osteopaths* Autumn, No. 5, 1978.
29. *Journal of the Society of Osteopaths* Spring, No. 6, 1979.
30. Kowalski, Tim J., "Osteopathy in Britain: An American Student's Perspective." Unpublished Manuscript, Michigan State University, 1981.
31. Larson, Magali Sarfatti, *The Rise of Professionalism: A Sociological Analysis*. Berkeley: University of California Press, 1977.
32. Leslie, Charles, "Introduction." Pp 1–12 in Charles Leslie (ed.), *Asian Medical Systems: A Comparative Study*. Berkeley: University of California Press, 1976.
33. Lin, Phyllis Lan, "The Chiropractor, Chiropractic, and Process: A Study of the Sociology of an Occupation." Ph.D. dissertation, University of Missouri, 1972.
34. McConnell, David G., Philip E. Greenman, and Richard B. Baldwin, "Osteopathic General Practitioners and Specialists: A Comparison of Attitudes and Backgrounds." *The D.O.* December, Pp. 103–118, 1976.
35. McKeon, L. D. Floyd, *Osteopathic Polemics*. London: C. W. Daniel, 1938.
36. Mills, Donald L. *Study of Chiropractors, Osteopaths, and Naturapaths in Canada*. Ottawa: The Queen's Printer, 1964.
37. Navarro, Vicente, *Class Struggle, the State and Medicine: An Historical and Contemporary Analysis of the Medical Sector in Great Britain*. New York: Prodist, 1978.
38. New, Peter Kong-Ming, "The Application of Reference Group Theory to Shifts in Values: The Case of the Osteopathic Student." Ph.D. Dissertation, University of Missouri. 1960.
39. Northrup, George W., "One Standard." *Journal of the American Osteopathic Association* 79:429–430, 1980.
40. *Osteopathy: The Story of Andrew Still House*. London: British Osteopathic Association, n.d.
41. Osteopathy in the United States and Michigan: A Staff Report from the Citizens on Education for Health Care for Presentation to the State Board of Education. *Citizens Committee on Education for Health Care,* August, 1967.
42. *Prospectus of the European School of Osteopathy*. Kent, England: European Europena School of Osteopathy, n.d.
43. *Prospectus of the London College of Osteopathic Medicine*. London: London College of Osteopathic Medicine, n.d.
44. Reed, Louis, *The Healing Cults*. Chicago: University of Chicago Press, 1932.

45. *Report of the Committee of Inquiry Into Chiropractic, Osteopathy, Homeopathy and Neuropathy.* Canberra: Australian Government Publishing Service, 1977.
46. Roth, Julius A., *Health Purifiers and Their Enemies.* New York: Prodist 1976.
47. Schiötz, Eiler, and James Cyriax, *Manipulation: Past and Present.* London: William Heinemann Medical Books, 1975.
48. Sharma, Sylvia L., and Paul L. Dressel, *Interim Report of an Exploratory Study of Michigan State University College of Osteopathic Medicine Training Program.* East Lansing: Office of Institutional Research, Michigan State University, 1975.
49. *Statistic Yearbook 1979/80.* New York: Department of International Economic and Social Affairs, United Nations, 1981.
50. Stevens, Rosemary, *Medical Practice in Modern England: The Impact of Specialization and State Medicine.* New Haven: Yale University Press, 1966.
51. _____, *American Medicine and the Public Interest.* New Haven: Yale University Press, 1971.
52. Twaddle, Andrew C., and Richard M. Hessler, *A Sociology of Health.* St. Louis Mosby, 1977.
53. Tyler, Richard H., "Osteopathy in Great Britain," *The Osteopathic Physician* February, Pp. 53–56, 1977.
54. Unschuld, Paul L., "The Issue of Structured Coexistence of Scientific and Alternative Medical Systems: A Comparison of East and West German Legislation." *Social Science and Medicine: An International Journal* 143: 15–42, 1980
55. Walsh, John, "Medicine at Michigan State (I): Educators and Legislators." *Science* 177: 1085–1087, 1972.
56. Wardwell, Walter L., "A Marginal Professional Role: The Chiropractor." *Social Forces* 30: 339–348, 1952.
57. _____, "Discussion: The Impact of Spinal Manipulative Therapy on the Health Care System." Pp. 53–58 in Murray Goldstein (ed.), *The Research Status of Spinal Manipulation Therapy.* Washington, D.C.: National Institutes of Health, 1975.
58. _____, "Social Factors in the Survival of Chiropractic: A Comparative View." *Sociological Symposium* 22: 6–17, 1978.
59. _____, "Limited and Marginal Practitioners." Pp. 230–250 in Howard E. Levine, Sol Levine, and Leo G. Reeder (eds.), *Handbook of Medical Sociology.* Englewood Cliffs NJ: Prentice-Hall, 1979.
60. _____, "Chiropractors: Challengers of Medical Domination." Pp. 207–250 in Julius A. Roth (ed.), *Research in the Sociology of Health: Changing Structure of Health Service Occupations,* Volume 3. Greenwich, CONN: JAI Press, 1982.

PHYSICIAN MALDISTRIBUTION IN CROSS-CULTURAL PERSPECTIVE:
UNITED STATES, UNITED KINGDOM, SWEDEN AND THE PEOPLE'S REPUBLIC OF CHINA

Marilynn M. Rosenthal and Deborah Frederick

I. INTRODUCTION

For many decades, an accepted assumption in health care system planning has been that a high physician-population ratio (P/PR) and an equitable distribution of a nation's physician manpower pool are important and desirable goals. The general reasoning has been that an increasing number of physicians will disperse themselves throughout a society so as to be equitably distributed among the

Research in the Sociology of Health Care, Volume 5, pages 101-136.
Copyright © 1987 by JAI Press Inc.
All rights of reproduction in any form reserved.
ISBN: 0-89232-597-6

population. This will logically lead to improved access to care and this, in turn, will result in improved health status. Numbers = Access = Health.

The issue of physician numbers and distribution has been a recurring one in the American health care system and continues as salient into the 1980s and 1990s. There is an extensive American research literature on this subject. However, it is rarely examined in cross-cultural context although comparative study is a powerful tool for understanding issues in one's own society. It provides a framework within which to separate out dynamics common to all Western, industrial nations (perhaps even developing nations) and those which may reflect more unique cultural histories or organizational arrangements [27]. So, for example, it is useful to inquire into the experiences of other health care systems, particularly those that are organized and financed in ways significantly different from the United States. Hence, the questions posed in this study are: How do organizational features of a health care system affect its ability to deal with the issues of physician maldistribution? and: what are the effects of physician distribution on the health status of the population? Drawing on available information from the United Kingdom (U.K.), Sweden, the United States, and the People's Republic of China (PRC), we present an initial attempt to describe policy and program evolution, changing definitions of the problem of physician maldistribution and relative ''success'' in solving geographic inequities.

The most recent document to discuss the problem of medical manpower and physician distribution in the United States, the Graduate Medical Education National Advisory Committee (GMENAC) Report [9], represents the most sophisticated American analysis of the subject to date. Created in 1976 under the Ford Administration to make recommendations to the Department of Health and Human Services on overall strategies concerning present and future supply and requirements of physicians, the Committee's report was published in 1980. Two important aspects of the report are: (1) the prediction of a physician surplus in the United States by 1990, and (2) the argument that medical education should be a major mechanism for influencing future doctor distribution. GMENAC also states that, in spite of the surplus, there will continue to be a marked *unevenness* in the geographic and specialty distribution of doctors. It recommends a reduction in medical school enrollments.[1]

The conventional measures of how a country is doing with reference to its physician manpower pool have been physician/population ratios. World Health Organization (WHO) Statistical Annals provide those ratios for the four countries discussed here and others (see Table 1).

Each of the countries has shown significant improvement in the period of time included, with the PRC establishing the most dramatic rate of change. These will be analyzed more closely later in the article. Suffice it to say that in worldwide perspective the United Kingdom and Sweden are somewhat above the European average, the United States leads the Americas and is comparable to Europe, and

Table 1. Physician-Population Ratios: Selected Areas and Countries

	1963+	1973+	1977–1978
Areas:			
Africa			1:5434
Americas			1:864
Asia			1:2877
Europe			1:552
USSR			1:289
Countries:			
Austria			1:428
Hong Kong			1:1144
India			1:3652
Japan			1:845
Korea			1:2088
PRC	1:40,000		1:2602
Sweden	1:950	1:630	1:563
United Arab Republic			1:243
United Kingdom	1:840	1:770	1:659
United States	1:690	1:6 0	1:595

1977–1978

World Population: 4,134,667,000
Total World Physician Stock: 3,342,587
World Ratio: 1:1,237

Note: The World Health Organization defines "physician" as: (a) Graduates of a medical school; (b) Active
participation in practice, teaching, administration, and research; (c) Assistant physicians, interns, residents,
house officers included.
Sources: World Health Statistics. Geneva: World Health Organization, 1980; 1976; 1966

the PRC does significantly better than India, the Asian country to which it is best
compared in terms of size and level of development. These ratios, of course,
provide only the most superficial of information. They reveal nothing about
physician distribution. That will necessitate a rather different level of scrutiny.

II. CHARACTERISTICS OF FOUR HEALTH CARE SYSTEMS

Since this discussion intends a preliminary exploration of the possible impact of
health care system organizational characteristics on physician distribution, a
quick sketch of the major features of the four systems is in order:

- *The United States:* a non-uniform multi-nucleus, free market health care
  system with a mixture of private and public financing and facilities, and

with a specialist-hospital-high technology orientation, with the majority of doctors in the private sectors [1].

- *The United Kingdom:* a centrally financed, centrally regulated and planned health care system with a balanced mix of general practitioners (GPs) and hospital physicians and surgeons, guaranteeing health care as a right of citizenship; hospital doctors are salaried; GPs are individual contractors to the National Health Service (NHS) [1]; there is a small private sector.
- *Sweden:* a national insurance plan tied to county-provided services (from county taxes) that has emphasized specialist-hospital-high technology services with shared national and local planning features and universal access; all doctors are salaried; patients contribute a small co-payment; there is a small private sector [1].
- *PRC:* an uneven, national and locally-funded system of care relying heavily on traditional and paraprofessional approaches and personnel. All doctors are salaried or receive work points [33].

All the systems are, of course, in a state of continual evolution. Generally speaking, however, we might agree that in terms of central government control over the health care system, the four can be shown on a continuum relative to each other (see Figure 1).

All four of these nations have, in the last three decades, concerned themselves with what they have defined as physician shortages and physician maldistribution, and they have established various policies and attempted to implement various programs in order to ameliorate physician maldistribution as they saw it. Brief histories and highlights of policy evolution in each country follow.

A. United States: Physician Manpower Policy

Shortly after World War II, Congress sought to increase the number of hospitals and medical facilities and thus effect an increase in the supply of physicians, through passage of the Hospital Survey and Construction Act of 1946, also known as the Hill-Burton Act. In theory, Hill-Burton would increase the number of hospitals and medical facilities in previously underserved areas and an increase in numbers of doctors would follow. However, there is evidence that Hill-Burton may not have been successful in this regard [6].

Figure 1.   Government control continuum.

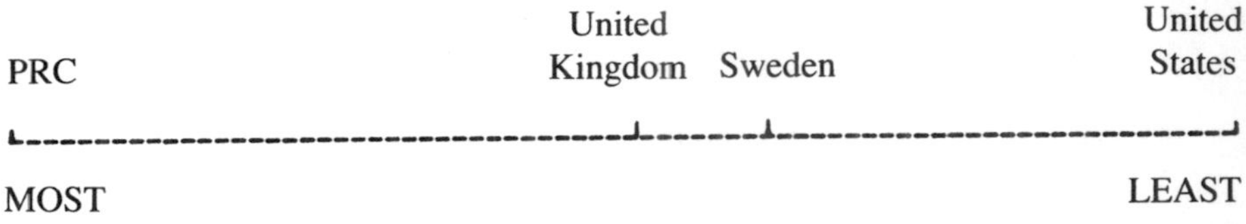

PRC	United Kingdom	Sweden	United States
MOST			LEAST

In 1963, Congress passed the Health Profession Educational Assistance Act (amended in 1968 as the Health Manpower Act), which increased funds for construction of medical schools and provided capitation grants to enlarge class size. A subsequent policy, the National Health Service Corps (NHSC), enacted in 1971, was established as an attempt to enroll health profession volunteers to serve in critical shortage areas. Through a well-financed scholarship program, the federal government would support a student through medical school if he or she agreed to practice in an underserved area in repayment for the cost of education [8]. Specifically, one year of service was required for each year of medical education funded through the NHSC. PL92-157, enacted by Congress in 1971, authorized medical schools to increase admissions of students whose backgrounds and interests made it likely that they would practice in rural and other areas experiencing severe shortages of medical personnel [4].

In response to a perceived adequate supply of physicians, 1976 saw passage of another Health Professional Assistance Act which attempted to control distribution with respect to both specialization and location and also made it more difficult for medical students to "buy their way out" of contracts agreeing to practice in underserved areas in exchange for financial assistance. Also in 1976, perhaps in response to the relative failure of the NHSC effort, a Health Manpower Act (PL94-484) made federal aid to medical schools dependent upon student commitment to practice in underserved areas and provided support for family practice residency programs [8].

The recently-released GMENAC report may give rise to policy initiatives aimed at effecting physician supply and distribution in the 1980s. GMENAC projects a coming surplus and calls for curtailment of medical school admissions and a continuation of voluntary efforts to address remaining manpower problems [9]. The current Republican administration has accepted the "surplus" analysis and is moving to reduce federal monies for medical education.

B. United Kingdom: Physician Manpower Policy

Accessibility to health care and, thus, the distribution of physician manpower came to the policy forefront after World War II, with adoption of the National Health Service Act, which made access to medical care a right of citizenship. Most manpower policy under the Act falls into two categories by recommending controls over the availability of training and practice posts and/or financial incentives. Some of the more notable manpower supply distribution policy statements, many in the form of "working party reports," are discussed below.

Control over Availability of Posts

The first postwar attempt to estimate medical manpower requirements was the Goodenough Report of 1944. It linked the interdependence of medical education and the NHS and concluded that an increase over the existing entrance quotas for British medical schools was needed in order to insure adequate physician supply and distribution [26].

In the early 1950s, the Cohen Report predicted a possible surplus of physicians but, several years later (in 1957), the Willink Report "corrected" those projections. It decried the inadequacy of available data regarding numbers of doctors, but went on to state that to 1961, production would be adequate, to 1979 it could be reduced and after that time it would need to be raised. It recommended an eventual reduction in student intake [26].

Ten years later, the Todd Report of 1968 provided both long-term and short-term assessments of medical schools to correct expected shortages. These recommendations were immediately implemented [26].

More recently, the 1976 Report of the Resource Allocation Working Party (RAWP) was an attempt to correct a gross imbalance existing in the hospital staffing levels of different regions and to link allocation of manpower with resource allocation [26].

Financial Incentives

The best examples of financial incentive policies are those used to effect GP distribution. Section 34 of the National Health Service Act creates a Medical Practice Committee, which authorizes general practitioner posts. Practice areas are measured according to accessibility: "designated," "open," "intermediate," and "restricted." A general practitioner choosing to practice in a restricted or oversupplied area will not receive NHS reimbursement. Included in this classification of areas is a system of financial inducements to encourage doctors to locate their practices in underserved ("designated") areas and those with high-need practice population (i.e., a high proportion of elderly, very young or disabled patients).

Recent Policy

The most recent policy statement, the Nabarro Report of 1980, advocates discontinuance of certain academic appointments that have grown up outside of central control, a limitation on the amount of time spent in specialty training, expansion of consultant (specialist) posts and a new mechanism for cajoling physicians out of the "bulge" areas into less desirable specialties and areas.

The overall effect of British manpower policy has been to increase the physician-to-population ratio approximately 17% between 1950 and 1980 and to increase the numbers of hospital specialists training for unpopular specialities while slowing down the growth in popular hospital positions. According to the Department of Health and Social Services (DHSS) in 1978, 5,500 additional GPs were still needed as well as 5,520 full-time hospital doctors to flatten disparities between the London Thames region and all other regions of England and Wales [22].

C. Sweden: Physician Manpower Policy

Between 1948 and 1972, the Swedish physician manpower pool increased sevenfold, though it should be noted that historically there have been fewer doctors in Sweden compared to other Scandanavian and European countries. Additionally, the number of medical schools increased and enrollments expanded two and one-half times during the late 1960s and early 1970s. During this time, the central government gradually assumed more control over the number and distribution of medical positions, concerning itself with increasing the numbers of physicians and at the same time controlling the number of positions available [10].

During the 1950s, a regionalized hospital boom took place, significantly increasing the number of hospital posts and outpatient positions in ambulatory care facilities. Further, in 1959, a Hospital Law abolished private beds and doctors' private hospital fees. During the 1960s, the central authorities began to consolidate their control over hospital staff positions. By 1969, the National Board of Health and Welfare (NBHW) was made responsible for all postgraduate medical training programs which put hospital positions under their jurisdiction. In the early 1970s, the Swedish Medical Association (SMA) began collective bargaining for physician salaries when the Seven Crown Reform abolished private fees for hospital outpatient services. At this time, the SMA was drawn into closer cooperation with the NBHW for medical manpower planning [10].

Since 1975 and in the face of continuing vacancies in both outpatient hospital posts and the impending problem in filling the GP positions created by a new emphasis on primary care in health centers, various groups have accelerated efforts to consolidate their positions. The 1975 Commission on Health and Medical Care legislation suggested that the County Councils have more power concerning medical manpower. This was endorsed enthusiastically by the 1979 Federation of County Council Congress (FCC) which "demanded" stronger measures to get doctors into vacant posts. At the same time, during the 1970s, the SMA collective bargaining created a new labor market situation. Arguing that other workers in the society have guaranteed 40-hour weeks, the same was gained for physicians, a reduction from previous 50–70 hour work weeks. In addition, Swedish doctors are now compensated for night and weekend duty with two hours off for every extra hour of duty. An intriguing by-product of extra duty compensation is a heated argument between the SMA and the FCC. The SMA has pressed for compensation in time off because of the marginal tax structure in Sweden; the FCC wants doctors to take compensation in money to avoid the need to hire extra doctors. The argument continues to date. Furthermore, the SMA has been actively promoting work in the private sector. This SMA strategy has had the overall effect of creating additional vacancies [32].

The most recent SMA/FCC/National Board of Health and Welfare negotiations have agreed that there will now be no new hospital posts anywhere in the country except in the shortage areas of psychiatry, long-term care and general practice in the burgeoning county health care centers. It is hoped that new doctors will be steered into vacant posts, particularly in general practice. This, of course, remains to be seen. Meanwhile, a recent SMA document, analyzing medical manpower, debates the dangers of the growing physician surplus in Sweden and projects a Physician/Population Ratio (P/PR) of 1:250 by the year 2014 [20].

In summary, the last 30 years have witnessed a steady and accelerated increase in numbers and a gradual increase in governmental control over the number and distribution of available posts as doctors become fully salaried employees of the evolving health care system. Theoretically, this should have eliminated most problems of physician maldistribution. However, during the same period, the medical profession and the SMA pushed for the establishment of an extensive hospital system, used uncontrolled and uncounted academic appointments and a "substitute" system to provide unanticipated alternatives for significant numbers of physicians, and developed a labor market strategy to create new positions where none existed before.

D. People's Republic of China: Physician Manpower Distribution

The physician manpower policies and programs developed in the People's Republic of China from 1950 to 1980 evolved within the context of a poor, Asian agricultural nation—in contrast to the Western, affluent, industrial countries we have been discussing. It also has a significantly different political economy, given the success of the Chinese Communist revolution in 1949. Since it has utilized some unconventional techniques to deal with its physician manpower shortage and distribution problems, it will be useful to examine its approach. We will also argue that certain dynamics in the United States, United Kingdom and Sweden can also be observed in the PRC. (Please note that statistics from the PRC are less reliable than those from the other three countries and are based on data, calculation and extrapolations that demand more than the usual skepticism applied to all such data.)

In the 1950s, the major strategies employed by the Ministry of Health were to double and triple the enrollments in existing medical colleges and universities [5]. As funds became available, the Ministry of Education built new schools and upgraded those already available. Appendix Table 7 documents an increase of 200–300% in enrollments and close to a fivefold increase in institutions. The Ministry of Health, since the inception of the PRC, also is empowered to assign positions to medical graduates just as all citizens receive job assignments in all parts of the labor force.

Mao Tse-tung also created an additional manpower policy in his 1950 address to the First National Public Health Conference held in Beijing when he legitimized 500,000 Chinese Traditional doctors of various types and declared that henceforth there would be a pervasive integration of Western-style and Traditional medicines. Also instituted at this time was the concept of the Mobile Medical teams which spent one to six months delivering care in remote and underserved areas of the country. These teams first were Peoples Liberation Army units. Later the concept was extended to teams from large urban hospitals [17].

Despite these efforts, physician maldistribution persisted into the 1960s, according to outside "educated" estimates [5]. The original problems had been formidable, of course, given the huge size of the Chinese population, the extent of poverty and disease inherited by the new government and the poverty of the nation. By 1964, the assessment of Mao and the central authorities was that the expansion of the physician manpower pool was moving too slowly and that serious maldistribution in rural areas persisted 15 years after Liberation. In conjunction with a period of time known as the Cultural Revolution, several programs were implemented simultaneously. First, medical education was cut in length of time, reduced from eight years to five in the most advanced institutions and from five years to three in others in order to speed up the number of students joining the ranks of practicing physicians. The medical school curricula were increasingly politicized [18; 7].

More dramatically, an enormous pool of health workers were created outside of conventional and professional channels. The Barefoot Doctor (BFD) program in 1965 is well-known in the West. Essentially, 1.8 million rural peasants were eventually chosen by their work comrades to receive from three months to one year of medical and prevention training in a variety of educational formats. They then provided medical and preventive care on a part-time basis, continuing to do agricultural work as well [29].

Evidence suggests that physician manpower strategies have now changed, particularly in the latter half of the 1970s, with the emergence of new national leadership committed to modernization and an emphasis on professional expertise.

Medical education curricula have reverted to their longer, earlier versions. Some 300,000–500,000 BFDs have been dismissed because of poor quality of care. The remaining 1.5 million are being professionalized—tested, certified and given further education to raise them to secondary physicians [29]. The new policy is that they will also become full-time salaried workers.

Existing manpower figures permit some insight into P/PR in the PRC. Appendix Table 7 establishes rough changes from 1966 to 1981 and provides a general view of what the BFD program has been able to accomplish by the 1970s based on limited descriptions of a variety of health units [29]. While there are no data comparable to that from the United States, United Kingdom and Sweden, it is possible to assert that the various physician manpower strategies employed by the PRC since 1950 have improved the P/PR dramatically. Recent WHO statistics (Table 1) show that the PRC is doing better than Asia in general, and 71% better than India, a nation with which it can be justifiably compared. Further, its rate of improvement is clearly the most impressive of the countries under consideration. A Fall 1981 statement from the Minister of Health provides some up-to-date numbers.[2]

In comparative terms, the strategies have involved the highest degree of social control and an element of compulsion that is not found in other health care systems. Lampton's study helps us understand the struggles over health policy between Chairman Mao who pursued a revolutionary ideology, and the medical profession which preferred a more cautious, conservative approach [14]. When Mao's position prevailed, it was with considerable disdain for the status of the medical profession. The current leadership, however, appears committed to the model of Western-style professional medicine and its value structure. So, current policy statements in the PRC indicate that the originally nonprofessional pool will be further professionalized and legitimized on terms acceptable to the PRC Western-style medical profession. This will increase the ranks of physicians (see Appendix Table 7). No other clear-cut policies have emerged to improve P/PR except that retired doctors may set up small, neighborhood private practices, and there has been renewed recruitment for traditional medicine education. The impact of these policies has not yet been determined.

E. Comparison of Characteristics

Overall then, the U.S. mechanisms to deal with professional distribution have emphasized increased hospital beds, federal monies for medical education and slowly increased enrollments, enlarging the doctor pool to create a "spillover effect." Essentially, the United States has depended on volunteerism in the medical profession and on market mechanisms. In the United Kingdom, the techniques have included central control of the number of top hospital posts and financial incentives and disincentives to GPs. In Sweden, control of positions and manipulation of medical school enrollments are employed in a system of what the Swedes call "steering."

Each national approach may be labelled:

United States	*United Kingdom*	*Sweden*	*PRC*
1. Market Mechanisms	1. Incentives	1. Steering	1. Assignment
2. Volunteerism	2. Control of Positions	2. Control of Positions	2. Innovation

Table 2.   Program Alternatives

	U.S	U.K.	Sweden	PRC
Financial Incentives				
1. Salary supplements		X	(X)*	
2. Subsidized medical education	(X)**	X	X	X
3. Goverment subsidy to purchasing power of poor locales		X	X	X
Enhancement Incentives				
1. Locate medical schools in needy areas	X	X	X	X
2. Build better facilities in needy areas	X	X	X	X
3. Raise status of shortage categories	X	X	X	
Recruitment Techniques				
1. Target groups admission policies	X			X
2. Increased admission to create spillover effect	X		X	X
3. Specialized training	X		(X)***	(X)***
4. Community-controlled recruitment				X
5. Foreign physician utilization	X (20%)	X (30%)	X (5–10%)	
Positional Incentives				
1. Control number of positions		X	X	
2. Position disincentives: tell where *not* to go		X		
3. Positional assignments				X
4. Positional rotation				X

Notes:

*now officially discouraged

**only to a small percentage of students directly through the National Health Service Corps; also through capitation to medical schools. The other countries provide 100% subsidy.

***recent

While emphasis has differed along with persistence and commitment (and these are of great importance), many of the same ideas have been tried, at least in the three Western countries. These have been grouped as "Financial Incentives," "Enhancement Incentives," "Recruitment Techniques," and "Positional Incentives" (Table 2).

Financial incentives include governmental monies to both individuals (for medical education) and communities (to afford physicians). Enhancement involves better distribution of medical schools and facilities to encourage localized medical practice, as well as improving the status of shortage specialities. Recruitment mechanisms are utilized to increase the manpower pool in general, and shortage specialties in particular. Positional approaches assert various levels of control over posts that physicians can occupy.

Major differences, compared to the United States, are that central authorities in the United Kingdom and Sweden control the overall number of positions available to physicians (only senior physicians in the United Kingdom). It should be noted, however, that both these countries permit private practice and that this alternative is not only viable but growing in both countries (primarily for hospital specialists in the United Kingdom) and therefore provides uncontrolled alternatives for practitioners. The PRC asserts central control through job assignments, government-determined increases in medical schools and enrollments, and the mobile medical team concept. It is the only country that utilizes very large numbers of unconventional practitioners, but these are slowly being socialized to a Western physician model.

If we refer back to the comparative continuum of control referred to earlier, we see more clearly the elements that constitute the legitimized and potential power of the various governments to influence physician distribution.

III. HOW SUCCESSFUL HAS EACH COUNTRY BEEN?

The major question remains: What is the relative success of the four health care systems in coping with their physician maldistribution problem? A variety of statistical sources reveal a number of answers (see Appendix Tables):

1. Overall, these four countries have improved their P/PRs significantly, with Sweden and the PRC accomplishing the greatest rate and magnitude of change. However, two countries have made substantial use of FMGs (foreign medical graduates: United Kingdom 30%, United States 20%) in order to accomplish this. See Table 3.

2. What about geographic distribution of these physician pools? The answer is surprising:until 1980, all three Western countries claimed continuing serious problems of physician distribution, and there are signs of persistent problems in the PRC. However, government strategies built up in the United Kingdom and in Sweden over at least one decade have reduced the GP distribution problems significantly in these two countries.

A. United States of America

Between 1960 and 1976, rural areas experienced little change in P/PR while suburban areas and small cities experienced the greatest improvement. A wide

Table 3. Changes in Physician-Population Ratio*

	1950	1960	1970	1980	% Change
United Kingdom	99	115	123	116**	+17.1
Peoples Republic of China		.27**		4**	+1500
Sweden	69	95	124	154**	+123.2
United States	149	148	156	171**	+14.8

Notes:

*P/PR: Physicians per 100,000 population

**Calculated by authors using data from sources below.

Sources:

U.S. Department of Health, Education and Welfare, *Health Manpower Source Book.* DHEW, 1964.

U.S. Department of Health, Education and Welfare, *Health. United States, 1978.* DHEW Publication No. (PHS) 78-1232 (Dec. 1978).

Roback, G. A., et al., *Distribution of Physicians in the U.S.* American Medical Association, 1971.

Wunderman, L., et al., *Physician Distribution and Medical Licensure in the U.S., 1978.* American Medical Association, 1979.

Anderson, Odin W., Ph.D., *Health Care: Can There Be Equity. The United States, Sweden and England.* New York: John Wiley and Sons, Inc. 1972.

Heidenheimer, Arnold J. and Elvander, Nils, eds., *The Shaping of the Swedish Health System.* New York: St. Martin's Press, 1980.

Statistical Yearbook 1968. New York: United Nations, 1969.

Eurohealth Handbook. New York: Robert S. First, Inc , 1980.

Monthly Bulletin of Statistics, March 1981. New York: United Nations, 1981.

disparity in P/PR continues within the United States, with the District of Columbia having the best ratio and Mississippi and Alaska the worst. Meanwhile, the number of medical school graduates doubled between 1950 and 1976, a period of time that saw a decrease in the number of GPs in the physician pool and a steady increase in specialists [9] (see Appendix Table 1).

B. United Kingdom

Here can be observed a general improvement of the P/PR between 1950 and 1978 but at a slower rate than the other three countries. (Actually, a slight decrease can be noted since 1978.) Increasing the number of medical students, raising the status of GP practice and controlling practice location has suddenly, in a two-year period, greatly reduced the number of GP posts available. However, new problems are looming in large inner cities because of the age structure of the GP pools [22]. Hospital consultant maldistribution persists on about the same level as it did twenty years ago in the same areas. In terms of absolute numbers, it has actually become worse. Medical school enrollments have increased but the medical profession is exerting new pressures to reduce student intake [11]. (See Appendix Tables 2, 3, 4.1 and 4.2)

When the physician distribution issue was reviewed with authorities in the United Kingdom in the Fall of 1982, some striking changes could be documented, particularly with reference to the distribution of GPs. While there were 100 "designated" (in special need) GP practice areas in 1979, there were only 15 in 1982—a dramatic reduction in a short three-year period of time [24]. Furthermore, there are documented reports of significant physician unemployment in the United Kingdom for the first time in decades: DHSS figures seem to be 1,000; the British Medical Association (BMA) claims 1,500 [25]. And the medical profession is pressing even more firmly to reduce the size of patient lists in each of the categories of areas [21].

In the U. K. situation, then, a combination of factors have come together over time to reduce GP maldistribution. These include government control of the number of practice locations (for an NHS practice), an increase in the status of GPs (by mandating three years of postgraduate "specialty" training), and an increase in the payments of GPs. All these have resulted in larger numbers of students choosing GP practice and hence beginning to fill up vacant practices. Finally, a recent redistribution of resources under the Resource Allocation Working Party (RAWP) formula has cut back the level of support for hospitals and medical schools in the "over-served" regions of the country. General cutbacks reflecting the worsening economic conditions of the country have also eroded money to the teaching hospitals. Finally, recent health workers' union strikes in hospitals have also tarnished the attractiveness of hospital practice.

By the same token, a 1982 update in the specialist hospital post situation reveals an altogether different picture emerging. In 1979, there were 481 consultant vacancies; in 1980 the figure was 627; in 1981 the figure was 1,070. This means that there has been a 122% increase in hospital vacancies in the highest posts in a three-year period of time [23]. It should be noted that the government has never had the power to control the number of hospital posts under the top consultant rank, so one might say a market approach prevails in those multiple categories. The vacancy rate at the consultant level may be further complicated by the agitation of the Junior Doctors Association to create new consultant posts to enhance their career opportunities. The junior doctors have also asked for a reduction in working hours. And of course the government still has no official say about the number of academically-related positions at any rank.

The system has indeed been able to take a sudden turn that has greatly reduced the number of GP vacancies in the country. It is possible, however, to look more closely at how this has been accomplished. It has not simply been increased numbers and control over where one can practice. Some rather simple figures show that the *characteristics* of the increased number of GPs have changed. Consider Tables 4.1, 4.2 and 4.3, describing gender of GPs and proportion born outside of the United Kingdom. See the discussion of GP characteristics in Section VI (Analysis).

Table 4.1. Percentage of Women
Admitted to U.K. Medical Schools

1968	25%
1969	26%
1970	28%
1975	35%
1978	38%
1980	40.7%
1981	42.6%

Source: UCCA.

Table 4.2. Percentage of Women at
Various Ranks in GP Practice, 1981

ALL GPs (England & Wales)	18%
Unrestricted Principals*	16%
Restricted Principals	36%
Assistants	55%
Trainees	34%

*Note: An Unrestricted Principal is a GP who provides the full range of general medical services and
whose patient list is not restricted to any particular
group of persons.
Source: DHSS 1981 data from Dobson.

Table 4.3. Percentage of Unrestricted GP
Principals Born Outside of U.K.

1968	11.8%
1973	16.6%
1978	18.5%
1981	26.0%

Sources: *BMJ* Article; DHSS, Dobson 1981.

C. Sweden

Sweden has the most favorable P/PR of the four countries. There has been a
sevenfold increase in the physician pool between 1947 and 1972 and a continual
increase is projected to 2010. However, in 1980, government documents revealed that one-half of the GP posts in some countries were vacant. Stockholm

County Council listed one-third of its GP posts as vacant [32]. The percentage of overall in-hospital vacancies had actually *increased* between 1974 and 1979. In Vasternorrland, one-half of the hospital staff positions in some specialities were vacant. Furthermore, 22% of other hospital positions were listed as occupied by temporary "substitutes" [15]. (See Appendix Table 5).

In addition, an undetermined number of unofficial posts have also been filled with substitutes (one source suggests over 1,000). Unofficial posts, or "black positions" as they are known in Sweden, are hospital positions created by the county councils in addition to their official allotment by the National Board of Health and Welfare. So, while the system was expanding in terms of positions and money, the rapid increase in the number of physicians had not yet solved the distribution problem.

Between 1980 and 1982, a dramatic change occurred in the GP vacancies. Almost all the Stockholm County Council GP slots have been filled and the situation is improving in other areas of the country as well. Hospital posts now show 7.9% vacancy nationally. Vasternorrland has 14% hospital posts and 4.2% GP posts vacant [12]. The figure for official hospital posts (nationally) that are occupied by substitutes is now 1,210. The unofficial positions have been challenged in the labor court and may now have to be made official, changing the overall number of positions available.

What appears to have happened in Sweden is again the confluence of several government strategies: heavy increase in medical school admissions, controlling new hospital posts, upgrading the status of GPs. New graduates appear to have snapped up the Stockholm GP positions and others around the country are slowly diminishing. It should be noted, however, that the private sector is becoming more aggressive, promising more opportunities there as well. Hospital vacancies persist as a national problem.

D. People's Republic of China

There are no known figures reflecting exact physician maldistribution. However, the PRC now has a P/PR that is better than the Asian average. Between the 1950s and the 1970s, they probably reduced their deficiency of physicians by 80% and increased their medical school graduates 1360% [5]. This means they compare favorably with most other Asian and developing nations. The creation of a pool of 1.5 million paramedics (BFDs) who are gradually being professionalized has been an unusual strategy to improve distribution for rural care.

Since all jobs are assigned in the PRC [3], we might assume there would be little distribution problem. However, a compilation of Barefoot Doctor/Population ratios reported by various study tours to the PRC in recent years indicates considerable disparity around the country [29]. And it has been established that local economic factors can influence the ability to support BFDs and, presum-

ably, other medical staff [14]. There is some disagreement as to how extensive
the rural medical cooperative system actually is. According to a 1976 report, 15–
20% of the rural communes do not have the cooperative medical funds which
provide a financial base for health care services [34]. However, a 1981 announcement from the PRC Ministry of Health suggests that 94% of the rural
counties are covered [31]. It should be assumed, nevertheless, that the problem
of maldistribution persists in the PRC as well. There may be less surprise about
this, however, than about persisting maldistribution in the United Kingdom,
Sweden, and the United States, given the enormous disparity in resources, stability and the ability to plan. (See Appendix Tables 6 and 7.)

IV. PROBLEMS IN MEASURING MALDISTRIBUTION

While it is widely held that physician maldistribution represents a major problem
for contemporary health care systems, little consensus has been reached as to just
what the nature of the problem is. Moreover, to date little progress has been
made toward determining at what point balance is reached, a requisite to any
definition of "maldistribution," a term which implies a deviation from some
acceptable state.

Two major obstacles stand in the way of defining both acceptable and unacceptable levels of geographic distribution of physicians:

1.   First, no uniform method has been devised by which to measure the
existing distributions of physicians and to calculate estimates of unmet needs.
2.   Second, little is understood about the relationship between medical resources and health. Does more health manpower—both physician and nonphysician—translate into improved health or do other factors beyond the control of the
medical profession determine the health status of a population? It is a well-
known fact that although the United States and Sweden spend roughly the same
proportions of their gross national products on health care and are comparable in
a number of other ways, such as level of technology and the degree of physician
specialization, a gross disparity exists between their respective infant mortality
rates in favor of the Swedes. Thus, should ways be found to achieve some
optimum level of medical manpower distribution, it is quite possible that the
populations' health status may not rise accordingly. Many, among them
Ginzberg [8], have pointed out that until the inequities of a society as a whole are
dealt with, neither equality of health or health care status can be expected.

Attempts have been made to improve upon the heretofore crude measures of
manpower distribution such as the P/PR [4; 9]. The variety of conceptual ap-

proaches is in itself testimony to the fact that one cannot really define mal-distribution as inequality or deviation from the average P/PR. The economic point of view sees maldistribution as the state in which demand for physicians' services exceeds the supply. Some define maldistribution or shortage as the difference between the supply of manpower and the number of physicians neces-sary to treat perceived medical needs. The political approach dictates that a shortage exists when the political leaders perceive that the public will pay more of their tax dollars to subsidize physician availability.

Recently, relatively sophisticated approaches to define optimum distributions of physician manpower have begun to develop, GMENAC recommendations for assessing availability of physician services advocate a complex system incorpo-rating such data as variance in need for hospital and physician services among populations, utilization rates of specific procedures and services by consumers, minimal acceptable P/PRs, maximum acceptable travel times and causal factors affecting physician location.

The RAWP formula, devised in 1976 by the Resource Allocation Working Party under the U.K.'s DHSS is another example of the more comprehensive attempts to develop means by which to assess need and allocate resources. This formula takes into account the composition of the population—e.g., age-sex makeup, indicators of the state of health of the population such as Standardized Mortality Ratios and Morbidity figures, utilization rates, environmental and occupational factors affecting health, population changes, and other economic and political factors [16].

Whatever method is used to determine adequate manpower distribution, it is clear that it must reflect a fuller understanding of the way in which health care systems and particularly physicians have an impact upon the health status of a population.

V. FRUSTRATIONS IN FORMULATING PHYSICIAN MANPOWER DISTRIBUTION POLICY

A review of physician manpower policy efforts in the three Western nations suggest that two phenomena take place that frustrate planning efforts to distribute physicians equitably:

1. The problem itself is evolving and definitions of maldistribution situations change;
2. Segments of the medical profession (and its organizational representation) find unanticipated ways to avoid going to locations they deem undesir-able; thev also develop negotiating strategies to expand opportunity in the face of expanding manpower pools.

Figure 2. Historical evolution of physician maldistribution.

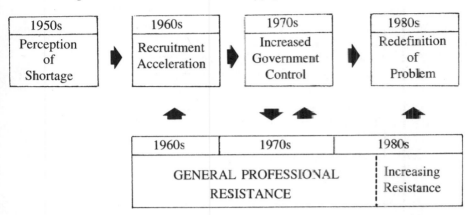

Figure 2 suggests a set of generalizations that may be made about what has occurred in the three Western nations.

After World War II, these governments became increasingly concerned with expanding the nations' supplies of physicians. Various forms of accelerated recruitment began to emerge in the 1960s buttressed by a variety of support programs. By the 1970s it became clear to the governments involved that more control was needed in order to induce, steer or promote voluntary distribution that would allow equity of access throughout a population. As government programs to encourage better distribution intensify, the medical professions intensify resistance, and new definitions of the problem itself begin to emerge. By 1982, however, government strategies in the United Kingdom and Sweden were beginning to have an effect. Time, then, becomes an important variable. At least GP vacancy rates are being sharply reduced although the "saga" is an ongoing one and the end is not in sight. This was the state of affairs, in the 1980s in the United Kingdom, Sweden and the United States.

The role of the profession is, of course, key in this process and merits special scrutiny and study. Particularly in the Unitd Kingdom and Sweden where the central authorities control certain positions, the medical profession has (1) created unanticipated "bulges" in academic settings which manage to negotiate special treatment for their institutions, and (2) physicians have managed to remain indefinitely as "substitutes" or in high training grade positions to avoid geographic areas deemed undesirable. In addition, (3) opportunities in private practice are expanding, and (4) increased numbers of women physicians mean an increase in part-time practice. This, along with medical associations' labor market strategies that change the parameters of maldistribution definitions, has countered increased social control. So, for example, acceptable patient load or "list size" is under consideration for reduction for GPs in the United Kingdom [22] and working hours cut approximately one-third in Sweden for all physicians [32]. Both techniques effectively create new positions—where none ever existed before—for the increasing number of physicians.

From the medical profession's point of view, it is argued that reduced patient load (in the United Kingdom) and reduced working hours (in Sweden) will produce higher quality patient care. Furthermore, doctors trained in high-technology, hospital-oriented medicine are loath to practice in areas and settings which they perceive as being unable to provide them with appropriate support. The profession also generally argues that their preference for settling in more urbanized areas of a country is very much like the preferences of the population in general.

In the United States, where government control over issues of this nature has always been weak, volunteerism and programs like the National Health Service Corps have affected only a small percentage of physicians. Increased federal capitation to medical schools while inducing increased enrollments, has not improved distribution. While recent research [30] documents improved physician distribution to smaller cities of the United States, the explanation appears to be that physicians are generally following the population trends in the United States. They are not making this new practice location choice because of government policies, programs or incentives. Furthermore, the current Republican administration is defunding those programs that have been put into place to influence physician numbers and distribution.

The position of the medical profession in the PRC and its relative influence is a special case. During the reign of Mao Tse-tung, the power of the profession went through periods of waxing and waning, depending on general political and economic issues and conditions [14]. But medical school enrollments and curricula were strongly manipulated by the central authorities and unconventional practitioners created and upgraded without the medical profession's enthusiastic support. The accomplishments in improved P/PR were remarkable but perhaps at great costs in quality of care. For example, the observations of some American physicians [19] have raised questions about BFD judgments, and the enthusiasm of visiting PRC physician-scholars in American medical schools for advanced medical technologies suggest the dated quality of their own current diagnostic and treatment levels. Now, new modernization policy sees renewed professional dominance influencing a return to more conventional medical education models and the professionalization of unconventional practitioners. The PRC emerges as a special case in this cross-cultural comparison and it is difficult to assess its meaning. Implied, however, is that very strong central control may produce more rapid results but at a cost.

This discussion would be remiss if it did not make special note of the use all three Western systems have made of foreign doctors. This is a complex and ethically potent issue that merits a more extensive discussion than is possible here. The need for "medical hands" has always been greater than the numbers produced in any of the three countries' medical schools despite admissions increases. There has been little coordinated planning between medical school intake and hospital need. It is true that the world's most advanced graduate medical training is found in countries like the United States and the United Kingdom and this is a powerful magnet for students from Third World countries to come to these two countries. However, it is also true that such medical migrations have been discouraged by special national legislation when it suited the Western nations' needs. Now that "indigenous" doctors are being produced in greater numbers, surpluses claimed and medical unemployment documented, national policy is changing, at least in the United Kingdom and the United States. New immigrant laws and tougher language requirements will make it increasingly difficult for foreign medical graduates or overseas doctors to practice. They flowed into the stream of medical manpower when the water was low; now as the native tide rises, their tributary will be walled off. What will happen in Sweden is not clear yet.

VI. ANALYSIS

The central issues that emerge in a cross-cultural study of physician maldistribution include the following:

1. Social definitions articulated by government health planners and administrators are in continuing conflict with those perceived by the medical profession.
2. Policy, programs and implementation are shaped by the political struggle that ensues from these conflicting perceptions. This suggests the strong likelihood that implementation may be a far cry from policy and programs. However, persistent control and pressure on the part of governments (where political change does not disrupt the program implementation) *does* appear to produce more equitable distribution patterns, at least for one type of physician GPs.
3. There is an evolution in understanding of the issue; that is, the need to control multiple variables and improve data collection; along with this is the recognition that time brings, and will always bring, changes in the objective situation. This has been noted in our section discussing problems in measurement.
4. There is also the need to recognize a worldwide culture of biomedical science and practice, with norms and values that transcend health care system organizational features. In all Western and westernizing societies, physicians have a deep loyalty to this culture and it shapes their behavior. As a high status

Figure 3.   Model of physician manpower distribution process.

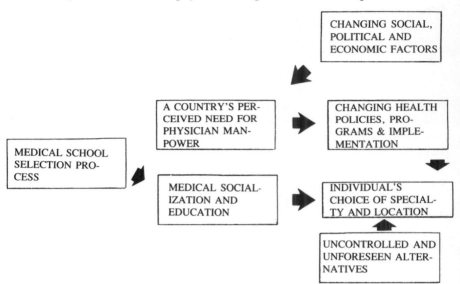

profession with a monopoly over knowledge that is valued by all societies, they are able to maintain control over their education, socialization and terms of work [2]. Even in the PRC where the medical profession encountered a powerful political force that disdained its "elitism," evidence suggests they managed considerable grass roots control over Chairman Mao's health dictums [28].

The macro-social process that takes place as a society addresses the issue of how many physicians it needs and the factors that influence choice of practice location (and specialty) may be modelled as suggested in Figure 3.

The most provocative of the boxes is, of course, the "uncontrolled and unforeseen alternatives" which seem to emerge primarily from the physician sector as government-perceived overall societal needs differ from professional choices.

There is always the difficulty of premature generalizations when one attempts to analyze the sociological dynamics of an ongoing process. However, we stand behind our general analytical framework. Using the analysis suggested in this article, we would want to watch very carefully the current actions of the medical professions (or its various subsections) in the United Kingdom and Sweden. For example, the Swedish Medical Association is mounting an increasingly energetic argument that there will be a dangerous surplus of physicians and is trying to get the Rikstag to reduce medical schools' places. It is also arguing that a certain number of hospital vacancies are needed for rotating continuing medical education purposes. Furthermore, medical students are dropping out or failing at

Swedish Medical Schools at a new and unusually high rate of between 5% and 10%.

A. How Much Difference Do Systems' Characteristics Make?

It can be said that in nationalized or rationalized (i.e., "planned") health care systems there is more agreement on government's legitimized role in defining and defending societal needs along with the profession's definitions. Rationalized systems also have a more stable structure for planning and for implementation. Administrative decisiveness and political courage to disagree with the profession may be enhanced. This legitimized structure makes it more difficult, but by no means impossible, for the profession to protect and promulgate its own definitions of appropriate physician distribution. If nationalized systems can sustain certain manpower policies over a protracted period of time (e.g., steadily increasing the number of medical students; controlling the number of certain positions) some reduction of physician maldistribution can be achieved. By 1982, the rationalized health care systems of the United Kingdom and Sweden achieved more equitable distribution of a *portion* of their physician manpower pool, although it may be noted that this is primarily the GP portion, not the highest in the medical profession's own internal status hierarchy. And this has been accomplished through an increase in the (still) "unconventional" doctor; women and foreigners. However, this makes the Numbers = Access = Health discussion even more salient as the persistent government push for equitable distribution of physicians is predicated on acceptance of the N = A = H assumptions.

B. Numbers = Access = Health?

This discussion cannot be concluded without recognizing that a new perception of the original assumption concerning the correlation between numbers of physicians, access and health has begun to emerge. This is a challenge to the concept of the Physician-Population Ratio as *the* significant factor in health outcomes for a population. J.R. Butler observed "Equity of (physician) distribution is that which yields equity of (health) outcomes" [4], thereby suggesting that the ratio formulation can be changed to: P/PHS = Physician/Population Health Status. One may suggest an even more radical change to: HC/PHS = Health Care/Population Health Status. Or, GW-HC/PHS = General Welfare-Health Care/Population Health Status.

Apropos of these proposals, it is interesting to contemplate the implications of the following comparative health statistics (see Table 5) relative to current P/P ratios.

It is not the purpose of this study to examine the correlates of health status, so Table 5 and its companions to follow are offered only to provoke further thought

Table 5. Comparative Health Statistics: 1980

| | Infant Mortality | Average Life Expectancy | | Physician Pop. Ratio | % GNP for Health Care |
		Female	Male		
PRC	12.8 (Peking)	Natl 69.5	66.9	1:2602	±4%
	11.3 (Ye County[3])	Shng 75.4	70.8		
Sweden	7.8	79	72.5	1:563	9–10%
United Kingdom	13.1	76.3	70.2	1:659	5–6%
United States	13.6	77.3	69.4	1:595	10.2%

Source: World Health Statistics, 1980 (Geneva, WHO)

And the most provoking figures in Table 5 are those from the PRC. With a sharply "inferior" P/PR and spending significantly less, they have comparable urban mortality rates and even some comparable rural figures. Among the Western nations, it can be noted that the United Kingdom's less favorable P/PR has not produced higher infant mortality or lower life expectancy figures compared to the United States with its more favorable P/PR. However, the additional important question Table 5 raises is whether the favorable Swedish P/PR is a major correlate of its impressive health status.

When changing rates of P/PRs are compared with rates of change for these two particular measures of a country's health status (infant mortality and life expectancy), some noteworthy patterns emerge. Just the three Western nations are compared in Table 6.

Looking at the United Kingdom, Sweden and the United States, the most powerful correlations appear to be between increased physician manpower and decreasing infant mortality rates, while none emerges relative to increased life expectancy. Obviously, all sorts of other socioeconomic variables are major correlates such as improved standard of living, improved public health, increasing average income and increasing educational levels. One must also observe that Sweden's impressive maternal and infant care programs are run, for the most part, by highly trained nurse-midwives, although obstetricians and pediatricians are responsible for the high-risk cases that could wreak havoc with Sweden's world-leading infant mortality rate. However, these tables do suggest the need for continued, careful consideration of where physicians do have a significant impact upon health status and where other factors may carry more weight.[4] The growing arguments that physicians and physician distribution may not be as significant to health status as assumed 20 years ago may be leading to too hasty conclusions. Equating numbers of physicians and access to them with macro-level health status may well be the wrong equation. A more appropriate correlation to examine is the impact of physicians on individual suffering and individual illness. How can we improve our methods for measuring medical diagnosis and

Table 6.   Comparison of Life Expectancy Rates, Infant Mortality Rates and P/PRs in the United States, Sweden and the United Kingdom, 1950–1980

Country	Year			
	1950	*1960*	*1970*	*1980*
United States				
Life Expectancy (Males)	—	67.4	68.0	69.4
(Females)	—	74.1	75.6	77.3
Infant Mortality	29.2	26.0	19.8	13.6
P/PR*	149	148	156	17:
Sweden				
Life Expectancy (Males)	—	71.3	71.7	72.5
(Females)	—	75.4	76.5	79.0
Infant Mortality	21.0	16.6	11.7	7.8
P/PR*	69	95	124	159
United Kingdom				
Life Expectancy (Males)	—	68.0	68.5	70.7
(Females)	—	73.9	75.1	75.3
Infant Mortality	31.4	21.8	18.1	13.1
P/PR*	99	115	123	115

Note:
*(P/PR = Physicians Per 100,000 Population)
Sources:
World Health Statistics, 1980. Geneva: WHO, 1980.
U.S. Department of Health, Education and Welfare, *Health United States, 1978.* DHEW Publicatior No. (PHS)78-1232 (December, 1978).
U.S. Department of Health and Human Services, *Health, United States, 1980.* DHSS Publication No. (DHS)81-1232 (December, 1980).

treatment outcomes for patients in the short, intermediate and long term? We must also recognize recent evidence that suggests impressive medical impact on reducing stroke and heart attack and controlling diabetes through preventive medical programs.

The introductory paragraphs of this study pointed to a basic assumption in health planning: that increased numbers of physicians, equitably distributed throughout a society, would lead to improved health status of the population. It then went on to examine how health care systems with distinctly different organizational features addressed the issue of physician distribution in their own societies. On one level of analysis it was found that the systems under study perceived similar problems of physician maldistribution and drew on a similar repertoire of programmatic solutions, although to significantly different degrees. In the two Western, socialized health care systems, the role and control of government was more directly salient, particularly in the control of positions that physicians can occupy. Yet because of uncontrolled alternatives, government efforts have been only partially effective in reducing the maldistribution problem. The explanations offered include conflict between government and the medical profession as to where physicians should practice, an evolving comprehension of appropriate distribution, and questions about the impact of medical care on the health status of a population.

Finally, the evidence concerning the relationship to health status is ambiguous. The Numbers = Access = Health assumption is clouded, particularly by evidence from the PRC, where Western-level health status statistics appear without Western-level P/PRs. Further, some evidence suggests that P/PRs may have an impact on some measures of status and not others. Meanwhile, the assumptions underlying the Numbers = Access = Health equations are increasingly called into question as nonmedical correlates of health are increasingly discussed. Health care systems, despite organizational differences, now face the common issue: how much of finite resources need go to physician manpower for maximum health status impact?

Appendix Table 1. United States: Non-federal Physicians, Civilian Population, Physician-Population Ratios and Rank by State, 1977

State	Civilian Population (7–1–77)	Non-federal Physicians (12–31–77)		Physicians per 100,000 Population		Rank of Physician Population Ratio by State	
		Total	Pt. Care	Total	Pt. Care	Total	Pt. Care
Alabama	3,666,000	4,330	3,687	118	101	45	45
Alaska	382,000	442	366	116	96	48	48
Arizona	2,270,000	4,651	3,552	205	155	10	12
Arkansas	2,134,000	2,506	2,081	117	97	46	47
California	21,618,000	50,088	40,001	232	185	6	5
Colorado	2,574,000	5,299	4,295	206	167	9	9
Connecticut	3,094,000	7,354	5,801	238	187	5	4
Delaware	577,000	936	787	167	136	27	21
D.C.	682,000	3,356	2,522	492	370	1	1
Florida	8,358,000	17,740	13,163	212	157	8	11
Georgia	4,988,000	6,928	5,875	139	115	36	36
Hawaii	838,000	1,709	1,379	204	164	12	10
Idaho	852,000	978	831	115	97	49	46
Illinois	11,205,000	19,592	16,103	175	144	19	13
Indiana	5,322,000	6,763	5,647	127	106	41	42
Iowa	2,878,000	3,490	2,917	121	101	44	44
Kansas	2,209,000	3,445	2,858	150	124	30	23

Appendix Table 1. (Continued)

State	Civilian Population (7–1–77)	Non-federal Physicians (12–31–77)		Physicians per 100,000 Population		Rank of Physician Population Ratio by State	
		Total	Pt. Care	Total	Pt. Care	Total	Pt. Care
Kentucky	3,422,000	4,516	3,743	132	109	38	39
Louisiana	3,893,000	5,614	4,696	144	121	32	31
Maine	1,075,000	1,684	1,334	157	124	24	29
Maryland	4,095,000	9,783	7,533	239	184	4	6
Massachusetts	5,770,000	14,299	11,226	248	195	3	3
Michigan	9,116,000	13,594	11,344	149	124	311	27
Minnesota	3,972,000	7,356	5,906	185	153	14	13
Mississippi	2,363,000	2,471	2,121	104	90	50	50
Missouri	4,777,000	7,458	6,046	158	127	23	24
Montana	755,000	955	847	130	112	40	38
Nebraska	1,549,000	2,240	1,840	145	119	33	34
Nevada	623,000	897	738	144	118	35	35
New Hampshire	845,000	1,512	1,172	179	139	18	20
New Jersey	7,301,000	13,349	10,777	183	148	16	17
New Mexico	1,174,000	1,781	1,396	152	119	26	33
New York	17,898,000	45,147	35,684	252	199	2	2
North Carolina	5,430,000	8,018	6,532	148	120	32	32
North Dakota	641,000	786	672	123	105	43	43
Ohio	10,689,000	16,633	13,978	156	131	25	23
Oklahoma	2,780,000	3,475	3,000	125	108	42	40
Oregon	2,373,000	4,378	3,560	184	150	15	14
Pennsylvania	11,775,000	21,234	17,413	180	148	17	16
Rhode Island	930,000	1,900	1,577	204	170	11	7
South Carolina	2,807,000	3,670	3,016	131	107	39	41
South Dakota	683,000	683	574	100	84	51	51
Tennessee	4,277,000	6,434	5,292	150	124	27	30
Texas	12,681,000	19,070	15,805	150	125	28	26
Utah	1,263,000	2,149	1,800	170	142	20	19
Vermont	483,000	1,049	809	217	167	7	8
Virginia	4,987,000	8,240	6,741	165	135	21	22
Washington	3,606,000	6,702	5,340	186	148	13	15
West Virginia	1,859,000	2,531	2,111	136	114	37	37
Wisconsin	4,650,000	6,984	5,842	150	126	29	25
Wyoming	402,000	466	380	116	94	47	49

Notes: Excludes physicians (3,619 Total Non-federal and 2,873 Patient Care) and population in Possessions (Canal Zone, Pacific Islands, Puerto Rico, and Virgin Islands). Population total does not add due to rounding.

Source: Goodman, Louis J., *Physician-Distribution and Medical Licensure in the U.S. 1977.* Chicago: Center for Health Services Research and Development. American Medical Association. 1979.

Appendix Table 2. United Kingdom

Region	Regional Doctors Hosp & GP Female (%)	Regional Hosp. Doctors Born Overseas (%)	Total Doctors Over 60 (%)	Total Doctors Over 50 (%)	GPs Over 65 (%)	GPs Over 55 (%)
Column #	1	2	3	4	5	6
Northern	12.85	39.66	8.71	30.75	4.54	24.45
Yorkshire	12.51	42.00	9.98	30.87	4.51	26.01
Trent	13.15	35.00	9.40	29.70	5.21	26.14
East Anglia	13.00	33.37	9.63	28.25	3.49	20.31
N. West Thames	19.86	31.59	11.04	31.59	10.38	31.23
N. East Thames	17.89	36.97	11.59	32.22	11.12	31.85
S. East Thames	15.81	32.63	10.71	33.09	7.95	29.36
S. West Thames	19.76	35.44	10.73	33.53	6.82	26.74
Wessex	13.47	24.59	9.43	30.14	4.15	22.80
Oxford	14.18	30.83	8.12	25.33	3.04	19.20
Southwestern	12.97	20.77	10.27	31.49	4.12	24.80
W. Midlands	18.62	39.71	9.84	29.50	6.04	25.33
Mersey	15.41	34.42	10.35	31.12	5.34	26.40
N. Western	14.61	42.00	9.18	27.03	5.62	24.61
Wales	12.94	35.98	9.08	30.48	4.81	21.01
Scotland	17.51	21.43	8.45	29.16	3.48	24.05
Great Britain	15.76	30.04	9.61	29.71	5.87	25.16

Region	Consultants & SHMOs Over 60 (%)	Consultants & SHMOs Over 50 (%)	Hospital Doctors Consultants or SHMOs (%)	Hospital Doctors who are Sen. Regs.	Total Doctor/ Pop. Ratio 100,000 Pop.	Unfilled Consultant Positions (%)
Column #	7	8	9	10	11	12
Northern	16.58	48.83	40.68	4.78	110.5	44.8
Yorkshire	15.62	45.67	40.23	5.28	103.5	45.2
Trent	13.33	45.28	37.86	6.95	93.5	42.8
East Anglia	13.47	46.13	40.55	7.89	105.6	46.3
N. West Thames	15.21	49.48	40.84	9.71	146.5	52.8
N. East Thames	15.73	53.29	39.89	8.35	138.6	50.3
S. East Thames	14.77	50.28	41.31	7.95	127.1	49.0
S. West Thames	15.69	51.31	42.90	4.06	121.8	50.4
Wessex	13.80	41.07	42.19	8.56	107.5	46.7
Oxford	16.70	46.41	38.04	9.68	112.2	45.8
Southwestern	14.62	46.16	39.35	6.84	107.2	50.3
W. Midlands	15.00	47.24	38.03	6.84	103.9	44.7
Mersey	17.07	52.22	38.33	6.15	111.9	44.5
N. Western	13.35	44.03	36.98	6.97	111.6	44.1
Wales	14.89	50.16	38.67	5.19	114.1	49.5
Scotland	13.89	47.75	36.74	7.99	160.3	57.3
Great Britain	14.59	47.62	38.15	7.66	118.6	48.0

Appendix Table 2. (Continued)

Region	No. Unfilled Consultant Posts	Pop. Growth 1975–90 (%)	Growth in Over 65 1975–90 (%)	Change in No. of Posts to Maintain 1975 Ratio in 1990	Change in No. of Posts to Take Each Region to 1975 Doc/Pop Ratio (118:6) in 1990	Change in No. of Posts to Take Each Region to Scottish Doc/Pop Ratio of 1975 in 1990
Column #	13	14	15	16	17	18
Northern	21	−1.5	+7.3	−52	−198	+1,482
Yorkshire	6	+0.6	+5.8	+22	−566	+2,067
Trent	8	+2.2	+12.9	+93	+1,259	+3,195
East Anglia	2	+18.1	+22.7	+341	−610	+1,486
N. West Thames	5	−7.0	+4.0	−356	−1,258	+90
N. East Thames	16	−7.1	−2.6	−366	−1,057	+384
S. East Thames	8	−4.7	−1.5	−215	−407	+925
S. West Thames	5	−3.8	+3.0	−133	−222	+933
Wessex	6	+9.5	+17.7	+270	−592	+1,800
Oxford	0	+17.5	+27.4	+432	−597	+1,674
Southwestern	0	+6.8	+16.9	+229	−613	+2,014
W. Midlands	14	+0.5	+16.1	+27	−792	+2,961
Mersey	4	−4.0	+4.5	−112	+48	+1,049
N. Western	13	−1.9	+1.1	−86	−194	+1,862
Wales	8	+4.5	+10.6	+142	−272	+1,476
Scotland	—	+1.2	+5.5	+100	−2,097	+100
Great Britain	—	+0.9	+8.4	+334	−700	+23,498

Notes:

1. Columns 1–12 are for 1975 data.
2. The population data used for Columns 14–18 was from a special mid-1976 population series (Home population) produced by the Office of Population Censuses and Surveys OPCS 1976 Based Special Series Subnational Population Projections. Equivalent data for Scotland and Wales was supplied by the Scottish Office and Welsh Office.
3. The total doctor stock referred to is based on our calculations of stock (see data appendix for further details).
4. The unfilled consultant posts referred to in Column 13 are those posts advertised for a permanent holder in the year 1st October, 1974 to 30th September, 1975 for which the appointments procedure has been completed by 30th September, 1975 but no appointment made. (DHSS Communication)

Source: "Doctor Manpower 1975–2000," Royal Commission on the National Health Service, Research Paper No 4 (London: HMSO, 1978) pp. 30–31.

Appendix Table 3.   United Kingdom: Distribution of Overseas Doctors

Year (30 Sept. for Hospital; 1 Oct. for GP)	Hospital Service All Staff	General Practice Unrestricted Principals	Hospital (Consultants)
	No. %	No. %	No. %
1968	8,291 (30.5)	2,657 (11.8)	1,204 (11.3)
1969	8,304 (31.4)	2,840 (12.5)	1,225 (11.3)
1970	9,021 (31.2)	3,034 (13.2)	1,286 (11.5)
1971	9,255 (30.8)	3,222 (13.9)	1,345 (11.7)
1972	9,888 (31.4)	3,445 (14.5)	1,409 (11.8)
1973	10,664 (32.5)	3,669 (15.3)	1,521 (12.2)
1974	11,261 (33.4)	3,905 (16.1)	1,651 (12.9)
1975	11,770 (33.3)	4,058 (16.6)	1,755 (13.3)
1976	11,356 (32.7)	4,288 (17.4)	1,881 (13.8)
1977	11,839 (31.8)	4,502 (18.1)	1,938 (14.1)
1978		4,681 (18.5)	

Source: "Medical Manpower, Staffing and Training Requirements," Report of County Council Working Party, *British Medical Journal*, 19 May 1979, pp. 1365–1367.

Appendix Table 4.1.   United Kingdom: Distribution of Doctors by Region

Region	Docter per 100,000 Pop.	Estimated Pop. Growth 1975–1990 (%)	Change in @ Region to Take Region to Scottish Dr.'Pop Ratio of 1975 in '90
Northern	110.5	−1.5	+1482
Yorkshire	103.5	+0.6	+2067
Trent	93.5	+2.2	+3195
East Anglia	105.8	+18.1	+1486
N.W. Thames	146.5	−7.0	+90
N.E. Thames	138.6	−7.1	+384
S.E. Thames	127.1	−4.7	+925
S.W. Thames	121.8	−3.8	+933
Wessex	107.5	+9.5	+1800
Oxford	112.2	+17.5	+1674
Southwestern	107.2	+6.8	+2014
W. Midlands	103.9	+0.5	+2961
Mersey	111.9	−4.0	+1049
N. Western	111.6	−1.9	+1862
Wales	114.6	+4.5	+1476
Scotland	160.3	+1.2	+100
Great Britain	118.6	+0.9	+23498

Note: According to "Doctor Manpower 1975–2000," Royal Commission on the NHS, Research Paper No. 4, in 1975 Scotland had the most desirable physician/population ratio; thus, the decision was made to use that ratio as an arbitrary standard to be attained in the rest of the United Kingdom.

Source: "Medical Manpower, Staffing and Training Requirements," Report of Council Working Party. *British Medical Journal*, 19 May 1979, pp. 1365–1376.

Appendix Table 4.2. United Kingdom: Distribution of Overseas Doctors in Great Britain

Year (30 Sept. for Hospital; 1 Oct. for GP)	Hospital Service (All Staff)		General Practice (Unrestricted Principals)		Hospital (Consultants)	
	No.	%	No.	%	No.	%
1968	8,291	(30.5)	2,657	(11.8)	1,204	(11.3)
1969	8,804	(31.4)	2,840	(12.5)	1,225	(11.3)
1970	9,021	(31.2)	3,034	(13.2)	1,286	(11.5)
1971	9,255	(30.8)	3,222	(13.9)	1,345	(11.7)
1972	9,888	(31.4)	3,445	(14.5)	1,409	(11.3)
1973	10,664	(32.5)	3,669	(15.3)	1,521	(12.2)
1974	11,261	(33.4)	3,905	(16.1)	1,651	(12.9)
1975	11,770	(33.3)	4,058	(16.6)	1,755	(13.3)
1976	11,856	(32.7)	4,288	(17.4)	1,831	(13.3)
1977	11,839	(31.8)	4,502	(18.1)	1,938	(14.1)
1978			4,681	(18.5)		

Source: "Medical Manpower, Staffing and Training Requirements," Report of Council Working Party. *British Medical Journal,* 19 May 1979, pp. 1365–1976.

Appendix Table 5. Sweden: Number of Instituted Positions and, of These Completely Vacant Positions Without Substitutes, 1981, (Distribution According to Health Care Area)

Health Care Area	Positions Hospital Care		Positions General Practice		Summary	
	No.	% Vacancies	No.	% Vacancies	No.	% Vacancies
Stockholm	962	2.0	498	3.4	1,460	2.5
Uppsala	87	16.1	68	10.3	155	13.5
Södermanland	166	16.3	83	15.7	249	16.1
Östergötland	353	8.2	121	18.2	474	10.8
Jönköping	186	12.4	127	13.4	313	12.8
Kronoberg	104	14.4	81	8.6	185	11.9
Kalmar	146	13.7	100	12.0	246	13.0
Gotlands Mun.	41	24.4	15	—	56	17.9
Blekinge	99	5.1	64	7.8	163	6.1
Kristianstad	187	8.0	113	8.0	300	8.0
Malmö Mun.	303	1.0	27	—	330	0.9
Malmöhus	490	2.7	209	5.7	699	3.6
Halland	112	6.3	77	6.5	189	6.3
Göteborgs Mun.	528	0.4	209	6.2	737	2.0
Göteborgs O Bohus	182	7.1	90	1.1	272	5.1
Älvsborg	240	11.7	149	16.1	389	13.4
Skaraborg	134	10.5	134	13.4	268	11.9
Värmland	182	14.3	129	12.4	311	13.5

(continued)

Appendix Table 5. (Continued)

Health Care Area	Positions Hospital Care		Positions General Practice		Summary	
	No.	% Vacancies	No.	% Vacancies	No.	% Vacancies
Örebro	230	14.8	131	25.2	361	18.6
Västmanland	168	13.1	117	29.1	285	19.6
Kopparberg	167	19.8	133	21.8	300	20.7
Gävleborg	191	14.1	137	18.3	328	15.8
Västernorrland	172	14.0	95	4.2	267	10.5
Jämtland	86	22.1	73	9.6	159	16.4
Västerbottan	254	9.5	100	17.0	354	11.6
Norrbotten	180	23.3	154	16.9	334	20.4
Karolinska Hosp.	329	1.2	15	(13.0)	344	1.7
Akademiska Hosp.	315	2.2	1		316	2.2
Total	6,594	7.9	3,250	11.5	9,844	9.0

Source: "Lakare, tjanster och vakanser 1981, LTV81," Socialstyrelson, 3/82.

Appendix Table 6.   PRC: Proximity to Cities and Barefoot Doctor/Population Ratios

Canton	Hangchow	Peking	Shanghai	Shenyang
1:1590	1:126	1:207	1:463	1:433
1:706	1:208	1:241	1:482	1:802
1:689	1:706	1:250	1:514	1:808
	1:710	1:220	1:1458	1:1078
	1:903	1:220	1:519	
		1:191	(Comb. 10 communes)	

City	Population	BFD/Population Ratios	
		Mean	Median
Peking	7.570 million (1/2 in suburban countryside)	1:221	1:241
Hangchow	980,000	1:611	1:706
Shanghai	10.8 million (5.2 million in suburban countryside)	1:729	1:514
Shenyang	3 million (including suburban countryside)	1:396	1:805

National BFD/Population Ratios
lowest 1:207
highest 1:1623
overall mean 1:650
overall median 1:514
national goal 1:500

PRC State Statistical Bureau, 1980: 1:616 (According to this source, this figure is the current national BFD/P ratio) from Chen, 1981.

Source: Rosenthal and Greiner, 1981.

Appendix Table 7. PRC: Development of Medical Manpower in the PRC

	1966*	1979**	1981***
Physicians	157,500	395,000	
Assistant Doctors	179,000	435,000	950,000ᵉ
Traditional Doctors		423,000	
Medical Assistants			
Midwives	44,000		
Nurses	193,000	421,000	
Dentists	31,500		
Pharmacists	21,000		
Jr. Pharmacists	52,000		
Technical Assistants			
Lab Technicians	52,000		
Barefoot Doctors		1,575,000	1,050,000ᵉ
Health Aides		4.2 mill.	

(current policy goals by 1985)

Notes:

*Adapted from: Cheng, Chu-Yuan, "Health Manpower: Growth and Distribution," in Myron Wegman, ed., *Public Health in the PRC*. New York: The Macy Foundation, 1973, pp. 139–157; and Taylor, Carl, "Report of a Trip to China . . .", Johns Hopkins School of Public Health, 1980.

**From: Chen, Pi-Chao, "Population Policy and the Rural Health System in China." World Bank Monograph, May 1981.

***From: Interview with Minister of Health, New China News Agency; Hua Chi 20, September 3 1981.

ᵉ estimated figures.

ACKNOWLEDGMENTS

Special thanks to Lenora Finn-Paradis for assistance in research for this paper.

Portions of this research were presented in the Medical Sociology Section, American Sociological Association, Toronto, Canada August 25, 1981. A version of this material, wihtout the PRC data, appeared in *Inquiry,* Spring 1984.

NOTES

1. A. The GMENAC report suggests the predicted surplus is the result of (1) expansion of American medical schools in the last two decades; (2) the increasing numbers of U.S. citizens studying in foreign medical schools who will demand entry back into the U.S. health system; and (3) the numbers of foreign medical graduates that come to the United States. It calls for a reduction of numbers in each of these categories.

B. GMENAC suggestions on using Medical Education to influence distribution can be exemplified by the following "Recommendations" taken from Vol. II:

- *Recommendation 18:* "role model development" aimed at changing the educational environment to stress positive aspects of practice . . . in underserved areas.
- *Recommendation 15:* some evidence that selective admission policies may improve. . . . geographic distribution of physicians.
- *Recommendation 19:* graduate medical education programs in family medicine should continue to be suggested as a strategy.
- *Recommendation 20:* incentives should be created to broaden residency education experiences to encompass training in underserved areas.

- *Recommendation 21:* replicate such programs as WAMI and WICHE (decentralized medical education programs).
- *Recommendation 23:* encourage medical education to consider number of programs, their size and geographic distribution of their graduates to better meet national and regional needs.

2.   To quote from the summarized news report: "China now has 109 medical colleges with a teaching staff of over 30,000. Since the founding of the New China, there were 406,000 graduates from medical colleges. Before 1949, there were only 22 medical colleges and 9,000 graduates in two decades" [From "Public Ministry Announces Achievements," *Survey of Mainland China Press,* 30 September, 1981 K 14 & 15]. It should be remembered that graduates from PRC medical colleges include students trained in five-year programs and students in two- to three-year programs (Assistant Doctors). Peter Chen, 1980, provides some medical manpower numbers obtained from the PRC Statistical Bureau:

	Total	*Population/Unit/Worker*
Hospital beds	1,932,000	503
Medical workers of which:	2,642,000	368
College graduated physicians	395,000	2,458
Middle-level physicians	435,000	2,232
Practitioners of traditional medicine	423,000	3,763
Nurses	421,000	2,306
Barefoot doctors	1,575,000	616

Source: S.S.B., 1980.
From: Chen, Pi-chai, "Population Policy and the Rural Health System in China." World Bank Monograph, May 1981, p. 97.

3.   Ye County in Shantung Province is an agricultural community of 827,500 with among the best health status statistics in the PRC. These have apparently been verified by the WHO [Taylor, 1981; Study Journal, 1981]. While there are no data to indicate that Ye is a "typical" county (indeed we may suspect that there are many rural areas with very poor showings), it does demonstrate what may be accomplished with dedication and limited resources in an agricultural community of a poor nation.

4.   A next step in examining the correlation between physician distribution and health status would be to break out each nation's infant mortality and life expectancy by region, province or district. These should be compared to regional P/PRs to see how the less well-served regions compare to national averages. In this manner, one could pursue a closer examination of impact of physicians on health status.

REFERENCES

1. Anderson, Odin W., Ph.D., *Health Care: Can There Be Equity? The United States, Sweden, and England.* New York: John Wiley and Sons, Inc., 1972.
2. Berlant, Jeffrey L., *Profession and Monopoly.* California: University of California, 1975.
3. Blendon, Robert J., *"Can China's Health Care Be Transplanted without China's Economic Policies?"* New England Journal of Medicine, Vol. 300, No. 26, June, 1979.
4. Butler, J.R., *The Spatial Distribution of Physicians in the United States: A Review of the Literature.* Health Services Research Unit, Report No. 24, Centre for Research in the Social Sciences, University of Kent at Canterbury, England, 1977.

5. Cheng, Chu-Yuan. "Health Manpower: Growth and Distribution" in *Public Health in the Peoples Republic of China,* Myron E. Wegman, et al., editors. Joshia Macy, Jr. Foundation: New York, 1973, pp. 139–157.

6. Clark, L. et al., "The Impact of Hill-Burton: An Analysis of Hospital Beds and Physician Distribution in the U.S., 1950–70," *Medical Care,* Vol. XVIII No. 5, May 1980, pp. 532–547.

7. Diamond, E. Gray. "Medical School Curriculum in the People's Republic of China." *Journal of the American Medical Association,* 236, No. 13 (1976): 1489–1491.

8. Ginzberg, Eli, *The Limits of Health Reform.* New York: Basic Books, 1977.

9. GMENAC, *Report of the Graduate Medical Education National Advisory Commission to the Secretary,* Department of Health and Human Services, Vols. I-III, DHHS Publication No. (HRA) 81-653, 1980.

10. Heidenheimer, Arnold J. and Elvander, Nils, ed., "Swedish Health Legislation: Milestones in Reorganization Since 1945," *The Shaping* of the Swedish Health Care System. New York: St. Martin's Press, 1980.

11. Interview. Dr. Roy Spector, Sub-Dean for Admissions, Guys Hospital Medical School. January 11, 1983.

12. "LàKare tjänster och vakanser 1981," LTV81. Socialstryelsen, 5/82. pp. 13–15. "Förslag till Läkarfördelnings program for Åren 1982–83," LP83. Socialstryelsen, December 1980.

13. Lampton, David M., "Performance and the Chinese Political System: A Preliminary Assessment of Education and Health Policy," *China Quarterly,* 75 509–539, 1978.

14. Lampton, David M., *Politics of Medicine in China: The Policy Process 1949–1977.* Colcrado: Westview Press, 1977.

15. LATT 79. Läkares Arbestider Ooh, Tjänster 1979, Del 2, Bilagatabeller. Stockholm: National Board of Health and Welfare, 1979.

16. Ludbrook, Maynard A., "The RAWP Formula," *Lancet,* 12 January, 1980, pp. 85–90.

17. Mao Tse-tung in "Directive on Public Health" in *Chairman Mao Talks to the People,* ed., Stuart Schram. New York: Pantheon, 1974.

18. Mao Tse-tung in "Medical Education and Health Services" *Red Medical Battle,* Aug. 8, 1965. Translated in Study of Mainland China Press. Supplement 198 30, 1967.

19. Mechanic, David and Kleinman, Arthur, "Ambulatory Care" in *Rural Health in the Peoples Republic of China.* Report of a Visit by the Rural Health Systems Delegation, June, 1978. Committee on Scholarly Communication with the People's Republic of China, US Department of NHS Public Health Service, NIH Publication No. 81-2124, Nov. 1980.

20. "Medical Manpower in Sweden, Supply and Demand: Subreport 1: Supply of Medical Manpower." The Swedish Medical Association, Stockholm, Sweden. Translated, April, 1981.

21. "Medical Practices Committee's Classification Areas," *British Medical Journal,* Vol. 282, April 4, 1981, p. 1170.

22. National Health Service Interview: July 1980. Department of Health and Social Services: Richard C. Longfield, Auditor, July 9; Irene Jones, Staff-GP Manpower, July 18; Alice Perkin, Staff-Medical Manpower, July 18. British Medical Association: Jon Ford, Staff, July 18; John Hopkins, Staff, July 18; Gary Webb, Staff, July 18. Royal College of Surgeons: Wilbert Webber, Asst. Administrator, July 19. NHS Medical Practices Committee: C F. Hayllar, Executive Secretary, July 22.

23. National Health Service Interview, Dr. Charles Dobson, Ph.D, Personnel Branch Department of Health and Social Services, Eileen House. September 29, 1982.

24. National Health Service. Interview, Deputy to Mr. Goodenham, Department of Health and Social Services, Medical Practices Committee Department, Evston Towers, October 1, 1982.

25. National Health Service Interview, Dr. Peter Wells, Staff, British Medical Association, BMA House Tavistock Square, January 12, 1983.

26. Parkhouse, James. *Medical Manpower in Britain.* Edinburgh, London and New York: Churchill Livingstone, 1979.

27. Przeworski, Adam and Teune, Henry, *The Logic of Comparative Social Inquiry*. New York: John Wiley and Sons, 1970.
28. Rosenthal, Marilynn, "Political Process and the Integration of Traditional and Western Medicine in P.R.C.," *Social Science and Medicine,* October 1981.
29. Rosenthal, Marilynn and Greiner, Jay. "The Barefoot Doctors of Rural China: From Political Creation to Professionalization," *Human Organization,* Vol. 41, No. 4, Winter 1982, pp. 300–341.
30. Schwartz, Newhouse, Bennett and Williams, ' Rand Corporation Study of Physician Mal-Distribution," *New England Journal of Medicine,* October 30, 1980.
31. Summary of Mainland China Press, "Public Health Ministry Announces Achievements." 30 September 1981, K14–15.
32. Swedish Interviews: August 1981. National Board of Health and Welfare: Christer Lindmark, Staff, August 5. Swedish Medical Association: Ulf Scholdström, Research Director, August 12. Federation of County Councils: Åki Jonsson, Staff, August 13. Stockholm County Council Medical Planning Board: Peteraf Geijerstaun, Staff, August 4; Naj Hammaingr, Staff, August 4.
33. Wegman, Myron, ed., *Public Health in the Peoples Republic of China*. New York: Josiah Macey, Jr. Foundation, 1974.
34. Wen, Chi-Pang, M.D. and Hayes, Charles W., M.D., "Health Care Financing in China," *Medical Care,* Vol. XIV, No. 3, March, 1976, pp. 241–254.

DIVIDED MEDICAL LABOR:

PHYSICIAN ASSISTANTS ASSESSED IN LIGHT

OF THE SOVIET FELDSHER EXPERIENCE

Ruth Breece Pickard

This paper will explore arguments regarding the continued viability of the physician assistant profession in light of important new developments in our health care delivery system. As a new order of dependent medical professionals, physician assistants have few parallels in this country. The long experience of their Soviet counterpart, the feldsher, will, therefore, be used to extend the perspective of the analysis.

I. THE PROBLEM

In the late 1960s some writers were calling the physician assistant movement the most important innovation in the delivery of medical care in this country since the turn of the century [117]. Barely 15 years later, however, the rosy outlook

Research in the Sociology of Health Care, Volume 5, pages 137-199.
Copyright © 1987 by JAI Press Inc.
All rights of reproduction in any form reserved.
ISBN: 0-89232-597-6

has become considerably clouded. In the fall of 1980, the Graduate Medical Education National Advisory Committee (GMENAC) concluded a three-year study with the prediction that by the year 1990 there will be an excess of 70,000 physicians in the nation [63:99]. While debate ensues over the efficacy of the GMENAC forecasting models [20, 97, 133, 169], in fact, far-reaching policy is already being effected on the basis of the Committee's findings. One factor cited as contributing to the anticipated doctor surplus is the steadily rising numbers of medical care visits being serviced by nurse practitioners (NPs), nurse midwives (CNMs) and physician assistants (PAs). To address this particular concern, GMENAC recommended that there be no further increase in the number of trainees of such non-physician providers. Supporting this embargo on competition, in June of 1981 the delegates to the American Medical Association's annual meeting in Chicago endorsed two pertinent measures: (1) to seek elimination of federal funding for the training of mid-level practitioners; and (2) to recommend that hospitals permit only licensed physicians to give physical examinations and to take medical histories from patients admitted for care [29].

In light of these developments, the future of physician assistants is now in question. Since the work of physician assistants is a limited subset of physician work and since under existing legal statutes, physician assistants may practice only by authority delegated through the licensure of the employing physician, it is pertinent to ask if there is any possibility for the new group to endure without strong professional endorsement. A narrow interpretation of the professional dominance principle often used to explain the division of medical labor [50] would lead to the prediction that loss of physician support will result in the elimination of the fledgling occupation. On the other hand, the current emphasis on cost containment in health care has led some to advocate increased reliance on PAs and other new health practitioners in the coming decade [25, 30, 39, 84].

It is too early to determine empirically the final outcome of these cross-pressures. This paper, through a comparison of the physician assistant movement with the lengthy experience of a similar mid-level practitioner group, the Soviet feldshers, will offer new insights on the controversy. The long endurance of the feldsher will be shown to be due to an adaptive response to the particular sociopolitical conditions of the Soviet medical system. Although health care arrangements in the United States are very different, it will be argued that recent shifts in power relationships combined with certain economic and social changes have created a climate which may now support the full institutionalization of an American middle-level medical provider.

The success or failure of any new occupation is bound to be tied to multiple determinants, but this paper suggests that the key to understanding any given outcome is contained in an analysis of the benefit potential for those who influence the ultimate policy decisions. First, a brief overview of the historical development and current status of physician assistants and of feldshers is given, with an emphasis on the identification of the particular conditions which have supported the continued existence of each group. Next, a comparison of several pertinent features of the cross-cultural counterparts is made. Finally, some implications for the future direction of the PA movement will be drawn from the parallels and contrasts between the two groups.

II. PHYSICIAN ASSISTANTS' GENESIS

A. Nursing Precedents

Charles L. Hudson, a physician with the Cleveland Clinic, is credited with proposing the concept of an assistant to the physician in 1961 [75]. Hudson envisioned a well-trained, but closely supervised, assistant who would be able to assume routine hospital tasks and, thus, free more of the physician's time for community practice. The idea was not entirely new. In fact, for many years physician-extending personnel had routinely carried out limited medical tasks in prisons and on merchant ships where few doctors were available [121, 37].

Nursing, in particular, has a long, yet rarely acknowledged history of assuming the overflow of medical work. It was not uncommon in the past for individual physicians who sought to carry out their practice more efficiently to assign apprentice functions to their nurse employees. Over time some of these informal job transfers, such as taking blood pressures and administering intravenous medications which were once considered strictly medical acts, became largely identified with nursing duties [21, 125].

The successful delegation of work to nursing personnel was held up by early proponents of PA training programs as a strong indicator of the feasibility of the concept. In fact, the designers of the first PA program, at Duke University, initially expected to draw their recruits from nursing ranks. This is not what happened, however. Nursing leadership, by then engaged in its own professionalization efforts, was little inclined to involve nurses in a new dependent practitioner role.

The uneasy relationship between nursing and the physician assistant occupation has its roots in this friction surrounding the attempts in the late 1950s of Dr. Eugene A. Stead, Jr., and Thelma Ingles, R.N., to launch a masters degree program at Duke aimed at preparing nurses as mid-level health practitioners. The proposed program met with strong resistance from organized nursing which felt it would undermine the heightening campaign by nurses to become more self-determining. The National League of Nursing condemned the endeavor for its insistence on using mostly physician educators and warned against the potential dangers of delegated medical practice. After failing in three consecutive bids for accreditation from the nursing agency, the fledgling program was dropped by the University [45].

B. Refocus and Success at Duke

Still believing in the utility of the physician assistant concept, Stead redirected his attention toward a program which would recruit ex-military corpsmen. To implement such a program, however, he needed funding. In a timely coincidence, a Duke colleague Dr. Herbert Saltzman was then in the process of submitting an application to the National Heart Institute (NHI) for support of a program to train physicians and paramedical technicians in research of hyperbaric medicine. The two medical educators agreed on a collaboration of efforts, and the NHI grant application which was subsequently submitted contained a proposal to train both specialized assistants for technical hospital service and general assistants to work with community-based primary care physicians. The approval of the grant in April 1965 provided the financial foundation which enabled the first PA training program to proceed. By the time the initial class began its study in the early autumn, however, the dual training goals had been dropped from the curriculum of the two-year program. Instead, the focus was centered upon the provision of a core education which emphasized the same theoretical underpinnings of basic sciences that the medical students at Duke were studying. It was anticipated that specialized preparation could be achieved later under the direction of the supervising physician and that such apprenticeship arrangements would be facilitated by the common knowledge base PAs would share with their employers [121].

C. Social Imperatives

Four students enrolled in an experimental project financed with piggybacked soft funds is hardly an auspicious beginning. Yet the movement took a tenacious hold and has steadily grown to a point where approximately 1,500 new physician assistants graduate from approved programs each year [3]. A considerable portion of the success reflected by the occupation's numerical increases is due, of course, to the foresight and perseverance of the early physician founders. But, it was a unique set of social imperatives erupting in this nation during the 1960s and early 1970s that provided the conditions needed to insure a climate receptive to the innovative concept. The pertinent social conditions, to be discussed in turn, include: rising support for expanded social entitlements; a perceived shortage of physicians, especially of those delivering primary care; a geographic maldistribution of resources; rising health care costs; rapid technological growth; and the availability of medical corpsmen returning in large numbers from the military service in Vietnam.

The restless mood of the 1960s with its explosive civil rights conflicts, student activism, women's movement, labor strikes, consumer boycotts, and the Vietnam War shattered the complacency of the period of post-World War II prosperity and sent the nation's leaders scurrying for means to contain the turbulence.

Under the Great Society programs of President Johnson sweeping social reforms were instituted, but an agitated public continued to press for even greater entitlements. In the health field, Medicare and Medicaid were passed as amendments to the Social Security Act in 1965 and they quite successfully reduced economic barriers to health care for approximately 35 million of the elderly and the poor [1]. Nonetheless the perceived failure of medicine to live up to rising public expectations for better care and more easily accessible care was widespread. By midway in the decade, health delivery needs had generated a flurry of legislation aimed at eradicating a severe maldistribution of health personnel. The Health Professions Education Act of 1963, the Nurse Training Act of 1964 and the Allied Health Professional Personnel Training Act of 1966 were three of the many bills passed in Congress during the period of time in which the Duke program was beginning to take shape. With their passage, federal monies were poured into new building construction, program upgrading, and expansion of enrollments in health professional schools.

D. Health Care Crisis

In spite of quickened government efforts to expand access through increased and redistributed resources, the term "health care crisis" used by President Nixon in his 1969 inaugural address became a popular media buzz-phrase for the various shortcomings still remaining in the delivery system. A perceived shortage of physicians received particular attention although the overall ratio of physicians to population was actually increasing at the time [8]. Butter [24], for example, notes that the 1962 physician-population ratio (136/100,000) was nearly identical to the 1920 ratio (134/100,000). Ten years later, however, the ratio had increased to 171/100,000 [12:12]. The enlarging supply of doctors was accompanied by a tenfold increase in biomedical research funding since the early 1950s [60:32]. Furthermore, massive expenditures under the landmark Hill-Burton hospital construction program had sharply reduced the acute shortage of hospital beds after World War II [94]. As impressive as these improvements were, the public's discontent with the medical system continued to build into the 1970s [86].

E. Specialty Maldistribution

Part of the persisting problem can be traced to an increasingly sophisticated public whose rising income and education levels contributed to heightened expectations and expanded demands on existing resources. A related but probably more important factor was the growing lack of fit between specific consumer wants and medicine's response. Ever since the Flexner Report in 1910, medicine had been growing more specialized. Whereas 70 percent of the U.S. physicians in 1940 had practiced general medicine, for example, by the early 1960s the proportion of active physicians in primary care practice had fallen to less than 20 percent [55:12]. During the same time that medicine was splintering into numerous, finely tuned specialty groups, the proliferation of third-party payment mechanisms after 1936 [56] shifted consumer demands toward an emphasis on first-contact, primary care service. With the financial onerousness removed from the decision making, many individuals were able for the first time to seek medical attention for relatively minor conditions. The dearth of primary care physicians became painfully apparent as a vast number of these recently insured consumers met with frustration in their attempt to take advantage of the new entitlements [4].

F. Geographic Maldistribution: Rural

The other facet of the maldistribution problem was the uneven dispersion of resources across geographical regions. Particularly notable was a severe shortage of all types of medical resources in the nation's rural areas. A crucial component in rural access was the difficulty of recruiting physicians to remote, sparsely settled areas. This difficulty was attributed to the reluctance of young physicians who had spent many years in a highly challenging, sophisticated training atmosphere to locate in communities with inferior hospital facilities, few opportunities for professional growth, and a limited range of cultural activities [116, 165]. In addition, rural practice often meant ponderous workloads, little leisure time, lowered colleague esteem and reduced income levels [164].

The problem of rural access was compounded by special need factors commonly found among residents of provincial areas. For example, among the approximately one-quarter of the country's total population which resided in nonmetropolitan areas, there was a relatively greater proportion of persons suffering with chronic illnesses, a higher rate of nonindustrial accident occurrences, generally lower family incomes, and increased per capita incidence of disability days [85, 152]. In addition, proportionately fewer rural than urban residents were covered by health insurance [28, 110].

G. Geographic Maldistribution: Urban

Urban areas, by contrast, were far better endowed with medical resources. While only slightly more than half of the nation's hospitals were located in metropolitan settings in the early 1970s, those hospitals contained approximately three-quarters of the total supply of hospital beds [12:27]. Consequently, disproportionately large numbers of highly skilled medical specialists, researchers, and associated health personnel tended to cluster near the large, complex urban health centers. These sophisticated facilities were further supplemented by a host of supportive health-related agencies and commercial enterprises offering services and therapies not usually found in smaller communities.

Although the broad spectrum of health services available in urban places offered definite advantages to city residents, there was another side to the picture which bore heavily on the crisis issue. Urban medicine, particularly that in inner cities, was highly skewed toward institutionally based medical specialties. Consequently, residents in an area heavily populated by highly trained and highly priced specialists were frequently without the services of a community-based primary care physician. The problem was particularly acute in poverty-stricken urban neighborhoods. Ginzberg [60:32] captures the seriousness of the situation with his observation that in the mid-1970s "there was not one pediatrician in Harlem and the ratio of private practitioners to population in the Chicago ghetto was about 1 for 5,000 people."

There was also a relative scarcity of group practices in urban areas which meant that patients were often compelled to deal with a highly fragmented system of referrals to different specialists in widely separated locations [136]. Particularly among the poor, moreover, a lack of affordable transportation facilities frequently impeded the search for needed care [9]. Adaptation to these constraining circumstances forced many inner-city residents to seek basic medical services in hospital emergency rooms, outpatient clinics, and a variety of Medicaid mills, some of which were sorely understaffed and underequipped [115, 123, 137, 167, 173].

As with rural residents, health needs were greater in core-city populations. In addition to lower incomes and lower educational levels, residents in these areas were apt to be older, members of a minority group, suffering from more chronic disease conditions, less knowledgeable about available health services and less apt to have a personal physician than were residents of more affluent communities [80, 87, 140].

H. Rising Costs

Concomitantly with the problems related to maldistribution of resources, this country in the late 1960s was experiencing a marked increase in health care expenditures. The percentage of the gross national product accounted for by expenditures for health care increased from 5.9 in 1965 to 8.5 in 1975, representing a greater than threefold increase in the absolute dollars spent [59]. The spiraling costs resulted from a complex set of social, political, and economic forces including generalized inflation which saw an 81 percent increase in the consumer price index between 1967 and 1977 and a disproportionate rise in the country's population of persons 65 years of age and older, who spend nearly three times more dollars for personal health care than the average per capita expenditure. Following the legislation which provided expanded entitlements for government financed care to the elderly and the poor, moreover, demand for all types of services rose sharply as reflected by the one-third increase in the annual total number of outpatient visits between 1970 and 1977.

Certain costs stand out as having had a disproportionate impact on the inflationary trends. For example, nursing home costs which accounted for only 3.3 percent of the total health expenditures in 1966, were responsible for 7.8 percent of the annual expenditures in 1977. Per capita outlay for hospital care alone rose from approximately $24.00 in 1950 to nearly $254.00 in 1976, reflecting an increase in the proportion to total personal health care spending from 33.8 percent to 40.4 percent in the respective years [105].

I. Burgeoning Technology

Closely interwoven with the rising costs and other facets of the health care crisis was the explosive production of medical technologies which accompanied this country's entry into the Space Age in the early 1960s. The rapid proliferation of sophisticated diagnostic and treatment innovations opened new vistas in the care of many previously intractable conditions. Collaboration between medicine, biology, physics, engineering and other scientific disciplines resulted in significant breakthroughs in the battle against certain diseases and the prolongation of lives. New medical specialties mushroomed to accommodate the esoteric requirements of the burgeoning techniques such as transplantation, dialysis, radiation therapies, electron microscopy, and similar developments in the various clinical, laboratory, and pharmaceutical fields.

Unfortunately the impressive technological revolution affixed a new set of complications and costs on the health scene as well. In part this was due to the actual expense connected with the more elaborate instrumentation, but technological distortion which led to unrealistically optimistic expectations among both consumers and providers was also responsible for a large share of the problems. Reacting to what Fuchs [54] termed the technologic imperative, physicians and patients began to rely increasingly on costly hospital care and the often unnecessary utilization of elaborate gadgetry. Disregarding the limited impact that health services actually exert on morbidity and mortality, society appeared to assume that the more technology was used, the better was the health care.

Technology bred new demands for even more specialized technology, producing a situation where it was outrunning the capacity of health institutions to adopt and utilize it fully. The resulting need for more health personnel with specialized technical training generated a rapid growth of new job categories and entirely new health occupations. By the early 1970s there were more than 200 job titles functioning in a typical hospital with new ones being added "almost monthly" [96:102]. Specialization, however, requires careful coordination if such non-specialized objectives as sensitivity to the anxieties of patients are to be met. As it had failed to check the runaway costs of technology, the system also faltered when it came to addressing these human needs for caring.

The psychological component of the doctor-patient relationship shifted as medicine became more bureaucratized and fragmented. Whereas in the past the doctor in a solo, fee-for-service practice had focused largely on the patients' interests, many of the new organizational arrangements which accompanied the technological advances put pressure on physicians to compromise certain patient interests in order to satisfy institutional needs for profit making and/or operational efficiency [99].

J. Vietnam Medics

In addition to the important effects of the resource scarcity, rising consumer demands, inflating costs, and an exploding technology, there was one other factor which played a vital role in preparing the conditions which would sustain the early development of the physician assistant movement. The involvement of the United States in the Vietnam War had led to the training of large numbers of military medical corpsmen who in the late 1960s began to return from active duty to resume civilian life. Hicks [72] estimated that approximately 30,000 of such medics were being discharged from the service each year during the late 1960s. The existence of this extensive body of previously trained and highly skilled health care personnel provided a fortuitous pool from which the fledgling PA occupation could draw enthusiastic recruits. The initial program at Duke and those emerging rapidly on its heels at Bowman Gray, Oklahoma, Yale, Alabama, George Washington, Emory and Johns Hopkins selected their earlier students almost exclusively from among the ranks of former military medics [47, 121]. This heavy recruitment of ex-military personnel fostered a mostly male image of the new occupation, an identity later derided by some nurses who saw issues of sexism mixed among various other interprofessional conflicts [144].

III. EXPANSION AND EVOLUTION OF THE PA OCCUPATION

A. Educational Programs

The timing of the PA movement's introduction was propitious and as publicity about the Duke program began to spread, enthusiasts in medical and educational circles across the country were quick to establish a variety of courses of instruction to prepare the new category of medical assistant. Enhancement of the success of these programs and a signal of the innovation's importance was provided by financial backing from some of the nation's leading philanthropic foundations [121].

At first there was little coordination of educational effort. Program length varied from a few hours to several years. Many schools adopted the Duke certificate model which originally divided a two-year program into nine months of didactic work and fifteen months of clinical rotations. By 1968 the first four-year, baccaalureate degree program appeared at Alderson-Broaddus College and in the following year a specialized postgraduate program was instituted by the University of Colorado School of Medicine [35, 111].

Program length was not the only aspect lacking early standardization. Faculties and facilities also varied widely. Many programs were conducted in medical schools with all-physician faculties but there were some which were organized as correspondence courses monitored by nonphysician educators. Student qualifications ranged from those of matriculants without high school diplomas to others bearing previous college degrees (74).

B. Military Programs

The military was one of the earliest adopters of the physician assistant idea. In 1966 the Marines launched the first program to train experienced medical corpsmen as PAs at the U.S. Public Health Service Hospital in Staten Island, New York [34].

As noted earlier, the military also figured in another fashion. In 1970 the U.S. Department of Health, Education and Welfare in cooperation with the Department of Defense initiated Operation MEDIHC (Military Experience Directed Into Health Careers), a program to counsel and recruit Vietnam veterans returning stateside who had received training and experience in health care delivery during their tours of duty. The idea was to assist military personnel with an interest in health careers in locating civilian employment or advanced training opportunities prior to their separation from the service. In turn, it was hoped that these persons with special skills would help to alleviate civilian personnel shortages. The program's considerable success brought Operation MEDIHC into the Division of Allied Health Manpower under the aegis of the National Institute of Health [36].

Discharged medical corpsmen also provided the base for the Medex (*Medicine Extension*) program which arose as the result of the efforts of Richard Smith at the University of Washington Medical School. In this and similar Medex programs to follow, the focus was on training the already skilled ex-medics to provide sorely needed service to persons in remote rural areas. In general, these programs involved a short, intensive classroom experience combined with a nine- to twelve-month supervised apprenticeship in the rural practice of a carefully selected primary care physician preceptor [33, 130, 155].

C. Government Involvement

In addition to the military programs, the federal government was increasingly involved in the training of physician assistants. Fisher and Horowitz [45:40–41] point out, for example, that of the 31 programs in operation at the start of 1972,

21 received funds from such sources as "the Office of Economic Opportunity, the Model Cities Program, the Veterans Administration the Public Health Service, the Department of Defense, and the Department of Labor." In June of that year, these authors note, the Bureau of Health Manpower (BHM) under the Health Resources Administration of the Department of Health, Education and Welfare stepped in. Acting upon the 1971 Public Health Service Amendment entitled "The Comprehensive Health Manpower Training Act of 1971," BHM took fiscal charge of 24 of these programs and initiated start-up contracts with 16 more. This federal involvement was in response to the Congressional mandate to find a solution for the problems posed by the resource shortage and maldistribution previously mentioned. The extent of the government commitment provided commanding evidence that top-echelon decision makers were impressed by the potential of the PA concept.

IV. CURRENT STATUS OF PAs

A. Education

Today there are more than 50 institutions which sponsor educational training programs for assistants to primary care physicians and at least three programs to train surgical assistants [7:10]. This is a record of some note given the active competition for funds to build and expand programs for the training of health personnel during the latter half of the 1970s. Most of the money flowing out of Washington during that time, as a result of legislation designed to increase the country's supply of physicians and other health care providers, was aggressively pursued by the larger, more politically powerful physician and nursing organizations. Nonetheless, the more than $21 million in federal expenditures allocated in 1979 for the training of physician assistants, Medex, and nurse practitioners attests to the considerable financial support the new middle-level providers are attracting [30:ix].

The settings for today's training programs vary from medical colleges and universities, to schools of allied health, community colleges and hospitals. Program length ranges from 12 to 45 months but is most typically of two years' duration. Competition for available class seats in PA programs is reportedly stiff with, on the average, only one out of five applicants being admitted. For any given program, both the length and the curriculum content are related to the admissions requirements for previous education and health care experience. According to the A.A.P.A. Profiles for 1981–1982 [7:2], more than 89 percent of PA students have had previous civilian or military health care experience and 46 percent held prior associate or baccalaureate degrees.

By 1981 slightly fewer than 11,000 students had graduated from PA training programs. Profiles of the more recent matriculants have changed considerably

from those of earlier students. Newer graduates are described as less likely than
in the past to be former medical corpsmen and to have no prior medical experience. In addition, they are more likely now to be female and to possess a
previously obtained baccalaureate degree than were their early predecessors
[122]. Although the literature on PA students regularly refers to them as older
and more mature than average collegians, such descriptions are relative. Among
the 1,126 PA student respondents in a survey of the class of 1977, half were
under 25 years of age and more than 80 precent were under age 30 [147:67].

B. Practitioners

It will be recalled that a major impetus behind the initiation of the PA movement was a perceived need for more primary health care services, particularly in
rural and inner-city locations. It was hoped by the early planners that PAs would
help remedy the specialty and geographic maldistribution of resources. There is
some evidence to suggest that these early objectives are being met. The Medex
programs, for example, have achieved an impressive record of deploying their
graduates to underserved areas [150]. Reports, moreover, indicate that approximately three-quarters of all PAs in this country are working in primary care
specialties while approximately half are located in rural areas defined as communities of 50,000 people or less and not in close proximity to a city [119, 122].
Recent comparable figures show only about 13 percent of physicians and 17
percent of nurses to be practicing in rural areas [179]. The optimistic success
implied by these figures may be overstated, however, as there appears to be an
increasing trend for PAs to seek work in fields and locations where remuneration
for their services is greatest, particularly in hospitals and in specialities such as
surgery, orthopedics, urology, and emergency care [11, 122].

Nationally, PAs are employed in all 50 states but tend to be located much more
heavily in the South than in other areas of the country [92]. An important
constraint in their geographical distribution is that, with the exception of those
employed in Rural Health Clinics, most physician assistants are limited in their
practice choices by the legal necessity for physician supervision. The matter of
location is compounded by the fact that general practice and family practice
physicians who are more likely than other medical specialists to locate in rural
areas [135] have recently been exhibiting increasing resistance to the PA movement [178].

An additional point that is not always made clear in discussions of resource
distribution is that the specialty of the PA and his/her supervising physician often
do not coincide. One national study which surveyed more than 3,000 PAs, for
example, discovered that while approximately 54 percent of the supervising
physicians were in primary care specialties, almost 83 percent of the PAs
claimed to be providing primary care service [42]. Thus, it appears likely that
some PAs may be hired to address the primary care problems which patients

bring to physician specialists. On the other hand, further research might reveal that specialists who employ PAs are, themselves, more oriented toward primary care practice.

V. CONTEMPORARY ISSUES

A. Personnel Projections

In 1978 the GMENAC Staff Paper on the Supply and Distribution of Physicians and Physician Extenders [64:66–71] projected there would be approximately 18,500 PAs in this country in 1990. A comparison with the projected figure of nearly 260,000 primary care physicians, shows that the new provider group is expected to constitute less than seven percent of the total primary care personnel. Overall, PAs will represent only about three percent of the total active medical care provider pool in that year. While this proportion is relatively small, the PA group would be about equal in size to the projected numbers in each of three physician groups: surgeons, ophthalmologists, and pathologists.

Leaving aside arguments about the efficiency of various forecasting models, it is evident that to be meaningful, projected supplies must be matched in some fashion with the degree of need involved. Yet there is simply no data now available which can be used to determine the need factor in the projection of PA supplies. Essentially, the planning problem hinges on the functional identity of physician assistants. If PAs are to be considered chiefly as a limited surrogate for the primary care physician during an interim period when the latter is in short supply, then the newest GMENAC findings would indicate there is little need to support continued production of these practitioners. On the other hand, if the PA is viewed as offering unique resources which complement the services of more traditional providers, it becomes feasible to suggest their market potential remains favorably broad. At the core of these disparate prognoses are factors of cost, reimbursement, productivity, performance and acceptability.

B. Cost

One of the reasons the physician assistant movement was able to attract favorable attention in its formative stage was that relative to the lengthy and very costly training involved in producing a physician, the training of a physician assistant was much less expensive. Studies in the mid-1970s set the net direct cost of training an individual PA at approximately 26 percent of the comparable figure for a four-year medical school education [76, 163]. Furthermore, when the opportunity cost, or additional output per year based on PA salary foregone during the extra years needed for M.D. training, is taken into account, the differential in training costs per practitioner is in excess of $113,000. In addition, the approximately $40,000 difference in the average annual salaries of primary care physicians practicing in partnerships and PAs strongly suggests that the utilization of PAs in place of MDs for routine primary health care could result in substantially reduced delivery costs [149].

Richard McKibben in 1978 reviewed the findings of numerous studies on the cost effectiveness of physician assistants and found that, in general, significant cost savings have resulted from the use of the new providers. Furthermore, he concluded that utilization of PAs is positively related with the total productivity of a medical practice. He cautioned, however, that there are a number of important qualifications to be considered with these conclusions. While PAs have been found cost-effective in various settings such as large group practices and in certain rural practices, for example, no general statements may be made about all practice circumstances. In addition, this author raises the crucial question: For whom will the employment of PAs be cost effective? In other words, to whom will the benefits of reduced practice expense accrue? If the reduced cost is not passed along to the health care consumers, the latter has little incentive to accept the delivery innovation. Along this same line, third-party reimbursement for the utilization of PA services would also be expected to depend on the cost-effect this utilization would have for the commercial insurance carrier or other government intermediary [30, 76, 145].

C. Reimbursement

Third-party reimbursement, or its refusal, has been a major barrier to the greater utilization of PAs to date. This country's health system relies heavily on third-party payments. Approximately 87 percent of Americans are covered by some type of health insurance. Of these, 78 percent are enrolled in private insurance plans while another 17 percent are covered by some form of publicly financed program. For those insured persons, 89 percent of hospital costs and 61 percent of physicians' charges are met by third parties [107]. Commenting on the magnitude of this phenomenon, a recent statement by former Health and Human Service Secretary Richard Schweiker noted that Medicare and Medicaid costs alone account for 80 percent of all federal health expenditures and 25 percent of all monies spent on health care in this country [148].

This extensive involvement of third-party mechanisms in meeting the personal health care expenses of the nation's consumers is a significant factor in the organization of the delivery of medical services. Few private or public health insurance programs provide reimbursement for the services of physician assistants as independent providers of medical care. Many do, however, reimburse the employing physician or institution for compensation of the PA's nonspecific, supervised service as part of the reasonable overhead of the practice costs.

Under the Social Security Administration's regulations, federal payments are generally not available for PA services other than those "incidental to" the physician's professional service. Medicare policy stipulates that if a PA performs a physical examination or other tasks identifiable as specific physician services, no reimbursement will be made. Medicaid policy, however, is less directly controlled by federal mechanisms and varies by state. In 25 states no reimbursement for PA services is allowed other than the overhead type of claim, but in 25 other Medicaid programs, some form of reimbursement policy for PA services does exist. Many of these latter programs require the immediate availability of a supervising physician as a condition for reimbursement, thus precluding any services a PA might perform in a visit alone to patients in hospital, home, or nursing care facilities or those performed in a satellite clinic setting [31, 107].

In 1977 the Rural Health Clinics Act authorized federal payments for PA services in certified rural health clinics even when a physician may be only available for indirect supervision. The payments for the PA services in this case are paid to the clinic, not to the physician assistant. It was hoped that this program would induce physicians in rural areas to employ greater numbers of PA and nurse practitioners and, thus, would greatly expand medical resources into seriously underserviced rural areas. The response of physicians to this new program, however, has been apathetic, one writer calling it "like spinach on the plate of an eight-year-old" [156].

Some authors [44, 107] identify the reluctance of private and public insurers to broaden the reimbursement coverage to PAs as concern that such action would increase service charges and further escalate the inflation of health care expenditures. Others [13, 30], however, point to the powerful influence physicians wield over both medical practice legislation and reimbursement policies, particularly those mediated through Blue Shield. The inference is that vested interests may be expected to exhibit resistance toward independent practice and direct reimbursement for physician assistants.

An extensive physician extender reimbursement experiment began in 1976 and carried out over two years by the Social Security Administration [57] resulted in recommendations that physician assistant services be eligible for reimbursement under Medicare, Part B (physician services) [82]. Although several bills were introduced into Congress to accomplish this change, in mid-1980 none had yet been passed into law [83]. Physician assistants, sensitive to the importance of the reimbursement issue for PA survival, have noted the incongruencies in a governmental policy that pours $100 million into the support of training programs for new health practitioners but at the same time limits their acceptance and effectiveness by withholding the vital support of the reimbursement mechanisms [175].

D. Productivity

From one perspective it would appear that if physician assistants are able to expand the volume of patients served in a given practice and at the same time to lower the cost of providing that service, then many physicians might consider employing a new provider as an attractive way to increase their margin of profit. On the other hand, with an increasing number of physicians now entering the market, some may perceive these same characteristics as a competitive threat to physician income. The issues involved are very complex. Among the vital aspects of the acceptance question are productivity and performance.

Numerous studies have attempted to assess the productivity of physician's assistants [88, 100, 128] but the various methodologies used have made comparisons of the results difficult. While in theory productivity measures change in total output produced by some change in production input, in practice such change can rarely be gauged with precision. In measuring the effect of an addition of a PA or other new health practitioner to a physician's practice, for example, few studies have attempted to account for individual attributes of the new provider such as aptitude and drive [132]. In addition, the frequent practice of using the number of patients seen as an indicator of productivity is unsatisfactory unless such factors as the number of patients presenting to the practice, the availability of support personnel, the other tasks assigned to the PA, the frequency and depth of physician supervision, and the preferred practice style of patient management are also taken into account.

In spite of such methodological constraints, findings from numerous studies [121, 132] support the contention that employment of a PA increases practice productivity. The precise extent of increase may vary by contingent factors, but, in general, evidence suggests that the fraction of a physician unit which a PA may be expected to replace ranges from about .50 to .75 [132]. This means that in order to be cost effective, the cost of employing a PA should be no more than about half of the cost of an MD. Schweitzer [149] has demonstrated that the PA cost is, in fact, considerably less than one-half the physician cost. To put this into broader perspective, consider that Fein [38] estimates that a mere three percent increase in total physician productivity would provide as much additional medical care as would an entire year's class of medical students. It seems reasonable to conclude, then, that any desired productivity increase can most efficiently result from utilization of the more cost-effective physician assistant alternative. This assumes, of course, the utilization of PA services as substitutes for more costly physician services. If, instead, the PA services supplement those of physicians, service expansion may increase the overall cost of health care.

E. Performance

The studies on PA performance have demonstrated that patient acceptance is related to the perceived quality of care provided [70, 114, 128]. Quality of care, however, is another term which defies easy definition. Although many components doubtlessly go into the meaning of the term, most writers seem to agree with Greene [65] that quality involves efficiency, effectiveness, accessibility, acceptability, and provider competence. In a comprehensive review of more than 66 studies on these various elements of quality, Celentano [26] concluded that the bulk of the evidence demonstrates that new health practitioners perform, overall, an acceptable level of care. Furthermore, within the generic task areas for which they are specially trained, the quality of care they provide is high when compared with that of physicians. More recent studies have corroborated these findings. Greenfield et al. [66], for example, found no significant variation in efficiency of care provided to two groups of patients in a single Health Maintenance Organization (HMO), one of whom was served by physicians and the other by physician assistants and nurses. Goldberg et al. [67] in evaluating the quality of care of 23 physician assistants and seven nurse practitioners practicing in Air Force primary medical care clinics, similarly concluded that PAs and NPs performed at least as well as physicians on 75 to 90 percent of the process-of-care criteria utilized in the study.

F. Acceptance by Physicians

Regardless of the evidence supporting the cost-effectiveness, the competence, and the productivity of physician assistants, their ultimate ability to make a lasting impact on the organization of medical care delivery in this country will depend, in large measure, on the willingness of physicians to utilize them and upon the willingness of patients to seek their services Voluminous literature coverage has been given to these topics.

Barriers to willingness of physicians to hire and share clinical responsibilities with PAs and other mid-level practitioners have been identified as: perceived threat to physician income, fear of legal liability, lack of economic incentives, lack of a clear working knowledge of NP and PA concepts [22, 168], reluctance to delegate responsibility, fear of patient response, concern over billing for services of NPs or PAs, limited space and/or facilities [162], reluctance to make the high personal commitment required, and preference for the status quo [49]. On the other hand, facilitators to physician use of PAs and NPs are identified as: increased productivity and efficiency [64, 159], cost containment [168], improved quality of care [170], higher income [119], reduced time requirements, enhanced authority, improved relationships with patients [49], and increased opportunity to focus on more difficult and/or more interesting medical problems [56].

Organizational and system correlates to physician acceptance of NPs and PAs have also been specified [49, 118] with those in group practice seen as more likely to favor acceptance than those in solo practice. As noted earlier, while mid-level practitioners are more likely than physicians to be located in rural areas [76, 108], the evidence to date does not show a greater willingness by physicians practicing in rural areas to use them [49].

Demographic variables which have been suggested in the literature to be related to acceptance are physician age, years since graduation from medical school, political orientation, and religion, with younger physicians, those who have more recently graduated from college, those with a more liberal political orientation, and those who are Jewish being more willing to utilize non-physician medical personnel [49, 98]. No evidence of a difference in attitudes toward PAs and NPs between male and female physicians was cited in the studies reviewed. Several researchers have, however, suggested a possible bias among male physicians in favor of the mostly male PAs as opposed to the female-dominated NP group [119, 146, 162].

An attitudinal variable which appears to be indirectly related to physicians' propensity to utilize mid-level practitioners is work satisfaction among the practitioners. If non-physician employees are satisfied with their working conditions, it is likely that this satisfaction will be manifested in good work performance, which in turn may increase the employer's positive attitudes toward their services. A major factor cited as a correlate to work satisfaction among medical care professionals is degree of work autonomy [17, 18, 26, 157]. In fact, studies reveal that those mid-level practitioners whose training is more extensive are least satisfied on the job precisely because they expect to be granted greater work autonomy than they actually experience. Work autonomy, moreover, is a function of willingness of the physician employers to delegate decision-making tasks, a behavior which, for many physicians, is seen as antithetical to the profession's traditional role of complete authority in medical decisions [58, 78].

As a measure of physician acceptance of PAs, Ramos [131:104] notes that 57 percent of the general AMA membership endorsed the concept. She points out, however, that some of the state affiliates not only do not endorse utilization of PAs, but have actively campaigned against the movement. A notable case in point is the situation in New Jersey, where to date the opposition of the State Medical Society has prevented the passage of legal sanctions which would provide the authority for physician assistants to practice in that state [3, 51].

G. Acceptance by Patients

Most studies of patients who have used the medical care services of PAs and/or NPs show a high degree of satisfaction with the care received [158, 162]. Patients vary, however, in their beliefs about the scope of tasks appropriately undertaken by mid-level practitioners [4, 90] and in their willingness to support independent professional status for these medical workers [16, 161].

The characteristics of patients which have been found to be most closely related to the acceptance of PAs and other mid-level providers are age, sex, social class, and prior exposure to such services [114]. Although inconsistent results have been reported, in general, those patients who are under 25 years of age, women, those having previous experience with PA care, and those from lower socioeconomic classes have been found to be more accepting. One point which may bear closer examination was raised by Lavin [89], who suggested that the conditions under which service episodes occur may be crucial to the acceptance issue. She suggests that patients who lack alternative resources may be more prone to feel as if the service of non-physician providers represents less adequate care, while those who are exposed to mid-level personnel in the context of a full-choice circumstance may be more accepting of the alternative. Hersey [71] had made a similar point earlier when he argued for a distinction between the use of PAs in rural areas and in inner-city ghettos. Since rural residents choose to live in remote areas, he claimed, they should be willing to accept as a consequence fewer high-powered resources. Urban ghetto residents are often denied full-physician services on a basis other than choice, however; thus, he concluded that PAs in these deprived locations may represent a true instance of second-class service.

Others have also been concerned with the possibility that services by PAs and similar non-physician providers represent a type of second-class medicine [136, 141, 166]. On the other hand, there are those who argue [95] that not only does the PA service not represent inferior care, but may actually be providing patients with more attention and concern for their problems than might be shown by an attending physician.

H. Acceptance: Other Health Care Personnel

In addition to physicians whose acceptance will determine the work opportunities and to patients whose acceptance will provide the work content and challenge, there is one other group with whom the PA will need to negotiate acceptance in order to perform the activities which constitute the work domain. In the daily schedule of patient care and related tasks, the PA will frequently need to interact with a variety of nurses, technicians, and office personnel, plus an assortment of hospital workers should he or she be among the approximately 75 percent of PAs involved in in-hospital activities at least part of the time [122]. Although the complexity of interoccupational contact will vary widely by setting and by negotiated job description, most physician assistants will be faced with the need to maintain harmonious relationships with other health care providers in order that the problems of the patients can be appropriately tended. The consequences of nonacceptance by other health personnel would be expected to range from minor annoyances to the outright blockage of access to the resources needed to carry out work activities.

The criterion found in one study [47] to be most crucial for determining acceptance was the competence of the new professionals, meaning their show of intelligence, initiative, and concern for their patients. Other factors identified in the same study were the willingness to work in areas exhibiting health personnel shortages, willingness to work in less well-supplied specialty fields, and flexibility to adapt to the real needs of the delivery system. In addition, there was a clear indication of the need to define the role of the new practitioners in a manner which would not infringe on areas previously considered the prerogative of other members of the health team and a need to educate physicians and other health personnel to the proper use of the new providers.

Actual experience of practicing PAs in attempting to win acceptance among other groups of health care providers has been mixed. Not surprisingly, roleset acceptance has been found highest among those other providers who saw the PA as carrying out tasks which visibly aided them in their own work.

Addressing the issue of professional territoriality among health care providers, Pluckhan [126] contended that the defensive actions of groups to protect their domains from outside invasion creates a major restriction on the potential for providing maximum health care to the public. She notes that the problem is a particular hazard when the lines demarcating work areas of health team members are hazy and the probability of members from one discipline overstepping another's territory is increased. Furthermore, she charges that overprotection of professional boundaries through the tool of licensure, the lack of interprofessional cooperation, and the reliance upon dogma and tradition rather than upon appropriate skill and capability for task delegation seriously hampers the efficient delivery of health servies. Coe and Fichtenbaum [27] identified the ambivalence and envy observed among other health care workers in their study as a result of the level at which PAs had been able to enter the health care system. When PAs burst upon the scene as "junior level" doctors, a considerable amount of professional jealousy was generated in those groups who had previously struggled to "work their way up by the bootstraps."

Without a doubt, the group in which territorial threat has aroused the greatest opposition to the new practitioners has been nursing. Numerous articles have been written about the problems which have developed between the two occupational groups. According to Andreoli [5], part of the difficulty stems from the fact that the PA concept was introduced during a period when nursing was already involved in a vigorous movement for professional and academic recognition. When the PA concept was formally introduced, nursing was deeply entangled in its internal struggles which focused on differences between the variety of levels in nursing ranging from diploma to doctorate level. Nursing took little official notice of physician assistants at first because their energies were directed toward building professionalism among their own members and gaining independence from medicine.

During the early period of the PA movement, the relationship between nursing and medicine was fraught with dissension [144]. The fact that PAs were the by-product of an antagonistic profession, then, could not have failed to increase the strain between nurses and PAs. An additional factor in that strain has been identified as the uncertainty over the role concept of physician assistants. The ambiguity about just who the PA is, where the PA fits in the pecking order of the medical hierarchy relative to nurses and physicians, and what the functions of the

PA are have all created anxiety among many nurses who must deal with the resultant role confusion [5]. Weiler [172] suggests an additional strain is posed by the transition occurring within nursing itself between the traditional emphasis of the role of a mother surrogate who is subordinate to the physician and the emerging roles of the liberated women and the independent professional.

Competition for jobs is another area of potential conflict between nurses and physician assistants. Some concern has been expressed that the PA movement will decrease valuable nursing personnel by the recruitment of the more ambitious nurses to the new occupation which appears to many to offer greater autonomy and expanded patient care responsibilities [45, 101]. The possibility that PAs will win prescription rights, moreover, is seen as yet another unfair advantage over nurses in the job market [139].

In the final analysis, the hostility between the two groups may be more apparent than real in spite of the abundance of inflammatory media accounts. Several sources have commented upon the relative concentration of nursing opposition at the top of that profession's hierarchy, while at the grassroots level, nurses and PAs exhibit little friction in day-to-day patient care activities [47, 106, 139].

VI. TRANSCULTURAL STUDY

Overall, the examination of the various developmental and contemporary conditions which have accompanied the PA movement results in conflicting forecasts of the occupation's future. The negative signs—which include the projected oversupply of physicians, the significant reimbursement barriers, and the serious interprofessional conflicts—are countered by a high level of patient acceptance, favorable indicators of performance, and the documented potential for significant reduction in primary care delivery costs. With such mixed signals, no clear-cut determination of the future of PAs is yet available. Furthermore, logical derivation from existing circumstances is likely to be overshadowed in the eventual outcome by political and economic contingencies existing outside the medical sector. The relatively brief existence of the new occupational group precludes any lengthy examination of their previous ability to adapt to changing conditions. A historical look at the extensive career development of the Soviet feldsher, then, offers a unique opportunity to shed additional light on the complex situation through an analysis of the experience of this Soviet counterpart within the context of its own medical system.

Attempts to utilize the experience of other medical care systems are inherently limited by the fit of the models being compared, however. As others have pointed out [19, 91], it is impossible to even formulate appropriate research questions without a thorough understanding of each of the cross-national cultures involved. While attaining the necessary familiarity may be painstaking, failure to

attend to this vital aspect in work spanning two or more countries may sabotage
the research effort. A likely result is misspecification of explanatory variables
which, in turn, leads to findings of spurious relationships and invalid
interpretations.

In general, comparative studies entail at least three cognitive requisites: (1)
precise delimitation of the particular conditions or subjects of interest; (2) careful
stipulation of the specific attributes of those subjects which will be used for
comparison; and (3) adequate accounting of the relevant contextual factors, be
they social, ecological, or temporal. Few assumptions can be taken for granted in
such studies. Cultural biases of the researchers and language differences requiring translation compound the risks of misinterpretation. Such language problems
take many forms. Grimshaw [68], for example, points to cultural differences in
word meanings (lexical), the grouping and organization of wording (syntactical),
and word pronunciations (phonological). The meaning of words, or conceptual
equivalence [6], rather than literal identity of terms appears to be the crucial
ingredient of comparative research.

In the area of health studies, particular difficulties are engendered by the lack
of uniformity across nations concerning what or who is included in any given
category of disease, health personnel or specialty group. Even morbidity and
mortality statistics often vary by base rates. Other sources of distortion include
the manipulation of outcome measures in response to political exigency.

In the face of such ambivalencies, it is impossible for comparative research to
achieve the level of methodological rigor attainable under more favorable conditions. The more dissimilar the societies under investigation are, moreover, the
greater the challenge is likely to be. Still, the potential of transcultural study for
testing hypotheses, for broadening perspectives, and for generating new ideas
may well outweigh the procedural limitations.

In the current analysis, since mainly secondary sources have been consulted,
the comparisons made must be interpreted with caution. Considerable cross-
checking of facts among references has been carried out, but there is no way at
this time to determine conclusively the accuracy of the information regarding the
Soviet medical system. Unfortunately, much of the work available in English
comes from the accounts of Americans who have observed in selected facilities
during what are usually very brief visits to the Soviet Union. In addition, documents originating from the Soviet Ministry of Health, while providing a wealth
of valuable detail, may well be expected to contain some measure of nationalistic
bias. The same, of course, may be said of some references used to examine the
American system.

VII. SOVIET MEDICINE

Since many facets of the Soviet medical system differ considerably from the
American medical system, and since, further, some understanding of these dif-

ferences is necessary for the interpretation of the feldsher role within the system, a brief overview of the organization of medicine in the USSR is given.

A. Cultural Features

The Union of Soviet Socialist Republics (USSR) has the largest land mass of any country in the world. Its land area covers 8.6 million square miles, which is almost 2.5 times larger than the land area of the United States. According to the Radio Liberty Research report (1980), the 1979 census counted approximately 262.5 million citizens, an increase of nearly 21 million persons over the 1970 census figures. The vast expanse of land which stretches across large segments of both Europe and Asia possesses almost every known natural resource. Although slightly greater than half its citizenry are Russians, in all there are more than 100 different nationalities in the population. To address the educational needs of such a diverse populace, the school system includes instruction in at least 61 distinct languages. One hundred thirty-six million people, or 62 percent of the population, live in urban areas. This represents an increase of 27.6 million urban residents since 1970. During the same period the rural population fell by 6.9 million. In some areas the rural loss was due, at least in part, to a policy of elimination of villages no longer considered viable by the central government [151:79-83].

The typical Soviet family is relatively small; 81.6 percent of all families consist of groups of two to four persons. Females make up 53.3 percent of the population, a sex ratio imbalance which is gradually correcting itself from the heavy losses of men resulting from World War II and the repressive campaigns under Stalin's government. The overall population growth has slowed markedly during the last decade to an average addition of only 2.3 million persons per year.

Demographic data such as these are crucial to the understanding of the organization of medical services in any given society. Policy makers who attempt to address a population's health care needs must have, in addition, considerable information on age distributions, dependency ratios, birth rates, death rates, and various morbidity statistics. Such data, while indispensable for health planning, is quite outside the more general focus of this paper. More pertinent to the analysis is the fact that the USSR is broken into 15 geopolitical divisions called *republics* whose boundaries also define the major divisions of the Soviet medical system. Ten of the republics are subdivided into 114 regions called *oblasts*, 6 territories called *krais* which contain an ethnic group large enough to constitute an independent oblast, 20 Autonomous Soviet Socialist Republics, 8 Autonomous Oblasts and more than 3,000 smaller administrative districts called *rayons*. The Russian Soviet Federal Socialist Republic (RSFSR) is the largest republic, containing 53.8 percent of the country's population. Some of the oblasts and krais in the RSFSR are further subdivided into 10 areas called *okrugs* which contain a recognized ethnic group but not one possessing national autonomy.

B. Political Structure

Understanding the complexities of these basic territorial partitions and their relationship to the medical delivery structure is additionally complicated by the tripartite arrangement of the Soviet state system. The power of this socialist nation was divided into three distinct, but closely interrelated, branches by the constitution written under Stalin's leadership in 1936: (1) the Communist Party of the Soviet Union, (2) the Parliament, and (3) the Cabinet. The first, the Communist Party of the Soviet Union (CPSU), is the decisionmaking branch that directs the policy governing all state organs. Under principles of democratic centralism, power is distributed in a pyramidal fashion whose base consists of the elementary cells or organizational units usually sited in the workplace. The cell members elect the rayon committee which, in turn, elects the oblast committee which then elects the republic committee. From the 15 republic committees the Congress of the CPSU is elected and from that body is elected the Central Committee in which the maximum authority of the Party is vested. The Central Committee maintains membership discipline, finalizes decisions, and holds approval power over all leading positions in government, enterprises and news media. It is composed of several commissions, including one on health and welfare. From the Central Committee 13 full voting members of the ruling Politburo are elected and they, in turn, elect the top leader, the Secretary General.

The legislative branch of the state system is the Parliament or the Supreme Soviet. Here, again, there is a power pyramid composed of councils of elected representatives at each divisional level from the village to the republic and centralized in the Supreme Soviet which meets twice yearly to act on proposed legislation. Out of session, authority is vested in the 37-member Presidium elected by the Supreme Soviet whose leadership resides in the President. The Supreme Soviet consists of two parliamentary divisions. One is the Soviet of the Union whose deputies are elected by the populace, with one representative for each approximately 300,000 citizens. The other division is the Soviet of Nationalities with representatives elected from the Republic Soviets. The two divisions have equal legislative rights and each has several committees, including one concerned with health and social welfare issues.

The actual execution of legislation is carried out in the third branch of the government, the Cabinet, whose 80 members are elected by the Supreme Soviet. Included in the Cabinet is the 30-member Council of Ministers, each of whom heads a government branch, as well as the leaders of various special boards and agencies. The head of this bureaucratic branch is the Premier who is selected by the Cabinet members.

C. Ministry of Health

One of the ministries in the Cabinet structure is the Ministry of Health which presides over most health sector operations. Planning and regulation functions are centrally dispensed through a broad network of ministries and health departments covering all levels of administration out to the most peripheral catchment areas called the *uchastok,* or neighborhood unit. Health research in medical care organization and delivery is usually generated through the Semaschko Institute. This central health agency is one of 15 units of the prestigious Academy of Sciences likened by Navarro [112:93] to the United States' National Science Foundation. The 300 or so institute professionals and their assorted advisory councils prepare standards for the development and distribution of medical personnel throughout the system. The staff and advisors are made up of the country's leading specialists in academic and clinical medicine.

The Union Minister of Health is the highest administrative authority in the Health Ministry. This position is always filled by an eminent physician who usually combines administration duties with a limited clinical practice. His[1] authority is delegated by the CPSU Executive Committee. Advising the minister is the powerful 30-member Medical Collegium composed of key persons in the Ministry structure, top medical administrators and researchers, representatives of trade unions, and Communist Party functionaries. The Collegium reviews and evaluates proposals originating from the Semaschko Institute.

Policy implementation flows downward from the Union Ministry throughout the administrative structure. Ministry-level decisions regarding norms of access and resource distribution are subsequently binding on all lower units in the health sector. A critical regulatory feature is lodged in the mechanisms for central financing. Both republic and oblast health sector budgets are largely funded with national government monies. Most of the operating expenditures of the health system are covered by funds from the union Health Ministry as is the bulk of capital investments for medical schools and postgraduate institutes. Capital investments for other health facilities, such as the oblast hospitals where most middle medical workers receive their training, come from separate republic or lower administrative funding sources, but they may also receive additional grants from the central government for construction and expansion when necessary. Actually, the operating budget at each administrative level is directly approved by the next highest authority unit but since approval decisions are based on the standards sent down from the Union Health Ministry, the central control is exceedingly great. Furthermore, it is important to remember that the plans produced by the Health Ministry are subject to the overall strictures of the total state budget developed as part of the national five-year plan by Gosplan, the central planning council for the State. Each completed plan of the Health Ministry must be approved by the full Council of Ministries which then submits it to the Supreme Soviet. Acceptance by the Supreme Soviet transforms the plan into law and it then is passed back down through the Cabinet bureaucracy for implementation.

The governmental centralism which is so crucial to the understanding of the Soviet medical system has been the key factor in the country's extraordinary economic development since the early part of this century. Although by Western standards the social amenities enjoyed by the average Soviet citizen are still deficient, the country has become one of the leading industrialized nations of the world. At a time when many countries are experiencing crisis-level unemployment, the USSR is seeking ways to mitigate a pending manpower shortage [151:78-2].

VIII. FELDSHERS AND THE HISTORY OF SOVIET MEDICINE

A. Comparative Specifications

International exchange is the basic concern of this paper. The question of interest is whether the experience of the Soviet feldsher can be used to refine the predictions regarding the future direction of the physician assistant movement in the United States. Having summarized briefly the contextual backdrop of Soviet cultural and geopolitical features, I will narrow the focus to an examination of the history and development of the feldsher occupation within the Soviet medical system. Since it is a major purpose of this paper to argue that occupations are both shaped and constrained by the broader system factors in which they are enveloped, the discussion will, necessarily, include references to those social, economic, and political forces which have pertinence for the understanding of the particular feldsher profile. Given the extensive history of this practitioner group, however, the explanatory framework must inevitably be drawn with broad strokes. Every attempt has been made to include those factors considered to have had a major determining influence on the developmental course of the feldsher occupation without miring the discussion with minute details of each era. What precision is lost, is thereby exchanged for a more clearly graspable sense of the total career pattern involved. The particular conditions to be described include the history of feldshers across various politically-defined time periods, the feldsher training programs, and the contemporary work roles of feldshers. Later, four specific features of these Soviet practitioners are selected for actual comparison with those of the American physician assistants. The units chosen for this brief analysis are: (1) controlling interests, (2) compensation, (3) role standardization, and (4) provider competition.

B. Military Origins

Late in the seventeenth century, under the direction of Peter I, the Great (1672–1725), a few hospitals in Russia began training medical personnel who would be utilized to minister to the needs of the army on the battlefield. Since physicians were in short supply, the country followed the lead of several Western European nations in preparing these special medical corpsmen called *feldshers*.

A few years later, Peter the Great, an amateur surgeon himself, began to instigate systematic health provision for the more privileged Russian civilians. In 1706, the first medical school was built in Moscow, thus ushering in the country's beginnings of scientific medicine. The new school, modeled after the famous Leyden Medical School in Holland, emphasized anatomy and adopted the modern scientific approach which viewed the patient mechanistically.

By the middle of the next century, there were approximately 10,000 physicians in the country, but only the nobility yet had access to their ministrations [113]. In 1861, with the liberation of serfs, Russia emerged as a modern state. Pushed away from the land by abject poverty and lured to the cities with the promises of industrial opportunities, the newly freed workers descended in hordes upon the urban centers. The massive migration resulted in appalling public health conditions.

In response to the needs generated by the liberation, Alexander II (1855–1881) launched a massive modernization campaign in 1864 which established the Zemstvo system of government. Zemstvos were local district assemblies charged with the responsibility of administrating programs of education, public health, charity and law enforcement. As a result of these extensive social reforms, the first large-scale organization of medicine in the world began to take shape. Part of the new campaign involved the establishment of formal training schools for feldshers. Although some of these schools were for military personnel, others trained middle-grade medical workers for civilian posts either in the zemstvo clinics or in the rural feldsher stations. Occasionally in the zemstvo and rural posts the feldsher worked with a physician as an assistant, but more usually she/he worked alone as the sole provider of medical care in the area. There was sometimes an additional midwife at these posts, but it was common practice for the functions of both feldsher and midwife to be carried out by a single worker. The zemstvos relied heavily on the feldsher services because they could be purchased for much lower wages than those of regular physicians [153].

At the turn of the century, Russia was still predominantly feudal. Control of the country was held by 1.4 percent of the population who were landowning nobility, bourgeoisie, petite bourgeoisie, and middle peasants with moderate rural landholdings. Medical facilities were yet the poorest in Europe [134]. This was partly attributable to the fact that religious and charitable foundations had never assumed care of the sick as they had done in most Western European countries. The network of health units established under the Zemstvo reforms extended medical care into areas previously without such services. But, although financed through taxation of the peasantry, the system still functioned primarily to serve the needs of the nobility.

Peasants toiling daily without hope of personal gain, and laborers oppressed by the wretched conditions of the industrial center of Moscow and Petrograd, finally began a series of uprisings which culminated in the October Revolution of 1905. Swift retaliation by the nobility resulted in the slaughter of thousands of workers. This brutally repressive response was accompanied by a series of cooptive measures designed by the Tsarist government to win support of landowning peasants called *kulaks*. Some of the measures constituted considerable improvement in civic freedom. Political parties were legalized, peasants and workers were represented in a newly created body to serve a consultive role in the parliament, limited social security coverage was effected for certain categories of workers, and mechanisms to provide credit to peasants for land purchase were established.

On the health front, the government increased its efforts to train much-needed medical care providers. By 1915 Russia had 65 schools for training civilian feldshers and feldsher-midwives with a combined student population of nearly 9,000. In addition there were 10 military feldsher schools operating at that time, most of which were located in central Russia [104]. The schools varied in curricula and in admission requirements, but most programs were three to four years in length. Graduates who passed a state examination were awarded a diploma and the title of feldsher. During the early years of the century there was considerable concern expressed by the medical community over the need to improve the quality of the training programs, but in part because the various middle-level schools were administered under separate civil service departments, the efforts to improve lacked coordination and the results were uneven.

C. Revolution and Civil War

As extensive as the cooptive measures were, they apparently fell far short of satisfying the masses who had so long suffered under the deprivations imposed by the Tsarist regimes. The burdens of World War I increased their misery, for it was the labor of the workers and peasants that financed the war effort and it was they who were sent to wage combat on the battlefields. In February 1917 a new, spontaneous uprising erupted which resulted in the overthrow of the 300-year-old Romanov dynasty and the beginning of the Soviet Revolution. The nearly bloodless uprising was led by the highly politicized workers in Petrograd who were composed of Bolsheviks, Mensheviks, and Social Revolutionaries. This group became dominated by the Mensheviks who later yielded power to the ideologically compatible Provisional Government set up by Alexander Kerensky in Moscow. Kerensky's main objective was to join the Allied surge to defeat the Germans; therefore, all political and social reforms were deferred in favor of a massive investment in the war effort.

Little relief was thus realized by the majority of the workers and peasants who continued to suffer a mean existence. It is hardly surprising that when the exiled leaders of the Bolshevik party—Lenin, Stalin and Trotsky—returned with their programs proposing utopian social reforms, they were met with widespread support from the greatly dissatisfied masses. The Bolshevik's platform called for an immediate end to the war and for a transfer of power from the Provisional Government to the elected councils, called Soviets, composed of laborers, soldiers, and peasants. To gather political strength, they demanded reforms which included an eight-hour working day and a program of social insurance protecting workers and the poor against unemployment and disability with costs to be borne by the employer.

The Provisional Government reacted swiftly to these threats, banning the Bolsheviks and imprisoning their leaders. Subsequently, in October 1917, the Bolsheviks (led by N. Lenin) rallied to overthrow Kerensky's leadership. Following the coup d'état, workers' committees assumed the operations of the factories, key industries were nationalized, and land was redistributed through peasants' cooperatives and state collective farms.

The transition of power was neither swift nor sure, however. For several years a civil war, referred to as War Communism, raged throughout the land. The Small Red Army led by Trotsky battled against a coalition of old nobility and Kerensky's government, who had considerable backing among the Allied forces. The effect on the populace was devastating. A food embargo by Western European nations left many starving. The country reeled under numerous epidemics. Typhus, relapsing fever, typhoid fever, plague, cholera, scarlet fever, measles and smallpox wended torturous, sprawling paths that left millions dead in their wake. Droves of urban residents fled the cities seeking food in the countryside.

Profound upheavals in the social and economic structure of the nation began to take place. Lenin's idealistic social security programs were inevitably compromised in face of the enormous challenges confronting the shaky new government. Circumstances changed so rapidly and erratically at first that the Bolsheviks sometimes found outcomes to be quite different from those they had planned. When civil strife subsided several years later, in 1920, state involvement in funding and administration of the social and economic sectors was much greater than the leaders had envisioned.

D. Setting Priorities

Minute documentation of the complexities of this period is well beyond the scope of the current paper. But, in essence, what ultimately transpired was a result of the recognition by the Lenin forces that in order to survive, the new government would need to adapt their policies to the hard realities. The Bolsheviks had signed a peace treaty with Germany in March 1918 with terms distinctly unfavorable to Russia. Furthermore, Lenin's expectations of general unification with the socialist forces among Western European countries failed to materialize. Instead, those nations sided with the old Russian aristocracy, and the Bolsheviks found themselves cut off from food and other much needed sources of aid. In response, significant revision occurred in Leninist strategy. Top priority was now given over to the rapid accumulation of capital supply: the building of socialist programs would need to await later opportunity. To accomplish this fundamental objective, all available resources were funneled toward the development of a vigorous industrial base. Initially this would require direct state intervention to insure success of the endeavor. In addition, state control was expected to provide the political cohesion and citizen support needed to legitimate the nascent system.

E. Proletarianized Medicine

Medicine played a leading role in the industrialization campaign. Worker health was of paramount importance to efficient production. It was crucial, then, to launch a frontal attack on the diseases plaguing the population. In 1918 the People's Commissariat of Health was established in the recently created Russian Soviet Federal Socialist Republic (RSFSR). As the world's first ministry of health [81], it was commissioned with the responsibility for all personal and environmental health facilities in the republic. Under the directorship of Lenin's close colleague Dr. N. A. Semaschko, the Commissariat's earliest concern was to increase and redistribute medical resources. Although there were 23,000 physicians in the country just prior to the Revolution, 92 percent of them were concentrated in the larger cities. At the same time, those cities contained only 17 percent of the population [113:12]. Physician services, long a prerogative of the urban elite, were further shrunken by heavy losses to disease and battle during the wars. Physicians led by their professional association, the Pirogov Society, had supported Kerensky's Provisional government. They were staunchly opposed to the Bolshevik leadership whose proposals for widespread health reforms posed a threat to the autonomy and the privileged livelihood enjoyed by the profession. Lenin's notion of medicine as a collective endeavor involving citizen participation in control and decision-making was at sharp variance with the bourgeois concept of an individualistic, biological medical model.

To weaken the power of the profession's opposition, Lenin sought to proletarianize medicine. A two-part strategy was employed to accomplish this objective. First, the universities were opened to groups previously denied access to higher education. Students of both sexes from all races and social classes were now granted admission. Children of working-class and peasant families were given preference in application to medical schools. At the same time, the existing network of feldsher schools was replaced by four-year technical feldsher-midwife colleges having upgraded entrance requirements. This was done to denounce the old system of different levels of care for the wealthy and the poor. Under the new plan, high quality service was to be available to all persons free of charge. In addition, since the primary and secondary education of many workers and peasants had been poor, special schools attached to the universites, called *rabochie fakulteti,* or worker faculties, were opened to prepare adult workers to enter the various higher-level training programs. Although tuition and stipends for basic living costs were provided by the state, the schools were only minimally successful in increasing the proportion of proletarian students in the medical curriculum since the better students were encouraged to go into the more prestigious fields of industrial science and engineering. Many of the students with proletarian backgrounds, moreover, experienced academic difficulties and soon there was great concern over falling standards of scholarship and program quality.

The other Leninist tactic designed to redistribute the power in medicine relied heavily upon the existing Zemstvo structure. Although the pre-Revolution Zemstvo network had functioned to increase the control of the Tsars over the populace, physicians had largely retained their economic independence under that system. There had been no compulsory assignment of doctors to Zemstvo units and few medical professionals had volunteered to practice for the typically modest remuneration provided under the council contracts. As a consequence, many of the Zemstvo health posts had been filled by feldshers who were themselves usually of peasant heritage and, thus, were ideologically aligned with socialist objectives. After the Revolution, the Bolsheviks manipulated this loyalty as a means of bringing the medical profession under state control. Not unexpectedly, party loyalty resulted in feldshers, rather than physicians, being assigned to many of the new health leadership roles.

The scattered, disorganized public health resources which had arisen after Alexander II's modernization reforms were now coordinated around a nucleus of medical-sanitary units. Insurance coverage, though far less broad than that proposed in early Leninist platforms, extended free health care to large numbers of workers. The free care combined with miserably poor conditions in the rural areas acted in concert to largely eliminate any market for private medical practice.

Cut off from its economic wellspring, the medical profession suffered a further blow with the establishment in 1920 of the all-Russia Central Council of Trade Unions. The feldshers, who early in the century had formed one of the first individual unions, instigated a drive to combine the forces of the various groups of medical workers. The successful upshot was an organization covering all categories of health personnel. The revolutionary leaders encouraged this union activity, seeing it as a chance to break the power of the elitist physicians. Under the new regime, membership in the union became a condition for employment in health posts. Since the poverty of the country made it nearly impossible for physicians to make a living on an independent fee-for-service basis, they were forced finally to capitulate to the unionization pressures. By this move, however, the doctors forfeited their independent power base and much of their prestige, giving the party leaders a major victory in their campaign to deprofessionalize and democratize the health sector.

F. New Economic Policy

In March 1921, the Tenth Communist Party established the New Economic Policy (N.E.P.) whose mission was to rebuild the economy so badly ravaged during the War Communism. The events following the Revolution had plainly indicated the country was not ready for the state capitalism which the leaders had envisioned as a preliminary to the eventual proletarian takeover of the forces of production and the final disappearance of the state. Under N.E.P., those enterprises judged to be vital to industrial development were to remain under state control, but all others would be denationalized. The production of consumer, rather than capital, goods would be encouraged and their regulation would be left to the forces of demand and supply. The banking system would be revamped. Taxes, prices, and wage rates would be determined by market factors but agriculture, electricity, mining, and services which were expected to strengthen production would be given special priority. State land was to be leased to private owners and peasants who were free to farm as they chose. To spur productivity, however, taxes on the leased holdings were to be inversely geared to production.

The New Economic Policy continued in effect throughout the period of formal establishment of the United Soviet Socialist Republic in December 1922 and up until Lenin's death in 1924. From then until the first *Pyatiletka,* or five-year plan, was instituted in 1928, N.E.P. was frequently challenged and modified, but it continued to serve as the basic blueprint for state policy. Years of social upheaval; shortages of food, skilled labor, and raw materials; sporadic and uncoordinated growth in some sectors; low wages; and, lack of capital reserves combined with the inexperience and relative ineptness of the new leadership to produce increased unemployment and rising inflation.

Medical services under N.E.P. returned largely to a fee-for-service, free-market structure. Only contract workers in industry remained covered under the revised social security plans. Non-wage earners were most often too poor to afford health care; thus, the market could not support individual medical practices and many doctors were left without work.

The priority given to agricultural production during this period, however, led to a reorganization of rural health services which constituted the beginning of the regionalization model. In 1925, the *uchastok* (neighborhood) unit was designated as the fundamental division for the delivery of primary health services. More specialized ambulatory and hospital care was made available at the *rayon* (district) level, while the most complicated and demanding medical problems were treated in highly specialized facilities at the *oblast* (region) level.

At the same time a dispensary system was established in urban areas. The urban system's focus centered on maintaining a healthy work force through preventive measures and record linkage which facilitated follow-up care.

G. Stalin: Preemptive Power

Emerging victorious from the lengthy internal clash of political factions following Lenin's death, Stalin began to set into motion programs whose foci were in sharp contrast with those which had operated under N.E.P. Stalin's leadership emphasized rapid, forced industrialization and agricultural collectivization. To achieve the socialist objective in such a vastly underdeveloped nation, the new Party rulers insisted that initially all other goals would need to be subordinated to the effort to amass primitive capital. The means to accomplish this objective would be found by exploiting the agricultural productivity of the peasantry in favor of industrial investment and by holding the level of consumption below the output of production. Furthermore, effective implementation of these policies would require a strong centralization of political control. The impact of these directives was to have profound effects on the nation's development for the next quarter of a century.

The guidelines for the Stalinist program were issued by the Fifteenth Communist Party Congress in 1927 in the form of a five-year plan. While five-year plans would continue to characterize the official notice of long-range objectives, it was the annual plan/counterplan process which formed the basic operating unit of Stalin's administration [175]. Each year the production goals formulated by the central leadership would be passed downward to the enterprises which would then send upward through the chain of command the inputs they would require to fulfill those goals.

When the first five-year plan went into effect in 1928, 96 percent of the land was owned by peasants [113:38]. Although the Party initially intended a gradual state takeover, bitter resistance from kulacks and peasants to the nationalization movement resulted in government retaliation and sharp escalation in farm acquisitions. By 1933, 93 percent of the land was collectivized, but 10 million resisters had lost their lives in the massive reorganization process. At first collectivization resulted in an overall decline in agricultural production; but, by the end of the second five-year plan in 1938, the profits from the marketable crops were being successfully diverted from the peasantry to stoke the fires of industry.

As was the case with collectivization, industrialization was swift but fraught with turbulence. Dissidents to the government's modernizing programs were quickly repressed. Using development models borrowed from the Western world, the Party created a highly technological bureaucracy which channeled the country's resources into a few favored industries: steel, machinery, and electricity.

Developments in health provision during the Stalin years were closely related to other changes occurring in the economy. Historic decisions made by the Communist Party's Central Committee at the beginning of this period, for instance, resulted in major transformations in the social security programs and these, in turn, determined the need for particular health resources. Reflecting the nation's critical manpower shortage, many of the social security revisions were designed to push all able-bodied nonworkers into the labor force. Thus, relief payments to the unemployed were sharply curtailed, previously retired persons were permitted to keep their pensions in addition to any earnings they could make if they returned to work, and mothers were induced to remain on their jobs through the combined reduction in maternity benefits and increased provision of child care centers.

In the health sector itself, the importance of maintaining a strong labor force was manifested through the creation of a system of factory health posts. Staffed by physicians, feldshers and other middle-level practitioners, these units were located in the work settings and were administrated by the industry management rather than by the local Soviets. They not only functioned to provide the workers with convenient access to primary medical care, they also served management as surveillance linkages designed to reduce employee attrition due to ill health and malingering.

The precedence accorded industrial productivity during this era far overshadowed any concern for a more equitable distribution of medical care services. The overriding principle encouraged the rewarding of greater benefits to those who added most to the production effort. The health needs of rural inhabitants, particularly those who were not part of the *kolkhozs,* or farm collectives, attracted little official concern from this government. An indication of this low priority was exhibited by the relatively meager salaries paid in rural physician posts.

The public health problems which accompanied the country's rapid urbanization, on the other hand, were accorded considerable attention. Sanitary engineering, which focused on environmental factors such as purity of water supply, crowded housing, and food handling, was given high priority. It was, in fact, combined with industrial health to form one of the three major functional service divisions identified as vital to the support of industry's growth. The other two divisions were maternal and child health service, and polyclinic curative care service.

After Lenin's death, medical education underwent a significant conversion, which also reflected the new emphasis on scientific expertise and specialization. Concern over the deteriorating quality of the academic programs under Lenin's open-door admissions policies led to the reinstitution of entrance examinations for medical schools. However, a quota remained in effect to assure that a definite number of places in the schools would be filled by students from working-class or peasant backgrounds.

In 1930, medical schools were transferred from administration under the

Commissariat of Education to that of the Commissariat of Health, thus reinforc-
ing the priority of medicine and the focus on specialization. Subsequently medical
schools were separated from the universities, curriculums were streamlined to
address more specifically the medical sciences, and 24 new schools were
opened.

In 1932 the State Institute of Experimental Medicine, later named the Semaschko Institute, was built. Within ten years the drive to expand the frontiers of
scientific medicine had resulted in the establishment of 222 more research
institutes.

During this time another series of changes in the medical school admissions
process began. First, restrictions which had severely limited the access of students whose parents were in engineering or in other technical fields were lifted.
Then, in 1935, a law was passed which made achievement levels on entrance
examinations the sole criterion for admission. In 1940, whatever little of the
democratization principle had survived in medical education, was erased with the
advent of two additional circumstances. First, tuition fees were levied on the last
three years of secondary education, making them beyond the financial means of
many families. Then, a labor draft pulled a disproportionate number of children
of manual workers away from the educational stream and into the labor pool.

In spite of this increasing emphasis on scientific expertise and specialization,
feldshers continued to play an important role in the medical delivery system. The
momentum of collectivization and industrialization produced a great need for
additional middle-level medical workers who could be independently responsible
for providing first aid and simple medical and preventive care in the work
setting. As a consequence, the number of feldsher and feldsher-midwife posts in
both the rural collectivities and the urban industries rose dramatically. In addition, feldshers were in great demand to fill many of the newly created public
health posts. To address these growing needs for mid-level personnel, the Government reintroduced three-year feldsher schools and added a program specifically to train feldsher sanitarians. By 1940, the health care system employed
nearly 96,000 feldshers.

The process of government centralization of health activities had stepped up
with the creation in 1936 of the All-Union Commissariat of Health which assumed national control over the still fragmented health sector. With this reorganization, all civilian health services were placed under the aegis of the
national commissariat which, in turn, was accountable to the Communist Party
Executive Committee. The country's World War II effort further increased these
formalization measures. Research activities then followed suit with their coordination in 1944 under the newly formed Academy of Medical Science. In 1946,
the commissariats, including that of Health, were redesignated as ministries, as
part of a trend to replace the revolutionary mantle with a more nationalistic one.
Even the term *Bolshevik* was discarded at this time [69].

As the organization of medical care became increasingly specialized and hierarchicalized, the hospital became the pivot of the delivery system. Partly because crowded housing conditions made home care and recuperation nearly impossible and partly because medical academicians came to equate good care with institutional medicine, a massive program of hospital construction was undertaken.

In 1947 the Polyclinic-Hospital Reorganization Act directed that the management of urban hospitals and polyclinics within the same administrative districts should be combined. Unification of the two types of facilities was designed to optimize the strengths of each by encouraging a rotation of resources between them. Urban specialists were sent periodically to practice for several weeks or months at polyclinic sites, while many polyclinic personnel were exposed to more sophisticated medical procedures in regularly cycled assignments to urban hospitals. What in principle appeared promising, however, in practice fell short of achieving the hoped-for balance. The conjoint arrangements largely favored hospital service as a result of the increasing importance placed on expertise and credentialling within medicine. Specialists, both clinical and academic, were now accorded greater prestige than were generalists, with those physicians who possessed the most highly technical, narrow skills claiming the most status. Likewise hospital practice which utilized expensive, highly advanced technologies were clearly ranked superior to outpatient practice.

While the class structure of medicine had shifted from bourgeois to proletariat and back to bourgeois as the result of reversing political strategies under Lenin and Stalin, the sexual composition of the medical work force grew steadily more feminized. The need for physicians to replace those lost during the Revolution and the democratization of higher education under Lenin had enabled large numbers of women to seek medical training. The personnel shortages during the 1930s, when most of the rest of the world was paralyzed by the Great Depression, and the serious drain of male workers during World War II, pulled even more females out of the home and into the labor market. Over the years, the Bolshevik's progressive civil rights platform encouraged this active participation by women in all phases of the industrialization buildup. Still, many women elected occupations which were compatible with their traditional supportive and nurturing roles. Thus, teaching and medicine drew disproportionately from the new labor reserves.

In the final analysis, Stalin's economic and social policies had been mainly determined by the material conditions of the country when he came to power. Economic improvement under this administration was impressive at the national level, but living conditions of the ordinary citizen remained bleak. Real wages declined by nearly one-half during the 1930s and over the years of the Stalin era, per capita income fell 25 percent [176:117]. At the time of Stalin's death in 1953, rural areas, in particular, lagged behind in the modernization push. The distribution of medical resources continued to be heavily skewed in favor of the urban centers. In spite of the reorganization scheme, for example, there were

2,000 rural districts without a single physician when the Kremlin oligarchs set about forming a new leadership structure [40:95].

H. Khrushchev: Populist Approach

Under Khrushchev, conditions began to change radically. In his speeches before the Twentieth Party Congress in 1956, Khrushchev established two precedents which would clearly delineate the direction of the new leadership's programs. First, he reinstated the old Leninist policies of peaceful coexistence with foreign nations and parliamentary resolution of internal disputes. Then, in an startling denunciation of the Stalinist personality cult, he exposed and condemned his predecessor's dictatorial strategies and ruthless crimes against the Soviet people. At the same time he affirmed the intent of the new leaders to work in collective cooperation.

These fundamental revisions in operational strategy signaled the beginning of numerous changes whose net effect would be to considerably ease the hardships of the ordinary Soviet citizen. From the beginning, Khrushchev made it clear that consumer goods and food staples would be given greater priority in the production scheme. In a complementary move, the industrial principle in medical services which had favored certain categories of workers was replaced with a sector system. The new policy assigned to a general physician the responsibility for the basic health care needs of all persons in a defined population. A sector might consist of a specific neighborhood, a given segment of a workshop, or even a small village. Feldshers, by now numbering around 272,000, played a major role in the new sector system. Though criticized by some for their lack of full medical credentials, feldshers greatly extended the access to primary health care.

In the labor sector, concern focused on reopening opportunities to the preferred occupations. As in Lenin's time, legislation was passed to facilitate the retraining and upgrading of the educational and employment skills of workers. Evening programs attached to universities and medical schools were reinstituted for adult learners, and students with peasant or laboring backgrounds were again given priority in the selection process. Tuition for the last three years of secondary schooling was discontinued, enabling many less privileged students to complete their studies.

The biggest shake-up to the economy came in March 1957 when Khrushchev announced a plan to decentralize industrial management. The extensive reorganization which went into effect in July of that year abolished 27 industrial ministries and 400 government bureaus. In their place a network of 100 *sovnarkhozy*, or regional councils, were created which had boundaries coinciding with the provincial authorities for health services. The regional councils were given the responsibility for implementing economic and social policy, including the delegation of management for various enterprises in their own region. The outcome was, essentially, the creation of a new managerial class with authority to wield considerable control on the local level. The scheme did not, in fact decentralize state power. What it did was consolidate the authority at the top levels under the aegis of the State Planning Commission so that the power now flowed down through the republic, oblast, and rayon administrative channels without first having to wind its way past the maze of competing ministries.

The late 1950s and early 1960s were characterized by national strife, both internally and externally. A pact between Khrushchev and Tito in June of 1956 smoothed a turbulent relationship with Yugoslavia but trouble erupted on another front later that year when the Hungarian Revolution broke out. Khrushchev's military intervention quickly quelled the revolt, but within months Khrushchev, himself, was the center of a Party shake-up in which he barely survived being ousted. Hoffman [73:75] notes that when Khrushchev's programs began to falter he was unwilling to accede to his Presidium colleagues, turning instead to appeal for the support of regional CPSU officials, scientific experts, and the public. While these tactics temporarily forestalled his downfall, his authoritarian and cavalier treatment of other top party leaders would ultimately prove his undoing.

Faced with the heavy burdens imposed by the massive destruction of industrial enterprises during World War II, and in spite of decreasing support for his idealistic but grandiose and poorly planned management programs, Khrushchev's reign was remarkably successful on certain counts. The intense concentration of resources in the scientific fields produced achievements in space technology, theoretical physics, mathematics and oceanography which bedazzled the rest of the world. In agriculture, considerable acclaim accompanied the program to develop chemical fertilizers and the daring Virgin Lands Project which opened to tillage 86,500,000 acres in southwestern Siberia and northern Kazakhstan. The importance of agriculture in this administration was further demonstrated when, in 1962, the CPSU was divided into two branches: the industrial and the agricultural. The salary of agricultural workers was increased and social security benefits were extended to cover these workers whose ranks numbered more than one-half of the country's total labor force.

Medicine during this period was demonstrating results from the applications of expanding scientific research. The infant mortality rate fell from 81 per 1,000 live births in 1950 to 26 per 1,000 in 1968. Malaria, smallpox, cholera and the plague were eradicated; tuberculosis and venereal disease were significantly reduced. At the same time, widespread construction of hospitals, pharmacies, and polyclinics continued to upgrade the quality and accessibility of health care resources.

Additional social policy changes affected the particular health-related issues of disability and retirement benefits. Disability benefits were increased and a new form for their allocation was put into effect. Under the revised disability plan, worker seniority and seriousness of the disabling condition became the main criteria for benefit determination. Retirement age was lowered to 60 years for men and 55 years for women with a corresponding rise in pension benefits that would allow older citizens to more freely choose to withdraw from the labor force.

I. Brezhnev: Scientific Management

Khrushchev's inevitable overthrow occurred in 1965 and, as might be expected, the policies of his predecessors have sought to redress the major criticisms leveled at his leadership style. The populist approach of Khrushchev gave way to Brezhnev's scientific managment style which restored the political prerogatives of official organs. The content of the new programs were similar to those which existed under the old leadership: detente with the United States and other Western nations, improved wages for workers, and increased use of advanced technology in production. Differences appeared, though, in the specific method of governing which became focused on the creation of a stable, cooperative means to ensure collective leadership. Change by increment, careful delineation of responsibility, and sensitivity to external influences largely replaced Khrushchev's tendency toward exaggeration and impulse. A key element, moreover, which generated a high degree of crucial bureaucratic acceptance, was the provision of career security for loyal and competent functionaries [15].

Premier Alexei Kosygin outlined these major reforms of the Brezhnev administration in the fall of 1965. At the same time, it was announced that the regional bodies would be replaced by a ministerial economic structure resembling that in existence at the time of Stalin's death. An additional series of changes provided managers of enterprises with greater latitude in resource use for achieving production targets, a new method for determining success indicators, increased amalgamation of enterprises, and a revised wholesale price structure. The course of the country's economic and social development over the ensuing 17 years was largely fashioned by these initial directives.

Prior to Brezhnev's death in 1982, organizational and departmental interests remained powerful through increasingly direct representation in the Politburo and in the Central Committee. But, the traditional Leninist idea prevailed that a conscious party leadership has the responsibility to impose its view of national interest on the "spontaneity of the masses" [80:81]. The trend continued toward increased managerial manipulation or organizational contributions in the support of collective goals. It was no longer thought necessary for the leadership to maintain a militant ideological stance.

In agriculture Brezhnev and Kosygin continued the intensification begun under their predecessor. The state farms now cultivate more land than the collectives. Today's farm, still very large, operates in a stable, socialist, quasi-market environment similar to the N.E.P. era of the 1920s [103]. The modern farmer, however, now enjoys a guaranteed annual wage, pension coverage, and considerably higher income as a result of the growth in productivity generated by expanded mechanization and increased research effort.

IX. FELDSHERS TODAY

A. Educational Programs

While it is too early to determine the effects on the medical delivery system likely to result from the brief Andropov and Chernenko administrations and the new Gorbachev administration, there is no reason to believe that feldshers will not continue to be a vital component of that system.

Today, for example, each of the 15 Union Republics has its own middle-level medical schools which operate under the direction of the individual Republic Ministries of Health in conjunction with the Ministries of Higher and Special Secondary Education and the local health authorities. In all, there are more than 650 special secondary educational establishments which train middle-level personnel. In addition to the approximately 150,000 feldsher student population, nurses, laboratory technicians, midwives, dental technicians, and dental mechanics receive training in these facilities. For the most part, the needs for middle-level personnel in each republic are met by the output of their own schools. The number of students admitted for training is based upon the calculated needs for the country and for the individual planning regions. A quantitative formula which takes into account various factors such as morbidity patterns, economic trends, and changes in the population structure is used to forecast future feldsher requirements; these are then integrated with the nation's larger health and economic objectives for a given planning period [104, 129].

There is brisk competition for places in today's feldsher schools with one source citing 15 applicants for each student position available [154]. Students who are admitted into the training programs must have completed at least eight years of general schooling and have passed an entrance exam. Maturity and aptitude for medical work are important selection criteria and only persons under the age of 30 are considered for admission. Once admitted, the student not only receives all training free of charge but most also receive a stipend from the government for living expenses.

The curriculum is standardized among the various schools and covers topics in three major areas: (1) general studies such as mathematics, chemistry, history, foreign language, and social science; (2) general medical studies including Latin, biology, anatomy, physiology, and pharmacology; and (3) clinical studies which rotate by disease category but are heavily weighted toward internal medicine, surgery, pediatrics, and midwifery/gynecology. The length of the course depends on the prior academic preparation of the student. Those students who have completed the full ten years of instruction, in the better-grade secondary schools, complete feldsher training in two and one-half years. Students with only eight years of prior secondary work, the standard length of rural schooling, spend three and one-half years in the programs. Overall, the coursework covers about 60 percent theoretical material and about 40 percent practical studies. The emphasis is on preparing personnel who can provide medical care in the absence of the physician including diagnosis, treatment, prescriptions, and carrying out of basic medical procedures [104].

Students move progressively through more challenging laboratory and practical experiences starting in specially equipped teaching units in the schools and advancing to training in hospitals, polyclinics, and other curative or preventive settings. Teachers in the medical and clinical studies are usually doctors, although feldshers and other middle-level personnel sometimes serve as instructors in the practical courses. The director of each program is always a physician, who is aided by an educational specialist.

Many American authors have commented on a unique feature of the feldsher programs which provides for mobility routes into medical schools [53, 109, 154]. Although the country's general educational system tends to channel rural youths into feldsher rather than medical schools [41], many feldsher students who come originally from the poorer-quality rural secondary schools are able to make their way later into the ranks of physicians. It is standard procedure that the top five percent of each graduating feldsher class be allowed to sit for the entrance examination to medical schools. During the late 1950s and the 1960s a number of medical institutes opened evening classes to further facilitate the movement of middle-medical workers into professional medicine. After two years in the field, graduate feldshers could enter these night courses while retaining their normal work positions. After serving three years in a feldsher post, they were eligible to apply for full-time medical study. Under these arrangements, about two to five percent of the practicing feldshers left their positions each year to enter medical training [154]. Approximately one-quarter of the country's physicians at that time had, in fact, had previous feldsher experience [53, 153].

Today, after completion of the regular training program, all feldshers are encouraged to continually upgrade their knowledge and skills by taking part in several types of post-diploma studies. Courses of various types are offered in all the Union Republics. These range from one-day in-service seminars to in-depth specialty programs of six months' duration. There are special courses to prepare workers for, among others, remote health posts, industrial posts, assignments on sea or river vessels, emergency care services, and care of children and adolescents. If the regular work schedule is disrupted by the course of study, the government provides a continued salary, travel expenses, and living expenses to the trainee in addition to paying for all of the training costs [104].

B. Contemporary Work Roles

The feldsher performs a considerable portion of the total health care service in the USSR. In 1975, for example, there were a little more than 425 million patient visits made to physicians. During the same year an even larger number of patients, nearly 437 million, sought care from feldshers and other paramedical personnel [142:74]. Even taking into account the difficulties of making such generalized comparisons without regard to specific provider group or presenting complaints, it is clear from such figures that feldshers and other middle-medical workers are critical to the Soviet delivery system. The feldsher, moreover, makes up about 22 percent of all health care personnel and is the only middle-level provider to carry out physician activities [142].

The actual tasks performed by individual feldshers varies by the work setting. In rural areas, feldshers staffing feldsher-midwife posts may carry out all the ordinary work of a primary care physician. It has been estimated that as much as 52 percent of the patient population in rural areas receive their health care entirely from feldshers [153]. To deliver this magnitude of service, approximately 90,000 rural feldsher-midwife stations have been established [142:72].

Where the population density is low, such as in small villages on the outskirts of a rural medical district or on state farms, lumbering centers and tractor repair stations, feldshers provide curative and preventive care, engage in sanitary and anti-epidemic campaigns, and serve as public health educators. They run outpatient surgeries, make home visits, apply first aid, participate in follow-up surveillance of the population, prescribe medications, and carry out any special treatment procedures prescribed by physicians. In some rural settings the feldsher makes simple lab tests and provides physiotherapy treatments. In others she/he runs outpatient services for gynecological patients and manages pregnancy cases, delivers babies, and cares for infants up to the age of one year. Referrals of more difficult medical problems are made to the rural district hospital whose senior physician holds authority over the medical activities of the midwife posts [43, 52, 148, 154].

While feldshers in rural posts practice quite independently of supervision, in urban settings they are considered primarily as assistants to physicians. Their roles in urban hospitals have diminished in recent years as the number of Soviet physicians has increased. Still, they are a vital part of the urban delivery system where they practice in polyclinics, industrial units, ambulance corps, sanitary-epidemiological stations, medical laboratories, and special category dispensaries such as those which treat patients with mental illness, tuberculosis, cancer or venereal diseases [53]. In the workshop district system, they may work under the supervision of an industrial physician or they may staff the health posts which operate as the primary units of the industrial health service. These health posts, located on the premises of industrial enterprises, are under the supervision of a physician from the factory medical department or from a district polyclinic. On a day-to-day basis, however, the feldsher independently performs initial-level emergency and preventive medical care for all workers in a specified section of the enterprise [104].

Urban feldshers also play important roles in school health services where they carry out day-to-day first aid, and preventive measures. Since there are no social workers in the Soviet medical system, moreover, urban feldshers often function in social-work-type roles [142]. In addition, there are a number of urban feldshers who work in teams with physicians and orderlies to provide emergency services from a network of specialized emergency treatment centers. These emergency teams, called *skoraya*, are organized by medical specialty areas so that the responsibilities of feldshers vary by the type of team involved [32]. In general, such assignments require a high level of skill in the use of sophisticated equipment and life-support techniques. The majority of these skoraya feldshers are males, incidentally, which is in contrast to the generally female composition of the various health care provider groups [160]. Overall, more than 75 percent of feldshers and about 72 percent of physicians are women and Soviet nurses are virtually all females [81, 153].

Feldsher sanitarians perform another set of functions which, again varies by the field of activity. These workers are generally based in a sanitation and epidemiological center which has the responsibility for investigation, surveillance, and analysis of public health problems. Feldsher duties in such positions might include such activities as routine inspections of water supplies, inspection of food handling procedures, laboratory work in bacteriology, chemistry or parasitology, epidemiological field surveys, or functioning as a health educator or medical statistician [104].

X. SELECTED COMPARISONS

Although it is rather commonplace to read in the journals of American medicine that the role of the Soviet feldsher is like that of the American public health nurse [53, 109], because of the great variety of roles involved, it is important when making such comparisons to specify not only what kind of feldsher is being referred to but also what kind of public health nurse. Whereas the rural feldsher and the Kentucky Frontier Nurse, for example, each assume large responsibilities for the independent delivery of primary health care, neither of these groups are truly representative of all feldshers nor of all public health nurses. A likening of the feldsher to the public health nurse in this country, furthermore, seems to direct the focus away from the essential medical functions of the Soviet practitioner. This, in part, reflects the previously acknowledged difficulty of attempting to draw similarities between occupational roles in different cultures. Such attempts are inherently limited by the fit of the models being compared. Unlike much of the work cited here which merely assumes the comparability of feldshers with physician assistants, this paper has presented a brief contextual framework of the separate medical delivery systems within which the middle-level workers of each country function. It, thus, becomes feasible to take into account the relationship of the particular medical assistant group and the totality of health resources within their respective systems.

These relative comparisons facilitate a more refined interpretation of similarities and differences because they, in effect, standardize the unit of measurement. For example, rather than try to show that some feldshers in their daily tasks carry out similar types of work as do some physician assistants, it is more revealing to point out that while there are about as many feldshers as there are physicians in the Soviet Union, the PAs in this country are outnumbered by physicians by a factor of nearly 30 to 1. Such figures clearly demonstrate a much greater societal dependency on the feldsher than on the physician assistant. Recognition of this enormous discrepancy in the societal dependency factor aids in establishing a more realistic comparative structure. While such information does not explain why the discrepancy is so wide, it certainly alerts us to avoid facile judgments based solely upon faulty assumptions of the functional equivalency of PAs and feldshers.

A similar type of contextual analysis may be applied to compare any number of features of the two groups. The four examined here are those thought to be most relevant for the projection of physician assistant viability: controlling interests, compensation, occupational identity, and provider competition.

A. Controlling Interests

Although the United States and the Soviet Union are each highly industrialized and economically advanced nations and each have similar health needs and similar technological capacities, their disparate political climates and economic priorities have resulted in distinct health care delivery structures. The feldsher is an employee responsible to a centrally planned and state-coordinated national health service, while the PA answers directly to the physicians who dominate the delivery of service in the decentralized medical market existing in the United States. This difference is crucial. It reflects basically different medical ideologies and ultimate power sources. In the USSR, the interests of the Communist Party determine the particular development and allocation of health services resources. In the United States, on the other hand, which resources will be available, in what amounts and in what configuration are ultimately determined by the economic goals of the more powerful segments of the country's medical marketplace. The reason the feldsher has become so firmly entrenched in the Soviet system is that the use of this special type of provider enabled the government leaders to allot scarce national resources in a fashion which would further their particular political objectives. The crucial question which must be asked, then, is whether the physician assistant will prove as valuable to the market interests in the United States.

The American medical market is an enormously complex system. Those segments most likely to chart the future course of physician assistants are the physician and nursing professions, hospitals and other facilities in which health care is delivered, banking and financial interests which provide capital for such facilities based upon profit potential, the insurance industry, business and industrial concerns which shoulder many of the health care costs for their employees, and consumers of health care services. In addition, governmental units affect these market arrangements. Elected representatives of the public are responsible for developing and implementing social policy on the provision of health care and for making spending decisions for massive public programs such as Medicare and Medicaid. They are also empowered to determine consumer options through the processes of licensure and regulation. Finally, the nation's intellectuals in universities and research institutes articulate with market forces through the provision of knowledge which assesses current and projected resources on such dimensions as efficiency, cost effectiveness, and public acceptability

None of these market segments functions independently from the others. While some are clearly more powerful, it is extremely unlikely that the self-interests of any single group could prevail without the support of at least some of the other segments. In the past, coalitions of physicians, hospitals, pharmaceutical firms, and insurers formed a powerful bloc which largely dictated market arrangements. Today, these traditional alliances are less certain. The public outcry against continuing cost escalation has heightened the possibility of large-scale governmental regulation. Attempting to avoid such external strictures, the various market sectors are utilizing new strategies which in some cases pose direct threats to the economic survival of former allies. Physicians in many areas of the country, for example, are setting up free-standing outpatient, emergency, and surgical clinics which are successfully competing with area hospital facilities, themselves heavily burdened by fixed overhead costs. Hospitals are responding by adopting business management and marketing programs aimed at economies of scale and services geared to consumer appeal.

In this current climate of market turmoil, it is impossible to be certain how each of the controlling interest groups is likely to act toward the continuation of the PA occupation. Clearly the projected oversupply of physicians has already resulted in the loss of some support from the dominant medical profession. Nurses, whose numbers are again exceeding market demands in some areas of the country, can be expected to join physician groups in opposing any measures which would grant independent licensure to PAs, give them prescription rights, or make possible direct reimbursement for their services. Pharmaceutical companies, hospitals, and insurers, on the other hand, may see the utilization of PA services as a way to extend markets and to control delivery costs. Business and industry are also quite likely to embrace the cost effectiveness of PA services. At the same time, though, labor unions and other special interest consumer groups, such as the elderly and minorities, are apt to strongly object to attempts to substitute PA services for physician services among their ranks if such changes are perceived as differentially lowering the quality of care available to them.

By themselves, the wishes of the elderly or the minorities may not have much impact on a profit-driven market, but the second-class medicine charge, not surprisingly, is being argued forceably by physician organizations as well. This popular ideological appeal for the highest quality of care, defined as physician care, to be available to all U.S. residents may persuade other powerful interests to side against continued growth of the PA movement. It seems more likely, however, that each separate interest group will weigh the economic impact of PAs on their own survival struggles and will act according to this projected cost/benefit outcome. Since the limited utilization of PAs has been demonstrated clearly to be cost effective in hospitals, in long-term care facilities, and in other institutional settings, where the power of physicians no longer goes unquestioned, it is entirely possible that such employer organizations and their economic allies may use their own considerable influence to support the continuation of the PA occupation. If this happens, then physician assistants may be able to outlast the currently ominous situation.

B. Compensation

The second issue raised by the study is that of compensation. The feldsher is employed by the socialist state to provide services financed from public coffers and made available to the nation's citizens without charge. His/her salary averages about the same as that received by the country's nurses [42] and is only slightly lower than that of a fully qualified physician [154]. Almost all educational expenses are paid for by the government, including living expenses during the training period. In addition, special financial and retirement benefits are provided as incentives to those who accept posts in underserviced rural areas. The government also funds the costs of continuing educational programs to insure the constant upgrading of knowledge and skill.

By contrast, the PA must negotiate wage and benefit remuneration for his/her services from the employing physician or institution. The mean salary of civilian PAs across all specialties in 1980 was $22,000, while the mean salary reported among all civilian physicians in this country in the same year was $80,900 [24]. Government funds have in the past provided much of the development and overhead costs of the educational programs, but most PA students have had to pay out-of-pocket monies for tuition, books and living expenses during the training period.

The economic well-being of physician assistants is plainly spliced to the issue of third-party payments. In the United States approximately 90 percent of the citizens are covered by some form of health insurance, but only those who are elderly, officially poor, or who fit in certain special-needs categories receive free or significantly reduced-fee coverage from the government. Utilization of the various types of health resources depend in large measure upon the reimbursement policies of the insurers. Both patients and potential employers are influenced in their decisions to utilize the serives of PAs by the availability of third-party funding. Although the new practitioners have made some gains in this area, they are still far from attaining full recognition by the various insurance mechanisms.

A quick resolution to the reimbursement problem is unlikely. Among today's rapidly changing forces, there are several indicators, however, that support the possibility of an optimistic outcome for physician assistants. Strictures on un-bridled reimbursement expenditures are arising on numerous fronts. Prospective payment caps on in-hospital procedures, increased copayment premium costs, requirements for pre-hospital admission reviews, and mandatory second-opinion consultations for elective surgery are among the new tactics being promoted by insurers to stem the runaway costs of medical care policies. Many business and industrial firms, unwilling or unable to shoulder the increasingly burdensome cost of employee protection benefits, are adopting self-insurance plans wherein the companies, themselves, assume the fiduciary risk and tailor the scope of coverage to both the particular need-profiles of their employees and their own profit requirements.

In addition to the various cost-shifting and expenditure-capping strategies currently underway, there appears to be growing interest among insurers in extending benefit coverage for selected preventive care measures such as stress-management supervision, for more cost-efficient delivery modalities such as outpatient surgeries and home care management, and for the services of less costly practitioners. The fate of physician assistants largely hinges upon the outcome of these current deliberations over compensation.

Physician assistant training is usually geared toward the assumption of routine medical tasks and there now exists voluminous evidence which demonstrates the proficiency of this skilled provider in the management of uncomplicated cases. Under certain conditions, if the insurance industry begins to reimburse separately the fees for PA services in these more mundane areas of medical work, it could stimulate increased interest in these practitioners. If, for example, insurers lowered reimbursement ceilings on procedures easily delegated to and performed by PAs, the profitability of physician performance of such tasks would decrease. At the same time, patients would be encouraged to seek out physician assistants for routine care, rather than having to pay the non-reimbursed portion of the higher physician fees.

Direct reimbursement for PA services in preventive care and chronic care where currently unmet need exists, would be likely to have an initial effect of increasing overall health care expenditures. Since many preventive and chronic care services are currently excluded by most existing insurance mechanisms, expanded reimbursement coverage over such services could produce an initial bulge in the demand for them. Over time, however, the greater attention to preventive measures and to more careful surveillance of routine chronic condi-tions would be expected to lower total health care expenditures as demand for the more costly treatment regimens necessary in acute and advanced disease states is consequently reduced.

C. Occupational Identity

The third factor for comparison is occupational identity. The highly centralized control of the Soviet network of educational facilities for the training of feldshers and other middle-level health personnel has resulted in a product uniformity quite unmatched by the diverse PA programs. Some American writers, such as Kaminski [79], have argued that such diversity among PA programs is a healthy indicator of growth and improvement in the new field. Many others [74, 139, 144], however, charge that the lack of program standardization is a major impediment to the attainment of a distinct occupational identity. Those holding the latter opinion maintain that without a clearly identifiable role, it is much harder for physician assistants to attain the professional endorsement and public acceptance needed to assure the group's continuance.

Although the tasks performed by rural feldshers differ from the more specialized functions of their urban counterparts and while the roles of urban feldshers vary by specialty post, there appears to be, nonetheless, little confusion about the placement of the feldsher position within the health care structure. At various periods the feldsher has been accused of being a second-class, or inferior-quality, doctor [109], but the much more prevalent interpretation of the role has been of a middle-grade or limited-function medical practitioner.

By comparison, the physician assistant role remains poorly defined. Often, neither physicians nor patients know what may be expected of the new providers [174]. PAs, themselves, are sometimes unsure of their identity as well. The confusion continues in spite of increased attempts in recent years to assure a minimum of educational standardization via accreditation and certification mechanisms. There appear to be three major reasons for the problem: (1) since PAs are often persons who have switched from other careers, the earlier identities may continue to affect the perception of the new role; (2) since the educational period is relatively brief and dominated by role models from other occupations, there is little opportunity for trainees to form a distinct role identity; and (3) since the practice opportunities must, in most cases, be negotiated individually, the resulting job descriptions may vary widely among disarticulated PA positions. Both professional associations, the American Academy of Physician Assistants (A.A.P.A.) and the Association of Physician's Assistant Programs (A.P.A.P.), have recognized the problems generated by the lack of role clarity and have directed considerable effort to alleviate them. Interestingly, however, to date there have been few attempts to incorporate formal role-identification courses into the educational curriculum. This differs, for example, from the directed efforts in nursing where students study nursing history and professional development as a standard requirement.

The lack of solid role identity has subtle yet far-reaching effects. When not only outsiders but the role occupants, themselves, harbor confusion over the PA identity, the questions of commitment to the role becomes salient. On the one hand, a lone physician assistant working among more traditional health care providers may lack identity reinforcement and a sense of belonging. To offset the alienating effects of these circumstances, such a person may attempt to identify more closely with the supervising physician. If the shift of loyalty to one's employer is great enough, the individual PA may be reluctant to affiliate with the more remote PA colleagues and may even resist organized attempts to counter the growing pressure from physician groups. On a broad scale, displaced commitment could weaken seriously the occupation's ability to defend successfully its so recently acquired stake in the medical sphere.

On the other hand, it is possible that the current challenge confronting physician assistants will provide an impetus for increased cohesion and group identity. The mutual imperative to join forces against external threats may heighten the awareness of commonalities and, thus, sharpen the occupational distinction. Increased political activity among PA leaders and expanded grassroots involvement in a united campaign for professional recognition are likely results of such polarization.

If PAs should persist in their failure to project a clearly defined role in the complex network of health care delivery tasks, the occupation's vulnerability to outside charges of redundancy and expendability will be amplified. In today's highly charged competitive atmosphere which is forcing even physicians to take stock of their previously unquestioned domain, the continued lack of unique claims could prove to be an insurmountable disadvantage for physician assistants.

D. Provider Competition

The final point to be discussed is this competition among providers. The relationship of the feldsher and the physician assistant to other health care providers in their respective systems is an important factor in the difference between the two groups. Although much of the success the PA has enjoyed in gaining favor among powerful financial and legal sources is due to the endorsement of prominent physician sponsors, recently there has appeared increasing evidence of a clash between the new occupation's economic interests and those of the rising numbers of physicians, particularly family and general practitioners and general pediatricians.

The threat from nursing, moreover, appears even stronger today than it did in the past. Organized nursing has grown increasingly sophisticated in its political efforts to define and protect its professional territory. There appears to be little doubt that this group will continue to resist the professional claims of PAs from which nurses seem to have nothing to profit. If the recent gains in achieving enhanced legal authority for specially trained nurses to diagnose and treat illnesses and to prescribe medications in the state of New York [102] are harbingers of nursing's future direction, moreover, it is reasonable to suggest that this group represents a formidable source of continuing opposition to the PA movement.

A third group whose territory is affected by physician assistants consists of those physicians who are foreign medical graduates (FMGs). As a result of the visa restrictions tied to the Health Professions Educational Assistance Act of 1976, the supply of FMGs has been sharply reduced. The drastic cutback has created a deficiency in house staff positions great enough to threaten substantial disruption of services in some large metropolitan hospitals, psychiatric institutions, and Veterans Administration facilities [62, 175]. Even though legal restrictions still hamper the full utilization of PAs in many institutional settings, such barriers could be overcome in the future as hospitals seek ways to compete with the rising numbers of profit-eroding, freestanding emergency clinics and ambulatory care centers. If these changes materialize, PAs would be in direct competition with FMGs for house staff positions.

Alternatively, the growing number of new physicians whose initial salary requirements may not exceed by much those of more experienced physician assistants, could mean a decrease in institutional reliance on both FMGs and PAs as hospitals opt to employ more resident physicians. The deciding factors in such circumstances will likely include issues of quality such as continuity of care, as well as strictly economic considerations. For example, the tenure of resident physicians in hospitals is relatively brief, necessitating frequent adjustments to staff changes. As a result, some hospitals may prefer to rely largely on physician assistants whose more restricted job options would assure their greater employment stability.

The fate of the PA occupation, then, is inextricably tied to the changes occurring among physicians, nurses, and institutional providers. Contrary to the benign acceptance of PAs which occurred during the era of personnel shortages, today neither physicians nor nurses can be expected to champion the cause of a practitioner group whose work is seen as encroachment in an increasingly oversaturated employment milieu. On the other hand, the competitive environment could generate greater support for PAs from hospitals and insurers who are motivated by falling profits to seek rational alternatives to the soaring costs of health care provision.

The situation in the Soviet Union is less sensitive to interprofessional struggles. An increased emphasis on specialization and highly developed skills combined with the availability of rising numbers of fully trained physicians, has resulted in a reduction in the number of feldsher posts in large urban hospitals and an increase in assignments of feldshers to special category polyclinics, industrial health posts, and sanitary-epidemiological stations. The many new hospitals being built throughout the rural countryside combined with increased incentives to induce feldshers to work in such facilities is expected to further accelerate the urban to rural shift [171]. Such adjustments to the resource allocation patterns are largely centralized political and bureaucratic matters where professional claims bear only indirect influence. Thus, competition with physicians is a relatively minor factor in feldsher survival.

Territorial problems between feldshers and foreign physicians or feldshers and nurses, moreover, are nonexistent. While there are special schools in the nation which train medical students from foreign countries, neither those graduates nor FMGs are utilized at all in the regular health care delivery system. With nurses, there is no rivalry because their duties and those of feldshers are quite distinct and tend to be complementary rather than competitive. The expanded medical role assumed by feldshers is in sharp contrast with the far more restricted responsibilities of nurses [109]. One author [53], for example, has described the duties of the typical Soviet nurse as being comparable to those of an office assistant or nurse's aide in the United States. Thus, neither group poses a threat to the other's occupational claims.

A crucial factor in the relatively uncompetitive structure of the Soviet system is the Medical Workers Union. This body constitutes the power base for all categories of health personnel. The single interest group differs significantly from the plurality of professional associations aggressively involved in seeking exclusive advantage in the United States system. When combined with the frequent overlap in work roles and a free-enterprise initiative, this multiplicity of separate interest groups in the United States encourages an atmosphere of contest, dispute, and protectionism. Until very recently the favorability conferred on physicians through tradition, training, and a long-entrenched nexus with financial and political powers has ensured their market hegemony. As a result of the persistent, ungovernable inflationary trends in health services costs over the last two decades, however, there is growing support for a major restructuring of the delivery mechanisms. Nearly all of the revisions currently under consideration would levy some measure of constraint or regulation or fee setting and resource utilization via curtailment of reimbursement policies and shifts in criteria for funding of capital investments, research, and educational programs. Although the final outcome of the revisionary efforts is far from settled, any solution which imposes added checks on the free market forces is likely to enhance the relative position of PAs and other mid-level practitioners.

XI. CONCLUSION

Throughout this paper there has been an attempt to describe the unique circumstances surrounding the development of the physician assistant occupation. After twenty years, the provider group seems poised at the watershed of massive changes in the U.S. medical delivery system. In an attempt to more clearly grasp the potential of the occupation, a comparison was made with a foreign counterpart, the Soviet feldsher. By using a contextual analysis of each provider group, it was possible to demonstrate many of their similarities and differences. Even more importantly, comparisons of the groups within the context of their own medicosocial systems, establishes a basis for using certain components from the lengthy experience of the Soviet feldsher to examine the projection of continued viability for the currently threatened PAs. Having traced the history of each occupation from very different roots to their present rather similar statuses, four features of comparison were selected to analyze the viability issue:

1. *Controlling interests.* While the feldsher has long served the interests of the centralized, state-controlled health service in the USSR, the physician assistant in the United States is employed by individual physicians in a decentralized, professionally dominated delivery system. Although the professional groups which represent physicians have recently withdrawn their earlier support of PAs, other factions of the medical market such as hospitals, businesses, and consumers are likely to champion the middle-level providers for their potential to help stem exploding health costs. Moreover, the huge infusion of capital into medicine from private and public coffers combined with the well-documented decline of public confidence in physicians [10, 50, 39] has sharply altered the traditional power configuration. It is no longer feasible for a lone interest group to control the system. Thus, while the loss of physician backing would pose a serious hurdle to PAs, it no longer sounds an automatic death knell for the new providers.

2. *Compensation.* The services of feldshers, as employees of the socialist state, are provided without charge to Soviet citizens. As part of the huge centralized delivery system, feldsher salaries are but one of the many factors which governmental controls hold in check. In contrast, both the services and fees of physician assistants are being perceived by some observers as costly additions to an already financially strained U.S. market. Much evidence suggests PAs will prove particularly cost effective in preventive care areas but the third-party reimbursement system, more geared toward immediate dollar returns, has been slow to include coverage for the services of these mid-level practitioners. This exclusion from the standard insurance mechanisms is currently the single greatest barrier inhibiting the growth of the occupation.

3. *Occupational identity.* In contrast to the feldsher who enjoys a firmly entrenched, well-defined position of integral importance to the Soviet delivery system, the physician assistant is currently caught in a state of identity confusion. Lacking independent licensure, PA work roles are largely circumscribed by physicians who vary greatly in their willingness to delegate tasks. If the tentative movement toward institutional sponsorship of PAs should gain momentum, a probable outcome would be increased standardization of work roles for the mid-level group. Not only would physician assistants, themselves, be in an enhanced position to negotiate increased control over their role boundaries and work performance, but policy makers who may support the greater utilization of PAs would likely find hospital administration channels more accessible to petitions from external interests.

4. *Provider competition.* Competition between provider groups has rela-

tively minor impact on the pattern of health care delivery in the Soviet system. In large measure this is due to the lack of redundancy in work domain. The roles of feldsher complement rather than compete with those of other Soviet practitioners. Encroachment of professional territory is minimized through strategic balancing of interests within the Medical Workers Union which is the solitary power base for all health personnel. When resources do overlap, as has recently occurred in some urban facilities, central administration is likely to redistribute career assignments in order to spread coverage to underserved areas and to reduce potential tension among providers. No comparable regulatory mechanism currently exists in the United States which would buffer the competition between physician assistants and other providers of health care. Lacking a powerful central coordinating unit, the various professional groups vie among themselves to establish work domains and market advantage. Not surprisingly, rising public demands for reining the unbridled costs of health care has led to even greater protectionism among the practitioners. Both nursing and physician groups have called for reduced reliance on physician assistants. At the same time, hospitals and other institutions appear to be stepping up their interest in the mid-level providers. If barriers to institutional employment and reimbursement are removed the utilization of PAs in such facilities could not only offset the results of physician opposition but lead to a greatly increased demand for their services.

In the final analysis the fate of physician assistants will be influenced by many factors in addition to the four selected here for critique. In certain respects, the present health care scene appears not to favor the future of physician assistants. The current administration's drastic reduction in federal funding for training programs for health personnel, its increased shift of monies into defense budgets, its transfer to the states of responsibility for many of the separate categorical health programs, its focusing on dismantling of much of the regulatory mechanisms, and its substantial reduction in Medicare and Medicaid programs [14, 124] would all be expected to have significant and probably negative effects on the PA occupation's present struggles to maintain early gains.

On the other hand, there are signs that the retrenchment policies of today may, in many ways, be as supportive of the PA concept as were the expansionist policies existent when it began in the 1960s. Alarmed by the increasing responsibilities being shifted into their own laps, consumer and business groups have stepped up their demands for curbs to the exploding price of health care. They are indicating a growing resistance to the traditional delivery mechanisms which allowed them little say in market decisions. These counterpressures appear to be shifting the balance of power in the health care system away from the long-entrenched professional dominance toward a more pluralistic arrangement. At the same time, evidence continues to mount that the PA offers significant potential for reducing costs of primary-level medical services while maintaining a high level of care. If, then, the consumer and business interests elect to revise their utilization patterns by increasing their reliance on the less costly PA services, the United States could witness a major realignment in medical labor. The long experience of the Soviet feldsher clearly demonstrates the tremendous capacity for extending a nation's primary health care resources through the rational utilization of middle-level providers, but until very recently there has been little impetus to adopt a comparable two-tier system of care in the United States.

The current climate in the United States is one of widening cognitive dissonance wherein spectacular scientific achievements holding forth the promise of a far healthier citizenry are accompanied by agonizing questions asking how the costs of such advancements are to be met. Within less than a decade, the venerable proscriptions against proprietary facilities, professional advertising, and public accountability have given way to a kaleidoscope of new for-profit services keenly geared to consumer demand. As a result, competition between providers today depends heavily upon marketplace advantage. In the case of health care, however, the usual market forces of supply and demand operate within a unique context of payment mechanisms and societal values. Since few consumers pay for health care at the point of purchase, third-party payers wield a disproportionate influence on resource availability. Given the profit motive of most insurers, it is not surprising that regardless of consumer need, limitations on reimbursement are placed on services which treat particularly costly conditions such as those associated with alcoholism and mental illness. In a related fashion, most insurers have been reluctant to cover services provided by mid-level practitioners. The rationale for this reluctance appears to be concern over the anticipated cost bulge which would accompany the start-up of such coverage. Thus, like many preventive care measures whose cost-lowering benefits take years to materialize, the potentially cost-effective PAs have been slow in attracting the benefit dollar.

The social values surrounding the distribution of health care exert additional constraints on the medical marketplace. The prevailing ideology in the United States during much of the last 30 years has been that health care is a right of all citizens. Although never fully realized in practice, the societal value for equal access to medical resources holds a strong grip on the public conscience. This appeal to equal access is currently being used by opponents of physician assistants who argue that the use of mid-level providers would lead to a second-class medical system for the poor of the country. Those making the second-class charge, however, rarely note the inequities of access currently suffered by the country's disadvantaged. It is reasonable to believe that many rural and inner-city poor who now have limited contact with health care providers would be pleased to have ready access to the services of a physician assistant. More to the point, the overwhelming evidence suggests that the care provided by today's physician assistants, within the limited scope of their training, is not only *not* of second-class quality but may even be superior to that furnished by traditional providers.

Perhaps now is the time, then, to consider seriously the proposals that suggest a two-level medical care system for the United States [61, 127, 138]. A division of labor in medicine could be based on the utilization of the least expensive personnel fully capable of carrying out a given function. The idea of sharing limited aspects of medical work between physicians and physician assistants offers not only the promise of expanding health care services to previously disenfranchised groups in society but would also insure that the more highly developed and costly skills of physicians would be optimally utilized in the more challenging medical tasks. The Soviet experience attests to the potential for such a scheme but the many differences between the delivery systems of the two countries suggest that, to be successful in the United States, the division of labor will need to accommodate vastly different economic, political and ideological realities.

ACKNOWLEDGMENT

This paper in a slightly different form and with greatly reduced detail was presented at American Public Health Association meetings, Montreal, Canada, November, 1982.

NOTES

1. According to Kaser's 1976 account [81], only one female has held the position of Union Minister of Health: M. D. Kovigina, in 1954–1959.

REFERENCES

1. Aday, Lu Ann, Ronald Adnersen, and Gretchen V. Fleming. Health Care in the U.S., Equitable for Whom? Beverly Hills, California: Sage, 1980.
2. American Academy of Physician Assistants. Membership Director, 1981–1982. Washington, D.C.: American Academy of Physician Assistants, 1981.
3. American Academy of Physician Assistants. Physician Assistant Fact Sheets. Information packet distributed by American Academy of Physician Assistants, Arlington, Virginia. 1981.
4. Andersen, Ronald, Joanna Kravits, and Oden W. Anderson. "The public's view of the crisis in medical care: An impetus for changing delivery systems?" *Economic and Business Bulletin* 24: 44–52, 1971.
5. Andreoli, Kathleen G. "Physician's assistants and nurse practitioners: A harmonious future." *The P. A. Journal* 6: 126–29, 1976.
6. Armer, Michael. "Methodological problems and possibilities in comparative research." Chapter 2 in Michael Armer and Allen D. Grimshaw (eds.), Comparative Social Research: Methodological Problems and Strategies. New York: John Wiley and Sons, 1973.
7. Association of Physician Assistant Programs. National Health Practitioner Program Profile 1981–1982. Fifth Edition. Arlington, Virginia, 1981.
8. Begun, James W. "Refining physician manpower data." *Medical Care* 15: 780–86, 1977.
9. Bergner, Lawrence and Alonzo S. Yerby. "Low income and barriers to use of health service." *New England Journal of Medicine* 278: 541–45, 1968.

10. Berlant, Jeffrey L. Profession and Monopoly: A Study of Medicine in the United States and Great Britain. Berkeley: University of California Press, 1975.

11. Bliss, Ann A. and Eva D. Cohen (eds.). The New Health Professionals. Germantown, Maryland: Aspen Systems Corporation, 1977.

12. Bobula, Joel D. and Louis J. Goodman. Physician Distribution and Medical Licensure in the U.S., 1977. Center for Health Services Research and Development. Monroe, Wisconsin: American Medical Association, 1979.

13. Bodenheimer, Thomas, Steven Cummings, and Elizabeth Harding. "Capitalizing on illness: The health insurance industry." Pg. 69–84 in Vicente Navarro (ed.), Health and Medical Care in the U.S.: A Critical Analysis. Farmingdale, New York: Baywood, 1975.

14. Brazda, J. F. Washington Report. The Nation's Health, 3, 1982.

15. Breslauer, George W. "Khrushchev reconsidered." Pp. 50–70 in Stephen F. Cohen, Alexander Rabinowitch, and Robert Sharlet (eds.), The Soviet Union since Stalin. Bloomington, Indiana: Indiana University Press, 1980.

16. Breslau, Naomi. "The role of the nurse-practitioner in a pediatric team: Patient definitions." Medical Care 15 (Dec.): 1014–23, 1977.

17. Breslau, Naomi, Alvin H. Novack, and Gerrit Wolf. "Work settings and job satisfaction: A study of primary care physicians and paramedical personnel." Medical Care 16: 850–62, 1978.

18. Breytspraak, Linda M. and Louis R. Pondy. "Sociological evaluation of the physician's assistant's role relations." Group Practice 18: 32–41, 1969.

19. Brislin, Richard W., Walter J. Lonner and Robert M. Thorndike. Cross-Cultural Research Methods. New York: John Wiley and Sons, 1973.

20. Budnick, Lawrence. "GMENAC estimates of physician shortages questioned." Letters to the Editor, American Journal of Public Health 71: 1171, 1981.

21. Brunner, Lillian S., Charles P. Emerson, Jr., L. Kraeer Ferguson, and Doris S. Suddarth. Textbook of Medical-Surgical Nursing. Second Edition. Philadelphia: Lippincott, 1970.

22. Burdett, Gaye L., Margaret Parken-Harris, Joan C. Kuhn and Gerlad H. Escovitz. "A comparative study of physicians' and nurses' conceptions of the role of nurse practitioners." American Journal of Public Health 68 (Nov.): 1090–95, 1978.

23. Carter, Reginald D. and Denis R. Oliver. "An analysis of salaries for clinically active physician assistants." Physician Assistant 7: 14–27, 1983.

24. Butter, Irene. "Health manpower research: A survey." Inquiry 4: 6–29, 1967.

25. Cawley, James F. and Walter A. Stein. "GMENAC revisited: Questionable assumptions and conflicting data." Physician Assistant 7: 161–162, 1983.

26. Celentano, David D. "Critical policy issues concerning new health practitioners—quality of care." Sociological Symposium 23 (Summer): 61–77, 1978.

27. Coe, Rodney and Leonard Fichtenbaum. "Utilization of physician assistants: Some implications for medical practice." Medical Care 10: 497–504, 1972.

28. Coleman, Sinclair. Physician Distribution and Rural Access to Medical Services: Executive Summary. Prepared for Health Resources Administration, DHEW (R-1887/1-HEW) by Rand, Santa Monica, California, 1976.

29. Chicago Tribune News Service. "Doctors bid to limit competition." Article in Akron Beacon Journal, June 12: A16, 1981.

30. Congressional Budget Office. Physician Extenders: Their Current and Future Role in Medical Care Delivery. Congressional Budget Office. Washington, D.C., 1979.

31. Cooper, David. "Current legislation as it affects reimbursement for P. A. services." The P. A. Journal (Winter-Spring): 25–30, 1974.

32. Cooper, John A. D. Report on Exchange Mission to U.S.S.R. on Health Planning and Medical Education, May 15–June 3, 1970 and Health Planning and Education of Health Professionals in the Soviet Union. Washington, D.C.: Associaion of American Medical Colleges, 1970.

33. Danforth, Nicholas. "The Current status of the MEDEX programs and their relationship to the physician's assistants concept." *Physician's Associate* (October): 123–32, 1972.
34. DeMaria, William. "The Marine physician assistant Program." *Physician s Associate* (October): 121–22, 1971.
35. Estes, E. Harvey and D. Robert Howard. "Potential for newer classes of personnel: Experience of the Duke Physician Assistant Program." *Journal of Medical Education* 45: 149–51, 1970.
36. Editorial Staff. "Operation MEDIHC." *Physician's Associate* (July): 63, 1971.
37. Federal Prison System. Facilities '78. U. S. Department of Justice, Washington, D.C., 1978.
38. Fein, Rashi. "An economist's view: Medical Manpower—a continuing crisis." *Journal of the American Medical Association* 201: 171–73, 1976.
39. Fasser, Carl. "Non-physician health care providers: A public policy for future health manpower." Paper presented at Conference on The Crisis in Health Profession's Strategy sponsored by National Health Council, Washington, D.C., 1981.
40. Field, Mark G. "American and Soviet medical manpower: Growth and evolution, 1910–1970." *International Journal of Health Services* 5: 455–74, 1975.
41. Field, Mark G. Soviet Socialized Medicine. New York: *The Free Press*, 1967.
42. Field, Mark. "Health personnel in the Soviet Union: Achievements and problems." *American Journal of Public Health* 56: 1904–20, 1966.
43. Field, Mark G. Doctor and Patient in Soviet Russia. Cambridge. Massachusetts: Harvard University Press, 1957.
44. Fisher, Donald. "The reimbursement challenge." *Physician Assistant & Health Practitioner* (December): 42, 44, 1979.
45. Fisher, Donald W. and Susan M. Horowitz. "The physician's assistant: Profile of a new health profession." Chapter 2 in Ann A. Bliss and Eva D. Cohen (Eds.) The New Health Professionals. Germantown, Maryland: Aspen Systems, 1977.
46. Fitzpatrick, Marsha. "The nurses versus the PA." *Physician's Associate* (July): 103, 1972.
47. Ford, Ann Suter. The Physician's Assistant: A National and Local Analysis. New York: Praeger, 1975.
48. Fottler, Myron D. "Physician attitudes toward physician extenders." *Medical Care* 17: 536–49, 1979.
49. Fottler, Myron D., Geoffrey Gibson, and Diane M. Pinchoff. "Physician attitudes toward the nurse practitioners." *Journal of Health and Social Behavior* 19: 303–11, 1978
50. Freidson, Eliot. Profession of Medicine. New York: Harper & Row, 1970
51. Frishauf, Peter. "Every PA knows someone in New Jersey." *Physician Assistant & Health Practitioner* (October): 9–10, 1979.
52. Fry, John. "Structure of medical care services in the U.S.S.R." *International Journal of Health Services* 2: 239–42, 1972.
53. Fry, John. Medicine in Three Societies. Guildford and London: MTP, 1969.
54. Fuchs, Victor. "The growing demand for medical care." *New England Journal of Medicine* 279: 190–95, 1968.
55. Funkenstein, Daniel H. Medical Students, Medical Schools and Society During Five Eras: Factors Affecting the Career Choices of Physicians 1958–1976. Cambridge, Massachusetts: Ballinger, 1978.
56. Garfield, Sidney, R. "The delivery of medical care." *Scientific American* 222: 15–20, 1970.
57. Gaus, Clifton, Stephen B. Morris, and David B. Smith. "The Social Security Administration physician extender reimbursement study: Anatomy of a quasi-experimental design." Pp. 341–51 in Ann A. Bliss and Eva D. Cohen, The New Health Professionals, Germantown, Maryland: Aspen Systems, 1977.
58. Geiger, H. Jack. "The illusion of change." *Social Policy* (Nov/Dec): 30–35, 1975.
59. Gibson, R. M. and C. R. Fisher. "National health expenditures fiscal year 1977." *Social Security Bulletin* 41: 3–20, 1978.

60. Ginzberg, Eli. The Limits of Health Reform. New York: Basic Books, 1977.
61. Goerke, L. S. Health Manpower, Action to Meet Community Needs. Report of the Task Force on Health Manpower. National Commission on Community Health Services. Washington, D.C.: Public Affairs Press, 1967.
62. Goodman, L. J. and L. E. Wunderman. Foreign medical graduates and graduate medical education. Journal of American Medical Association, 246, 854–858, 1981.
63. Graduate Medical Education National Advisory Committee. Summary Report. Vol. I. U. S. Department of Health and Human Services Publication No. (HRA) 81–651, 1980.
64. Graduate Medical Educational National Advisory Committee. GMENAC Staff Paper #2: Supply and Distribution of Physicians and Physician Extenders. U. S. Department of Health, Education, and Welfare. Health Resources Administration. DHEW (HRA) 78–11, 1978.
65. Greene, Richard. Assuring Quality in Medical Care. Cambridge, Massachusetts: Ballinger, 1976.
66. Greenfield, Sheldon, Anthony Kamaroff, Theodore Pass, Hjalmar Anderson, and Sharon Nessim. Efficiency and cost of primary care by nurses and physician assistants. New England Journal of Medicine 29, 1978.
67. Goldberg, George A., David Maxwell Jolly, Susan Hosek, and David S. C. Chu. "Physician's extenders' performance in Air Force clinics." Medical Care 19: 951–65, 1981.
68. Grimshaw, Allen D. "Comparative sociology: In what ways different from other sociologies?" Chapter 1 in Michael Armer and Allen D. Grimshaw (eds.), Comparative Social Research: Methodological Problems and Strategies. New York: John Wiley & Sons, 1973.
69. Gunther, John. Inside Russia Today. New York: Harper & Brothers, 1958.
70. Henry, Richard. "Use of physician's assistants in Gilchrist County, Florida." Health Services Report 87: 687–92, 1972.
71. Hershey, Nathan. "Legal issues concerning the physician's assistant." Physician's Associate (October): 110–14, 1972.
72. Hicks, Nancy. "Returning medics no longer spurned as civilian health aides." The New York Times, December 13, 1970.
73. Hoffman, Erik P. "Changing Soviet perspectives." Pp. 71–92 in Stephen F. Cohen, Alexander Robinowitch, and Robert Sharlet (eds.), The Soviet Union Since Stalin. Bloomington, Indiana: Indiana University Press, 1980.
74. Howard, D. R. The history, utility and greater advantages of the term 'physician associate.' Physician's Associate, (January), 4–5, 1972.
75. Hudson, Charles C. "Expansion of medical professional services with nonprofessional personnel." Journal of American Medical Association 176: 95–97, 1961.
76. Institute of Medicine. Costs of Education in the Health Professions: Report of a Study. Washington, D.C.: National Academy of Sciences, 1974.
77. Institute of Medicine. Report of a Study: A Manpower Policy for Primary Health Care. National Academy of Sciences, Washington, D.C., 1978.
78. Jeffers, James R., Marie F. Bognanno and John C. Bartless. "On the demand versus need for medical services and the concept of 'shortages.'" American Journal of Public Health 61: 46–63, 1971.
79. Kaminski, Katherine D. "Liberals vs. conservatives." Academy Opinion. Physician Assistant and Health Practitioner (August): 58, 1979.
80. Kane, Robert L., Josephine M. Kasteler, and Robert M. Gray. The Health Gap: Medical Services and the Poor. New York: Springer Publishing, 1976.
81. Kaser, Michael. Health Care in the Soviet Union and Eastern Europe. Boulder, Colorado: Westview Press, 1976.
82. Katterjohn, Karl. "Medicare reimbursement." Legislation, Health Practitioner (November/December): 14, 1977.

83. Katterjohn, Karl R. "Legislation: Reading the juggler's moves. ' *Physician Assistant* (May): 16, 18, 1980.
84. Kentucky State Health Planning Council. Preliminary State Health Plan, July 1 1983–June, 1986. Cabinet for Human Resources. Frankfort, Kentucky, 1983.
85. Kibbe, David. "Issues in physician recruitment to rural areas." *The Journal of the Maine Medical Association* 70: 268–70, 1979.
86. Knowles, John H. "Doing better and feeling worse: Health in the United States." *Daedalus* 106: 1–7, 1977.
87. Kosa, John. "The Nature of Poverty." In John Kosa and Irving K. Zola, (eds.), Poverty and Health, A Sociological Analysis. Revised Edition. Cambridge, Massachusetts: Harvard University Press, 1975.
88. Lasdon, Gail S., W. Steven Mork, David A Major, Wilbur W. Oaks, and Harold Kretzing. 'Physician time per patient reduced by the use of physician's assistants in two practice settings." *The P. A. Journal* (Winter) 27–31, 1974.
89. Lavin, Bebe F. "The Public and Care by Non-Physicians." In Challenges and Innovations in U.S. Health Care. Boulder, Colorado: Westview Press, 1981.
90. Lavin, Bebe F. and Marie R. Haug. "The public and care by non-physicians: Health policy considerations." Unpublished paper. Kent State University, Kent, Ohio, 1978.
91. Lenninger, Madeleine. "Towards conceptualization of transcultural health care systems: Concepts and a model" Pp. 3–22 in Madeleine Lenninger (ed.), Transcultural Health Care Issues and Conditions. Philadelphia: F. A. Davis Company, 1976.
92. Light, Judy A., Mary J. Crain, and Donald W. Fisher. "Physician assistant: A profile of the profession, 1976." *The P. A. Journal* 7: 109–23, 1977.
93. Luckey, E. Hugh. "The United States." Pp. 157–76 in John Z. Bowers and Elizabeth F. Purcell (eds.), The University and Medicine: The Past, the Present, and Tomorrow. New York: Josiah Macy, Jr. Foundation, 1977.
94. McCarthy, Carol. "Planning for health care." Pp. 346–70 in Steven Jonas and contributors. Health Care Delivery in the United States. New York: Springer, 1977.
95. McKibbin, Richard C. "Cost-effectiveness of physician assistants: A review of recent evidence." *The P. A. Journal* 8: 110–15, 1978.
96. McNerney, Walter S. "The role of technology in the development of health institution goals and programs." Pp. 101–12 in Morris F. Collen, (ed.), Technology and Health Care Systems in the 1980's. National Center for Health Services Research and Development. DHEW Pub. (HSM) 73–3016, 1972.
97. McNult, David R. "GMENAC: Its manpower forecasting framework." *American Journal Public Health* 71: 1116–24, 1981.
98. Mechanic, David. "Factors affecting receptivity to innovations in health-care delivery among primary-care physicians." Pp. 69–87 in Politics, Medicine, and Social Science. New York: Wiley and Sons, 1974.
99. Mechanic, David. "The growth of medical technology and bureaucracy: Implications for medical care." *Health and Society, Milbank Memorial Fund Quarterly* 55: 61–78, 1977.
100. Mendenhall, Robert C., Paul A. Repicky, and Richard E. Neville. "Assessing the utilization and productivity of nurse practitioners and physician's assistants: Methodology and findings on productivity." *Medical Care* 18: 609–23, 1980.
101. Mereness, Dorothy. "Recent trends in expanded roles of the nurse." *Nursing Outlook* 18: 30–3, 1970.
102. Merritt, R. State health reports. *The Nation's Health*, (August), 7, 1982.
103. Millar, James R. "Post-Stalin agriculture and its future." Pp. 135–54 in Stephen F. Cohen, Alexander Rabinowitch, and Robert Sharlet (eds.), The Soviet Union Since Stalin. Bloomington, Indiana: Indiana University Press, 1980.

104. Ministry of Health of the USSR. The Training and Utilization of Feldshers in the U.S.S.R. Geneva: World Health Organization, 1974.
105. Misek, G. I. (ed.). Socioeconomic Issues of Health 1979. Monroe, Wisconsin: American Medical Association, 1979.
106. Morgenstern, Robin. "PA-nurse paranoia: Reality or myth?" *Health Practitioner* (September/October): 10, 1977.
107. Morris, Stephen B. "Third party payment for the services of the assistant to the primary care physician." The *P. A. Journal* (Summer): 72–77, 1977.
108. Morris, Stephen B. and David B. Smith. "The distribution of physician extenders." *Medical Care* 15 (December): 1045–57, 1977.
109. Muller, James, Faye Abdellah, F. T. Billings, Arthur Hess, Donald Petit, and Roger Egeberg. "The Soviet health system." *New England Journal of Medicine* 286: 693–702, 1972.
110. Murrin, Kathleen L. "Laying the groundwork: Issues facing rural primary care." Pp. 3–29 in Gerald E. Bisbee, Jr. (ed.), Management of Rural Primary Care-Concepts and Cases. Chicago: The Hospital Research and Educational Trust, 1982.
111. Myers, Hu C. *The Physician's Assistant*. Parsons, West Virginia: McClain, 1978.
112. Navarro, Vicente. "The political economy of medical care." Pp. 85–112 in Vicente Navarro (ed.), Health ad Medical Care in the U.S.: A Critical Analysis. Farmingdale, New York: Baywood, 1975.
113. Navarro, Vicente. Social Security and Medicine in the U.S.S.R. Lexington, Massachusetts: Lexington Books, 1977.
114. Nelson, Eugene C., Arthur R. Jacobs, and Kenneth G. Johnson. "Patients' acceptance of physician's assistants." *Journal of American Medical Association* 228: 63–7, 1974.
115. Olendzki, M. C., R. P. Grann, and C. H. Goodrich. "The impact of medicaid on private care for the urban poor." *Medical Care* 10: 201–06, 1972.
116. Parker, Ralph C., Jr. and Andrew A. Sorensen. "The tides of rural physicians: The ebb and flow, or why physicians move out of and into small communities." *Medical Care* 16 (February): 152–66, 1978.
117. Pellengrino, Edmund D. "Forward" in Ann A. Bliss and Eva D. Cohan (eds.), The New Health Professionals. Germantown, Maryland: Aspen Systems Corporation, 1977.
118. Perkoff, Gerald T. "An effect of organization of medical care upon health Manpower distribution." *Medical Care* 16: 628–40, 1978.
119. Perry, Henry B. "Physician assistants: An overview of an emerging health profession." *Medical Care* 15: 982–90, 1977.
120. Perry, Henry B. and Bina Breitner. "An analysis of the specialty and geographic location of physician assistants in the United States." *American Journal of Public Health* 68: 1019–21, 1978.
121. Perry, Henry B. and Bina Breitner. Physician Assistants: Their Contributions to Health Care. New York: Human Sciences Press, 1982.
122. Perry, Henry B. and Donald W. Fisher. "The physician's assistant profession: Results of a 1978 survey of graduates." *Journal of Medical Education* 56: 839–45, 1981.
123. Pesznecker, Betty and Mary A. Draye. "Family nurse practitioners in primary care: A study of practice and patients." *American Journal of Public Health* 68: 977–80, 1978.
124. Peterson, H. N. Changing federal and state relationships—a new era in health? *Journal of the American Medical Association*, 245, 2169–2170, 1981.
125. Pickard, C. Glenn, Jr. "Midlevel practitioners: Nurse practitioners and physicians' assistants." Pp. 129–40 in John Noble (ed.), Primary Care and the Practice of Medicine. Boston: Little, Brown and Company, 1976.
126. Pluckham, Margaret L. "Professional territoriality: A problem affecting the delivery of health care." *The P. A. Journal* (Summer): 41, 1974.
127. Poe, William. "Medical care and changing times." *Physician's Associate* 1: 78–80, 1971.

128. Pondy, Louis R., Jeffrey M. Jones, and John A. Braun. "Utilization and productivity of the Duke physician's associate." *The P. A. Journal* (Winter): 32–58, 1974.
129. Popov, G. A. Principles of Health Planning in the U.S.S.R. Geneva: World Health Organization, 1971.
130. Pulsipher, Vaughn L., Hilman Castle, and Robert L. Kane. "A report of the findings of a model developed to assess and predict physician/MEDEX match stability." Proceedings of the Second National Conference on New Health Practitioners, March, New Orleans, Louisiana, 1974.
131. Ramos, Maryann. "The physician assistant as change agent." *Health Practitioner and Physician Assistant* (June): 104–05, 1979.
132. Record, Jane Cassels. Staffing Primary Care in 1990: Physician Replacement and Cost Savings. New York: Springer, 1981.
133. Reinhardt, Ewe, E. "The GMENAC: Forecast: An alternative view." *American Journal of Public Health* 71: 1149–57, 1981.
134. Roemer, Milton I. "Highlights of Soviet health services." *Milbank Memorial Fund Quarterly* 60: 373–406, 1962.
135. Roemer, Milton I. Rural Health Care. St. Louis: C. V. Mosby, 1976.
136. Roemer, Milton I. Social Medicine: The Advance of Organized Health Services in America. New York: Springer Publishing, 1978.
137. Roemer, Ruth, Charles Kramer, and Jeanne E. Frink. Planning Urban Health Services from Jungle to System. New York: Springer Publishing Company, 1975.
138. Rosinski, Edith F. "Education and the role of the physician." *Journal of the American Medical Association* 222: 473–75, 1972.
139. Rubin, Larry A. "Quest for unity," Editor's Message. *Physician Assistant* (November/December): 14, 1976.
140. Rudov, Melvin H. and Nancy Santangelo. Health Status of Minorities and Low-Income Groups. Pittsburgh: Centers for Health, Education, and Social Systems Studies. DHEW Publication No. (HRA) 79–627, 1979.
141. Rushing, William A. and David L. Miles. "Physicians, physicians' assistants, and the social characteristics of patients in Southern Appalachia." *Medical Care* 15: 1004–13, 1977.
142. Ryan, Michael. The Organization of Soviet Medical Care. Oxford, England: Basil Blackwell, 1978.
143. Ryan, T. Michael. "Primary medical care in the Soviet Union." *International Journal of Health Services* 2: 243–53, 1972.
144. Sadler, Alfred, Blair Sadler, and Ann Blessa. The Physician's Assistant Today and Tomorrow. New Haven: Yale University, 1972.
145. Salkever, David S., Elizabeth A. Skinner, Donald M. Steinwachs, and Harvey Katz "Episode-based efficiency comparisons for physicians and nurse practitioners." *Medical Care* 20: 143–53, 1982.
146. Schachtel, Bernard P. "The pediatric nurse practitioner Origins and challenges." *Medical Care* 16: 1019–26, 1978.
147. Schneller, Eugene S. and Jesse A. Simon. "A profile of the backgrounds and expectations of the class of 1977." *The P. A. Journal* 7: 67–72, 1977.
148. Schweiker, Richard. Comment quoted in Cleveland Plain Dealer, January 22: 10-A, 1982.
149. Schweitzer, Stuart O. "The relative costs of physicians and new health practitioners." Pp. 53–67 in Jane Cassels Record, with others, Staffing Primary Care in 1990. New York: Springer Publishing Company, 1981.
150. Segal, Richard, William Wilson, Michael Hogben, Bernie Asahina, Richard Murlock, and Peter Gerity. "Deployment-A six year perspective." *The P. A. Journal* 7: 198–204, 1977.
151. Sheehy, Ann and Sergei Voronitsyn. The All-Union Census of 1979 in the USSR. Munich: Radio Liberty Research Bulletin, 1980.

152. Sheps, Cecil and Miriam Bachar. "Rural areas and personal health services: Current strategies." *American Journal of Public Health* 71 (Supplement): 71–82, 1981.
153. Sidel, Victor W. "Feldshers and 'feldsherism': The role and training of the feldsher in the U.S.S.R." *New England Journal of Medicine* 278: 934–39, 1968a.
154. Sidel, Victor W. "Feldsher and 'feldsherism' (concluded): The role and training of the feldsher in the U.S.S.R." *New England Journal of Medicine* 278: 987–92, 1968b.
155. Smith, Richard A. "Medex: A demonstration program in primary medical care." *Northwest Medicine* 68 1023–30, 1969.
156. Stalker, Tim. "Fourth annual AAPA constituent chapter officers workshop-selling the profession." *Physician Assistant and Health Practitioner* 3: 57–62, 1979.
157. Stamps, Paula L., Eugene B. Piedmont, Dinah B. Slauitt, and Ann Marie Haase. "Measurement of work satisfaction among health professionals." *Medical Care* 15: 337–52, 1978.
158. Stead, Eugene A. "Manna from the physician's assistant program: A source of nourishment for medical educators." Pp. 161–72 in Judy Graves (ed.), The Future of Medical Education. Durham, North Carolina: Duke University Press, 1973.
159. Stewart, Charles T., Jr., and Corazon M. Siddayas. Increasing the Supply of Medical Personnel. Washington, D.C.: American Enterprise Institute for Public Policy Research, 1973.
160. Storey, Patrick B. The Soviet Feldsher as a Physician's Assistant. John E. Fogarty International Center for Advanced Study in the Health Sciences. DHEW Publication No. (NIH) 72–58, 1972.
161. Storms, Doris and John G. Fox. "The publics view of physicians' assistants and nurse practitioners." *Medical Care* 17: 526–35, 1979.
162. Sullivan, Judith A., Christy Z. Dachelet, Harry A. Sultz, Marie Henry, and Harriet D. Carrol. "Overcoming barriers to the employment and utilization of the nurse practitioner." *American Journal of Public Health* 68: 1097–1103, 1978.
163. System Sciences, Inc. Nurse Practitioner and Physician Assistant Training and Deployment Study. Final Report. Bethesda, Maryland: *System Science*, 1976.
164. Tanaka, Argustus M. "Problems facing rural physicians: Do the boondocks really need docs?" *Federation Bulletin* 65: 3–9, 1978.
165. Taylor, Mark, William Dickman, and Robert Kane. "Medical students' attitudes toward rural practice." *Journal of Medical Education* 48: 885–95, 1973.
166. Terris, Milton. "False starts and lesser alternatives." *Bulletin of the New York Academy of Medicine* 53: 129–40, 1977.
167. Torrens, P. R. and D. G. Yedvab. "Variations among emergency room populations: A comparison of four hospitals in New York City." *Medical Care* 8: 60–75, 1970.
168. U. S. Department of Health, Education, and Welfare: National Center for Health Services Research. Nurse Practitioners and Physician Assistants: A Research Agenda. Summary of the proceedings of a conference held June 21–22, 1977, in Warrentown, Virginia. DHEW (PHS) 79–3236, 1978.
169. U.S. Department of Health and Human Services. Third Report to the President and Congress on the Status of Health Professions Personnel in the United States. January. Hyattsville, Maryland: DHHS Publication No. 82-2, 1982.
170. Vacek, Pamela M., Taka Ashikaga, John H. Habry, and Janet P. Brown. "A model for health care delivery." *Medical Care* 16: 547–59, 1978.
171. Vezyukov, Zyacheslav. Dobeda Collective Farm, U.S.S.R., Interview at Northern Kentucky University, Highland Heights, Kentucky. July 17, 1984.
172. Weiler, Philip G. "Health manpower dialectic—physician, nurse, physician assistant." *American Journal of Public Health* 65: 858–63, 1975.
173. Weinerman, E. Richard, Robert S. Ratner, Anthony Robbins, and Marvin Lavenhar "Yale studies in ambulatory medical care V." Determinants of use of hospital emergency services." *American Journal of Public Health* 56: 1037–60, 1966.

174. Weston, Jerry L. "Ambiguities limit the role cf nurse practitioners and physician assistants." *American Journal of Public Health* 74: 6–7, 1984.

175. Whitman, N. A. The prospective effect of Public Law 94-484 on graduate medical programs. *Journal of Medical Education,* 53, 841–843, 1978.

176. Wise, Jarrett M. "Third Party reimbursement." *Physician Assistant* (November/December): 37–38, 40.1976.

177. Wright, Arthur W. "Soviet economic planning and performance." Pp. 113–34 in Stephen F. Cohen, Alexander Rabinowitch, and Robert Sharlet (eds.), The Soviet Union Since Stalin. Bloomington, Indiana: Indiana University Press, 1980.

178. Yankauer, Alfred. "Who shall deliver primary care?" *Editorial American Journal of Public Health* 70: 1048–50, 1980.

179. Editorial staff comment. *Physician Assistant and Health Practitioner.* (Oct.): 88 1979.

MOROCCAN IMMIGRANTS AND HEALTH CARE IN THE NETHERLANDS:

A CONFRONTATION OF CULTURAL SYSTEMS

Ingeborg P. Spruit

I. INTRODUCTION

In the past, densely-populated Europe was more accustomed to the phenomenon of mass emigration than mass immigration. The extensive labor (im)migration which took place in this part of the world during the last 30 years imposed considerable problems on countries such as the Netherlands, Belgium, West Germany, Switzerland, France and Great Britain.

Although there has always been migration among the Western European countries and it has certainly not been uncommon to admit foreigners into one's

Research in the Sociology of Health Care, Volume 5, pages 201-247.
Copyright © 1987 by JAI Press Inc.
All rights of reproduction in any form reserved.
ISBN: 0-89232-597-6

society, never before had these countries counted such a large number of non-European immigrants among their population.

After World War II, the new composition of the political map (refugees), the disturbed demographic balance and the economic reconstruction (the need for labor force), and the many colonies that became independent, influenced the changing migration policy [23]. Especially in France, Great Britain and the Netherlands, large numbers of foreigners were admitted or actively recruited to migrate temporarily. Shortly after the war this was compensated for by emigration of the indigenous population as well as by a rapidly expanding labor market. However, even before the admissions policy became more rigid because of the economic recession, there were signs that there would be many more societal problems than expected because the hired labor force turned out to be rather human.

Health care was one of the last sectors in society in which people openly realized that there were problems in dealing with (im)migrant laborers and their families. The first medical professionals to encounter nearly unsolvable problems were the occupational and social security physicians, quickly followed by the family doctors. Then psychiatrists began to recognize difficulties and finally even hospital staff, reluctantly, has found that it must deal with unfamiliar issues raised by clients from alien cultures.

In this article attention will be focused on one of the largest immigrant categories in the Netherlands, the Moroccans. The central theme will be: In this country with high-quality medical care and one of the best systems of social security and health insurance, medical care seems to fail in dealing with Moroccan immigrants. The immigrants, from their point of view, seem to disapprove of Dutch medical care and value their own health care. In order to understand this situation it is necessary to examine several important factors: the migration history, the social position of the immigrants in Dutch society, and the medical systems of their country of origin.

I will describe in succession:

1. Societal setting of the problem and background information: the composition of ethnic groups in the Netherlands; a short overview of origins and types of migrants; settlement, social position and integration.
2. The health care structure and common difficulties in health care in the Netherlands for health care personnel and for the immigrants.
3. The health care structure and its strong cultural bases in Morocco's urban and rural areas, which differs from the Dutch system.
4. Hypothesized origins of the difficulties of providing health care to Moroccan immigrants in the Netherlands: a) origins in the migrants culture (e.g. illness perceptions, illness behavior) and migration problems (social causes of illness), b) origins in health care itself: immigrant health care as

a mirror for western medicine, c) origins in society: migration history and social position.

II. IMMIGRATION AND IMMIGRANTS IN THE NETHERLANDS

The Netherlands have a long and outstanding tradition of admitting foreigners. In the 18th and 19th centuries it was known as a port of refuge for categories and individuals who were persecuted in their countries for political reasons, religion, or unaccepted scientific theories.

Between the two world wars impoverished Germans, Chinese, and others found their way to this country. Some of them strongly maintained their own cultural identity (Chinese, Jews), others assimilated into Dutch society (Germans, Poles). The majority managed to maintain themselves socially and economically at the same level as the indigenous population. After World War II, 250,000 immigrants came from Indonesia (1949) after this colony successfully attained its independence. In 1951 another 12,500 came from the South Moluccan islands for the same reason. In 1956 a contingent of Hungarians fled to Holland when their revolt failed, and in other years many other refugees have followed from countries of widely varying cultures. None were considered to be immigrants by the Dutch government. They were called "repatriants," "temporary sojourners," and "refugees." Having a population density of 419 inhabitants per km^2 (1981), the Dutch government fundamentally did not want the country to permit immigrant status. An important consequence of the policy of not considering immigrants to be immigrants was that there was no policy at all concerning foreigners who came to stay.

A. Actively Recruited and Spontaneous Migrants

The business boom that reached Western Europe in the 1950s reached the Netherlands relatively late. Therefore, it was one of the last countries that started to recruit foreign or "guest" workers. The pattern, however, was the same as in other Western European countries.

In the beginning recruitment was done chaotically by the firms that needed hired labor. However, this soon led to undesirable developments—unacceptable recruitment procedures and "spontaneous migrants" who, hoping for good fortune, started to wander to and through Europe. Soon the government took action to control migration. From 1960 on authorities regulated the provision of foreign workers to industry. For this purpose, government officials entered into contracts with the governments of the various "recruitment countries." The first contract that *temporarily* allowed foreign hired labor to work in the Netherlands was concluded with Italy in 1950. In succession, similar contracts were concluded with Spain (1961), Portugal (1963), Turkey (1964), Greece and Morocco (1966), and Yugoslavia and Tunisia (1970).

Apart from these "temporary" migrants, 61,000 nonrecruited Surinamese came to the Netherlands between 1973 and 1975 because this colony was scheduled to become independent in 1975, by which time the inhabitants would lose Dutch citizenship.

In 1981, 14.2 million Dutch lived in the Netherlands, of whom about 180,000 Surinamese and 35,000 Moluccans (who are legally Dutch) are considered ethnic minorities because they strongly preserved their own culture and ethnic identity. In addition, there were 520,000 foreigners of many nationalities, 350,000 of whom came from the recruitment countries. The largest immigrant categories from these recruitment countries are the Turks (138,500) and the Moroccans (83,000).

The share of the immigrants in the total population in the Netherlands is like most of Europe on average, but in no country (except France, perhaps) was migration so heterogeneous in origin. Other differences are that the immigration "shape" is between that of the United Kingdom (predominantly postcolonial immigrants) and of most continental countries (predominantly labor immigrants). Because of a relatively prolonged humane policy which permits family members to join the migrant worker, the share of economically nonactive immigrants is larger.

B. From Migration to Immigration?

The migrants from the recruitment countries were hired as *temporary* labor, and officially are *not* considered to be immigrants. They are referred to as "ethnic minorities" or simply "migrants." Most of the immigrants themselves do not consider themselves to be immigrants either, despite living in the "guest country" for 10 to 25 years or more and having their families with them and their children born in it. They came to earn and save money in order to return with greater wealth to their native country.

Originally (1965–1975) the migration from Morocco to the Netherlands was considered to be circular, as Van Amersfoort (79) points out, based on Price's typology [59]. This is a type of migration in which mainly married men migrate while the other members of the (extended) family remain behind in the country, having a double source of (poor) income. Most of the Moroccan immigrants in the Netherlands originate from the extremely poor and traditionally rural Rif and Chleuh areas. These areas have an old migration tradition because of high unemployment and lack of income. Those from the Rif, for example, have for decades migrated to the French agriculture areas in Algeria.

After arrival, many migrants suffered severely from homesickness. Research in West Germany showed that after three months about one-fourth of the migrants showed negative mental reactions to the migration; these increased to one-third after 18 months. Most of their complaints were of a depressive nature: feeling uncomfortable and cast down, lack of appetite, decreased libido, diffuse physical complaints, and extreme loneliness [34]. It is, so to speak, "against their will" that most of the migrants became immigrants. The push-pull model [65, 82] tries to explain why these huge streams of migrants came into existence, but there are no models to analyze why they turn into immigrants. Common explanations are the existence in the guest country of: (a) an initial belief in continuing economic growth and the migrants' role in the economy (cheap labor), which offered them plenty of employment and sufficient opportunity to obtain a residence permit that would go with employment (b) a well-established social security system, parts of which apply to migrants; (c) lack of efficient control of illegal (formerly "spontaneous") migrants; and after a few years, (d) the possibility for the (nuclear) family to be united with the migrant. Less commonly mentioned, but no less important factors are: (e) insufficient opportunity for the migrant to save money because life in the guest country was more expensive and labor paid less than was expected; but also (f) because the number of (extended) family members who had to be given support in the native country grew steadily; (g) the economic slump in the fatherland caused even more unemployment there; (h) reduced opportunity for small scale investments; and (i) the disruption of family, social, and economic life in villages from which nearly all of the men emigrated.

C. Integration

The "fiction of temporarity," as it is commonly referred to in the Netherlands by both the government and the immigrants, is considered to be an important impediment to integration of these labor immigrants into Dutch society. The government did not make any provision to facilitate their adaptation. The norms for admission were founded exclusively on labor-market criteria. There was no coordination between policy decisions and practice. So there were, for example, no measures at all in important areas such as lodging, instruction and education, or encouragement to learn Dutch. Only in the case of severe, obvious problems was ad hoc action taken in the form of some kind of social work. Social and demographic consequences were not even considered when the first announcement about family reunion was made. The migrants themselves did not want to integrate into, let alone assimilate, Dutch society. Their life centered around sacrifices in order to be able to return: a very segregated life of double jobs and/or extremely heavy work; contacts confined to fellow countrymen; no investment of money or energy in relaxation, social contacts with colleagues, friends, neighbors, or others in the guest country, or even in efforts to learn Dutch [1]. In their own words: "mind is full up, body is tired" [57].

Yet, even before the ink of the last recruitment arrangement was dry, it became obvious that the Dutch people did not welcome all these "guest-workers" as wholeheartedly as did the government and industry. Negative feelings became stronger when the migrants no longer were housed in sheds and dwellings of the contracting firms, but had to find lodging on the free market. Because of their concentration around industrial settlements, they landed in the old districts of towns and cities, where the disruption of social life was not long in coming. In these already socially vulnerable districts, historically short of housing and provisions, Dutch inhabitants were confronted with an explosive increase of foreign house-hunters. Moreover, these house-hunters had a very different pattern of life, which also became disrupted because of the absence of their families and familiar ways of living and because of their ignorance of big-city life. Race riots occurred on a small scale. Political pressure groups developed to protect the migrants' interests.

It may have been the myth of being a tolerant population, or the memory of the Jews in World War II, and it certainly was the political inability to recognize the existence of *im*migrants that influenced the continued absence of government action to try to alleviate this social disruption by providing means of support. Officials denied that such huge and sudden changes in the population structure could cause problems. There were moral admonitions: the guestworkers do the dirty jobs, the guestworkers save our economy. "Whose economy?" asked the people in the old districts, doing dirty jobs themselves and still remembering poverty from their own experience, "Not the poor man's economy." As for the migrants, only their work productivity was respected. As human beings, they had to fight for themselves in this civilized bureaucratic jungle. "They asked for hired hands, they got people," their spokespersons said. In the meantime the second generation grew up, socialized as "temporary" sojourning foreigners with their own cultural identity. In reality they are displaced, feeling foreign in their fatherland as well as in their "guest" country.

D. Immigrants' Place in Society

Although the recruitment of foreigners has been stopped, the number of immigrants is still growing. This is partly caused by the reunion of families, partly by marriages of young immigrants living in the Netherlands with a partner out of the country of origin, but most of all by fertility. The Turks and Moroccans (often lumped together because of their Islamic religion) in 1979 formed 1.5% of the population, but the percentage of live births among them was nearly 4% of all live births.

The result of this 25 years of unplanned development is often referred to as a "multiracial society." Social scientists, however, have rejected this term [6, 79]. Researchers note that it usually takes three generations before the process of immigration is completed and the immigrant's place in society may be considered to be rather definite. This phase has not yet been attained in the Netherlands.

The present transitional phase is better characterized as a mosaic of several coexisting societies, in which each ethnic group (including the indigenous) stresses the importance of preserving its own culture, the migrants are collectively readily recognizable and have the lowest social positions, and assimilation to the "guest culture" is rejected as much as is the growth of a "new" culture by reciprocal acculturation (melting pot).

Meanwhile, the process of forming ghettos appears to be irreversible. The changes in the town and city districts where many immigrants live are not only changes into a greater ethnic and cultural pluriformity but in the sex composition (surplus of men), the age composition (relatively young), degree of education (from analphabetic to low), occupational level (heavy and unskilled labor), and in the percentage of unemployed people (relatively high). This change in district characteristics refers not only to the immigrants, but also to the Dutch who could not or did not leave the area. Still, the process of fitting the foreigners in is left to the free play of social forces, with the historically known result of downward mobility of the weakest social groups.

The unequal spread of immigrant settlement influences, in an unforeseen way, family doctors' practices, hospitals, and pharmacies, as well as the types of problems that occur in medical care. In the old districts of the five largest cities and a number of smaller towns, there are general practices with over 80% foreign patients. Even more problems, however, face general practices with fewer foreign patients and those practices whose foreign population is of rather heterogeneous origin, partly because most doctors find it impossible to deal with a great diversity of cultures and languages.

III. DUTCH HEALTH CARE AND PROBLEMS IN THE CARE OF MOROCCAN IMMIGRANTS

A. The Health Care System in the Netherlands

The structure of the health care system in the Netherlands has never been regulated, so most health care provisions developed freely. As a result, the system is quite complicated and unstructured. Lay people (patients) as well as professionals (doctors) readily get lost in it. Most intra- and extramural health organizations are privately established, nonprofit institutions. General practitioners, pharmacists, and many of the specialists are privately organized professionals. A remarkable wealth of services exists because religious and nondenominational groups were able to organize their own health and welfare provisions. A fully developed social security system entitles everyone to professional health care, a side effect of which is that an unknown number of consumers are channelled into the health system with problems of a (somaticized) psychosocial nature. Because of this, many health care professionals, as well as managers, consider the system inadequate as an input filter. This refers to indigenous Dutch as well as the immigrant population.

Access to Medical Care

The medical care systems providing personal care to the population are made up of a loose federation of some 2,000 autonomous institutions and about 12,000 privately established professionals (specialists not included). The social security laws guarantee that practically no financial barriers prevent consumers from receiving adequate health care, and that illness, injury, or other disabilities do not lead to poverty, since the system of benefits is linked to minimum wages.[1] Roughly 70% of the population (low and lower middle class) are publicly insured against the costs of medical treatment and loss of wages due to sickness. The remaining 30% (higher middle and upper class) is privately insured. Since the population's share of the cost of this insurance is automatically deducted from their wages, there are no direct costs in obtaining medical care and medicines[2] when falling ill. This holds equally for every inhabitant, Dutch or (im)migrant, who works in the dependent labor force up to a certain, yearly indexed, wage limit.

Professional density (1980) per 10,000 inhabitants is: 5.7 specialists in 27 officially recognized specialties, 3.7 general practitioners, 3.5 dentists, 0.4 midwives and 0.8 pharmacists. Pharmacists supply most of the medicine on doctor's prescription. Patients can initiate only primary care (family doctor). Thereafter people who are in need of specialist care are channelled through the various institutions by the medical profession. The more specialized the institution, the more overwhelming the technology, the less humane doctor-patient contact, the more disease- (but less patient-) oriented, and the greater the separation from local services. The institutions all have their own boundary controls and medical responsibility and there is an upward pressure by consumers as well as by factors in the family doctor's personality, type of practice, and the growing medical knowledge in general. For the patient who remains in the system, this may result in a steadily growing number of physicians taking care of him/her and a growing number of medical acts (sometimes the very same examinations conducted by every responsible professional), advice, and prescriptions, which are not necessarily compatible with each other. Doeleman [15] sketched the movement of clients as shown in Figure 1.

Public Health Care and Preventive Services

Public health care is provided by public and by privately organized local authorities. The school health services reach all children at primary school and many at secondary schools. The most important private organization is the "Cross Society." Their public health and district nurses care for bedridden patients and they are very active in child health, including well-baby clinics, clinics for preschool children, and home visits and care for the old and the

Figure 1. Direction of client progression through the professional systems. With slight modifications, by the author, taken from: Doeleman, F. (15: 52).

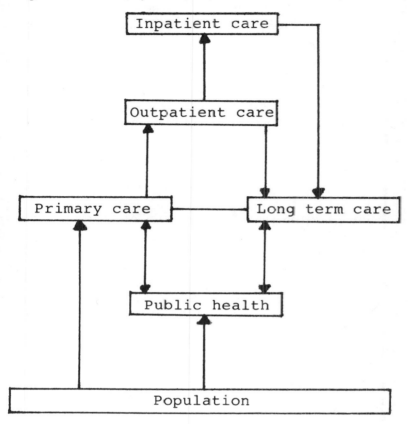

infirm. Nearly all young mothers visit the well-baby clinics. Overall, 90% of the children are vaccinated. It is suspected that this percentage is somewhat lower among immigrant children, but a relatively large percentage of immigrant mothers also visit the well-baby clinics [33, 80].

There is still a well-established network of tuberculosis control clinics that has been fairly effective in prevention and early treatment of tuberculosis among immigrants. (Tuberculosis is rare among the Dutch). A quite different service is provided by occupational health care and social security health care. Occupational health care is predominantly a prevention service to improve working conditions. About one-third of the working population benefits from these services. Social security health care has a strong juridical component. Their best-known task, with which everyone in the dependent labor force is familiar, is control of sick leave and determination of disability benefits when sick leave is prolonged for more than a year. Because of the separation of care and control, occupational health care and social security health care (like all preventive services in the Netherlands) are not allowed to provide medical treatment. When curative care is needed, the consumer has to be referred to his family doctor. This generally confuses the consumer about the (works' and security) doctors' roles and may readily lead to conflict.

Community mental health is provided by child guidance clinics, socio-psychiatric services, family guidance bureaus, services for alcohol and drug addicts, and psychotherapeutic institutions. A few of these are government operated; the majority are privately organized. Consumers may go directly to these centers (if they are aware of their existence) without being referred by a general practitioner.

B. Dutch Health Care and Moroccan Patients: Discovery and Description of Problems

In relation to immigrants, public health attention focused initially on preventing the importing of diseases that had already disappeared in The Netherlands. Before being permitted to migrate, every legal migrant was medically examined in his own country. This examination was intended mainly to test his suitability for labor and to screen him for contagious diseases. In The Netherlands a "specific" examination by the works' doctor often followed, testing his fitness for the work he had been hired to do. Family members legally joining the migrant later on were also medically examined. Many illegal migrants also received medical attention (depending on the individual doctor's views), especially when this was

Cartoon 1. Source: Buitenlanders Bulletin (Foreigners Bulletin), *8* (1), 1983, 10.

needed for vaccinations or contagious diseases. The effect that was intended by these measures was achieved: Public health is generally the same as it was before, there were not outbursts of epidemics, and imported rare diseases are very seldom a medical problem [18].

Two side effects, however, were not intended. First, the complexity and intensity of the problem of attending to foreign patients was initially underestimated. It was the current opinion that "medical care for the migrants was sufficiently taken care of by government measures and would not give further problems" [29: 331]. Did it not concern mainly young, medically selected people, who came into a country where health care is well organized, where the institutions are easy to reach and the medico-technical quality high? An eventual language barrier was not given much attention because "this need not impede objective diagnostics" [29: 331].

Another side effect is seen in the immigrants, as illustrated in cartoons 1 and 2.

Cartoon 2. Source: Van Dam, A., Ik zie, ik zie, wat jij ook wel ziet; 150 satirische tekeningen. (I see, I see, what you see too: 150 satirical drawings), Kampen, Kok, 1978.

They may feel that The Netherlands made them sick, especially when their illness is prolonged: "They took my vitality and when I had given it all and did fall ill, I was put aside as garbage." This explanation fits into the Moroccan magico-religious views on causes of illness and it is affirmed by their social relations and their place in the social structure. So these preventive measures have become a factor that now gives rise to many juridical procedures and high costs when immigrants' claims on sick leave or disability benefits are not granted [42, 85].

Because the economic issues of migration were the major concern, the first research done were studies to compare sick leave of foreign and Dutch workers. The results were not meant to obtain a comparative indication of the health status of both population categories, but to get some indication of the economic costs of employing migrants. No conclusions had been reached before the record of nationality had been removed from the sick-leave registration in order to protect the individual's privacy and to prevent even the glimmer of racial discrimination.

Discovery of Problems

It was only late in the seventies that frequent and regular signals began to come from medical practitioners, reporting nearly insoluble problems with immigrants. Nowadays, essays of widely varying quality, conferences and special issues in medical journals give attention to this subject.

Four main topics can be isolated out of a body of literature of over 200 titles. Three of those topics concern problems of medical personnel, only one concerns problems of patients. These main topics are:

1. Problems in attending patients by those who provide medical care. These signals are mainly subjective experiences of individual doctors, nurses or other (para)medical personnel, who describe unsystematically observed impressions out of their own practice.

2. Elucidations of these problems. A large part are more or less stereotyped explanations of individual medical assistants based on popular, popularized-scientific, or selectively perceived social science studies. A small part consists of preliminary scientific elucidations (mainly by medical anthropologists) based on research that is still in its early stages.

    Explanations for most difficulties are nearly always thought to be found in the immigrant's "deviant" (for the Dutch) culture, in addition to some victim-blaming. Only two or three authors pay attention to the immigrants' social position, the structure of health care and the nature of medical services.

3. Possible solutions, especially emergency solutions for the most important problems. Here too, only a small portion of the authors look toward a scientific approach. Most personnel feel pressed to find quick answers to

urgent questions. A structural approach is not often pursued. One merely encounters descriptions of more or less successful trials by individual doctors in handling difficulties that they thought pressing, and descriptions of adjustments they made in their medical practices. This not only concerns family doctors' individual practices, but also hospitals [2, 63], where specialists are confronted with the same problems. It even concerns social security and occupational health care institutions, which are pre-eminently suited for well-organized structural approaches.

4. Remarkably little attention is paid to problems that patients may experience in their search for care. These problems are mainly highlighted by foreign social workers in case descriptions, or emerge when the workers were counseled to explain why patients cause problems and how the problems might be solved.

Currently, the common view in medical care is that (a) "the" foreign patient costs extra time and extra money, (b) that he is referred too often and often unnecessarily from family doctor to specialist, from specialist to another specialist and from that specialist to psychiatry, and (c) that in the end he is more difficult to cure than the Dutch patient. In psychiatric care this opinion is even stronger than in somatic medical care, and it is considered quantitatively (as far as foreigners are concerned) a large problem.

Community mental health organizations complain that foreigners do not wish their type of help. They have very few foreign patients. Only the "Cross Society" and well-baby clinics report a rather positive attitude of foreigners toward their type of care. However, to maintain this satisfaction they must make greater efforts than their limited manpower permits.

This opinion is based mainly on unsystematic observations in individual practices and subjective reports of medical personnel. Meanwhile an impressive process of rethinking is taking place in medicine. The previously predominant biomedical conviction—that (Western) medicine, being universal and not substantially influenced by culture-bound factors, would be able to take care of all medical problems because of its technical expertise—is being questioned (as far as foreigners are concerned). This process was first marked by a general tendency to put all difficulties down to the language barrier (in the purely technical sense). More recently, we find commentators often saying that "after reducing the language barrier, the whole range of postponed problems manifests itself in full scope" [67].

In the same period (late '70s) the government began to realize that most of the (im)migrants would remain permanently. Two ad hoc solutions for the most urgent problems were financed: (1) interpreter telephone centers for doctors who cannot understand their patients, and (2) an educational center, one important task of which is the production of visualized translated medical prescriptions, and another one is educating the Dutch on immigrants' cultures.

Research

A few small-scale studies quantify some of the problems that health-care personnel experience and underline the impressions that came out of practice. In 1974, Paes [58] conducted a study among family doctors in Utrecht, a middle-size town where many immigrants live. A general practice in an old district can include patients of six or more nationalities, speaking just as many different languages. Slightly over 58 percent of the family doctors felt that their relationship to foreign patients was problematic. They found their relation to Moroccan patients the most so, followed by that with Turkish patients. The two most frequently mentioned problems were: good doctor-patient contact is impossible, and it is impossible to get a good patient history, expecially a differentiated patient history.

In a 1982 study [74], 30 percent of a sample of pharmacists all over the Netherlands and 38 percent of their assistants experienced problems regularly in contact with foreigners. Seventy percent of the pharmacists and 46 percent of their assistants thought that many foreigners took prescribed medicines in a wrong way. One example of seriously wrong medicine use is the oral intake (sometimes even including the packet) of medicines intended for external use.

In another study, 47 out of 112 occupational health services reported experiencing problems in assisting foreign workers. Hoolboom [36] found a significant correlation between the existence of special provisions for foreigners and the experience of problems, as shown in table 1. He also found that of all ethnic categories, Moroccans and Turks are considered to be most difficult to adequately care for.

Van Groenestijn and Epker [84] remarkably found that few social security health personnel had serious problems dealing with foreign clients. However, a closer look reveals that personnel usually consider it possible to fulfill their goal, but experience quite a lot of trouble while moving toward their goal. Compared to other health care personnel, they also appear the least self-critical in evaluating the results of their decisions.

Perception of Causes and Types of Problems in Medicine; The Doctors' View

There appears to exist a somewhat implicit, but clear and consistent, perception of a vicious circle into which medical care has fallen [75]. This is described in Figure 2.

The heart of the process is that it is impossible to establish a good doctor-patient relationship, because the foreign patient is so different that the doctor and patient do not understand each other. The doctor is unfamiliar with the patient's culture and cannot communicate with him. Nowadays these communication difficulties are not considered to be due exclusively to the language barrier, but

Table 1. Correlation of provisions for and problems with foreigners in occupational health services. Source: Hoolboom, H. (36: 211).

Problems

Provisions	yes	no	total
yes	34	27	61
no	13	8	51
total	47	65	112

also to differences in mimicry, behavior, perceptions, roles, attitudes, and mutual expectations. In current health care opinion, these communication difficulties influence nearly all aspects of medical intervention.

Factors in the Patient's Culture-Bound Behavior

Much attention in medical care to migrants goes to descriptions of the deviant behavior of the patient during consulting hours (especially the presentation of complaints and help-seeking behavior) and his illness career.

- With respect to illness and cause-of-illness perceptions, it is noted that foreign patients cannot make the soma-psyche distinction, that they do not recognize psychosocial causes of disease, and that they do not accept responsibility for their own life-situation, illness, and healing. Foreign patients are generally considered to be noncompliant.
- With respect to complaint presentation, it is noted that foreign patients do not make straightforward statements, but use an incomprehensible symbolic language. Their feelings of shame and their taboos lead them to refuse necessary diagnostic and therapeutic techniques. This extends to examination of body parts which are taboo and to the use of some medicines, to verbalization of feelings or life events which are felt to be negative, e.g., decrease of potency, family conflicts, having one's honor and prestige attacked by behavior of one's family or by gossip, or by situations in which one failed to fulfill one's role prescriptions. In general, their experience of pain is considered to be different ("they cannot localize their pain," nor "specify their complaints"). Most personnel state that Moroccans exaggerate pain, but others state that they undergo heavy pain stoically, so acute pain syndromes are often not recognized.

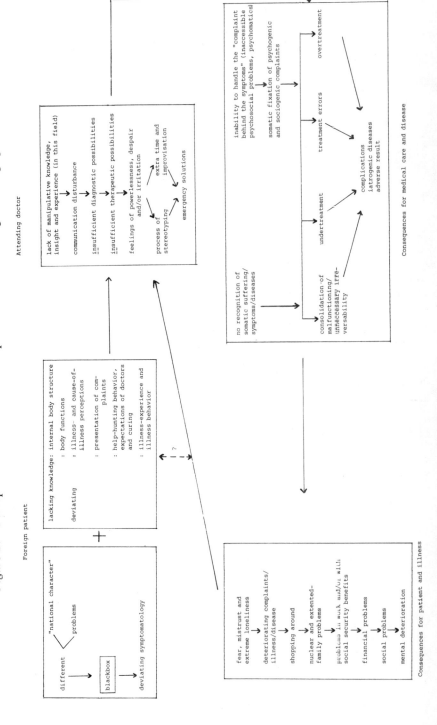

Figure 2. Perceptions in health care of the problem chain in caring for foreign patients.

Foreign patient

Attending doctor

different → "national character" → problems

blackbox

deviating symptomatology

+

lacking knowledge : internal body structure
            : body functions

deviating : illness- and cause-of-illness perceptions

: presentation of complaints

: help-hunting behavior, expectations of doctors and curing

: illness-experience and illness behavior

lack of manipulative knowledge, insight and experience (in this field)

communication disturbance

insufficient diagnostic possibilities

insufficient therapeutic possibilities

feelings of powerlessness, despair and/or irritation

process of stereotyping

extra time and improvisation

emergency solutions

fear, mistrust and extreme loneliness

deteriorating complaints/illness/disease

shopping around

nuclear and extented-family problems

problems in work and/or with social security benefits

financial problems

social problems

mental deterioration

Consequences for patient and illness

no recognition of somatic suffering/symptoms/diseases

consolidation of malfunctioning/unnecessary irre-versability

inability to handle the "complaint behind the symptoms" (inaccessible psychosocial problems, psychomatics)

somatic fixation of psychogenic and sociogenic complaints

undertreatment

overtreatment

treatment errors

complications iatrogenic diseases adverse result

Consequences for medical care and disease

- With respect to lack of knowledge of the body and bodily functions, it is noted that they do not have "any" (read: western/biological) image of things not visible on the outside of the body.
- Limburg-Okken and Limburg [47] elaborated theories of Moroccan western psychiatry [3, 37] in which the body and the way the body functions take the position of the individual identity of the Moroccan. According to this theory (among illiterate Moroccans) the body primarily functions as language and vehicle of the mind.
- With respect to deviant care-seeking behavior and the expectations of doctors and curing, there are detailed criticisms, such as: "They do not understand telephonic arrangements"; "They always come with a lot of family members." This disrupts the doctors' daily routine. Behaviors that influence the therapeutic process to a greater degree are: (a) the tendency to consult several doctors for the very same complaints ("they want their diagnosis to be checked," many family doctors conclude), (b) shopping around when relief is not quickly attained; and (c) the use of divergent medicines prescribed by many doctors (this may very well include medicines with adverse interactions and medicines from other countries which are unknown locally or considered noxious). It is frequently stated that foreigners tend to repeat their appeal for help to the same doctor for the very same complaint too frequently, but it is also noted that calls for help may come too late. There is unanimous opinion that foreign patients want "instant" cure with powerful medicines, preferably injections, and that they expect the doctor to be "omnipotent." A therapy that does not give immediate relief nearly always leads to noncompliance. The opinion is also unanimous that the patients mistrust their doctors
- With respect to deviant illness experience and illness behavior, it is generally stated that Moroccan patients are too dependent, are immoderately afraid of illness, and cannot be motivated to return to work when they have complaints that do *not* cause work disability ("when a Moroccan receives medicines, he immediately thinks he cannot work"). In general they are often considered to react "strangely" toward illness, often with the underlying suggestion that many of them are malingerers or at least exaggerate their condition.

Assisting Foreign Patients

When communication is not possible at all, doctors may consider 'veterinarian medicine' the only possible thing to do, referring to the limited diagnostic information that can be gathered from examination of the body only and at most some facial expressions or painful exclamations. This is felt to be undesirable, especially when patients experience acute pain. Family doctors, for example, are afraid to miss an acute appendicitis, in case of sudden and extreme abdominal pains. In such cases they tend to overtreatment and reassurance of themselves by sending their patient to the hospital. Another commonly mentioned difficulty is the examination and diagnosis of babies and small children, about whom the parents cannot communicate. Panicky telehpone calls may come in the middle of the night from frightened parents who behave as if the child is going to die, when in the doctors' opinion it is not serious and the patient can just as well come to his practice during the day. Repeated calls "for nothing" can diminish the family doctor's willingness to pay home visits [19].

In general, overtreatment may considered to be the most common reaction of medical personnel whenever they are uncertain about a diagnosis. This not only happens when no verbal communication is possible, but also when its quality is poor.

Difficult to handle are complaints that involve some change of behavior. This refers mostly to chronic as well as to relatively "small" complaints. An example is advice on a child which is forced to (over-)eat by an uncertain and nervous mother, who lacks the expertise and advice of elderly experienced mothers in her in-group. Such a child may react by (hysterical) refusal to eat, heavy crying, nervousness, and vomiting. It is difficult to educate a Dutch mother in such circumstances to be more easy on feeding habits, it is impossible to do that to a Moroccan mother. Overheated rooms and overdressed small children are also commonly seen. This may result in dry and irritated mouth and nose, coughing and crying. It is readily confused with having a cold, for which the parents expect to get medicines and not advice to change their health habits. Examinations of patients at home may be difficult when the patient exaggerates his pain and complaints in front of his family (who are present as much as possible at all medical examinations) in order not to lose face. The doctor who tries to tell the family that there is nothing seriously wrong with the patient may face threats and thus may prefer to refer the patient to a hospital, if only to reassure the family. This may occur, for example, in cases of hyperventilation. The reason for referral to a hospital then is not the doctors' uncertainty of the diagnosis, but the patients' fear of dying 'because of heart failure' or because of the threat of the family.

Undertreatment and treatment errors are more common when doctors diagnose a complaint as originating in psychosocial problems. Complaints that have a social background, e.g., problems at work, financial troubles, problems with family in the home country, housing problems, or/and problems with sick leave are considered impossible to handle. Doctors are sometimes expected to do something about these problems for their patients. Some indeed try to do something, as far as their capacities go, but many refuse.

Health problems that include psychosocial aspects are very often aggravated by problems with sick leave or disability benefits. There is no common behavioral reaction of physicians toward such problems, because there are few institutionalized behavioral expectations in such cases and because the situational context may differ very much. Family doctor Dorrenboom describes one reaction toward such a problem in the case of his patient El B., a 48 year old Moroccan [19]. Dorrenboom says that his patient complained to him that he was always tired and had continuous back pains. Besides, for several weeks he had not been able to follow the work rhythm of the machine in the factory where he worked. Only this latter message about the patients' workload gave the doctor some clue on complaints that he had already known about for a long time but never understood properly, because he writes: "reading over this patients' records it appears that he had already complained for a long time about his back, his belly, his breath, his knee, his nose, and reading back to the beginning it appears that he once complained about sexual impotence, about four years ago. However, he always pitied himself so much and so aggravated his physical complaints that it hampered the understanding and willingness of his doctors to help. Anyway, in his registration I find notices like: 'Commedia dell'arte', 'impossible to examine', 'no atrophy, can work', 'aggravation!'. However, now my eyes are opened, because he can tell me in understandable terms that he cannot work up to the machine rhythm, and I realize that he is simply worn out before his time and that his complaints were indications of physical and mental overload'' [19: 91–92].

Then the doctor describes how difficult it has always been to examine this patient physically ("he always deliberately tensed his muscles, loudly demonstrating his pains, so that it was impossible to feel his back", "he would not allow me to bend his knee") and he describes that he considered some complaints (hyperventilation) unimportant; other ones (pain in nose) were incomprehensible for him, and the sexual complaint was not treated and no reason given (possibly inaccessible).

Now the doctor considers two clusters of stress factors existing in his patient: (1) psychosocial stress: work in shifts, living in a boarding house under bad conditions, not enough money to visit his wife and children in Morocco, (2) "medical care stress": the social security doctor had sent him back to work several times before he finished his physiotherapy (massage), which the family doctor prescribed because of his back pain, and the doctors who treated him probably showed their negative feelings toward his complaints.

Although the family doctor discussed this analysis with the social security doctor and despite the fact that they agreed that EL B was physically older than his age indicated, the latter sent him back to work, because otherwise he would have had to have been considered for disability allowance and become completely outcast. There is no elucidation why admission of disability pension would make the patient an outcast, nor a description of the patient's reaction. The final decision is that when the patient falls ill again, they will more readily grant him sick-leave.

Factors in Symptomatology and Illness

A current analytical starting point in medicine is the patient's behavior from the moment that he contacts the doctor. Little attention is paid to factors influencing the immigrant's health status and the decision to consult the doctor. Nevertheless, the symptomatology and illness pattern is considered to deviate from the Dutch one. This symptomatology is quite vaguely described as prevalence of more psychosomatics. The reasons for this vague observation appears to be threefold: (1) The opinion on psychosomatic complaints among immigrants is not founded on observations of well-described symptoms, but on the current medico-reductionist practice of assuming their existence when demonstrable somatic disorders are excluded. (2) Doctors find it difficult to interpret their patients' vague complaints, even if they have some knowledge of his/her cultural background. They often cannot estimate which parts of the patient's story are medically important, how the problem originated, or which reality lies behind what symbolic language. (3) There is no research that, for example, systematically goes over patients' written histories in order to try to discover regularities or frequencies of complaints, or studies that might give more insight about the health of the population.

Examples of serious treatment errors illustrate the severity of the difficulties in medical care. However, there are no figures on morbidity, mortality, or iatrogenic diseases. Information exists only on the health status of foreign infants and toddlers. There are increasing indications that children of foreigners are less healthy than native Dutch children [16, 87]. Results show greater frequency malfunctioning hearing, skin infections, and bronchial tube infections. Rickets, which had disappeared completely in the Netherlands, is prevalent again [55]. One cause of many of these problems is an unhealthy lifestyle, originating in ignorance and a culture that did not develop customs to protect its members against the Dutch climate.

Out of the life-event literature and literature on social change, we may assume that the observations of the importance of psychosocial factors of illness theoretically make sense. There are also studies on psychosocial processes that influence the health status of immigrants, e.g., failure to recover from culture shock, goal-striving stress, discrepancies between own position and reference group, social isolation, high demands of the new culture on the migrant and a confusing complexity of behavioral alternatives in the new culture, which prevents adequate adaptation [73]. Failure to fulfill important culture-bound roles in the Moroccan kinship system is shown to lead to serious health problems among a rather high percentage of the immigrants [81]. This includes failure as a member of the extended family, e.g., toward family members remaining behind in Morocco in poverty, and failure as a member of the nuclear family. There are also more "conventional" variables known to influence health: bad housing; dangerous, heavy work and overwork; financial problems; and immaterial factors such as uprooting, identity loss, homesickness, and belonging to the under-class. Health and food habits, disease, and health history (unemployment, pover-ty, child labor, juvenile undernourishment), personality [40, 41], and genetic factors (preferences for marriages with close kin) also influence people's health. However, they do not specifically lead to psychosomatic complaints.

Manageability of Factors for Assisting Patients from Another Cultural Background

Most of the above-mentioned factors influencing health status are difficult to manage in medical care. Medical care can intervene to a small extent only if it concerns individually changeable circumstances. However, even then medical intervention seems failure-prone. Two interrelated factors appear to influence this. (1) Western assistance (especially for psychosocial problems) serves the individual. However, Moroccans are socialized to accommodate the group. Or-ganizationally, structurally, and emotionally their life is directed toward the group. This refers most of all to people who grew up in rural Moroccan areas. (2) The smallest organizational social unit is the family, and medicine is familiar with delivering family health care. However, in attending to the family, medical assistance is confronted with a very different, patriarchally colored, family pat-tern. This impedes efficient help to men, but even more to women and children, as soon as values, norms, attitudes, or behavior are included in the advice on problems, conflicts, or diseases. In cases with a strong ethical component, deci-sions have to be taken that are almost impossible to accept either by the doctor or by the patient. Moreover, social change and acculturation processes affect norms and values to an extent that every decision may appear wrong. An abortion case described by Sieval [67] may serve to illustrate this.[2]

A young woman and her father come to a gynaecologist to ask the doctor for an abortion for the daughter. The daughter says nothing, so the doctor wishes to see the young woman in the absence of her father, otherwise she will not feel free to speak. The doctor learns that the father wishes an abortion because a quarrel between the young woman and her mother-in-law ended in such gossip that the good name and honor of the young woman's father is seriously in danger. Therefore he demanded that his daughter abandon her husband. Then it turned out that she was pregnant, so he demanded an abortion. The woman herself was quite satisfied with her marriage and pregnancy. The woman insisted on having the baby supported by the feeling that the doctor would help her. But her social position is very weak. Her husband disappears and her father repudiates her, since she does not obey him. Initially, a foster family is found for the woman and her child, but they cannot afford the cost of living for them. She is denied social benefits and she cannot find work because she has a baby and is analphabetic. The woman is neither materially nor mentally able to support herself outside the family. With a young baby she will not find another man.

Social-medical support that would have been efficient for a Dutch patient has the opposite effect on a foreign patient, despite the fact that the doctor speaks her language and knows her culture. According to traditional cultural values, the doctor should not have granted the woman's wish, but rather her father's. According to her new but fragile values, the woman's wish should have been granted, but there is no social structure to enable her to live accordingly.

Causes and Types of Problems: The Patient's Views

The immigrants themselves are less well organized, internally divided, and have fewer outlets such as conferences and journals. Above all, however, they are laymen, unable to present their case. Their views are mainly presented by social workers of their own nationality. Many of these are chronically overworked because of the overwhelming and unsolvable problems. "As a Moroccan social worker, I feel like being a wastebasket. Medical personnel deposes in me the hopeless cases that they cannot handle. I am far less educated, but because I am a Moroccan I am expected to bring the solution" [77]. Moroccan patients feel that their complaints are not understood or not even taken seriously, that they are treated very distantly and impersonally and that they are discriminated against. Many of them do not trust medical professionals. They are afraid they will not be treated properly but are afraid to remain ill. Many idealize their fatherland, and in the Netherlands they feel lonely, deceived, and in despair.

The problems social workers describe often complement the health care workers' perceptions. This is illustrated in the next case of a Moroccan patient, describing his struggle to get his disease recognized [78].

Occurrence 1: Jilali has been in the Netherlands since 1965. He always did heavy physical labor. His wife and nine children live in Morocco. He falls seriously ill in 1977, the first time since he has been in the Netherlands.
Occurrence 2: Neither the family doctor nor the specialist find any sign of a disease. After two months of sick leave, he is summoned to go back to work.
Occurrence 3: Jilali's complaints persist. He suffers from pain in the chest and heart palpitations. He is afraid. He stays home again and gets fired. He legally protests against his rejection of sick leave benefits, but loses.
Occurrence 4: Jilali goes to Belgium, where the doctors 'find' a heart disorder. He goes back to his Dutch doctor with the X-ray photos. They do not recognize his disease. It is 1978 now.
Occurrence 5: Jilali has been warned in Belgium of the serious consequences of his disease and he leaves for Morocco to get treatment. He loses his social security/unemployment benefits. He legally objects, but the objections are not recognized. He temporarily returns to Morocco for treatment.
Occurrence 6: Jilali has to sell his house in Morocco to pay for his treatment. The Moroccan doctors consider him to be seriously ill, but he does not recover before he runs out of money. He returns to the Netherlands and gets the lowest welfare benefits, by which he cannot support his family. He borrows more money. The doctors do not recognize the Moroccan diagnosis. It is 1979 now.
Occurrence 7: Jilali feels he has failed everyone. He lost his honor and prestige, his family disrespects him, he has serious financial and health troubles, he also believes his body fails him. He can only regain his health if at least one Dutch authority recognizes his illness. He collapses mentally and again goes to see the doctor. He is sent to a psychiatrist, who cannot find abnormal mental functioning (considering his difficulties). The psychiatrist sends him to another specialist.

Occurrence 8: In 1980 Jilali ends up in a Dutch hospital with a serious heart disease mentally broken.

Not all cases end in an obvious somatic disease. Some remain under psychiatric care, others are lost from the sight of medical services.

Even less research is done on problems of patients than on problems of medical personnel. In a small research project in the province of North Holland [60], it was found that three percent of the Moroccans consider their own health to be better since they have been in the Netherlands, 55 percent think that their health was better when they still were in Morocco, and 44 percent think there is no difference in their health status. Nearly half of the researched population experienced difficulties with one or more doctors: 45 percent had difficulties with their family doctor or specialist, 40 percent had difficulties with social security personnel and 34 percent with the work's doctor.

Evaluation of Described Problems

There has been too little research in health care to quantify the described problems. Besides, the situation is complex and continuously changing. Description of the problems may suggest that successful coping and adaptation hardly exist among Moroccans. This conclusion is certainly wrong. Medical care and social work are "problem offices"; people without health complaints or other complaints do not come to see them. Only general population research can reveal the real proportions of problems as well as the prevalence of disorders.

It is questionable whether there is really so much "deviant help-seeking behavior." Among Dutch patients there are also dissatisfied people looking for alternative ways of treatment. It is not known how big the differences are in dissatisfaction and search for alternative care between the Dutch and the immigrants. However, from some descriptions we may conclude that there are some real behavioral differences in showing dissatisfaction. A few examples may illustrate this.

- Dutch patients may prefer to consult alternative medicine in case of minor disorders (in which case it is not so harmful), or in case of lethal disorders where patients feel desperate. Often these patients accept the doctor's diagnosis, but not his treatment, or they look for additional treatment, e.g., a natural diet, homeopathic medicines or acupuncture.
- Foreign patients appear not to accept the doctor's diagnosis and in that case they do not look so much for alternative treatment, but expect their doctor to give them another (Western medical) treatment.
- Dutch doctors as well as patients consider it impolite to consult two or more family doctors for the same complaint, as well as to force their family doctor to refer them to a hospital at the time of the first complaint, or when

they themselves failed to take the prescribed medicines, but foreign patients are described as tending to do so.

However, it is not known whether striking and time-consuming phenomena appear to be frequent only because they impressed the observers (observation bias). It is also questionable whether there is really as much "deviant symptomatology" as medical personnel suppose. There is considerable disagreement about the definition of psychosomatic and psychosocial complaints, so it is not known what its prevalence is among native Dutch patients nor what its prevalence is among immigrants. Vague or strange constellations of complaints may appear less frequent or less strange in Dutch patients, because the doctor is accustomed to these type of complaints or because he can imagine the complaint behind the complaint because doctor and patient share the same symbolic language. It is not certain whether the immigrants' behavior and their words are properly interpreted. Nevertheless, the observations do tell us how health care personnel experience problems. They constitute the framework within which the patients' complaints are being interpreted. In these terms the experience is an important social reality, setting the frame of reference of medical acts. It is also clear that the nature of many complaints, the way in which patients present them, as well as divergent attitudes, beliefs and stereotypes of doctors and patients, hinder the diagnostic process. This in turn brings about illness-stimulating processes, such as somatic fixation of psychogenic or sociogenic complaints, as well as "psychologization" of somatic complaints. The effect may be that efficacious treatment begins (too) late, impeded by irreversible complaints or iatrogenic diseases, not to mention the human misery in the migrant families, the rising costs of medical care, and the increased feelings of uncertainty and impotence among doctors as well as patients.

IV. SYSTEMS OF MEDICAL CARE IN MOROCCO

Morocco became an independent kingdom in 1956 after 44 years of French colonial rule. The wounds of the colonial past and the current suppression of people who are against the government policy have resulted in continuous political unrest. Culturally as well as linguistically Morocco is a pluriform country. The differences between rural and urban areas are substantial. It is estimated that approximately 75% of the Moroccan immigrants originate from rural areas and 25% from towns and cities [60].

The Arab townspeople speak Moroccan Arabic and are more highly educated. In their modernized lives, tradition is less dominant than in the villages. Western medical care and hospitals exist only in urban areas. The countryside is inhabited by various Bedouin peoples, speaking various (nonwritten) Bedouin languages. Illiteracy is high and many people (especially women) do not understand Moroccan Arabic, which adds to their geographical isolation. The traditional social order is the patriarchal extended family, in which (grand)parents, their sons, and unmarried daughters live together. There is a clear social hierarchy according to gender, birth-number, and position in the family, and there is a strict division between the male and the female world. The male world is the outside world. Everything that occurs outside the house is the responsibility of the man. This includes the behavior of his family members. The tasks and contacts of the women lie inside the house. There too, the man has the decisive power, but a woman, especially an elderly woman who has had children, is certainly not without rights and power.

Social control in the villages is very strong. Moroccan culture is described as an "honor and shame" culture [5, 81, 83]. The acquisition of honor and respect by correct and proper behavior is a central value for Moroccan men and women, and the loss of honor and respect may have serious social consequences for the individual and his kinfolk and may be experienced as traumatic. Manners and polite phrasing are important and related to a vast and complex structure of values, norms, and sanctions. Ninety-four percent of the Moroccan population professes Islam, a religion that heavily influences various aspects of social life and daily existence. The law too is based on the Qur'ān, and many forms of traditional medicine are founded in religion.

Several systems of medical care exist in Morocco. Each system functions independently. There are, however, important and recognizable shared origins and overlaps in these systems, and some authors prefer to speak of one pluriform system. However, for the patient they function alongside each other and have rather clear-cut tasks. The latter are mainly recognizable by their visual differences in ways of healing. It is not always unambiguously clear what constellation of complaints belongs to what way of healing or treatment.

The medical care system is indeed quite different from the Dutch system, even if it is complex in itself. First of all it is important to discriminate between western and traditional medicine in Morocco. Thereafter distinctions will be made among the latter.

A. Western Medicine

When the French left the country in 1956 there was hardly any western health care left [13]. In the cities there were some privately established doctors with private practices, hardly any Moroccan nurses, and no medical educational institutions at all. In 1962, the first medical facility was opened in Rabat, followed a few years later by a second in Casablanca. Western health care had to be built up from scratch. The government's aim was to establish a network of hospitals and dispensaries. The most modern and well-equipped hospitals are part of both universities and were built in cities. Smaller and simpler regional hospitals were planned in the 40 provinces (serving 45,000–60,000 people each) and the vast rural areas have to be served from simple medical centers and dispensaries.

Nowadays there are about 2,000 doctors in Morocco and 20 million inhabitants. That is 1 doctor per 10,000 inhabitants (in the Netherlands there are 9.4 doctors for every 10,000 inhabitants). Of those 2,000 doctors, however, about 800 are privately established and care for the well-to-do. So the density of doctors is higher for the well-to-do and lower in the poorer areas of towns and cities and in the rural areas.

There is one (government) hospital bed per 600 inhabitants; in the Netherlands there are 5.25 per 1,000 inhabitants; but in Morocco the spread of these is unequal too. Besides, there are only 1,200 doctors to take care of these 33,000 beds, that is one doctor per 27.5 beds.

All graduated doctors are obliged to work for the government for two years, in lieu of military service. Officially, government health care is free of charge. In reality, however, many services have to be paid for (e.g., injections that the doctor supplies privately, the use of a blood-pressure meter, getting clean sheets in the hospital, etc.), either because the government did not supply their doctors with anything but a stethoscope and/or because they like to get some extra earnings on top of their low wages. Besides, Moroccans are convinced that free services are inferior to ones that are paid for, so they prefer to pay anyway. Because of the circumstances under which Moroccan doctors have to work, they can for the most part pay attention only to life-threatening and acute situations. Diagnostics are rudimentary and patient follow-up is unknown. Most of the doctor-patient contacts are one-time visits and prescription of strong medicines in large quantities is the usual outcome.

All in all, this means that the average Moroccan, especially in the country, never comes into contact with Western medicine, or at most once in his life because of a traffic accident or other life-threatening situation at which a doctor happened to be at hand. For all other situations and medicine prescriptions he may go to a pharmacist (who also gives "medical" advice and sells every medicine that he can lay his hands on), to the local market, or preferably, to a traditional healer in whom much more faith is placed. Benyoussef and Wessen [4] concluded that in Tunisia (which, together with Morocco and Algeria forms one culture area, the Maghreb) there is a direct relationship between modernization of the population and the use of Western medical care. This type of care is a scarce commodity, it is culturally only partially assimilated, and it must compete with other forms of care.

B. Traditional Medicine in Morocco

Descriptions of traditional medicine often refer to the whole of Northern Africa, and in most cases to the Maghreb which is considered to be one cultural area. Few studies are done in Morocco itself.

Throughout the centuries, healing traditions have undergone various influences, depending on the social structures and ideas of an epoch. Before the Islamic world view triumphed, the nomadic culture of the Bedouins prevailed. In the early Islamic period this developed into a pluralistic magico-religious system of healing [31, 89]. With the rise of tribal agrarian states (660–950 A.D.), the Galenic humoral medicine of Greece was introduced by Arab Scholars (Yunani tradition). The interpretation of dreams, a tradition which up until now is very important, belonged in those times to the religious sciences. Dreams are considered to be a powerful diagnostic and therapeutic vehicle. The highly developed Arab science delined after the twelfth century, but its medical system in the present attenuated form remains the basis of Moroccan beliefs and practices, still reflecting the various ancient traditions despite the colorial and present European influences.

Coherence of Healing Power and Cause of Illness

In the Bedouin world view, elements such as spirits (*jnun*), sorcery and the (evil) eye were powerful and feared agents of illness and misfortune. The power of magic was used to counteract them. Bedouin medicine also included treatment by diet, drugs, and the manipulation of impurity by bleeding, scarification, and branding. These features became crystallized and legitimated by the Qur'ān and Hadīth. The Prophetic medicine added to this system important laws on hygiene, bathing, drinking, sanitary regulations, marriage, and circumcision, which for the Muslim today are still just as important as they were in the past. These laws are not only important in the prevention of disease, but also may be a cause of illness. The dilemma Moroccans face when they have to go to a (foreign) hospital can be an illustration of the latter. In many Dutch hospitals some adjustments are made for Moroccan patients (such as not serving pork), but otherwise the patients have to conform to hospital rules. For a faithful Moroccan this means that it is not always possible to obey some of the religious rules as he learned them in his village, such as not eating meat that is not ritually slaughtered, or washing after defecation or before praying. This is important because a man or woman who does not obey the Prophet's laws will lose *baraka* (vitality, everything in life that is on the positive side of the life forces), which may endanger his life. A healthy man or woman may afford to lose *baraka* to a certain extent for a certain time and can regain it. A sick man, however, has already lost a lot of *baraka* and this additional loss will "make him even less" (less of baraka) and this may very well be beyond salvation. So, unless God decides otherwise, he will slowly 'decrease' until death. Another danger of this loss of *baraka* is that he may become an easy victim for a spirit (*jinn*), because spirits preferably invade weak people.

Prophetic medicine also added the healing power of the Prophet himself, inheritable by his descendents, and it added the healing power of the words, letters and numerology of the Qur'ān to prevent and treat illnesses. In line with these additions were additions in features that make people ill: not following religious laws (*fard*) and prohibitions (*haram*) of the Qur'ān and the use of wrong words, expecially if these are "heavy" words. The latter are words that are heavily loaded with emotions that make people think of the bad side of life. The full scope of these words can be heard only in the mourning rituals. How central in life and vivid these elements are is wonderfully illustrated by the description of a conversation given by Creyghton [11].

> "Ummzin's brother has t.b.c.," they tell me, "that is why Ummzin cries so much." After a few days, new, more confidential information is given to me in a low voice. "Beneath the disease he has another disease, the real disease, *zjeied*. With this disease he is paying for something (retaliation) because he collapses every day and in the evening he recovers a little bit. Why did he always say so many bad things? (heaviness of the word). Now he is lying there with a mountain on his breast (punishment). And his body becomes heavy. He is beginning to decrease (of life) like a mountain on which it rains and the earth washes away. You know that the heart, the liver, the kidneys and everything inside is linked by tubes, don't you? Death is cutting those tubes one by one. When the dying person complains that the legs become heavy and the heart jumps too much, then the heart tube will soon be next. Soon the heart will fall, too."

The humoral medical system is far less elaborate in today's Morocco. What remains of the full Galenic system is practically confined to the opposition of heat and cold. There are hot and cold foods and environmental factors whose imbalance in the body produces hot or cold illnesses that are treated by foods of the opposite quality. Moroccans agree on what are hot and cold illnesses but not on the food classification, although most Moroccans are able to name at least a hundred food items as hot or cold.

The humoral medical system is fundamentally a secular, empirical science that is health-oriented and primarily concerned with the inner experience of the body in relation to the environment. The Prophetic system is its opposite. It is illness-oriented and it relates illness and misfortune to psychosocial factors. As in Christianity, in Islam there are many religious variations in interpretations of the Book. Religious practices and interpretations differ in the various Islamic countries, in various areas and in social classes. The beliefs of the devoted villager differ as much from the scientific explanations of the Qur'ān and the well-educated Muslims as those of the Christian uneducated villagers from the theologian in his religion. In villages the belief system includes a larger body of Bedouin magical survivals than in towns, but they have been integrated into the dominant religious world view. Prophetic medicine derives its authority from Islam and those values dominate.

Cause of Illness and Help-Seeking Behavior

The complexity of the traditional medical system and its interactions with the social structure and the belief system make the Moroccan face quite different decisions when falling ill than do the Dutch. Apart from self-help and lay referral, the average Dutchman usually only has to consider whether or not he will consult his family doctor. Once he has consulted him, he will be further channeled through medical institutions by the medical profession, if necessary. The average Moroccan has to make a choice out of a variety of healers, on top of his decision whether or not to consult a healer. When he needs further help, he has to channel himself through the systems. It is his own responsibility to choose the next healer. To make his choice, he has to classify his symptoms and he needs to know which healers are within reach (financially and geographically). In addition, the choice of a type of healing is directly related to the type of treatment it offers. To make his choice, the patient has to "diagnose" the probable origin of his complaints himself. This diagnosis is not dependent only on the type of complaint, as in Western medicine, because the origins of the very same complaints may differ substantially. Some origins of illness are more dangerous and more shameful than others, so there also is an important psychological and social factor in this process. Greenwood [22] classifies illnesses by cause and the tradition they are based upon. Jongmans [39] classifies them according to the various levels of harm induced by the supposed origin of the complaints, which results in different levels of "heaviness" of the illness (the heavier the origin, the more serious the disease). These classifications are combined in Figure 3.

God and the material or mechanical causes of illness are the least shameful origins of disease. 'Heavier' illnesses are caused by people trying to hurt their fellow people ("folk illnesses"). The eye (*el-âin*) is a glance of envy or ridicule (loss of prestige) that is retrospectively diagnosed as a cause of illness or misfortune. New, young, growing, and successful beings are most vulnerable to it and the responsibility lies fully in the victim. Accordingly, it is an effective means of social control and internalization of values, such as not being greedy, proud or ostentatious. Sorcery (*es-shor*) is deliberately practiced by an enemy, often used to harm people or their property and to influence affection between men and women. The practice and accusation of sorcery is most often seen in conflicts within the family [21].

Even "heavier" is a supernatural origin of illness which is caused by spirits (*jnun*) or (dead) holy people (*marabouts*). In orthodox Islam, maraboutism is considered superstitious and villager-like. But the cult of the holy, which is very close to maraboutism, is widely accepted. Holy places and holy people, and their ghosts, can heal people as well as make them fall ill, especially the "second class" holy people, who are more concerned with profane matters and people than the first class ones, who are more concerned about religious values. Far more virulent, however, are the *jnun*, the spirits. They are hostile to people and they can attack them in several ways. They may cause illness or madness, they may try to inhabit a person (possession) or they may just torment him. They are capricious, vengeful, libidinous, obscene, demanding, and violent. They preferably attack weak people. A large body of custom relates to their avoidance and propitiation, and to places and circumstances where they are likely to be encountered.

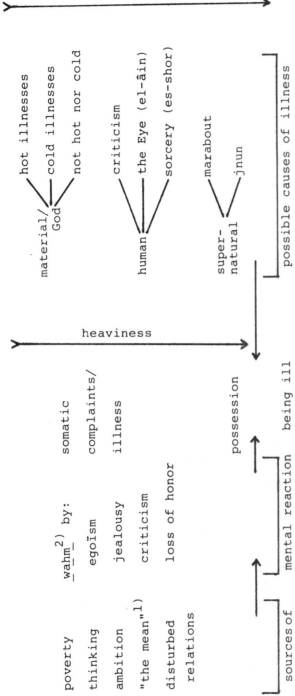

Figure 3. Illness classifications and causes of illness in traditional Morocco.
Sources: Jongmans, D. G. (39) and Greenwood, B. (32).

1) symbolic referral to fertility problems

2) wahm is described in the Arab dictionary as: imagination, concept, gloomy foreboding, hypochondria, fear of illness, etc. Wahm leads to sleeplessness, brooding, dreams, lack of appetite and absent-mendedness.

Everyone prefers that his complaints not have a *wahm* (stress), human (psychosocial) or supernatural origin, because somatic complaints are the least dangerous and give less rise to loss of prestige and honor. Therefore, whenever circumstances allow, one will pick such an origin. However, when the onset of complaints occurs soon after an undesirable event, other origins may be difficult to exclude. This may be the case, for example, when the complaints are preceded by a shameful quarrel or public insult or when they are preceded by disobeying a religious rule or custom, or by exposure to circumstances in which you are known to be vulnerable to magical attacks.

Types of Healing and Healers

The variety of healing actions and healers, as well as their therapeutic principles, are schematically presented by Greenwood, as shown in Figure 4.

The most important healers in Morocco are the *fqih*, the *attar* and the *cherif*. In strictly mental illnesses the *Hamadsha*, a religious brotherhood, also performs healing practices.

Herbal remedies are very popular in Morocco and they can be prepared either at home or bought from the *attar* (herbalist). His consultation and treatment is derived from Arabic medicine and local folk tradition and includes medicines that are imported from the Middle East and India as well as locally grown plants. Herbalists prepare medicines used in the humoral as well as in the Prophetic systems.

The *fqih* (scribe, learned man) is someone who studied the Qur'ān and Hadīth. He usually knows whole parts of it by heart. One of his functions can be the practice of Qur'ānic magic (*hekma*), influencing events and relationships by supernatural means. He prepares talismans (*hajib*) for varying purposes, counteracts the Eye (*el-âin*) and sorcery, exorcizes spirits and can treat any illness. A very common practice for minor illnesses is the use of texts of the Qur'ān written on a piece of paper that has to be laid on injured parts of the patient or swallowed after having been put in water. The *cherif* (pl. *chorfa*) is a holy man or woman who claims descent from the Prophet and is therefore certain to possess *baraka*. The healing power of the *chorfa* is explained by their inherited *baraka*, or by their means of expelling cold (in the humoral sense). Their power is associated to the cult of the saints. People who have no money or are not seriously hurt can also choose this type of healing by paying a visit to a local shrine or holy place. However, this is not as powerful as visiting a *cherif* [17]. *Chorfa* may have inherited *baraka* to only one or two specific illnesses, or possess techniques of branding, scarification, and bleeding at prescribed points of the body, depending on the organs involved in the illness. Other *chorfa* possess general *baraka* against any illness, which they heal with their saliva or shared food, or by performing healing ceremonies and spirit exorcisms.

A special place is taken by the *Hamadsha*, members of a Moroccan religious

Figure 4. Choice of healing in Morocco.
Source: Greenwood, B. (32: 221).

CHOICE OF HEALER	HERBAL	HUMORAL	PROPHETIC QUR'ĀNIC MAGIC	PROPHETIC COUNTER-SORCERY	PROPHETIC SIMPLE BARAKA	PROPHETIC CUTTING BRANDING	PROPHETIC EXORCISM	WESTERN MEDICINE
Self, family, neighbor	+	+						
Barber, cupper		+						
*Bonesetter/ surgeon	+	+						
Midwife	+	+						
*Toothpuller	+	+						
*Herbalist (attar)	+	+		+				
*Market medicine seller	+	+		+				+
*Fqih			+	+			+	
*Cherif/brander					+	+	+	
Religious brotherhood					+		+	
Visit to saint's shrine					+			
Womens' cults				+			+	
*Doctor, nurse								+
Missionary								+

*May be full-time professional healer

232

brotherhood claiming descendence from two holy men of the seventeenth and eighteenth centuries. Their self-mutilation is one of the reasons for their special reputation. In contrast to other North African brotherhoods, they are not so much concerned about the mystical relation to God, but merely about curing people who are possessed by demons. According to Crapanzano [9], they are rather successful in healing features of mental illnesses and hysterical or functional paralyses, deaf-mutism, blindness, severe depressions, nervous palpitations, paraesthesis, and possession. However, they avoid treating diseases with a somatic cause which can be diagnosed by western medicine (e.g., epilepsy). The crux of their technique is social rehabilitation of the individual, using rituals in which the community or family members must participate. Dancing (*hahdra*) and trance are central in their ceremony. After being cured, the patient necessarily becomes a member of the brotherhood, since he cannot live healthily any more without sharing their baraka.

To Greenwood's scheme one could add the interpretation of dreams, which is based on Prophetic principles and the desire to have dreams which answer questions. According to Kilborne [43], this can be done by the individual with the help of his family, or by going to holy places or to a holy man (the *cherif* of *marabout*). Similar to words and disobeying religious prescriptions, dreams may advise and cure (good dreams), or may harm you and make you sick (bad dreams). Jongmans describes how migration and dreams influence illness in North Africa and Van den Berg describes how dreams may influence misfortune and disease in the immigrants.

> Otman has two sons in Europe, but they did not do anything for him. His neighbor also has two migrated sons, who made their father rich. But Otman still lives in an ordinary hut. Otman became jealous of his neighbour because of his wealth and since then he became ill (*wahm*). His knees are painful (disturbed father-son relation; taking a child on the knee is recognition of fatherhood) and his mouth and nose bleed (symbolic complaints connected to too much jealousy). The medicines of the doctor did not help him. The villagers know he can get well only when his sons behave correctly by sending him money, so that jealousy will leave his heart. Only then will the doctor's medicines help [38].

Migration (indirectly) caused the father's illness. The father's illness in turn may cause dreams and illness in immigrants, as Van den Berg describes:

> A Moroccan panicked when he got a telegram stating that his father was very ill (his fault) half a year after his wife and children joined him in the Netherlands. "If this continues," he said, "I will have to send my wife back. I cannot manage here and send money to my father. My father appears to me in my dreams." This Moroccan, who was already in bad health, changed to an even heavier job in order to be able to fulfill his obligations and get rid of his dreams [81].

Many Moroccans who cannot live up to their obligations toward their parents fall ill (often stomach complaints), sometimes indirectly because of taking too much or too heavy work, but also directly because the dreams continue to come and they begin to worry and become frightened.

Ambivalence in Diagnosing Causes of Disease

In practice, illnesses are often not easy to classify as originating from one or another cause since the demarcation lines fluctuate. Greenwood describes the origins of illness as a continuum, with humoral imbalance at the one end and spirit possession at the other. "But Moroccans do not recognize the separate systems or the pluralistic nature of *dua musselman:* they are pragmatists and a hypothesis is validated by a cure" [32: 232]. In terms of behavior this means that a Moroccan who does not experience relief after having visited a healer, will look for another healer or another type of cure since it is possible that either he misclassified the origin of his illness or the healer was not qualified enough.

Greenwood also noted that elements of western therapy are being incorporated into the Moroccan belief system, mostly in addition to the humoral system and particularly when diets are part of the treatment. So penicillin is considered a very hot medicine because of its success in cold illnesses, X-rays can reveal the site of cold, blood samples can remove it and injections insert heat directly.

Recent developments in Morocco and the penetration of Western technology, bringing Western economic, social and cultural values, have induced social change and influenced traditional values and patterns of living The social structure as well as the internalization of norms and values are affected by it, with tradition and modernization conflicting or competing.

Traditional medicine did not escape the effect of this process by change. Greenwood sees a slow progression toward a greater importance of the humoral view of health and erosion of the supernatural world view. New, hitherto unknown problems arise, such as identity problems, alcoholism, suicide, and diseases with which traditional medicine is not familiar [46] and that are ascribed to Western influences [24]. These processes of acculturation and change differ between Moroccans in Morocco and Moroccan immigrants in the Netherlands.

V. ORIGINS OF PROBLEMS IN DELIVERING HEALTH CARE TO IMMIGRANTS

There is a clearly recognizable tendency in medicine to ascribe most of the problems in health care delivery to the immigrants' culture and their "deviant" behavior. The study and knowledge of Moroccan medical beliefs and care certainly can help us to understand the problems and the potential conflicts that arise when Moroccan immigrants have to depend upon medical care in the new country. The tendency for medical shopping may result from the "dua musselman," the pluralism in Morocco's medical systems, and we can recognize the preference for "strong" medicines that give immediate relief, and for injections and X-rays, that Dutch doctors report to exist. It is also easy to understand that they lack resources for help when they feel threatened by evil human or supernatural causes of illness, which may result in feelings of abandonment, loneliness, dependency, fear, or panic. Illness, culture, and healing are strongly interwoven. Without understanding culture, many illnesses are incurable. When we go deeply into the culturally rooted behavioral rules and internalized values of honor and shame, we can understand Moroccan difficulties in discussing failure and domestic problems, even in a medical setting. In traditional North African medical care, such matters are not discussed with the patient, but redress of the lost honor and prestige is offered by symbolic acts. The usefulness of cognitions by verbalization and reformulation of problems as used in Western therapy is Western culturally bound and even within the Western countries its success varies for the different social classes. Luria [49] asserts that this is influenced by the differential (but no less effective) use of cognitive functions and abstraction by people from different educational levels.

Creyghton [10, 12] shows how usefully the concept of symbolism can be applied to this situation. She analysed the sharing of symbolic language in a culture and its communicational value and influence on the acceptability of therapy. Her description refers to the therapy of a Tunesian *meddeb* (in Morocco called *fqih*). The consultation of the meddeb is nearly wordless, when he advises a father on the cure of his daughter, who was "shaking" and had "bounded hands" (not literally). The origin of the illness was diagnosed to be: (1) she fell ill on Thursday afternoon and (2) she was hit by a *jinn* when she went to get water out of the well. This diagnosis contains a twofold (contradictory) message: an accusing one and one that pleads for innocence. The accusational part of the message is toward the father of the young woman: you do not let your daughter go out for water on Thursday evening because it is common knowledge that the *jnunn* are very active and dangerous at that day and time, especially near wells. The pleading part is: in every household you can run out of water at an unconvenient time and water is very essential. Toward the girl the double meaning is: you could know that *jnunn* were to be encountered, so you did not say enough prayers while getting the water, and: *jnunn* are that violent late on Thursdays that they can hit you despite many and powerful prayers. This way the *meddeb* never accuses a patient of failure or even suggests failing inadvertently, thereby never being the one who makes the patient lose his honor in front of the community, which is a very central value in (rural) Northern African life. Western doctors (including psychiatrists) do not give such beautiful double messages, respecting the patient's dignity. The double meanings of our doctors are culturally interpreted by their foreign patients as one single (accusing!) meaning: your illness is only in your mind, and you will fail if you do not cope better. Such a message appears rude and impolite and does not show respect for the patient's essential values.

In acculturational situations, traditional medicine may face as much difficulty as western medicine, either because the type of problem is unfamiliar so that there is no healing tradition at hand, or because the social environment is not as functional for symbolic healing as it was before or is even absent where traditional patterns are uprooted. However, in acculturational situations, knowledge of cultural roots can also help us understand problems; for example, difficulties in verbalizing complaints if shame and eventually self-blame go together with loss of honor and prestige. Such an example is Achmed's case, which was neither understood in Belgium, where he lives, nor in Morocco.

> Achmed had vague abdominal complaints which the Belgian doctors diagnosed as heart rhythm disturbances. Achmed was not relieved by this diagnosis and became so aggressive at home that he went to live on his own. Then, however, he became self-destructive. He tried to solve this problem by returning to Morocco with his family. This did not bring relief either and after severely beating his wife, he was admitted to a psychiatric institution. When he was able to return to Belgium, the same vague abdominal complaints caused him to return to the doctors. An anthropological consultant was called for help and he made a symbolic language interpretation. He asked Achmed if he happened to have potency problems. "This complaint could not be verbalized in the family context; he could only express it symbolically" [86]. After being understood, Achmed was very relieved and treatment could start.

Many other aspects of culture can help us to understand problems. From their Islamic background, we may understand the immigrants' resistance to the use of suppositories and rectal examinations, because these are associated with homosexuality which is disapproved of. From the social structure with its strict division between the male and the female world and its related norms for interaction, we may understand women to be shy or reluctant when facing certain medical examinations, there are Western medical practices in Morocco [7] in which North-African and Spanish doctors report that women undress readily when necessary. It appears that in his practice people were able to discriminate between the old and the new and the appropriate behavior for each of them. However, there are also observations which do not seem to make cultural sense, such as the reported resistance to sampling blood (while "let blood" is common practice in Morocco), or the denial of nonsomatic origins of disease.

Ascription of all problems in health care to cultural differences would deny the migration status of the immigrants and it would impoverish the complexity of the relationship between social factors, illness, and healing.

Studying the relationship between western and traditional medicine, Foster [26] noted years ago that even though local disease theories change very slowly, the pragmatic and essentially empirical attitude of many persons enables them to rapidly alter or accept different medical practices or behavior. Shiloh affirms: "the impression from studies of culture change is that people are practical to an unexpected degree. If, with their own eyes, they can see results that they recognize as beneficial to them, then regardless of their understanding of the reason, and notwithstanding local tradition and belief, many persons will add to the old by accepting the new" [66: 244]. This is not a unique finding. Repeatedly researchers came to the same conclusion in rather different settings and countries [22, 45]. Young reaffirmed in 1981: ". . . tradition-focused explanations tend

Figure 5. Factors influencing medical care for immigrants.

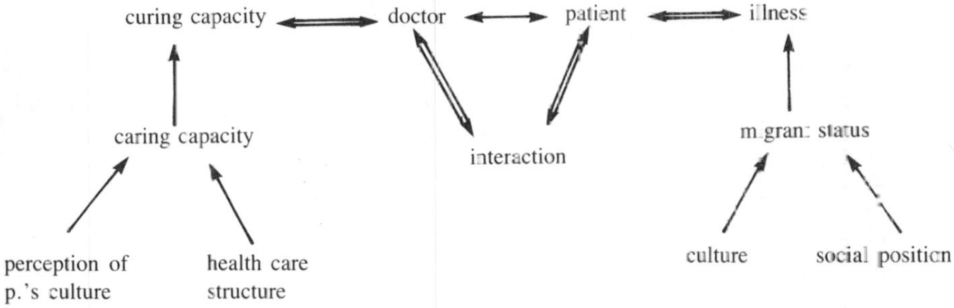

curing capacity ⟷ doctor ⟷ patient ⟷ illness

caring capacity

interaction

migrant status

perception of p.'s culture   health care structure

culture   social position

to place the responsibility . . . with the people and their way of life, *rather than with the providers of health care.* . . . The major empirical finding [is] . . . that traditional medical beliefs and practices do not represent a primary barrier to the use of a physician's treatment . .TH.'' [92:506].

Medicine's perception of the problem cycle (Figure 2) is essentially only a provider's view on delivering care to foreign patients, despite its focus on communication/interaction processes. From a recipient's point of view the problem cycle has to include health care factors too (71). This is shown in Figure 5.

Structural Elements in Health Care

"The unequal position of the [immigrated] person in health care can be illustrated by many everyday examples. Public health personnel and family doctors have insufficient knowledge of the [immigrants'] problems. Besides, the [foreign] patient asks much of the family doctor's time. . . . Medicine prescriptions, the ways to take medicines and the ways to supply medicines do not take the [immigrants] into account. . . . Specialists do not have sufficient time for the slower reacting [foreigner]. . . . The . . . functional structure of hospitals is not functional for [immigrants]. This applies to polyclinics of general hospitals too. It is all too complicated and it goes too quickly. . . . Referral possibilities do not exist sufficiently or are not being used'' [69: 163].

This description of the geriatrist Sipsma refers as a matter of fact to the elderly. Appropriate replacement of the words immigrant or foreign, where Sipsma wrote elderly or older, may serve to illustrate that these deficiencies are not isolated cases, but structural deficiencies in taking care of the "nonaverage" people. They may be special categories of people, but are a very large percentage of the patient population. This is certainly not a uniquely Dutch problem. It is inherent to Western medical care and can be found in varying intensity in many Western countries. However, besides the organization of health care, which this description fits, there are more factors influencing it to be ill-suited to cope with the variety of needs of divergent population categories.

Schillemans [64] analyzed a few behavioral attitudes of the medico-technical cure-centeredness of Western medicine in the process of care, which he hypothesized are the origin of the somatic fixation of complaints. They are: (a) the absence of manageable knowledge and of the capacity to intervene outside a somatic frame of reference, (b) the inability to positively handle (existing models of) latent doctor-patient conflicts [28, 51]. (c) the idea that all the patients' problems need a solution from the doctor, and (d) the idea that useless examinations (e.g., examinations to check an uncertain diagnosis, examinations to reassure the patient, elaborate examinations in order to exclude somatics in psychosocial problems) are not harmful to the patient. A Moroccan's view of his medical treatment [76] may illustrate such a process.

Abdullah is a modern Moroccan and skilled laborer. He had suffered for some time from moderate back and stomach complaints, when he was fired in the laundry where he worked. Shortly after that he got severe headaches. The family doctor told him that there was nothing wrong with him, he was just a little overwrought and when he took the prescribed pills he would soon recover. The doctor did not know that Abdullah was out of work and Abdullah considered it impolite to tell him that without being asked. A good doctor would not diagnose him to be overwrought since he was out of work and a worker with less education does not, by such a message, "tell" the doctor straight to his face that he doubts the diagnosis. When the doctor asked whether he liked it in Holland, he politely answered "yes" and the doctor did not ask further questions.

After two months Abdullah had seen his doctor four times and to his complaints he added sleeplessness, loss of appetite, and a general feeling of weakness. He repeatedly had to ask the doctor for physical examinations, which the doctor did reluctantly. The fifth time, Abdullah wished to be referred to a specialist, because he was very worried and angry. In the hospital he waited very long; then the doctor saw him a few minutes and before he realized it, he was out in the corridor again, with a bunch of papers in his hand. For nearly half a day he was busy having his blood taken, providing urine, and being X-rayed. With all this technology, it would take two whole weeks before the doctors could figure out what was wrong with him. Then the specialist told him: "Your blood is o.k., we cannot find anything in your urine, your blood pressure is good and your stomach is better than mine. Calm down a bit and take these pills." A month later the same process was repeated by another specialist in the same hospital. Abdullah was by then convinced that he had something serious and that the doctors would not tell him. He might have an ulcer, or maybe even cancer. During the last visit he paid to his family doctor, the doctor asked him about Morocco and said that he could refer him to a psychiatrist, but that he advised him to return to his own land to get rid of his problems. Abdullah, however, is convinced that he is not mad, but, because he is seriously ill and unemployed (and in his neighborhood racism is expressed openly), they just want to ship him off to his native country and do not care about his disease.

Perceptions of Culture and Psychosomatic Complaints

A disturbed equilibrium between cure and care negatively influences the system's alternatives to cope with new, unknown problems. The incapacity to handle psychosocial information and its second-rate position lead to stereotyping or simply not listening to the patient, and to a poor result in problem solving.

The avoidance of somatic fixation of psychosocial complaints currently has high priority in medicine, although the change of approach is rather difficult to implement. This medical priority to avoid somatization is in line with the supposed prevalence of "more psychosomatics" in the immigrants' illness patterns. However, it is not in line with the immigrants' perception of the problems in health care [88]. Moroccan social workers emphasize rather the opposite: undertreatment and psychologization or "culturalization" of somatic complaints. The next case is an illustration of culturalization [76].

> Houria had joined her husband in the Netherlands about a year before she went to her family doctor because she had severe abdominal pains. Her Dutch was very poor, so her husband did all the talking. Her family doctor had taken a post graduate course on migrants and was aware of the importance of their culture. When he could not find a somatic disorder, he assumed a lack of contact opportunities for Houria. Indeed, her husband confirmed that they did not have family in town, that she did not like to go out in the street alone and that she was a very religious woman. The doctor then, wrongly, assumed that the complaints arose from the religious principles and the cultural norms of women's place in society and referred the couple to a Moroccan social worker. However, the couple refused and went to another doctor. It took nearly a year and several doctors before it was found that the couple had fertility problems.

Two important errors can be made, after discovering the importance of culture in illness and healing: (a) to relate *all* problems and incomprehensible behavior to culture, and (b) to gain a stereotyped image of culture which leads to wrong assumptions about the possible background of complaints.

The lack of basic research in health care has been fertile soil for four other major misconceptions which add to the errors mentioned above:

1. narrowing of the meaning of culture to religion and exoticism (e.g., confusing folk wisdom with Qur'ānic rules; explaining all cultural values from Islamic principles; overattention to spirit possession).
2. mixing up information of different cultures (e.g., most doctors make no distinction between Turks and Moroccans because they are both Muslims. There are even doctors who do not discriminate between Turks and Spaniards).
3. assumption of uniformity within a culture (e.g., all Moroccans are devoted Muslims; all Moroccans are illiterate; all Moroccans believe in supernatural causes of illness).
4. failure to discriminate between deviant behavior in a culture and the normatively accepted behavior (e.g., women are not allowed to speak to male doctors; Islam permits men to beat up their wives and children; Moroccan women have no rights).

These four misconceptions have led to observation and interpretation errors, such as Moroccans do not want their blood taken because of superstition, and Moroccans do not recognize psychosocial origins of illness. Such misconceptions have far-reaching consequences. Stereotypes develop and the individual person is not recognized behind his culture. The many individual and situational variations that are so important for a differential psychosocial history to estimate the individual's coping mechanisms and their relation to illness (such as the degree of religious devotion, degree of modernity, family relations, job constraints, coping with migration, life-style, health-habits, neighborhood constraints, etc.) are ignored under the heavy load of cultural assumptions.

Another result of the absence of basic research is the lack of a frame of reference for the interpretation of data. Well-founded but fragmentary scientific explanations which are valid within a certain context are applied to other situations. Houria's case is an example of wrongly applied knowledge, and there are many more. There is enormous pressure on researchers to formulate only explanations immediately applicable to common problems with migrants as encountered by medical personnel.

There is also valid scientific information that is not utilized at all. This applies to information: (1) on strongly-held stereotypes which existed before the information was gathered, (2) that is so general that it has to be applied differently in various situations, (3) that is difficult to use outside a somatic frame of reference, (4) that would cost the doctor extra time when applied. Examples of such information are the descriptions of important Moroccan values on politeness and its influence on the presentation of complaints. Darrot [14] explained that patients often politely offered him "head" complaints first, because he was "a doctor of the head." Eppink [24] explained that patients may first present an exaggerated complaint in order to find out how the doctor reacts to a patient who is not paying him. However, there are no case descriptions which show how the doctor handled the first complaint politely in order to discover the real complaint. Indeed, most case descriptions show all therapeutic guns to be fired at the first complaint presented. Several other authors [25, 46, 56] stress that psychosocial aspects of complaints cannot be treated without first giving full recognition to the somatic part of the complaint. However, most case descriptions show that many physicians give two conflicting messages in the very first contact: (1) you are not ill, "nothing is wrong with you" (2) you get pills and/or you may be referred to a specialist. This message is to many Moroccans as clear as an overt statement that: "you are a malingerer" or that: "I do not want to spend much time with you."

The persistent myth that Moroccans do not recognize nonsomatic origins of illness is the most serious example in the above context. Not only does it have far-reaching consequences for therapeutic decisions, but also on choices of topics for research.

Discussion of the Management of Problems

Research on the recipient's view of problems is necessary to reveal concrete barriers to medical care [8]. Otherwise, medical personnel will never gain a proper concept of the interaction process between them and the migrants and the way it is influenced by their own behavior and by the patient's perception of this behavior. Young summarizes that: "Properly constructed decision models have been shown to account for actual behavior with a high degree of accuracy in a variety of domains. Since they provide a view of the [immigrant's] logic involved in choices, and not just data upon which to infer that logic, they are particularly well suited for use when the aim of the research is to inform policy makers and planners in concrete terms of the factors influencing, or likely to influence, the target population's acceptance of new alternatives. They also have the advantage of producing quantitative estimates of the effect of specific factors" [92: 506].

Elimination of stereotypical explanations should also have high priority. Attitudes and behavior patterns are quicker set than changed and may unnecessarily influence medical care to second and even third generation immigrants. Such elimination of stereotypes includes the practice of health care personnel to ascribe all patients' attitudes, behavior, and problems to their culture instead of also considering the consequences of migration, social position, health history, risk factors, or interaction patterns in medical care. It also includes getting proper information on the prevalence of psychosomatic complaints and on the immigrant's 'denial' of psychosomatic origins of complaints. Došen [20] showed that lack of confidence in Dutch medical care existed in 60 percent of a sample of Yugoslavian patients with somatic or psychological complaints. Dutch medical personnel assume this lack of confidence exists to a significant extent only among Turks and Moroccans. This error is probably due to observation bias, influenced by the stereotypic image of Turks and Moroccans and to failure to pay attention to the patient's point of view. Lack of confidence is considered to go with Moroccan and/or Turkish attitudes and beliefs. However, if this belief can be found among immigrant patients of many nationalities, it may have more to do with their immigrant status.

There is a vast body of literature, especially in psychiatry and ethnopsychiatry, that shows how strongly diagnoses are influenced by the way in which patients present their complaints and by their familiarity with the language in which they present them. Behavioral interpretation may influence even the type of disease that is diagnosed [48, 52, 61, 62, 93]. In other countries with large and divergent immigrant populations, a vast body of literature exists on the (apparently widely) assumed "somatization" of complaints by immigrants and the "lack of recognition of psychosocial origins of illness." Comparative analysis proved fairly successful in tracing recipients' views of the origins of illness in such widely different studies as on Mexicans or Chinese in the U.S.A., and Eastern European immigrants in Israel (35). In many cases it turned out that the supposed denial of psychosocial origins of disease was founded in ethnocentric observation bias [27, 30, 90].

If properly rendered, western medical care has been shown to be widely used in other cultures. However, especially in (properly diagnosed) mental or psycho-social origins of illness, traditional medical care that is assimilated in the culture often proved to be more successful than western medical care. This may apply to acculturational situations only to a certain, unknown, extent. Experiments with specially developed provisions for such situations show different results, depend-ing on the proper connection of the new model to the acculturational situation (53). In Dutch medical care, there has been a considerable effort by individual health care workers to render satisfactory care to immigrants. Physicians, nurses, social workers, and public health personnel who ''invented'' new adaptive mod-els of care report far more positive results and satisfactory relations with their patients (75) than those who stuck to their familiar modes of service. The lack of a structural framework to impose on such innovations in a wider context certainly accounts for the limited results of their efforts to improve the overall quality of medical care.

Management of the problems in health care for immigrants will depend on the extent to which intervention in these problems is possible. Several difficulty levels for intervention can be discerned:

1. Problems resulting from the inability of individual medical personnel to deal with culture and psychosocial factors can be affected. Lack of knowl-edge can be redressed by education and post-graduate courses. However, thorough understanding of the variety of cultures which the various ethnic categories represent may be considered as impossible as understanding all their languages. Therefore, organizational solutions will have to comple-ment such education. Efficacious education aims at knowledge that is sufficient for proper diagnosis of a type of illness and further referral to or cooperation with bilingual personnel capable of handling the cultural, migrational and acculturational variables. Problems as a result of medical personnel's lack of interest in or even resistance to dealing with foreign patients are far more difficult to influence and they further stress the need for organizational solutions.

2. Problems resulting from the organization of health care are manipulable. However, efficacious management demands careful study of existing pos-sibilities and eventually the development new structures which are useful and acceptable to both medical personnel and immigrants. Successful initiatives of individual medical workers offer useful models. The same applied to descriptions of solutions in other countries that are comparable to the Dutch situation and to descriptions of doctor-patient, or traditional healer-patient contact, in the original culture. The important understand-ing and sharing of symbolic language and acts has been described and its communication value and influence on acceptance of therapy analyzed in the North-African situation [10]. The value and importance of this subject has been explained [54, 91] and empirically applied successfully in differ-ent situations with various ethnic categories [44, 50, 63].

3. Problems resulting from the dominant biomedical (cure vs. care) approach are difficult to handle within a limited period of time. Although this approach is in the process of change, such changes are usually slow and the outcomes are difficult to predict. Indirectly they can be influenced by education and by stimulation of research. Research aimed at manageable implementation of psychosocial/cultural variables in healing is still underdeveloped. However, without such general expertise, diagnosis as well as therapy will remain difficult when such variables play an important role in illness and illness perceptions.

4. Problems resulting from the immigrant's place in society are probably the most difficult to handle. Discrimination and its consequences, such as constant fear (health hazard) and mistrust (influencing interaction also in the doctor-patient relationship) in the immigrant are one example. Other examples are the "permanent temporarity" of the immigrant's stay in the Netherlands and the strong social control among them, preventing adequate coping. These have negative consequences for their adaptive reactions and other emotional strains. In addition, this type of problem is reinforced by the type of problems mentioned in (3) and vice versa.

Aiming at solving the whole range of problems will certainly lead to disappointing results. However, there is enough knowledge to establish models and start to influence the negative vicious circle at the level of health care organization and education that is most susceptible to change.

NOTES

1. Under the pressure of high unemployment, the automatic link between benefits and minimum wages has decreased since 1984.
2. In 1983 government started a trial to make people pay a small amount of these costs, up to a certain limit a year.
3. This case is taken from a practice concerning Turkish patients, but the described dilemma is applicable to the Moroccan context too.

REFERENCES

1. Abu Gahzaleh M. B. Enige ziektebevorderende factoren bij Marokkaanse werknemers in Haarlem en omgeving. (Some illness-stimulating factors among Moroccan employees in and around Haarlem). *Haarlem, Opl. Middelb. Soc. Arb.*, 1974.
2. Bedaux T., and Van der Zijde G. Turken en Marokkanen in het ziekenhuis (Turks and Moroccans in the hospital). *Medisch Contact, 36*, 1981, 281–284.
3. Bennani J. *Le corps suspect: le migrant, son corps et les institutions soigrantes.* Paris, Galilée, 1980.
4. Benyoussef A., and Wessen, A. F. Utilization of health services in developing countries— Tunisia. *Soc. Sci. & Med., 8*, 1974, 287–304.
5. Bourdieu P. The sentiment of honour in Kabyle society. In: Peristiany J. G. (ed.), *Honour and shame, the values of Mediterranean society*, London, Weidenfeld & Nicolson, 1965.

6. Campfens H. The integration of ethno-cultural minorities: a pluralistic approach; *The Netherlands and Canada: a comparative analysis of policy and programme*. Den Haag, Staatsuitg., 1979.
7. Choffat F. Aït Baha u Baha; étude de santé publique dans un village Moroccain. *Psychopathologie Africaine, 4*, 1968, 329–382.
8. Clark M. *Health in the Mexican-American culture*. Berkeley, Univ. Calif. Press, 1959.
9. Crapanzano V. *The Hamadsha: a study in Moroccan ethnopsychiatry*. Berkley, Univ. Calif., 1973.
10. Creyghton M. L. Communication between peasant and doctor in Tunisia. *Soc. Sci. & Med. 11*, 1977, 319–324.
11. Creyghton M. L. Ziek-Zijn en ziektegedrag in Noord-Afrika (Illness and illness behavior in Northern Africa). *Med. Cont. 32*, 1977, 500–502.
12. Creyghton M. L. Betekenis van het ziek-zijn in Noord-Afrika (Meaning of being ill in North Africa). In: Spruit I. P. et al. (eds.), *Gezondheidszorg en Turkse en Marokkaanse migranten*. Leiden, Boerh. Comm. Postacad. Onderw., 1982, 89–96.
13. Croes H. F. Systemen van gezondheidszorg in Marokko (Health care in Morocco). In: Spruit I. P. et al (eds.), *Gezondheidszorg en Turkse en Marokkaanse migranten*. Leiden, Boerh. Comm. Postacad. Onderw., 1982, 83–88.
14. Darrot J. Aperçu des institutions psychiatriques et de l'epidemiologie dans l'Ouest Algérien. *Inf. Psychiatriques, 48, 1972*, 873–887.
15. Doeleman F. The health care system in the Netherlands. *Comm. Medicine, 2*, 1980, 46–56.
16. De Leeuw-Vringer A. Gezondheidstoestand van Nederlandse en buitenlandse kinderen; bevindingen bij p.g.o. (Health status of Dutch and foreign children). *Tijdschr. Soc. Geneesk., 61*, 1983, 898.
17. Dermenghem E. *Le culte des saints dans l'Islam Maghrebin*. Paris, Gallimard, 1954.
18. De Vries P. L. *Aspecten van de problematiek rond buitenlandse werknemers*. (Aspects of the problems with foreign employees). Almelo, G. G. & G. D., 1977.
19. Dorrenboom G. *Arts en buitenlandse werknemer*. (Doctor and foreign employee). Utrecht, Bunge, 1982.
20. Došen A. Het gastarbeiderssyndroom; een onderzoek bij Joegoslavische migranten. (The guestworkers syndrome; research among Yugoslavian migrants). Maandbl. Geestel. *Volksgezondh., 38*, 1983, 387–394.
21. Dwyer D. H. Images and self-images. *Male and female in Morocco*. New York, Columb. Univ. Press, 1978.
22. Elling R. H. Medical systems as changing social systems. *Soc. Sci. & Med., 12B*, 1978, 107–115.
23. Entzinger H. B. Migratie en minderhedenbeleid in Europees perspectief. (Migration and policy toward minorities in European perspective). In: Van Amersfoort J. M. M., Entzinger H. B. (eds). *Immigrant en samenleving*. Deventer, Van Loghum Slaterus, 1982, 20–39.
24. Eppink A. "Bezeten" Marokkanen; demonen in de praktijk van de Nederlandse arts. ("Posessed" Moroccans; demons in Dutch medical practice). *Med. Cont., 37*, 1982, 513–517.
25. Fernandez R., and König F. Gezondheidszorg en Turkse en Marokkaanse migranten. In: Spruit I. P. et al (eds.), *Gezondheidszorg en Turkse en Marokkaanse migranten*. Leiden, Boerh. Comm. Postacad. Onderw., 1982, 199–203.
26. Foster G. M. Guidelines to community development programs. *Publ. Hlth. Rep., 70*, 1955, 19–24.
27. Foster G. M. Medical anthropology: some contrasts with medical sociology. *Soc. Sci. & Med., 9, 1975*, 429.
28. Freidson E. *Profession of medicine*. New York, Harper & Row, 1971.
29. Gastarbeiders en gezondheidszorg (Guestworkers and health care). Editorial. *Med. Cont., 32*, 1977, 331.
30. Gaviria M., and Stern G. Problems in designing and implementing culturally relevant mental health services for Latinos in the U.S. *Soc. Sci. & Med., 14B*, 1980, 65–71.

31. Gran P. Medical pluralism in Arab and Egyptian history: an overview of class structures and pilosophies of the main phases. *Soc. Sci. & Med.*, *13B*, 1979, 339–348.
32. Greenwood, B. Cold or spirits? Choice and ambiquity in Morocco's pluralistic medical system. *Soc. Sci. & Med.*, *15B*, 1981, 219–236.
33. Gunning-Schepers L. *Well-baby and well-child care in multicultural communities in Amsterdam*. Thesis, Baltimore, 1979.
34. Häfner, H., Moschel G., and Öztek M. Psychische Störungen bei Türkischen Gastarbeitern. Eine prospectiv-epidemiologische Studie zur Untersuchung der Reaktion auf Einwanderung und partielle Anpassung. (Mental health of Turkish guestworkers). *Der Nervenartz*, *48*, 1977, 268–275.
35. Honig-Parnass T. The effect of latent social needs on physician utilization by immigrants: a replication study. *Soci. Sci. & Med.*, *16*, 1982, 505–514.
36. Hoolboom H. Mogelijkheden van bedrijfsgeneeskundige begeleding. (Possibilites for occupational physicians). In: Spruit I. P. et al. (eds.), *Gezondheidszorg en Turkse en Marokkaanse migranten*. Leiden, Boerh. Comm. Postacad. Onderw., 1982, 209–225.
37. Ifrah A. *Le Maghreb déchiré: tradition et migration*. Paris, La Pensée Sauvage, 1980.
38. Jongmans D. G. Het denken over gezondheid en ziekte in Noord-Afrika, een transcultureel perspectief. (Thinking over health and illness in Northern Africa, a transcultural perspective). *Tijdschr. Soc. Geneesk.*, *55*, 1978, 805–807.
39. Jongmans D. G. Verbal presentation in post-graduate course. Leiden 1981/1982.
40. Kabela M. Spaanse migranten bij een Nederlandse psychiater. (Spanish migrants at a Dutch psychiatrist). *Med. Cont.*, *35*, 1980, 24–30
41. Kabela M. Psychiatrische bepaling van arbeics(on)geschiktheid bij Marokkaanse werknemers in Nederland. (Psychiatric judgement of the fittness to work in Moroccan employees in the Netherlands). *Tijdschr. v. Psychiatrie*, *24*, 1982, 665–678.
42. Kabela M., and Van der Meer Ph.J. (eds.). *Ziek of niet ziek: maar nu bij Marokkanen*. (Ill or not ill: Moroccans). Muiderberg, Coutinho, 1983.
43. Kilborne B. *Interpretations du rêve au Maroc*. Paris, La Pensée Sauvage, 1978.
44. Kleinman A., and Sung L. H. Why do indigenous practitioners successfully heal? *Soc. Sci. & Med.*, *13B*, 1979, 7–26.
45. Kleinman A. *Patients and healers in the context of culture*. Berkeley Univ. Calif. Press, 1980.
46. Limburg-Okken A. Identiteitsonzekerheid bij Marokkanen. (Identity uncertainty among Moroccans). *Maandbl. Geestel. Volksgezondh.*, *36*, 1981, 625–634.
47. Limburg-Okken A., and Limburg J. J. M. De betekenis van somatiseren bij Marokkaanse patienten. (The meaning of somatisation among Moroccan patients). *Ned. T. Geneesk.*, *126*, 1982, 892–895.
48. Littlewood R., and Cross S. Ethnic minorities and psychiatric services. *Soc. Hlth. & Illness*, *2*, 1980, 194–201.
49. Luria A. R. *Cognitive development; its cultural and social foundation*. Boston (Mass.), Harvard Univ. Press, 1977.
50. Marsella A. J., and Pedersen E. P. B. (eds.). *Cross-cultural counseling and psychotherapy*. Oxford/New York, Pergamon, 1981.
51. Merton T., and Barber E. Sociological ambivalence. In: Tiryakian E. (ed.), *Sociological theory; values and sociological change*. New York, Free Press of Glencoe, 1963.
52. Murphy H. B. M. Migration, culture and mental health. *Psychol. Med.*, *7*, 1977, 677–684.
53. Nann R. C. *Uprooting and surviving; adaptation and resettlement of migrant families and children*. Dordrecht, Reidel, 1982.
54. Needham R. *Belief, language and experience*. Oxford, Blackwell, 1972.
55. Nijhuis H. G. J., Zoethout H. E., and De Jong G. M. De terugkeer van een volksziekte: rachitis. (The return of a common disease: rachitis). *Tijdschr. Soc. Geneesk.*, *60*, 1982, 846–850.
56. Örücü H. Psychosomatische klachten. (Psychosomatic complaints). In: Spruit I. P. et al. (eds.),

Gezondheidszorg en Turkse en Marokkaanse migranten. Leiden, Boerh. Comm. Postacad. Onderw., 1982, 125–128.

57. Özüm E. Y. Problemen van buitenlanders bij het opvolgen van voorschrifter en het voorkómen daarvan. (Problems of foreigners in following patient prescriptions and how to prevent them). In: Spruit I. P. et al. (eds.), *Gezondheidszorg en Turkse en Marokkaanse migranten.* Leiden, Boerh. Comm. Postacad. Onderw., 1982, 31.

58. Paes A. H. P. *Gastarbeiders en hun huisartsen.* (Guestworkers and their family doctors). Utrecht, Inst. Huisartsgeneesk., 1974.

59. Price Ch. The study of assimilation. In: Jackson J. A. (ed.), *Migration.* Cambridge, Cambridge Univ. Press, 1969.

60. *Prov. Comm. Buitenl. Werknemers.* Positie van de meditterane werknemer in de Noord-Hollandse samenleving. (Position of the Mediterranian employees in the North-Holland society). Haarlem, 1975.

61. Riedesser P. Psychische stoornissen bin buitenlandse arbeiders in de B. R. D. (Mental disorders among foreign workers in Western-Germany). *Maandbl. Geestel. Volksgezondh., 29,* 1974, 285–295.

62. Risso M. Der Einflusz des magischen Weltbildes auf die Gestaltung geistiger Störungen bei Süditalienschen Patienten. (The influence of perception of magic on mental disturbances in South-Italian patients). In: *Beitrage zur Vergleich. Psychiatrie. Part II.* Basel, New York, 1967, 155–173.

63. Rubin J. C., and Jones J. Falling-out: a clinical study. *Soc. Sci. & Med., 13B,* 1979, 117–127.

64. Schillemans L. Gezondheidszorg voor de buitenlander; uitdaging en toetssteen. (Health care for the foreigner; a challenge and a test). *Metamedica, 58,* 1979, 3–9.

65. Shadid W. A. *Moroccan Workers in the Netherlands.* Thesis, Leiden, 1979.

66. Shiloh A. The interaction between the Middle-Eastern and the Western systems of medicine. *Soc. Sci. & Med., 2,* 1968, 235–248.

67. Sieval Z. Spreekuur voor Turkse vrouwen. (Consulting hours for Turkish women). *Med. Cont., 32,* 1977, 506–508.

68. Sieval A. Het vreemde ziekenhuis. (The strange hospital). *Metamedica, 58,* 1979, 9–12.

69. Sipsma D. H. Advies inzake de ontwikkeling van de sociale geriatrie. (Advice on the development of social geriatrics). *Tijdschr. Soc. Geneesk., 58,* 1980, 162–168.

70. Six M. J. A., Örücü H. A., and Botros A. Migratie en geestelijke gezondheid; een literatuurstudie. (Migration and mental health). *Maandbl. Geestel. Volksgezondh., 36,* 1981, 645–655.

71. Spector T. E. *Cultural diversity in health and illness.* New York, Appleton Century Crofts, 1979.

72. Spruit I. P. (ed.). *Gastarbeiders en gezondheidszorg. een impressie van problemen uit het veld.* (Guestworkers and health care, an impression of problems in medical practice). Leiden, I.S.G., 1979.

73. Spruit I. P., de Cultuurschok in het aanpassingsproces. (The cultural shock in the adaptation process). In: Spruit I. P. et al. (eds.). *Gezondheidszorg en Turkse en Marokkaanse migranten.* Leiden, Boerh. Comm. Postacad. Onderw., 1982, 147–156.

74. Spruit I. P., and Van der Kruijk, R. Communicatie met Turkse en Marokkaanse patienten in de apotheek (Communication with Turkish and Moroccan patients in the pharmacy). *Pharmac. Weekbl., 118,* 1983, 471–475.

75. For the construction of the vicious circle described in Fig. 2 a content- and proceedings analysis was made of questions and discussions of physicians in medical conferences and post-graduate educational courses (as well as of those in small-scale educational sessions of locally organized family doctors and hospitals):
    1977 *Study conference of the Royal Dutch Medical Society (K.N.M.G.) on Guestworkers and health care,*

1978 *Dutch session on foreigners and health care in the conference of the European Union of Social Security Health Care (UEMASS)*,

1980 *Session on foreigners and health care in study conference on Health Care in the Big City*, Royal Dutch Medical Society (*K.N.M.G.*),

1981/1982 Postgraduate courses: *Health Care and Turkish and Moroccan migrants.* Boerhaave courses, Leyden State University,

1983 *Study conference Migrants and mental health care.* Dutch centre for public mental health (NCGV).

76. Case in which the author was consulted.
77. Tounssi M. *Verbal communication in post-graduate course.* Leiden 1981/1982.
78. *Case of M. Tounssi, Moroccan social worker,* given to the author.
79. Van Amersfoort J. M. M. Immigrant en samenleving: een terreinverkenning. (Immigrant and society: an exploration). In Van Amersfoort J. M. M., Entzinger H. B. (eds.), *Immigrant en Samenleving.* Deventer, Van Loghum Slaterus, 1982, 7–19.
80. Van Bekkum-Van Vliet E. W. *Verslag van het consultatie-bureau voor Turkse en Marokkaanse kinderen te Delft.* (Report on the well-baby clinic for Turkish and Moroccan children in Delft. Scriptie, Leiden, NIPG-TNO, 1981.
81. Van den Berg-Eldering L. Falen als oorzaak van stress bij Marokkaanse arbeiders in Nederland. (Failure as a cause of stress in Moroccan workers in the Netherlands). *Med. Cont., 32,* 1977, 495–499.
82. Van den Berg-Eldering L. *Marokkaanse gezinnen in Nederland.* (Moroccan families in the Netherlands). Alphen a/d Rijn, Samson, 1979.
83. Van der Meer Ph. Gezins—en familiestructuur, eer en schande in Noord-Afrika. (Nuclear and extended familystructure, honor and shame in Northern Africa). In: Spruit I. P. et al. (eds.), *Gezondheidszorg en Turkse en Marokkaanse migranten.* Leiden, Boerh. Comm. Postacad. Onderw., 1982, 141–146.
84. Van Groenestijn X., and Epker Y. *Kommunicatieproblemen van GAK medewerkers in contacten met buitenlandse werknemers.* (Communicational problems of social insurance personnel in contacts with foreign employees). Amsterdam, GAK/S&O., 1980.
85. Van Kasbergen H. *De nadelige resultaten van het niet-onderkennen door medici van socio-psychosomatische klachten bij Marokkanen, in relatie tot hun uitkeringen en gezondheid* (The negative effects of non-recognition of socio-psychosomatic complaints of Moroccans by physicians, related to social security and health). Driebergen, De Horst, 1981.
86. Van Mol M. *Case presented at the Royal Dutch Medical Society (K.N.M.G.)* conference on Health Care in the Big City. 1980.
87. Verveen-Keulemans E. M. *Enkele aspecten van de preventie en curatieve zorg voor het jonge buitenlandse kind.* (Some aspects of prevention and medical care for young foreign children). In: Spruit I. P. et al. (eds.). Leiden, Boerh Comm. Postacad. Onderw., 1982, 175–184.
88. Visser J. Buitenlanders over gezondheidszorg. (Foreigners opinions on health care). *De eerste lijn, 8,* 1983, 4–7.
89. Westermarck E. *Ritual and belief in Morocco.* London, Macmillan, 1926.
90. White G. M. The role of cultural explanations in "somatization" and "psychologization". *Soc. Sci. & Med., 16,* 1982, 1519–1530.
91. Wilden A. (ed.). *System and structure, essays in communication and exchange.* London, Tavistock, 1977.
92. Young J. C. Non-use of physicians: methodological approaches, policy implications, and the utility of decision models. *Soc. Sci. & Med., 15B,* 1981, 499–507.
93. Zwingman C. A., and Pfister-Ammende M. *Uprooting and after . . . .* New York, Springer. 1973.

EVIL EYE OR BACTERIA:
TURKISH MIGRANT WOMEN
AND SWEDISH HEALTH CARE

Lisbeth Sachs

This article concerns how women from a rural community in Turkey cope with sickness[1] in a setting that is new to them, a Stockholm suburb in Sweden.

Having encountered the conditions experienced by these women and their families in the villages of central Anatolia, one tends to assume that the move to Sweden was nothing but a change for the better. Similarly, knowing the Swedish statistics, a look at the figures for child morality and disease in the Turkish communities between Ankara and Konya may at first convince one that people from there who come under the aegis of the Swedish health service feel pleased and grateful that the basic problem of health care has been solved. Here I shall show that the adjustment undergone by the Turkish women and their children in Sweden does not necessarily follow a course we find logical. Despite its good international reputation, advanced technology, insurance system, and so on, the Swedish health care system is not always attuned to the health problems of

Research in the Sociology of Health Care, Volume 5, pages 249-301.
ISBN: 0-89232-597-6

Turkish women. Health care problems cannot be resolved by relying solely on scientific medical technology and Swedish policy in this field. This article exposes an incapacity in encounters with people who, in spite of having what we consider a negative environmental and socioeconomic foundation, already possess a more or less functional health care system. It also indicates ways in which aspects of the Swedish health care system have unforeseen consequences for these people, as well as how they perceive and use the system in new, "unorthodox" ways.

The women who are the subject here undergo a form of adjustment which to some extent can be described with the aid of my interest in sickness as a cultural category. The women's actions in connection with sickness provide a guide to their perceptions and interpretations of the world around them. It is, moreover, on account of this world that they become "ill."

The problems concerned the child welfare and district pediatric center in Tensta, a Stockholm suburb with a large group of Turks from the district of Kulu in central Anatolia. The Turkish women and their children differed so much from Swedish patients in their behavior and symptoms that the medical personnel felt somewhat powerless.

The doctors found that certain medical problems were unusually common. There was an over-representation of intestinal infections, above all those with a specific bacteriological and parasitological cause. Such infections frequently occurred when the immigrant returned from a visit to Turkey. Chronic inflammation of the ear (otitis) was common, too. Many children, moreover, seemed to fall short of the Western standard for growth and weight gain. Although they did their best to tackle the medical problems, the doctors felt unable to practice the type of care they considered to be effective.

This, briefly, was the situation that confronted me when, in the late autumn of 1976, having reached an agreement with the doctors, I started to consider the questions that I might explore in my capacity as an anthropologist. It transpired after a long period of observation at the child welfare center, participation in the daily life of the Kulu women and attendance at numerous illness processes[2] in and outside the Swedish health care system, that the encounter between Swedish health care and the Kulu women was far more complex than I could imagine.

Whereas the doctors questions chiefly centered on the ineffective nature of their meetings with Kulu patients, I was equally concerned with what happened before and after these meetings. I wanted to follow illness processes from start to finish in order to assess how the encounter with Swedish health care affected the Kulu women's experience and perception of illness. Might not the encounter with Swedish health care influence the way in which illness processes arose and developed among these women and their children? Did these women's attitude to their earlier forms for health care undergo a change in Sweden and, if so, how did they adapt to Swedish health care?

Besides being interested in processes, I wanted to explore the part played in these processes by the Swedish doctors. Perhaps it would also be possible to say something about the behavior of the doctors in light of their cultural antecedence.

My subject matter inevitably raises questions to do with development, migration, political, and economic differences between Sweden and Turkey, with their attendant health-care ideologies, ecological conditions, their influence on the human organism, and so on. Such large matters cannot be discussed in the present context, but it is clear that a national ideology of health care, like the general health of the population, is bound up in many respects with ecological, physical, and economic conditions.

But there is more to it than this. Having migrated from a rural community in a developing society to an industrialized welfare society, many Kulu women feel that their health here is poorer that it was in Kulu. Their health can hardly be determined solely by factors, such as material conditions, which cannot be controlled or avoided. Health is also susceptible to factors in their culture.

Culture refers here to "what goes on inside people's heads," their shared ideas and conceptions, values, and standards, as well as the related actions. Actions confirm the internal reality, just as behavior and objects acquire significance as the embodiment of ideas. All this occurs at both a conscious and a subconscious level.

The Swedish doctors were worried that the behavior pattern of the Kulu women, whom they considered to be ignorant of physical and biological relationships, might be bad for their children's health. Yet tentative results from studies by the doctors suggest that disease and mortality among Kulu children do not exceed the average for Swedish children. My account of how the Kulu women nevertheless largely rely on their culturally based ideas when dealing with illness and health care may therefore promote a new view of their competence and a reappraisal of the causes of ill health among them and their children.

The Kulu women go through a process in which their previous experience, e.g., of child mortality and sickness rates, serves as a basis for actions and explanations when symptoms and changes occur in Sweden. They do not, any more than other people, let a serious illness pass unnoticed. Illness always elicits a response, made up of actions as well as questions about its significance. The women from Kulu are in a situation that is new to them and their actions accordingly reflect the way in which their perception of illness—in terms of responsibility for the illness and the efficiency with which it is treated—changes by degrees. This means that one can observe and describe the process of change which these women undergo in the course of illnesses in Sweden (in this case during the period 1976–81, which is my ethnographic present).

I. SECTORS OF CARE

We turn next to the various encounters which may occur between the Kulu woman and the various kinds of specialists who are included in her health care system. Within the system, ways of thinking and acting may vary situationally.

The home, the locale of a folk healer, or a large modern hospital are all settings of different types, with different expectations and rules for treating sickness.

It is not the fact that she utilizes Swedish health care that is of principal interest, but how she does so. Swedish health care is only a limited part of her total health care system. To explicate this we can subdivide the health care system into three sections, i.e., into what Kleinman [30:49] calls the popular, folk, and professional sectors.[3] For the present purpose I prefer to refer to these as the personal, the folk, and the scientific sector.

The personal sector in this scheme comprises the individual, the family, relatives, friends, and the informal network of nonspecialists in general. This is where all illness is first perceived, expressed and interpreted. The folk sector includes specialists in Kulu and its surroundings, specialists who employ methods that are entirely magical as well as incisions, cuppings, and other techniques. These specialists in the folk sector belong to the women's Turkish sociocultural environment and have a large part of their conception of reality in common with her. That is to say, they share similar ideas but have different fields of competence in their joint culture.

The scientific sector, finally, contains specialists who are trained in and practice natural science. These physicians may belong to a large, bureaucratic organization for health care or function as private practitioners. They may have access to scientific apparatus and medicines but this cannot always be taken for granted. For the Kulu woman, the scientific sector, with its physicians and health care, exists in Turkey as well as in Sweden. Although these physicians subscribe to the same scientific explanations for bodily processes, their different environments may cause them to act very differently.

Each health care sector has its own way of influencing the development of an illness process. The attitude of the women to illness and health care is a key factor in their adjusment to a new life.

A. Sickness, Illness and Disease

The Swedish word *sjukdom* is used both for changes, discomfort, pain, nausea, etc., perceived by the individual and for disorders identified by physicians. This word also covers the context of a person who is sick in a social perspective, i.e., a deviant social role. Everyday usage in other languages is often similar. In medical anthropology, however, the terms illness and disease have been used in an attempt to distinguish these aspects of sickness [18;29;38;19;20].

I adhere to these terms here as far as possible and use sickness as the general concept.

Illness stands for whatever a person perceives as ill health. It is these individual experiences of discomfort that have to be communicated in some way if the person in question is to be regarded by other as ill. Illness accordingly implies changes in a person's social function as a consequence of perceived physiological and/or psychological changes. As an anthropologist I am concerned primarily with illness, as this is the aspect for which data are most accessible.

The direct observations a Swedish physician can make in encounters with patients whose language and means of expression he understands are likewise manifestations of illness in the sense used here. Illness comprises expressions for the subjective perceptions (symptoms) which are not necessarily visible (pain) but are communicated, verbally or otherwise, in a culturally prescribed manner. In addition, however, the physician may discover things of which the patient is unaware (signs, e.g., such changes as fever, anemia, elevated blood pressure, cellular changes, and so on). He can do this even without understanding the patient's language or means of expression. He does not even need the patient's active assistance. The symptoms are communicated in a different way. In the case of infants, for instance, illness is communicated by nonverbal expressions of discomfort.

In order to claim that illness is occasioned by biological changes—that disease is present—one therefore needs objective evidence of what is going on in the body. It is only competent specialists in the scientific sector who can obtain such evidence, above all with technical aids. A physician also needs to communicate his assessment to the patient as well as to colleagues. He does this in the form of a diagnosis, i.e., the disorder is named and classified with the aid of biomedical disease categories. The diagnosis accordingly rests on a foundation of biological knowledge, but to arrive at it the physician usually has to rely on a wide spectrum of information. In the next section diagnosis is considered as classification in each of the present systems of ideas.

B. Diagnosis as Classification

Referring to diagnosis as classification implies that sicknesses are placed in different categories in accordance with the composite experience, ideas, and conceptions of the actors concerned. The way in which people name, describe, interpret, and classify sickness is also pertinent to the way they treat it.

As diagnoses are founded in people's socially constructed perception of reality, they may vary between as well as within health care systems. Swedish physicians base their diagnoses predominantly on their scientific knowledge, acquired in a special sociocultural environment. This environment also influences their interpretation of such knowledge, and consequently it differs from that of doctors with the same type of knowledge in other environments [30:55].

When a physician cannot establish a diagnosis that matches the patient's symptoms, i.e., the illness for which the patient has applied for help, one can say that illness is present without detectable disease. In other cases it is illness which prompts the physician to detect a disease and then they are both present. But can disease be present without any manifestations of illness?

Health checkups are an accepted part of Swedish life. They are performed

regularly at birth, during pre-school and school age, in connection with pregnancy, at "critical" ages for cancer, during old age, and up to death. Such a
checkup may uncover a disease even though the individual is not ill. It may, for
instance, reveal a patch on a lung, a cytological change in the neck of the womb,
unduly high or low blood pressure, etc. In such cases the physician bases a
diagnosis, not on symptoms presented bv the patient, but on the signs of disease.

Let us now turn to the Kulu woman's diagnostic process and consider the
similarities and differences in her way of looking for a name and an explanation
for symptoms. Symptoms are categorized by Kulu women with the aid of the ill
person's manifestations and their assessment of the situation's gravity. They
neither need nor are in a position to examine the body more than superficially.
Some symptoms derive their names from folk categories, others from scientific
categories. Irrespective of its name, however, the diagnosis at which the women
arrive is invariably linked to the symptom's case. The women look for this by
asking, "Why just me, just now?", a question that reflects the idea that the
cause of all accidents, including illness, lies in external forces that attack and
weaken the individual's resistance. Having established the cause, steps can be
taken to neutralize or eliminate it. This can be accompanied by treatment of the
symptom.

This suggests that there is a substantial difference in how sickness is both
diagnosed and treated by a Swedish physician and Turkish woman. The former's
diagnosis relies mainly on pathological processes, whereas the latter is chiefly
concerned with the cause. The difference is largely a consequence of the distinction between illness and disease. I will state the problem here and return to it later
in connection with descriptions of other cases.

When a Kulu woman feels healthy she is by definition not ill. It is not until
symptoms materialize that she looks for an explanation, a name, a way of getting
well. If illness, i.e., some form of symptom, is the sole criterion for sickness, the
woman can have a disease and still experience well-being. Illness and well-being
are a pair of opposites, while disease and well-being need not be incompatible
[44:1037]. A further complication arises when a woman who is ill wants to have
her symptoms confirmed by a Swedish physician, who may look for disease
without finding any. Thus the presence of disease does not presuppose illness
and vice versa.

We now know that Kulu women do not include disease in their diagnoses.
They start from a symptom, determined socioculturally, and incorporate it in a
system of ideas, constructed in part on a foundation of magic. Representatives
for the folk sector in their health care system do much the same. The folk healers
may, of course, form opinions and diagnoses which differ from the women's in
their personal sector. The crucial difference is with the scientific sector's representatives, whose diagnoses can take cognizance of disease as well as illness,
assuming that they understand the latter. It they do not, their diagnosis can be
based solely on disease.

Turkish physicians in the scientific sector often have to base their diagnoses on illness alone because many of them lack the aid for establishing disease. In their interpretation of illness, however, they use knowledge about disease and a biomedical classification system.

These observations indicate that it is physicians in the scientific sector who are specialists with a potential for treating both illness and disease. As we shall see, in reality it is not particularly common that they do so.

When the women move between two communities that are as disparate environmentally and socioculturally as Kulu and Tensta, they have to confront many new questions. These include questions about the causes of illness and the effectiveness of treatments. The two environments also give rise to different symptoms among them and their children. As a result, the functions of specialists are questioned or sometimes reinforced. In order to arrive at an understanding of the sociocultural environments in which the women live in Kulu and Tensta respectively, these environments will be described next.

C. The Women of Rural Anatolia

What sort of life did the Kulu women who moved to Europe leave behind them? The tradition that influenced the first generation of immigrant women from Kulu is being tranformed in many ways, and part of the reason lies in the scale of the emigration. This affects the women who are left behind by emigrant husbands, as well as those who accompany their husbands [15;1].

The traditional way of life, common to Anatolian persons, has been decribed in ethnographic reports since before the mid-1960s. Accounts of ecologic, economic and social conditions are to be found in monographs on villages and small towns.[4]

Although it is difficult to generalize from these ethnographic presentations, before discussing the Kulu women's health care system in Sweden I shall try to outline the rules for social life with which these women grew up.

In large parts of central Anatolia the peasants have long been accustomed to a subsistence economy or a combination of this and a money economy. Women account for a large share of production and their burden is heavy. They work in the fields, with certain regional variations, participate in harvests, carry home water and firewood, prepare fuel from cow dung, water and care for the animals, cook, sew, and manage the home and children. A women's work in this type of economy is unpaid and is regarded as a way of life rather than an occupation. When asked whether they worked, peasant women in such an economy invariably answered "no" [25;4].

Self-sufficient peasant families are not so common any more in the Kulu district, either where the traditional pattern has been altered by modern technology or where production is part of the national economy. Farm mechanization and national markets for crops have made survival difficult for small family farms in large parts of the Anatolian plateau. Several of the families that have moved to Sweden belonged to such small farms whose land was sold to large agricultural enterprises.

With mechanized farming, female labor in the field becomes redundant. The consumption economy that results from large-scale operations involves ready-made articles in the form of bread and other food, clothing, fuel, and so on. This can be seen as an advantage for women in that it relieves them of heavy burdens. At the same time, however, it may upset the balance between women and men and their respective contributions to production.

The peasant women still have a heavy load, but the whole day can now be spent inside the home. It is here that rules of life, largely based on the Islamic code, are inculcated [15:138]. This is where a child, a girl, and a young woman learn their future rights and obligations.

The family aims to marry off its daughters to honorable men and families. At 14–17 years of age a daughter exchanges her family for an environment—often strange, sometimes hostile—where as a *gelin*[5] she is exploited for the heaviest household tasks.

A *gelin* belongs to the female collective in the new family. She has learnt that the men and the older women in the family are to be respected. There can be no questioning the ideological foundation for this respect or the social order to which it gives rise [15:131–168].

It is the men who decide all questions to do with matters outside the household, e.g., whether the women may visit a household in another village or consult a healer or physician. The family's joint economy is also controlled by the men.

The sexes are separated not only during the day, when the men leave the household, but also in the evening when they have returned. Women and children often eat and spend the evening in each other's company, as do the men. The younger women serve the food and mind the children; they seldom sit at the table.

A young woman also has to learn the tasks involved in running a household. Her models and judges are the other women around her. She learns to handle family disputes and to deal with illness and accidents. Many of these women become highly skilful in traditional healing, magic, and soothsaying [21:235,43:22].

The woman's world—the time she spends without her husband in the company of other women—has a particular social structure, a system of obligations and rights based on age, number of children (sons in particular), skills and efficiency, relationship to the men of the family, and conduct in terms of honor and shame. Women participate in social activities, ceremonies and rituals that are set apart from the male world. This means that women may have considerable freedom of action in a household of this type [cf. 21:255]. One can say that the limits are imposed by the men but that the room to maneuver within these limits may be very great.

The ways in which illness is to be perceived and expressed are something that women learn from an early age, in close touch with other women and subject to the limits set by the men. They acquire, consciously and subconsciouly, the expressions that induce a reaction from those around them and help to relieve their discomfort. Children mind their younger siblings, carrying, feeding, comforting, and tending the smallest. Above about 5 years of age, a child's reactions to the symptoms of younger siblings may also help to form the adult sick-role pattern.

Young women are not supposed to display pain or symptoms of illness to men, including their own brothers and father. A sexually mature woman should not disclose problems that have to do with her sex. Birth pains are not to be revealed to a man; if an older man is present, young women giving birth for the first time may endure labor for a considerable period without showing that they are in pain.[6]

Older women and those with several births behind them learn to control pain until it can be expressed legitimately. Even when she is ill, a woman's condition has to be very serious before she will be absolved from her everyday responsibilities. The manifestations of illness which indicate that a woman has given up and is asking for help are often very tangible and dramatic. Expert help may be difficult to obtain, assistance from outside the household is costly, and the woman's contribution is essential for the survival of the household. Moreover, the matter of who is entitled to display symptoms of illness and whether when and to whom they may do so is regulated in relation to the woman's age and her social position in the household.

Among themselves the women give expression to their troubles, pain and bodily complaints while continuing to function in their everyday roles. When illness behavior starts to express something that others definitely consider calls for treatment, a process is initiated in the personal sector of the women's health care system that may lead on to the folk and scientific sectors.

The farming communities have been caught up in the structural changes in the Turkish economy and the drive for mechanization and economies of scale. The family pattern had started to change and adopt new forms to satisfy new requirements even before the era of emigration to Europe [cf.28:261–271]. Large composite households have disintegrated into smaller units of the nuclear type, with or without functions in common, and this has been accompanied by the emergence of other types of family [31;8:219–241]. When young families break away from the extended family for some reason to function on their own, the woman—lacking the support of the other women in her husband's family—may turn for assistance to her own mother. Newlyweds who live with the woman's parents are looked down on; even so, many families have opted for this alternative [28:263].

The changes in Turkey are by no means confined to the rural parts of central Anatolia but they are compounded there by the number of men who emigrate

from the villages without their women and children [15;1;28]. Emigration does
not necessarily result in an improved material standard for those who still live in
the villages. They may be better off as individual consumers, in that every family
has some member in Europe who sends back money and saves up for land,
buildings, and capital goods. But the general standard in the village is liable to
suffer. The price of a bride and the cost of a wedding, with gold, gifts, musi-
cians, a cirsumciser, food, and so on, escalate because prices are pushed up by
the "capitalists" from Europe.

Medical resources and the general state of health show no signs of changing, at
least according to studies from other parts of central Anatolia where conditions
are similar [6,33].[7] As a preliminary to describing the life of the Kulu women in
Sweden, I shall now consider the part of their background that has to do with the
health care system, chiefly the scientific and folk sectors, which are also utilized
by the emigrants.

D. Health Care in Turkey and in Kulu

In Turkey, as in most countries, professional physicians and health care resources tend to be concentrated in the cities. In 1965, which was roughly when
people started to leave Kulu, 45% of the physicians in Turkey were attending to
the health of 10% of the total population. These physicians, of whom 60% were
specialists, were to be found in the three largest cities: Ankara, Istanbul and
Izmir. At the time the country had 22.6 hospital beds per 10,000 persons
[48:1492]. In the province of Konya, which includes Kulu, there was only one
doctor to service 7,332 persons and as many as 608 persons per hospital bed (see
Table I).

Some other figures which may be relevant here are listed in Table 2.

In Kulu district there is one small hospital with 15 beds, located in Kulu town.
There are three general practitioners, a dentist, a pharmacist, and 10 nursing
personnel (including 7 nurses and aides, of whom 5 function as midwives); they
are attached to the hospital and also cope with ambulatory cases. In addition, the
district has 3 private practitioners and 5 privately owned pharmacies.

Exact figures for child mortality in Kulu are not available but the area in which

Table 1. Population of Turkey

Census of:	Total population (1000s)	Rural population (per cent)
1935	15,158	76,5
1945	18,790	74,6
1955	24,065	70,8
1965	31,391	65,6
1975	40,347	58,4

Table 2. Worker Emigration to Europe Broken Down by the Area of Turkey from Which the Individuals Emigrated (per cent)

Area	1962	1963	1967	1968	1969
a. Istanbul	52,9	40,6	20,6	11,4	5,4
b. Ankara		5,7	5,1	3,3	4,8
c. Izmir		4,3	5,5	4,0	4,6
Total for a, b, c		51,1	32,2	18,7	14,8
Other areas		48,9	67,8	81,3	85,2

Source: (48:1623)

the district lies has a rate of 214 per 1000 and life expectancy at birth there is 48.3 years [36]. There has been no prophylactic health care apart from campaigns against tuberculosis, malaria, trachoma, and so on, and certain vaccination programs. Perinatal health care is available only in the large cities and more densely populated areas, and then only for a small section of the population [26:53].

Health care is free of charge only for persons who are insured via their employment. This inevitably excludes the peasant population. As health care is based in many respects on commercial interest, it tends to be beyond the reach of the rural population—the large cities are far away and they cannot afford to spend large sums on health care. As we shall see, these and other circumstances oblige the people of Kulu to rely on personal and folk health care to a large extent.

E. Scientific Health Care

Everyday symptoms and signs such as fever, diarrhea, headache, and cough are generally either ignored or treated at home by the women without seeking any advice or expertise. If the women need some scientific medicine that they know is effective against persistent symptoms of this kind, they turn to the pharmacies that sell certain drugs without a prescription.[8] Shops where food is sold may stock antibiotics and analgesics. The women can get advice about which medicine they need from shopowners as well as pharmacy staff. Whether the drug is an antibiotic or a painkiller, it will be taken until the symptom subsides.

Prudent shopkeepers lay up a stock of these medicines for the winter. They can then supply the villagers when the road to the distant city is blocked by snow and rain.

If the symptoms are sufficiently alarming and the family is relatively well off, scientific and folk health care are used side by side. The sequence depends on the nature of the symptom and what its cause is believed to be. When a family has resolved to consult a scientific doctor, it is up to the head of the family to decide the where and when. It is usually a doctor in Kulu who is consulted first. If the case is difficult he will recommend a hospital or a specialist in Konya or Ankara. The Kulu women regard the large hospitals as dangerous places where people die.

If a hospital is held to be definitely the last resort for an illness process, it may well be that patients arrive too late. This opinion results in people putting off visits to hospital still longer. The journey, moreover, takes at least two hours, the clinics are overcrowded and patients have to wait a long time.

Being afraid of hospitals and seeing the task of scientific medicine as being to relieve pain and other discomfort, Kulu women turn in the first place to private practitioners. The women are favorably disposed towards these physicians, who live up to their expectations as regards role behavior and medicines.

Let us see how a consultation can run with a doctor in Konya. The patient, whom we can call Güldis, is 25 years of age and is staying in Kulu with her children to see her parents. Knowing that she would be coming to Kulu, she has been waiting to consult a doctor for several months, notwithstanding an aching pain below her ribs. Her father promised to accompany her to Konya as soon as he had a day free. This involved a further wait of three weeks and then the trip was made because the father wanted me and my husband, who were his guests, to see Konya.

Having entered the street, we go in without more ado to a doctor whose name seemed familiar to Güldis's father. Ascending a narrow staircase and entering a small, cold room, we find a woman and a man already waiting. When we have sat down, only a few minutes pass before a man in a white coat and horn-rimmed spectacles enters the room. He greets us and then hands a thermometer to the waiting woman, who is sitting next to us with her husband. She takes the thermometer and is told by the doctor, who addresses her husband, to place it in her armpit. The woman, who is wearing numerous layers of clothes and has a large shawl round her head and shoulders, makes frantic efforts to do as she is told without having to shed any garments. Meanwhile the doctor asks Güldis and me to come into another, very small room. This is furnished with a desk, three chairs, a table with some instruments against a wall, a couch with a screen in front of it and a small bookshelf. The doctor asks us to sit down and starts to talk with Güldis about her pain--where it is, what it feels like and how long she has had it. Güldis replies by describing and pointing to the place where it hurts. He asks Güldis to sit, fully dressed, on the couch and feels her abdomen and back for a long time in silence. When she has returned to her seat in front of the desk he explains that she has an inflamed gall bladder and he will prescribe medicine to put an end to the pain. He also says that she ought not to drink so much coffee and tea and should not eat nuts (Güldis is holding a bag of sunflower seeds and pistachio nuts, which she has been munching unceasingly).

Güldis has just nodded in response to this. Now she asks if she may go to the lavatory, whereupon the doctor takes a small tin mug from the table, on which there is also a machine of some kind and a small microscope, and asks her for a sample of urine. During her absence he tells me that Turkish women from Germany and Sweden bring all of their problems to him when they visit their native community in the summer. Many of their aches and pains have a psychological cause. This they do not understand and they expect to get tangible help, preferably in the form of injections. Güldis has trouble with her gall bladder in addition to pain of nervous origin.

We are offered coffee by the doctor and when Güldis returns with the tin mug, he goes to the table, places the mug on the machine and presses a button. The mug starts to rotate, the noise is deafening and we sit in silence until he turns off the machine. He then takes a glass slide, rubs it with a linen rag, dabs it with the content of the mug, inserts it in the microscope and leans forward to take a long look. After a while he gets up and gives us a meaningful nod—the urine contains bacteria.

The doctor sits down and writes out a prescription for five different drugs: an analgesic, a diuretic, an antibiotic, vitamins, and a tranquilizer. With a gesture towards the window he indicates that there is a pharmacy across the street to which we can go to obtain the drugs. We return to the waiting room, where the doctor speaks to Güldis's father, who pays him, and we prepare to leave. The doctor has brought the tin mug with him and now gives it to the woman who has been sitting in the waiting room, and asks for a sample of urine. I have not seen him clean it out.

We go to the pharmacy and buy the medicines. Güldis's father has paid out more than 300 lira all told, which for him is a large sum. She talks about the doctor's diagnosis and is pleased that he understood her illness and had been able to provide her with a remedy for it.

After a day or so Güldis feels that the pains have ceased. She soon forgets that she has been ill and stops taking the medicines, which she saves in case similar symptoms occur in the future.

The Kulu woman finds this kind of visit to a professional practitioner satisfactory. She feels that her illness has been recognized and accepted; it earned a diagnosis that warrants medication and after a time the latter proved effective in eliminating the symptom, her pain. She finds the doctor skilful—he could tell which medicine she needed "just with his hands". By not asking too much, performing a test in her presence and telling her just what to do to get well, he has come up to her expectations. The doctor in turn does what he can to oblige his patient. He knows that the women who have migrated to Europe somatize all kinds of complaints and troubles. But he also knows that they will neither understand nor accept a psychological explanation. In order to achieve an intelligible interaction with the woman and please her, he performs a ritual that may well be a standard practice for most patients: he establishes that the urine contains bacteria. Other than that the gall bladder is giving trouble, an opinion which may or may not be based on realistic suspicions, he has a confirmed biological change of a bacteriological nature on which to construct his treatment. By detecting a disease he legitimates the woman's illness, for himself as well as for her.

The scientific doctors are regarded by the women in Kulu as alternative specialists. The treatments, diagnoses, and medicines which these physicians provide satisfy the women's need for alleviation of symptoms. In a sense, these women look at scientific medicine and magic actions in the same way; both are considered to have an inherent ability to eliminate something evil.

F. Folk Health Care

Magical treatments are performed exclusively by folk healers, of whom there are plenty throughout Anatolia [10;2;17;50]. The oldest kind of magician whose knowledge and powers are used to treat illness is known as a *hoca* (pronounced hodya).

A *hoca* is a teacher versed in scripture who serves in mosques and schools for teaching the Koran. He functions as a prayer-leader and an interpreter of the Koran. In rural areas these men have frequently acted as confidants and spiritual guides. Their authority and knowledge have conveyed the impression of a person in touch with God.

The pronouncements and decisions of a *hoca* have often gone unchallenged on account of his ability to read and write. For those who consult him, his social significance is equivalent to that of a Swedish physician for a Swedish patient. He plays an important role in legitimizing illness, above all when this is associated with a breach of norms or other deviations.

Reading the Koran as a means of curing illness is strictly secondary to the tasks of a *hoca*. However, the divining power which a *hoca* displays by interpreting the Koran has always been regarded by the peasant as something sacred and curative. The Koran is the repository of all secrets about life and death. By reading the Koran a *hoca* can divine how illness has arisen and identify the evil forces that have been involved.

The term *hoca* is also used for persons with no religious training who have the art of healing as their principal occupation. The *hocas* whom the women in Kulu consult are mostly of this type, which is also known as *cinci* or *büyücü*. Persons who do not deign to use their services, or do not admit to doing so, may refer to them somewhat disparagingly as *üfürükcü* ("he who blows'"[9]). As the Kulu women use the term *hoca* even for these healers and magicians, I shall do so here.

The therapeutic power of a *hoca* derives not from the knowledge acquired from a formal training but from his ability to employ magic. His activity has been banned in Turkey ever since the reforms of Atatürk. While using the Koran, moreover, he contravenes the rules about magic that are laid down there.

The women in Kulu ususally go to a *hoca* whom someone has recommended. During my stay in Kulu in the summer of 1977 there were several situations that occasioned such a visit. One of them concerned a boy who had undergone a transformation when the family made the trip from Stockholm to Kulu for his wedding. He suddenly refused to marry the girl who had been chosen for him since childhood.

The entire clan assembled to discuss what had happened to the boy. Being convinced that the boy had come under an evil influence on an earlier occasion, it was agreed that he would have to be treated by a *hoca*. His father decided to take him to a *hoca* in a village some kilometers away.

The content of the visit to the hoca was formalistic. All those involved in these consultations know what is happening and what it signifies. The father and son get a signal to go into the *hoca* after a friend, who has visited him before, has entered first and given an account of the case. They stand in front of the magician, who does not address them directly but starts to read from the book in front of him. The father and son go and sit against one of the long walls of the room, which is completely unfurnished. They sit on a carpet with a cushion behind their back and appear to be completely at ease with what is going on. Everyone is silent except the *hoca,* who reads continuosly. There is no direct verbal communication between him and the visitors.

Having read for some time, the *hoca* takes a piece of paper on which he writes a few lines, places it in a bowl of water and resumes his reading. After awhile he holds out the bowl to the boy, who drinks the water. This procedure is repeated twice, first to burn the writing and blow the smoke over the boy and then to sew in the paper in a small bag of cloth and attach this to the boy. The boy and his father believe that the power in the words from the Koran will restore him to his normal self.

The same type of treatment can be obtained for illness, but it is then usually accompanied by other forms of folk health care or scientific care.

This example illustrates the social function of the magician: he absolves the boy from responsibility for norm-breaking behaviour. As is the case with illness, the *hoca* confirms that his client has been attacked by an external force that only his treatment will cure. The diagnosis in this example—an evil force has struck the boy—is confirmed and made explicit by the joint treatment in the course of the ritual. In the event of illness a *hoca* may also recommend that his client should see a scientific doctor in conjunction with a visit to him. Cases involving a breach of norms never reach another specialist. They are handled exclusively in the personal and folk sectors.

The chief feature of encounters between a *hoca* and his client is the writing of amulets or *muska.* [10] There are other folk healers who may perform magic treatments but they combine these with more technical methods. Such healers are know as *ocak.* [11]

I have not been able to establish how many *ocaks* there are in Kulu and its surroundings. It is clear, however, that they are available for every conceivable condition and that the Kulu women and their families have no difficulty in reaching them. The remuneration of a *hoca* and *ocak* varies in size and nature in the same way as the fee of a scientific physician. In some cases there is no payment until a treatment involving several visits has been completed; in others, payment is made each time. Besides money, remuneration may take the form of gold, carpets, china, and other capital goods.

An *ocak,* who may be either a man or a woman, is often a specialist in a particular illness and is considered to have inherited knowledge and ability from either parent. In many cases the power is said to derive from some ancestor's contact with the particular evil that causes the illnesses which the *ocak* is then a specialist at curing. An instance of this is *alci,* an *ocak* whose speciality is curing the illness *albasması,* which can be equated here with the disease puerperal fever. Some relative once managed to stick a pin or the like into *alkarısı,* the evil witch who causes the illness.

Much more could be written about the activities of *ocaks* in Kulu and its surroundings, supplemented with descriptions of other folk healers whose services concern accidents, love disputes, and breaches of norms. The pertinent point here, however, is the plentiful supply of various specialists in the folk sector of the women's health care system and the fact that the healers are considered to cure a wide variety of named illnesses. The healers treat the Kulu women and comply with their wishes in a manner that these women expect. Their common culture means that these health care encounters are of great therapeutic importance.

G. Struggling against Evil Forces

Like other people, the women from Kulu have ideas about what the world is like and how it functions. This system of ideas includes a belief in natural causes. The knowledge and perceptions of such causes are incorporated in a cognitive structure that was erected and developed in Kulu's sociocultural environment. The cognitive structure that most of these women have in common also contains explanatory theories about illness, accidents and death (all such events are considered to be of one kind). As new generations grow up and spend their adult life in a new environment, these theories are liable to change. Among the first generation of immigrant women from Kulu, the shared cognition and its theories about causality live on to a large extent as a source of order and predictability in all the vicissitudes of life.

In their search for causes of illness and misfortune, the Kulu women draw on their conception of the world, including its religious and magical aspects. Their actions in connection with illness may be clear manifestations of these ideas.

The women consider that their lives may be affected by a variety of phenomena. On the one hand there are those which can be classified as mediated forces. Examples of these are misfortune that strikes through targeted actions of a person or spirit (*büyü, cins*) as well as evil forces, transmitted by a person more inadvertently (*nazar*), and the force inherent in the will of God. On the other hand, there are unmediated forces such as heat, cold, moisture, wind, sunlight, and so on.

Before reviewing the mediated forces that cause illness, misfortune and death, I shall briefly describe how mediated and unmediated causes are related. For the women perceive these phenomena, not as the separate entities presented here, but as interrelated parts of a whole system of ideas, a repository of explanations for specific events and situations.

Besides providing infallible rules for daily life, Islam can be of assistance in clearing up special circumstances connected with illness. Help in this respect can also be obtained from the spirits and beings that are sometimes associated with Islam - various *cins,* which are considered in the next section.

Nazar, the evil eye, is not associated with Islam but the content of the Koran may be involved in the way in which *nazar* is averted. For the Kulu women, *nazar* is a natural, animate explanation for a great deal of life's complexities.

The next section deals with *büyü,* a large field that contains all kinds of magic: magic that harms or that purifies, heals and cures, magic that is evil and magic that is good, magic as a cause of misfortune and magic as medicine and remedy.

II. CAUSES OF MISFORTUNE, ILLNESS AND DEATH

Different cultures generate different explanations as to why people become sick and die, why the rain destroys the harvest and why a house is destroyed by fire. The philosophy of the Kulu women provides alternative ways of explaining events that occasion anxiety, disorder or a threat. These alternatives are integrated into the system of ideas which these women mobilize to varying degrees to cope with problems in their daily life.

The causal explanations the women use are, as mentioned already, of two types, mediated and unmediated—and these are not mutually exclusive.

When a child falls ill in the cold of winter or heat of summer, a Kulu woman reasons that an unmediated force, that is to say, the cold or the heat, has entered the child, causing it to be ill. At the same time, many children survive the winter and summer without falling ill from the cold and heat; neither is her child ill every winter and summer. Accordingly she has to consider why the cold or heat has afflicted just her child at this particular time. The answer to this question— why something has happened that does not happen to everyone on every occasion—lies in the omnipresent mediated causes: *cins,* the evil eye or magic.

The way in which the Kulu women explain, for instance, why a boy has fallen as he ran down a staircase that has a faulty step, is reminiscent of such explanations in ethnographic accounts of other communities [16:63–83]. The boy has run up and down stairs many times before and now, suddenly, he falls. Why? Because he ran too fast? No, he ran no faster than usual. Because the step is faulty? It's been that way a long time and he has not tripped on it before. It must have been some evil force that caused the boy on this particular occasion to trip and hurt himself as he ran down the faulty stairs.

The mediated causes in their world of ideas provide the Kulu women with the missing link between two mutually independent phenomena. When matters which generally function smoothly covary in a way that contradicts the usual order of things, mediated causes serve a logical function in the explanation.

The belief of these women in mediated causes does not conflict with their insights into cause and effect. Their conception of the world is as real to them as ours is for us. One cause may be impersonal and therefore nonsocial, while another involves a medium and is therefore social, with different implications. On some occasions when something happens, the women may concern themselves exclusively with the causal component that is relevant socially.

As pointed out earlier, events that are disturbing or unfamiliar prompt the Kulu women—like anyone else—to look for an explanation. When a member of their group falls ill, they try to identify the cause of the illness. In this they are assisted by the etiology, which also underpins their actions. An etiology invariably takes the form of a narrative. It is anchored in time, episodic, and may refer to a period before the illness struck.

> "My child was afflicted by *nazar* when he was a year old. She had a lovely red dress, which accentuated her white skin. A women admired her. That night she got a fever that lasted two days. We called on a woman near Kulu who is *ocak*. She did *kurşun dökme* and gave us the water. My daughter's fever disappeared but she has been thin ever since. She is often ill like this."

Such etiologies have certain features in common with myth. They relate events analytically, giving certain facts more weight than others. Social facts are communicated in ways that all those involved understand and which indicate the sort of relationships that exist between the ill person and the community. Like certain etiologies, a myth can "provide a point of reference in the past beyond which one need not go" [13:350].

Mediated forces, besides supplying answers to the question "Why just me?", provide the Kulu women with a key that prevents their world and society from appearing chaotic. They perform a similar function by clearly indicating that the women are not to blame. The concept of an "evil eye" supports the view that no blame for an illness attaches to the person who is ill. Neither is a woman to be blamed if her child is ill. The scientific "bacteria theory", on the other hand, usually explains how a disease has been incurred, but when it helps to explain why, often does so in terms of responsibility and blame. A Swedish doctor might voice his opinion as follows:

> The Kulu women do not look after their children. They leave them unattended so that they burn themselves and as they fail to have them seen to, the burns become infected. When older

children are diseased, no effort is made to keep them away from a baby. The chances of
infection are high. As I see it, hygiene is not as it should be among the families from Kulu and
this contributes in the highest degree to infections.

The blame for an illness, whether of a child or of the woman herself, is a burden
that clearly fails to invest the illness period with a narrative that fits the women's
reality. Their social relationships and their actions for maintaining these have to
be assimilated in their etiologies.

A. Islam

Innumerable sources have influenced the way in which the Kulu women
construe the world and everything that happens to them and their families. There
are no clear dividing lines between these sources. Their impulses merge to form
the fund of experience and insights that is manifested and modified in these
women's daily life.

I start with Islam because lifestyles and specific rules are invariably attributed
explicitly to the common religion. The Kulu women never question the existen-
tial presence of God and the view that everything is ultimately ordained by Him
is one to which they all subscribe as entirely self-evident. When asked what their
religion means in their lives, the women usually answer, "What else is there?"
God is the fount of all truth and all decisions affecting men; all good and all evil
are manifestations of His will. He has given man the Koran as a guide. God
knows best and humans cannot influence His will. It does not occur to the Kulu
women to wonder why God acts as he does. They simply say, "That's how it
is." The rules for the ideal Moslem life, as expressed in the Koran, become
commonplace for the Kulu women as religion fuses with their experience of how
everything is related and how the world works.

The knowledge of the Koran that the Kulu women acquire is constantly being
modified and reinterpreted. Those who attended a Koran school in childhood
learnt certain prayers by heart and were instructed to follow certain religious
rules, such as the daily prayer, *namaz*. Of the mandatory rules for Moslem life
that are incorporated in the five pillars of Islam, it is chiefly prayer that plays an
active part in the life of the Kulu women (Sura II from Medina, Koran; cf.
[35:34]). The older women pray five times a day; the younger ones say that will
start doing so when they are older. But prayer is also used as a force to influence
events, for preventive as well as curative purposes, and it then has a different
significance.

In Kulu the religious life is part of the women's daily round, and they see
nothing unusual in looking for help and explanations for accidents and sickness
in religious terms. However, trying to explain why a child is seriously ill, or why
a close relative has died or been involved in an accident, is not just a religious
concern for these women. Several of their conceptions and methods of treatment

have little to do with Islam. Some of the resultant causal connections and explanations are quite unconnected with religion. Let us now take a look at particular causes which the Kulu women can invoke as alternative explanations for misfortune and illness.

B. Cins

Certain spirits, known in the singular as *cin* (pronounced djin, Arabic Jinni), can afflict people directly, eliciting symptoms that the Kulu women immediately attribute to them. *Cins* are the spirits whose association with religion is most explicit. The Koran recognizes their existence.

A *cin* may be male or female (Koran, Sura VI). *Cins* are believed to live in the community and have their own leaders (*beys* and *padisahs*). All their deeds are done at night and they withdraw to their own territory when the cock crows. During the night they assemble at mills, public baths (*hammams*), old abandoned buildings, ruins, graves, under large trees, and so on. By day they sleep by rubbish heaps, privies, muddy pools, under roofs, and the like. This means that even during the day people must take pains not to disturb or irritate them. Among other things, one must not urinate on rubbish heaps or pools of water. When people go to the privy or other places that are dark and dirty, they say *destur*, "excuse me" [10:91].

All unidentified spirits can be labelled *cins*, and the women have seen them in human and animal forms. According to the women, *cins* occasionally reveal themselves to human beings but only to one person at a time. They are harmless unless something makes them angry, in which case they "strike" and may even kill a person.

The disguises that *cins* employ vary—a black cat, a black dog, a lamb, an eagle, etc. They may also take the form of a gigantic human figure, white-skinned and thin, or a beautiful woman, a daughter-in-law (*gelin*), a dwarf, or a wrapped-up infant. They constantly change their disguise and on some occasions may take the form of an object. Fickle and omnipresent, they afflict people in a rather arbitrary way. Dramatic events are often explained as the work of *cins*. A person who faints or has an attack of convulsions has clearly been struck by a *cin*.

There are also *cins* that afflict people in a particular way. They induce terror, paralyze, come only at night, in a particular season, on a certain day and so on. Examples of such *cins* are: *kara-kura, alkarısı, cadı, çarşamba karısı* and *albiz* [10:91–95]. In the forty days after childbirth, known as the *lohusa* period, a woman is liable to contract *albastı* or *albasması*.

Albasması has been translated by a Turkish sociologist as "a raid of red" [10:95]. This condition is caused by *alkarısı* or *alkadın*, translated by the same person as "the woman of red". *Al* signifies red here. The word *albasması* has also been traced back to the work-stem *alp* = alf, a kind of demon or *cin* that has appeared in various contects in shapes that resemble a combination of human and animal forms, or as a dead person.

To the Kulu women *alkarısı* is a witch, a woman with long fingers and nails and a great deal of hair, or a small, fat woman with tiny hands. Dressed in red with large breasts, she frequents stables, rivers, and springs. *Alkarısı* is usually active at twilight. According to the Kulu women she comes to a person who has just given birth and wants her lungs. Many women tell of relatives and friends who have been visited by *alkarısı* and they frequently claim to have seen her themselves on various occasions. She comes to women when they are alone, sits on the bed and waits for them to fall asleep. The infant may be threatened, too. Those who have felt her approach relate that she ultimately sits on their chest and tries to extract their lungs in order to eat them or hurry off to put them in water. They say that it is her breath that makes them hot. Everything turns red, they feel as though they can neither cry out, speak, or breath. Many Kulu women have died at the hand of *alkarısı* when they have contracted *albasması*, her affliction which can seldom be cured.

To ward off *alkarısı* a woman has to observe certain rules during the forty days after childbirth. Women in Kulu generally do so meticulously. They refrain from going outdoors and are particularly careful not to be left alone at any time of the day or night. The room in which they lie must not be dark, and they should sleep with the Koran under their pillow. Other measures—such as having one of her husband's garments on the bed and a needle, scissors or other pointed object within reach—vary with the circumstances and the state of the woman. Most women tie a red ribbon to the bed during the *lohusa* period. This is said to afford protection from *alkarısı*.

Alkarısı dreads objects that are sharp or made from metal, which is why the woman has them by her during these forty days. Some of those who have seen *alkarısı* have managed to pull her long hair until she has promised not to afflict their family. A person who has managed to pierce *alkarısı* with a pin becomes a specialist in treating *basması*. Such a healer, male or female, is known as *alcı*. Many women have stated that a family member or relative has seen *alkarısı* with a lung in her hand and that, as a result, they have an *alcı* in their family. An *alcı* can forbid *alkarısı* to enter or approach their land or to take an object or person belonging to their family. During the *lohusa* period an *alcı* usually calls to declare *melúne cabuk git* ("evil being, depart"). If a woman or her child is struck by *albasması*, the alcı describes a ring round them and recites prayers.

C. Nazar

Conceptions of an evil eye are to be found in conjunction with a variety of religious outlook and social systems. In anthropological literature the evil eye has been compared with witchcraft, since the capacity for visual transmission of an evil influence is associated with certain individuals or a particular group

[39:311;37:279;22:152]. It is generally considered that the evil eye refers to envy and jealousy on the part of one who casts evil glances [23:165–186;40:201–207]. Ideas about the evil eye existed long before Judaism, Christianity, and Islam. The Koran does not mention it explicitly but a verse that is frequently cited runs as follows:

In the name of God, the Merciful, the compassionate
Say: I take refuge with the Lord of the Daybread,
from the evil of what he has created,
from the evil of darkness when it gathers,
from the evil of women who blow on knots,
from the *evil of an envier when he envies*

(Koran, Sura CXIII, my italics; [5:362;35:435].

Nazar is constantly present in the lives of the women in Kulu. A belief in *nazar*, i.e., the evil eye, is found throughout Turkey, to varying degrees among different groups in society. A notable feature of *nazar* in this word is that its power can be transmitted by anyone at any time. One can never be sure of having it under control or of foreseeing when it will strike. But there are many ways of trying to ward off *nazar* and of treating afflicted persons.

A *nazar* requires a human agent, and there is often speculation about who this may be in a particular case. Kulu naturally has its deviant persons, such as those with blue or green eyes and fair hair, who may be suspected of having looked at a child who has fallen ill. But it is just as conceivable that the force was transmitted by the child's mother. *Nazar* usually strikes in conjunction with statements that something or someone is beautiful and successful. If such statements are not accompanied by protective measures, the power may be transmitted to the admired object or person.

The Arabic expression *Maşallah* (''in the name of God'') is used in Turkey by all categories of people, in cities as well as rural areas, after a word of praise or an admiring look. Even a glance without any words may thus suffice to transmit this evil force.

Preventive measures against *nazar* and treatment of symptoms elicited by this source can, for instance, involve concealing the subject, as when outsiders are kept away from a *lohusa* and her infant for forty days after delivery. Another form of protection involves making the subject unrecognizable to the the source of power, e.g., making a child ugly by adorning it with objects that are considered ugly, dressing it in worn-out clothes or daubing its face with black patches. The Kulu women use such measures to ''deceive'' the source of power by transforming what they consider to be *nazar's* targets—the weak, beautiful and successful—into their opposites. A third group of protective measures, finally, involves placing an obstacle between the source of power and the subject. A *nazarlık* (= anti-*nazar*) or a *muska* is attached to the child or whatever is to be protected. Such obstacles attract the evil power to themselves, thereby diverting it from the person or object that carries them.

D. Büyü

Much of what happens to the Kulu women is explained by them with the aid of such phenomena as *cins* and *nazar*. Both these phenomena are conceived as evil forces that necessitate protective measures. When such measures are of no avail, one needs to know how to treat the symptoms which indicate that the forces have struck. Like their preventive methods, the treatments used by the Kulu women are based on magic, *büyü*. Various events requiring measures on the part of the women, can also be caused by *büyü*.

To clarify *büyü* as a phenomenon we shall consider prevention, methods of treatment and causes of accidents in terms of positive and negative magic. The women use the concept of *büyü* to explain accidents of various kinds. They do not employ it when describing magic methods they use themselves. On a theoretical level, however, this concept comprises all actions that by magical means are intended to prevent or alter a course of events for better or worse. A Turkish sociologist has made a distinction between positive and negative *büyü* [10:128]. As used by the Kulu women, however, the concept invariably has the latter sense, which is equivalent to sorcery. When sorcery is to be practiced, a magician, *büyücü*, is often called in. As the concept "positive *büyü*" does not exist for the Kulu women, I shall avoid it and talk instead about positive magic versus *büyü*, which refers here to negative magic.

Magic is largely confined to the world of women. The men with whom I have talked on the subject have not displayed much insight or an awareness of the vast knowledge in this field that the women possess. The women, on the other hand, have taught me how they use magic actions and indicated that this is a necessary, self-evident part of their daily life.

Büyü as a cause of illness and other kinds of misfortunes refers chiefly to negative magic. This kind of *büyü* indicates that someone has employed magic objects and actions without any moral justification. Such actions are dictated solely by a desire to harm someone. All the women condemn them. Such *büyü* generally has to do with events like crop failure, accidents, serious illness, and death, for which there is no explanation in terms of *cins* or *nazar*. Negative magic, *büyü*, is much more diffuse than positive magic, perhaps because it frightens the women so much that they dislike talking about it. When what I call positive magic is used, the women describe the procedures they have performed. Media are used, usually in the form of *muska*, when practicing positive magic. By invoking *büyü* to account for what has happened, moreover, no blame attaches to the women or those nearest to them. The medium serves as a catalyst, transmitting power when one is impotent.

The instrument that is used most when practicing magic—as prevention and treatment but also in connection with *büyü*—is *muska* [cf.17,10].

Muska comes from the Greek word *nusha* (which means "something written"). This refers to the writing that people carry about as protection against evil forces, usually in the form of short prayers, images or number and words with a magic significance. A *muska* is written by a *hoca* and can be used as general protection against illness and accidents.

In summary, one can say that a common feature of the explanations that the Kulu women provide for events that upset their daily life is that the causes are located outside people, not inside. The causes may be personal or impersonal but their basic significance is the same—they strike people from outside without the victims incurring any blame for this. When "God gives" an illness or "takes" a child, when "*cins* strike" and make a woman afraid and weak, when "*nazar* hits" a child so that it falls and hurts itself, or when someone practices *büyü* and "takes" a woman's husband from her, the situation does not include anything in the form of a consciously accepted act or fantasy involving blame. The resolution and responsibility of the Kulu women are unrelated to their anxiety and fear, as they are to illness, accidents and death.

III. KULU IN TENSTA: MIGRANTS IN THE WELFARE STATE

The Kulu women came to Sweden as a temporary measure, a necessary evil, and constantly longed to return home. As things turned out, however, their stay lasted longer than they had ever imagined. The women and grown-up children started to work for money, like the husbands, and the Swedish allowance was available for young children. As residents in Tensta, the families were catered for by the social services there. Many of the Kulu families found it almost incomprehensible that in Sweden there was no need to suffer poverty on account of illness or unemployment. In such situations the family economy could be maintained by means of insurance systems and social assistance.

The Kulu men came to Sweden in order to work and take back some of the affluence. Some of them were therefore confused to find that so much seemed to be there for the asking. It was not just the existence of insurance to cover circumstances beyond one's control; various situations also entitled one to financial assistance. Free child-minding was provided in conjunction with free instruction in the Swedish language and alphabetization courses. Having given birth, one could stay at home with the infant for a whole year with a maternity allowance. Occupational training could be obtained under the auspices of the National Labor Market Board. There was an allowance for children under 16 and a pension for the elderly. On top of all this, the social welfare office in Tensta helped to pay for food and rent if for some reason people could not manage on their own.

The Kulu women have not been able to comprehend Sweden's economic system and very special social morality. The social reforms and full insurance systems are seen and interpreted by them in the light of their own culture and their earlier life in Turkey. In their conception, some components of the Swedish system are gifts, while other are rights enjoyed by all Turks. As described later, some of the social benefits have served to found a new form of sick role.

The move from Kulu to Sweden has enabled the families to improve their status compared with many of their relatives and friends who still live in Kulu. In Sweden they belong to the working class, performing unqualified jobs, such as cleaning and washing-up, in service industries, but it is chiefly with the remaining families in Kulu that they compare their situation [cf. 4:56–79, 146–149].

Life in Sweden affords a multiplicity of experiences for the Kulu women. A suburb like Tensta, which houses more than a thousand Turks from Kulu, contains a piece of their native district. Large families and kin groups have assembled there. Many women are therefore able to go on living a traditional life in the confines of their household. But there is also a sociocultural environment to which the women have to relate in one way or another. New roles are required, new forms for family life, and the world around them has a different scale of values concerning women and men, bringing up children and caring for the aged. Because some of their ideas and conceptions of reality are frequently questioned in their new surroundings, the Kulu women have become more consciously aware of them. As they encounter values which contrast markedly with their own, the women find it necessary, for instance, to indicate more explicitly to their children what is right and wrong.

This does not mean that in every situation the women reinforce their earlier ideas about what is right and proper. Much that they come across in the new setting is integrated into their system of ideas. They may adhere to earlier conceptions in conscious utterances, while their actions bear witness to the change that is constantly taking place. This ongoing process of adjustment is particularly evident in connection with sickness, accidents, and death.

A. The Kulu Families in Tensta

The dwellings in Tensta are so organized that the women spend more time with their husbands than they did in Kulu. The entire family is often assembled when the men are at home. The narrower scope for interaction between the sexes is not entirely to the women's advantage. In Kulu their life was more separated from that of the men and they formed collectives with other women. It is now much more common for the women to live in nuclear families, with no other woman in the household. It is true that the women call on each other daily but they spend less time working at home, partly because many of them have a paid job elsewhere. When they visit each other and men are in the dwelling, the women invariably sit in the kitchen.

In Sweden the Kulu women also meet away from home. They may see each

other at their workplace and commute in groups. Many women attend some form
of instruction together in the afternoons—a course in alphabetization or Swedish. They meet in waiting rooms at the child health center and the maternity
center, where they pass the time in talk. All kinds of news is exchanged in this
way.

In these ways the collective, domestic life in Kulu has dissolved and acquired
new forms since the women moved to Tensta. This is true in particular of the
women in nuclear households who have a daytime job away from home. Moreover, older women who spend the day at home and live in joint extended
households no longer have the company of their daughters and *gelins*, since most
of the younger women go out to work. Getting used to the new forms for
interaction with other women, as well as with men, is more difficult for some
women than for others. They have developed various forms of buffer mechanisms to preserve their traditional life.

The most tangible change which the move to Sweden has imposed on the Kulu
families arises from the women going out to work. This means that, to some
extent, the younger children spend the day in Swedish institutions such as day
nurseries, playschools and after-school centers.

Several Kulu women find children more of a problem in Tensta than in Kulu.
The youngsters cannot be left alone at home or in the streets and open spaces, as
they could in Kulu. The authorities in Tensta have a say in how the women look
after their children and react if they are left alone. Besides considering it wrong
to pay someone to look after children, many of the women are reluctant to leave
this to Swedes. The children may get the wrong kind of food and learn about
things that are unsuitable. As one women commented, "When children start
saying *no* to their parents, they've started to become Swedish".

For various reasons—such as encouragement from husbands to take a job, the
feeling that children are more trouble than in Kulu and that minding them costs
money if it cannot be arranged internally, coupled with access to an active
contraceptive service at maternity and child welfare centers and hospital birth
clinics—a number of Kulu women have procured contraception or had a legal
abortion with or without the approval of their husband. They consider that two or
three children are enough.

Still, several of them are worried that if they do not give birth to additional
sons, their husband will leave them for a new wife. Older women shrug their
shoulders and say there's nothing to be done, children come from God. To them,
moreover, children are insurance against old age and can lend a hand in the
household. Besides which, many of the older women have given birth to more
than ten children, of whom only five or six have survived. Experience of Kulu's
high child mortality helps to explain why many Kulu women are so opposed to
contraception.

Preventive measures have also been adopted by some young, unmarried wom-
en, who experience entirely new forms of companionship at school and at work.
Their situation, however, is more complicated because marriage with the man

selected by their family presupposes that they are virgin. Doctors sometimes receive agitated mothers, who demand to have their daughter examined to ensure that her maidenhead is intact. If it is not, an operation is called for to restore it. The alarm expressed by the older woman reflects her awareness that an unmarried daughter who has lost her maidenhood is a disaster for the family. It destroys the family's honor, the reputation of the father as the protector of his womenfolk.

Slowly, however, even these strict rules are being modified. The young women and men from Kulu who live in Tensta choose a partner from their own group in consultation with their families. Many matches have been arranged since childhood, with intermarrying cousins as the ideal. If a young woman with a Swedish work and residence permit marries a man in Kulu, he too will be entitled to a work and residence permit in Sweden. Unless one already has parents, children or a spouse in Sweden, this is the only way at present of being allowed to settle in Sweden from Kulu.

Immigrant controls in Sweden[12] have meant that a woman from Kulu who has a Swedish work and residence permit is highly prized. Among the Kulus such a woman is said to have a "golden passport" and this has put up the price which her family can expect when she is married off.[13] Combined with the economic and political problems in Turkey, immigrant controls have generated a huge demand for young, unmarried women, just as women who have lost their husband or divorced in Sweden have no difficulty in remarrying, which was more or less unheard of previously. One woman in Tensta whom two husbands have rejected for being childless is still an attractive person to marry on account of her "golden passport."

Many of the older women had little need of money in their daily life in Kulu. Their attitudes to money and the values it represents is evident in the way they speak about the family's general economy. They talk with pride about everything they have been able to buy in Sweden and show off TV, stereo and video sets, china, tablecloths, and the family car. It is chiefly to each other that they display these possessions. Improving one's status in Kulu by means of material wealth is one of the purposes of living in Sweden.

To the staff at Swedish institutions, however, these women exclaim anxiously that everything is so expensive, that they have difficulty making ends meet, and cannot afford clothes for their children or sufficient food. While admitting to each other that they have never been so well off materially as in Sweden this stance of having a hard time is a reflection of, above all, the attitude they encounter among Swedish social and health care authorities. People there refer to immigrant families as poor, their women as oppressed, and the children as neglected. The families get the impression that Swedes think they are to be pitied. While in Sweden they have learnt that they require various forms of help and assistance. Having been capable peasants in an adverse environment who have managed to break away and start afresh in a distant city, they are now seen as a handicapped group.

It should be noted that, compared with several other groups of immigrants in

Sweden, the Kulus are in a unique situation. They have a large network of relatives and former neighbors, besides being able to return home each year to convey a favorable picture of their life in Sweden to those whom they left behind. The happiness and companionship among the women is seldom expressed outside their homes. And when a Swedish doctor, nurse or social welfare officer calls, their identity as Swedish immigrants comes to the fore, thereby confirming the institutional assessment. The Kulu women respect the institutional staff and try, consciously or otherwise, to live up to the expectations that have been formed among the personnel at various institutions.

The Swedish community have come to perceive the Turkish families as a problem, not least with reference to health care. The Turkish way of life was considered to conflict with many Swedish norms. One general effect of this Swedish reaction has been that various institutions make a deliberate effort to inform, support, and assist this group of immigrants in accordance with official policy.[14]

Implicit in this policy is the view that immigrants are entitled to maintain their cultural antecedents. This has given rise to measures that seem to be designed to prepare the families for possible repatriation rather than adjustment to either a Swedish or a more pluralistic society.

That the goals of immigrant policy, e.g., freedom of choice, have been severely tested is evident from explicit Swedish expressions of alarm and dismay over "malnutrition," "cruelty to children," "child marriages," "oppressed women," "analphabetism," "child criminality," and "child labor."[15] Meanwhile the families have gradually shifted more and more responsibility onto Swedish institutions. "If corporal punishment is not allowed, how should children be brought up? No wonder they commit crimes when we have not been allowed to keep them in order the way we want to. So Swedish society must also take the consequences. It would never have happened in Kulu. Everyone keeps an eye on everyone's children there and children respect their parents." In this situation the children, moreover, have learnt to turn to the social service center for support in conflicts with their parents [cf 9:152–164].

In the midst of all this, several of the women try to reconstruct an ordered existence, a legitimate way of returning to their home and a more traditional life. This is the theme of the next section.

B. Changing Roles for the Kulu Women

Tensta is a complete entity for many Kulu women, a place that has everything one requires, so there is no need to travel. They regard Tensta as their new "village." The few occasions on which they are obliged to leave their Swedish village concern childbirth and illnesses that necessitate a visit to a hospital in the center of Stockholm. On such occasions Tensta relates to Stockholm as Kulu to Ankara.

One Kulu woman who has spent five years in Tensta has left the "village" only three times, once to have a child, once to visit her child at a hospital in Stockholm and once for a trip to Kulu for her son's wedding. In Tensta she feels closer to Kulu than she does to Stockholm.

Other women are away from Tensta all day, travelling by underground or bus to jobs in other suburbs or in Stockholm. It is chiefly these women's roles that have changed substantially. But most of those who do not go out to work have also acquired several new roles. They are pupils at alphabetization or Swedish-language courses, they are patients, e.g., giving birth in a Swedish hopsital, and they are clients and consumers of social services.

For the women who go out to work, life has been split into two spheres. In the sphere of employment they are permitted to travel early in the morning and late at night to unfamiliar places and to do this, as well as to work, in the company of strange men. In the family sphere, on the other hand, they are not allowed even to visit other Turkish families in the evening without a male escort from their household. This sphere is still governed by the traditional rules of the Islamic code.

The women are expected to travel and work in groups. The ideal employment is a "key job," i.e., one where they have a key and clean the office, school, or other premises before or after normal hours. This is a way of isolating the women as far as possible while they are at work. Such jobs however, are not available for all the women and the others work instead in restaurants and hospitals.

By and large the men seem to have accepted the fact that their women are employed in public places, far from home and their own surveillance. The women have found this more difficult. For many of them there is a conflict in having to make a financial contribution to the family's future in the new country while preserving the family honor by keeping away from strange men. The men have coped by seeing employment and the home as two distinct spheres, subject to different rules. This has not been equally feasible for the women.

Many women resort to a new role to relieve them of responsibility in the job sphere. Finding the situation troublesome and even against the rules, many women use this role as a buffer. The role is bound up with the Swedish system for health insurance and the view that women should contribute to the family economy. It is also closely connected with how the women feel in Sweden, their physical and mental well-being, and the extent to which they are entitled to live out their symptoms. It is a fact that many women feel ill more or less continuously. A Swedish way of relating to illness has been adopted, which the women call "sick fund" (the Swedish word, *sjukkassa*, refers to the public health insurance offices which disburse sickness benefits). When a woman relinquishes responsibility for her work outside the home, she says, "I sick fund" (*ben sjukkassayım*). Neither the form nor the content of the Swedish term can be expressed in the Kulu women's own language; "to sick fund" means that one has a legitimized sick role that enables one to stay at home and work in the household without an appreciable loss of income.[16]

As Swedish doctors consider that many of the women's symptoms are psycho-somatic, getting a sick role legitimized at a Swedish hospital is not always easy. The complaints experienced by the women are not perceived as disease and do not necessarily result in an assessment that the woman needs a rest from her job. Such situations will be analyzed later.

Pain constitutes a new symptom for many women, one that they never had in Kulu. The symptom is not sufficient to absolve them of their household tasks. Consequently they may not even consult their immediate family before turning to a Swedish doctor to get the sick role legitimized. The same applies when, for instance, they are attending a literacy course and get a pain in the head, stomach, or back; they may then ask the teacher or some other Swede to help them to reach a doctor. This means that the woman omits the stage in an illness process that customarily gives the immediate family the right to decide which type of illness the symptom represents, whether it should absolve the woman from responsibility, and which expert should be consulted for this particular symptom. An encounter with Swedish health care under these circumstances will be highly unsatisfactory for the woman if her symptom is not perceived as sufficiently serious to be certified as sickness.

In the course of time the women have found their way to doctors—at hospitals or in private practice—who understand their particular situation and consider that their symptoms justify sick leave. They have also managed to find veritable charlatans, who charge a high fee for issuing a certificate without troubling to make an examination.

The women have also realized that in this way they can become "sick," i.e., assume a role in Swedish society that was entirely unknown to them previously. For people in Sweden this role is perfectly legitimate, though it is used in very different ways by different categories. The Kulu women deviate in that they conceive this sick role as differing somehow from illness proper. It relates primarily to life in Sweden.

Noting that the various cultural institutions of the Kulu women function as these women expect does not suffice as a description of their logic. The institutions must also be examined in connection with transition, adjustment, and change, that is to say, when they fail to function as the women expect, with a view to understanding how the women interpret these situations. By explaining functional failures in their institutionsl setup, the women reestablish an orderly reality. New actions and explanations help to reshape their environment. A case in point is the phenomenon "to sick fund"; this serves as a buffer that may diminish conflicts. It is not as easy, however, to incorporate other parts of Swedish health care so as to maintain an orderly, functional life.

The women do feel ill in Sweden, in some cases more so than they did in Kulu. Their new environment allows them to heed their symptoms, besides providing the financial support to which everyone in the community is entitled. But it is only the scientific sector of their new health care system which can

establish just how ill they are and whether it is reasonable that they should use the
sick role as a buffer in this situation.

IV. SCIENTIFIC HEALTH CARE IN TENSTA

In Tensta itself, where the proportion of immigrants is one of the highest in the
country, the Kulu women have access mainly to outpatient care. Such care is
organized in Sweden into primary care districts, each with around 10,000 to
50,000 inhabitants. Each district has one or more health centres. In Tensta,
primary care is delivered in the form of a district pediatric clinic, a child health
center, a maternity health center, a gynecology clinic, a dental center, and a child
and youth guidance center. Neighboring Rinkeby has a district medical center for
adults with several physicians on its staff.

Nowadays outpatient care aims at an integrated approach that permits the
simultaneous provision of medical and social assistance. Outreaching and preventive measures should be a major element and the need for aftercare and
rehabilitation must be taken into account. Teamwork is seen as a means of
achieving an optimum service, with collaboration between doctors, district
nurses, assistant nurses, physiotherapists, occupational therapists, psychologists,
and other personnel. The extension of general medical services has been and still
is restricted mainly by the supply of general practitioners.

Two other forms of decentralized care are known as district care and domicili-
ary care respectively. They are staffed by district nurses, assistant nurses and
nursing aides.

The general medical service consists mainly of unspecialized outpatient care,
psychiatric as well as somatic. It usually also includes various forms of preventive care, examples of which are the maternal and child health services and the
school health service, as well as duties at nursing homes and consultant tasks in
the social services.

The area covered by a general practitioner is known as a medical district.
Since 1971 each county is divided into such districts by the Medical Services
Board. The boundaries are being coordinated with those of the municipalities,
and today the two usually coincide. Outpatient care is usually provided at medical centers staffed by one, two, or three general practitioners.

A. Functions of Outpatient Care

The maternal health center in Tensta is one of 623 in Sweden (1978) where
women can get a pregnancy confirmed and obtain pre- and postnatal care. The
center also has a general advisory service and handles matters to do with family
planning. More than 90% of all pregnant women in Sweden register at a maternity health center, with an average of 12 visits per pregnancy. Practically all
deliveries take place in hospital at a maternity ward (in 1978 less than 0.1%

occurred in the patient's home with a midwife in charge). Psychoprophylactic courses, conducted by midwives in the district, are also well attended.

One of the goals of maternal health care is the early detection and treatment of risks and complications in mothers and infants by means of health supervision during pregnancy and after birth.

In Sweden the low maternal and perinatal mortality rates are attributed in part to the expansion of child and maternal health services and the improvement in hygiene and general standards during the past five decades. In 1975, for instance, only two mothers died in connection with childbirth and perinatal mortality was 10.4 per 1000.

The child health centers, of which there were 1,512 in 1978, are likewise in touch with 90 percent of all children born in Sweden. Among preschool children, i.e., between 1 and 7 years of age, the figure is around 70 percent. The checkups arranged by these centers include vaccination against certain diseases.

Besides supervising immunity, the child health centers are intended to provide advice about dietary matters, consultation concerning a child's upbringing and growth, and a control of physical and mental health in the early years. It is the child health center that is in the best position to detect physical and mental irregularities.

All births are reported at once to a child health center. The infant should be taken to the center for a checkup roughly 10 times in the first year, three in the second and twice a year after that until it reaches school age (7 years), when the school health service takes over. Nurses from the child health center also make home calls at certain intervals: as soon as a mother and her baby have returned from hospital as well as later for particular reasons, e.g., if the mother has failed to keep appointments for some time. All children have to undergo a checkup at four years of age. This covers hearing, eyesight, speech, teeth, nutrition, physical and mental development, and general appearance. On this occasion the child is also asked to draw something, e.g., a person, and the doctor assesses speech development by talking with the child.

At the major hospitals, outpatient care consists of clinics for certain specialties and emergency receptions. In the Stockholm region the specialist clinics are spread out over several hospitals, so that a patient may have to alternate between these. Doctors at the district centers or hospitals refer patients to a particular specialist for an examination or treatment. In this metropolitan region one may have to wait a long time for an appointment. Moreover, as each hospital serves a particular area, it can refuse patients who belong to other areas. The major hospitals do not each have all the specialties. Consequently, a patient has to apply to a particular hospital for one disease, while for another he may have to go to a different hospital.

In addition to the general practitioners in primary health care and the specialists and general physicians at the major hospitals, the health care system in Sweden includes a small proportion of private practices. Most of these are in the large municipalities and they account for around 15 percent of total outpatient care.

The initial anxiety concerning the Kulu families, particularly their children, has died down. Still the special measures to which these families were subjected when they arrived in Tensta have had a lasting impact on Swedish health care as perceived by the women.

In investigations and programs for social services, immigrant families are equated with Swedish families with "special need." The child health personnel worked vigorously at first to get the Kulu women to bring their children for a checkup. Once the women realized that Tensta, just like Kulu, had a "small hospital," they also started to visit the health center as and when the need arose. This center, however, is not a hospital for children who are ill; it has a supervisory function and receives children who are healthy. The Kulu women saw no need for this. They were in fact allowed to bring ill children to the doctor who presided at the health center, but only when he was working a block away at the district pediatric clinic and then only by appointment, which had to be arranged by phone.

Many difficulties and a great deal of irritation arose if the women arrived at the wrong time or on a different day, when they considered that they needed help. An interpreter was available only by appointment.

When they applied for health care, the women were chiefly interested in meeting the doctor. They might bring some problem to the health care center and have to make do with the nurse, who could not prescribe medicine. Many of their visits to the health center failed to elicit the help they had expected.

The difficulties in getting health care to function for the Kulu families and their children were a disappointment for the staff at the Tensta center. For one thing, the Kulu women failed to attend at the center's hours for health checkups, vaccination programs and so on, neither did they come when called on to do so. The staff sat and waited, phoned and sometimes called in person to bring women and children to the centre. For another, when women did come without any prompting, their children were usually so ill that the staff were afraid that they would infect other children who had come for a checkup. Neither were the staff always sure what disease the Kulu children had contracted. Some symptoms were unfamiliar to them, though mostly it was a question of intestinal infections, parasites, infected ears and eczema. The staff also had difficulty communicating with the women "who understood nothing; neither could they read nor tell the time."

Ultimately the situation at the child health center become impossible and after great internal difficulties, the staff began to alter their routines. Restrictions were modified and it became possible, among other things, to bring sick as well as healthy children to the center. The whole setup was made much more flexible, besides being adapted to the needs which immigrant families had demonstrated in their ways of seeking care. Thanks to support from the Swedish Save the

Children Fund, a Turkish woman from Istanbul was employed as a contact assistant. She functioned as an interpreter and go-between, accompanied families to hospitals, called at their homes and arranged appointments, reminded them about appointments and was generally helpful. Whenever she was not at the child health center, the Kulu women did not come. Her presence meant a great deal for the subsequent work of the staff.

B. The Health Care Encounter and the Illness Process

In Sweden the ideas the women share about illness, misfortune, and death are exposed to many influences, not the least encounters with Swedish health care. This is a collective process. Everything that happens to the woman and her children in our case study below is discussed in the Kulu group and may either reinforce or weaken its ideas and attitudes. One may ask what it is that causes the health care system of the women to survive and be reinforced and what causes it to be perceived as a failure. One must also ask why Swedish health care is considered effective in some instances but not in others.

Let me briefly recount the life of the young woman, whom I have chosen to call Fadime.[17]

Fadime's Story

Fadime was born in 1960 and grew up in the town of Kulu. She has a sister and two brothers, all younger than herself. Her father died when the children were quite young, and since then her mother has managed on her own. Fadime's mother has continued to breed sheep and till the soil, chiefly as a market gardener. She is a personality in Kulu, a deviant woman who drives a horse and cart, does business and goes her own way. Men have lived with her at times but she has not remarried. In recent years the two sons have taken over some of the farming but one still sees the mother at the reins on the dusty roads around Kulu.

As the eldest child, Fadime had to manage the youngsters and do housework from a very early age. Her mother expected her at the same time as a paternal aunt who was pregnant, and the two women had planned that their children, who turned out to be a boy and a girl, would marry. Fadime accordingly grew up in the knowledge that her cousin was to be her husband. This did not happen, however, because Fadime's life changed in many respects after the death of her father. Fadime's mother refused to submit to her mother-in-law and the relationship broke down. The cousin subsequently married another young woman; Fadime's mother had other plans for her daughter.

When Fadime reached puberty she stayed for some months with a maternal aunt in Ankara. There she was attracted by clothes and makeup and wore what was fashionable in the city. She was 13 years of age and caused a stir when she returned to Kulu. After becoming interested in a young man, she asked her mother's permission to marry him. The mother did what she could to comply with her daughter's wish. About a year passed before the wedding could be arranged. Her future family had already migrated to Sweden and after the wedding she started her life as a *gelin* in Tensta.

The father-in-law had been against the marriage from the start on account of the reputation of Fadime's family in Kulu, but the son was so insistent that in the end he gave way.

Fadime arrived in Tensta in 1974 and had lived there for just over four years when my field work started. As a young *gelin* she ranked lowest in her new family. She did whatever domestic chores she was told to do and continued to function as a daughter, albeit in a household of strangers. When Fadime joined the household it consisted of her parents-in-law and their five sons, plus the eldest son's wife and small daughter. The youngest son was only 5 years old and two of the others were of school age.

During the day there was no one at home. The father-in-law worked as a dishwasher at a restaurant in Stockholm, accompanied by the eldest son when there was a lot to do. Fadime's husband tended the paths and flowers in a churchyard outside Stockholm in the mornings and worked at a pizzeria in the evenings; he came home after Fadime had gone to bed and left before she got up. Fadime's sister-in-law had a job as a nursing aide at a Stockholm hospital where she had worked ever since her arrival in Sweden.

Fadime became pregnant quite soon and gave birth to a son after barely a year in Sweden. To start with she stayed at home, doing the housework and minding the children. For a year after the birth of her son she received the maternity allowance, which she handed over to her father-in-law. It astonished her that one could earn money without doing anything. With the birth of her son, things started to change for Fadime. The baby was her parents-in-law's first grandson; they were proud and looked after the boy as they saw fit. But the baby also led to growing tension between the two daughters-in-law.

Fadime's sister-in-law is the daughter of a large, respected landowner in Kulu. Many members of her father's family have migrated to Sweden and she has spent a lot of time with them right from the start. She maligned Fadime to her parents-in-law as well as among her relatives and friends.

When the baby was one year old, the father-in-law considered that Fadime should go out to work in order to bring in money. One of his brothers arranged a job for her at a hotel in Stockholm where the brother washed dishes and other women from Kulu worked as cleaners.

In Fadime's words:

> When I arrived at the hotel we started by cleaning the rooms and toilets. We had to make the beds with clean sheets, remove all the dirty ones and clean baths and toilets which the people had used. I vomited throughout the first week. But then it got better.

Fadime handed everything she earned to her father-in-law, who managed the household finances and gave his wife the money that could be used to buy food, etc.

When Fadime had been in Sweden for just over two years her husband returned to Turkey for 21 months of military service. Fadime's second pregnancy had started; she continued to work but developed back trouble, whereupon a Swedish doctor sick-listed her for the last four months of the pregnancy. She stayed at home to look after the family's three small children while her mother-in-law worked as a school cleaner in the afternoons. The three children were the youngest son of the mother-in-law, Fadime's son, and her sister-in-law's daughter.

Fadime felt unwell during the pregnancy; she disliked being alone during the day and felt threatened, uneasy. When her time came she was very frightened and it seemed to her that something was wrong with everything to do with her delivery. Although she got a second son, it did not make her at all happy. She found the baby small and thin, too weak to suck her milk and a constant fretter. For her stay at the maternity clinic she had taken a copy of the Koran, her *nazarlık,* a small scissors, and one of her husband's pullovers. When the lights were turned out at night she was frightened and lit her bedside lamp, at which the other women in the room complained. Fadime was convinced that she saw *alkarısı* outside the window; she felt hot and could not breath normally. She lay awake in fear the whole night. When her baby was brought in by the nurse in the morning he had scratches on his face, so she knew that *alkarısı* had attacked him, too. She decided to go home immediately.

The doctor at the clinic said that she had a slight fever and would not be allowed home until it had subsided. She then phoned her mother-in-law to get the family to fetch her. She related that *alkarısı* had been there, that the room had to be in darkness at night and she did not dare to keep the Koran under her pillow when the staff came round to make the beds. She was quite certain that she would get *albasması* if they did not fetch her so that she could obtain *kırklama* (a ritual bath) for herself and the baby.

The father-in-law came to fetch Fadime, accompanied by his wife. This caused a commotion because the baby had not been examined by a pediatrician and could not be discharged before it was clear that everything was in order. The doctor informed the father-in-law that, with the aid of an interpreter, the staff would talk with Fadime and calm her down; he explained that she had a slight temperature, possibly due to milk congestion, and would definitely get best care and rest at the hospital. The father-in-law still considered that she should return home and would be cared for better there. The doctor then allowed Fadime to leave, alone and at her own risk, but the baby had to stay at least until the following day to be examined.

Fadime was in despair at having to leave her son behind but was too frightened to stay on at the hospital. Safety home, she received *kırklama* from her mother-in-law and prepared for her son's return the following day. All that night Fadime thought she saw *alkarısı;* her mother-in-law and sister-in-law sat by her in turns. The sister-in-law had a patrilinear relative who had seen *alkarısı* outside Kulu one night and managed to grasp her long hair, whereupon she had promised never to strike a member of his family. As the sister-in-law now belonged to her husband's family, however, she was less confident and felt frightened, too. Many women in Kulu had died of *albasması.*

Next morning the father-in-law went back to the clinic to fetch his grandson. The doctor repeated that the baby would be discharged at the father-in-law's risk and that a nurse would call as soon as possible to lend a hand.

Fadime considered that all was not well with her baby boy. She was sure that *nazar* had struck while he was on his own. She felt that he was never like her other son. For the first few months he would not eat in spite of all her efforts. He was thin and listless. The nurse from the child health center fetched Fadime and her baby and took them to see the doctor; he found the boy thin and suggested that Fadime should give him a little food more often rather than everything at once.

Fadime continued to believe that her boy had been struck by *nazar.* She did not allow any stranger to see him and kept him indoors. Her mother sent a *muska* in an envelope from Kulu. For five months after the boy's birth, the father-in-law stayed at home on account of protracted headaches that were so severe that he could not see. He lay in the living room most of the time and was not to be disturbed. Fadime supplied him with food and tea and kept the youngsters out of the way. When he occasionally left the flat, Fadime was able to smoke, watch television or listen to a tape of Turkish music that she had received from Kulu. During this period she never left the flat.

Fadime and her mother-in-law suspected quite soon that the baby was suffering from *kurbağacık.* His fontanel was depressed and pulsated, there were small white lumps on the roof of his mouth and a dark streak on his back, all of which indicated that it must be *kurbağacık.* He seemed to get smaller and smaller, had continual diarrhea, and was tired and listless, eating hardly anything. Several relatives who saw the boy agreed that it must be *kurbağacık.* The illness exists only in Kulu and has never been heard of by people who have not lived in that district. The women say that it can be fatal and that children can be injured for life. Only certain *ocaks* that have specialized in the illness can cure it. This cannot be done by doctors in Kulu, Konya, or Ankara, nor by Swedish doctors, who do not know what it is.

The father-in-law decided to take his grandson and Fadime back to Kulu, to get *kurbağacık* treated at Kuşhisar. Meanwhile the nurse from the child health center called again and asked Fadime to bring her four-year-old for a checkup. An appointment was arranged and the nurse phoned in the morning to remind her. Fadime took both her children to the center, where she encountered the doctor.

Returning from the center, Fadime was distressed and frightened. She could not forget the blue eyes and fair hair of the nurse or the latter's admiration of her son. Fadime is fearful of *nazar;* the nurse did not know that she ought to have said *maşallah.* Having attached several *nazarlık* to the child, she waited for her mother-in-law.

When the mother-in-law came home, Fadime showed her paper from the doctor and related that he told her to take the baby to a hospital. The mother-in-law replied that her husband must decide but added that there was certainly no point in going to see a Swedish doctor who did not know what is wrong with the boy; in any event, they cannot help him in Sweden.

A couple of days later the father-in-law left for Kulu with Fadime and her son. There they turned immediately to the woman who is *ocak* and a specialist in incisions for *kurbağacık.* The woman held the boy's head, made small incisions round the fontanel, placed chicken liver on them and bandaged the head. When she removed the bandage after a time, the fontanel was no longer depressed. Fadime could see for herself that the treatment had been effective and driven *kurbağacık* out of her son. She felt happy and grateful to the *ocak* and resolved to bring gifts next time she visits Kulu. The boy has also received a *muska.*

Fadime spent no more than a week in Kulu, where she looked after her father-in-law in his house. She managed to visit her mother once only and as her father-in-law was present, there was little she could say. Back in Tensta, Fadime soon found that the baby's digestion was in very bad shape. After a short time both children got pains in their ears and cried all night. Accompanied by her brother-in-law, Fadime took them to the emergency clinic at a hospital in Stockholm; penicillin and nose drops were prescribed and Fadime obtained them at the pharmacy. The elder boy took his medicine but the baby refused and Fadime did not want to force him, particularly as the medicine would not have any effect since a power was preventing him from getting well. She had to get rid of the evil power first but did not know what to do because the *muska* did not seem to be potent for more than a few days or weeks at a time.

The elder boy recovered but the little one deteriorated and the day came when he could not be aroused. This frightened Fadime, who was alone at home with all the children. With the baby wrapped in a blanket, she took the underground to a hospital in Stockholm, leaving the other children behind. At the hospital the doctor told her they had to keep the baby for some days to give him nutrition and fluid. They placed him in a bed and attached tubes to his body. Fadime returned to the other children and waited, frightened and unhappy, for her mother-in-law, to whom she said that she wanted to take the boy back to Kulu. He still had *kurbağcık* and would no doubt have to be treated again. She also thought there was something else as well this time. She believed that the power of the *muska* has diminished, so that the boy needs a new one.

After a week the father-in-law fetched the boy from the hospital, where the doctor said that he had lost fluid, seemed to be undernourished and must have had diarrhea for a long time. Back at the flat the boy was calm and seemed content but Fadime did not think he was any better. The mother-in-law and sister-in-law both consider that he was much better than he had been for a long time but Fadime did not see it that way. She referred all the time to his skinniness and apathy. She wanted him to get well so that she could leave him by day and go back to work.

The holiday season came round and the father-in-law made the journey to Kulu, taking Fadime and his grandson with him. Fadime had the boy treated again by the *ocak* and found him much better afterwards. Having spent the summer in Kulu, she returned to Tensta, where the boy became worse.

This procedure was repeated a third time in the two years during which I followed the family. Fadime made the trip to Kulu again after she and her husband had separated from his parents. On no occasion has she considered that Swedish doctors or visits to hospital have helped her boy. She believes that he will die and that nothing helps. She interprets his symptoms differently from time to time but always in terms of an evil power, *nazar* or *büyü*.

Fadime's dream is to earn a lot of money. She wants to learn how to drive a car and then drive to Kulu to show everyone there how successful she has been in Sweden. Without telling anyone she has managed to save some money, which she keeps in the sewing machine, to which she has the only key. When someone she trusts travels to Kulu, they take the money to her mother, who sets it aside for her. Fadime wants to buy gifts for *ocak* and *hcca* with some of it. Her plans for the future amount to having plenty of money.

Originally everyone in Fadime's new family had intended to invest in Kulu and ultimately move back to a good life there. According to her father-in-law, this could only be done if they all worked hard and stuck together. They had to save together; he would look after the money and invest it.

The sons, however, grew reluctant to hand over everything they earned to their father; they wanted to set aside some of it for themselves. The outcome was that the family split up. Each of the two eldest sons moved into a separate flat in Tensta. The separation was tumultuous and for Fadime the move changed a great deal. If she went back to work there would be no one to look after the children, which would mean leaving them at a day nursery. This she does not want to do; it costs too much and one cannot tell what will happen to the children. Making ends meet is more difficult, moreover, when there is only one pay packet to cover the rent and other expenses.

Fadime and her husband incurred debts on the television and stero equipment that they are buying by installment. They discovered that all the money they earn was required for their needs in Tensta; saving is out of the question. At times Fadime has to apply for social welfare assistance; she obtains a housing allowance as well as money for food and clothes.

Her father-in-law refuses to accept that his sons have left him. He cannot get over the disgrace for the family. The mother-in-law calls on the quiet to see her grandchildren, bringing food and sweetmeats and invariably crying when she leaves. The sons are no longer under pressure to earn more in order to invest in land and buildings in Kulu; after a time they both became unemployed and lived on social assistance. Fadime's sister-in-law went out to work, leaving her daughter at a day nursery. She hands her husband a little money from time to time but keeps most of what she earns and saves a little. Her intention, she says, is to make a trip to Kulu. Fadime's husband started playing cards with other Turkish men and is away at night. Sometimes he brings them home and keeps Fadime and the children awake all night. It happens that the men are accompanied by Swedish women.

When tired and angry, Fadime has occasionally shouted at her husband and been struck by him. When she was visiting a hospital where her son lay, the doctor and nurses noticed she had a black eye. They informed the district medical officer, who sent a nurse to call on her. Staff from the social service center have also visited Fadime and all are agreed that she should get a divorce. But Fadime does not see this as a solution; for her there is nothing remarkable in all that has happened.

The chief difficulty with Sweden for Fadime is that the children are not well and she cannot get the care and assistance that she wants when they are ill. Several of her Turkish friends consider, on the contrary, that children are better off in Tensta than in Kulu, whereas they themselves are worse off. In Kulu they did not experience all the headaches and stomach pains that trouble them now.

Fadime relies entirely on the stock of knowledge that the Kulu group possesses about illness and health care. When something happens she turns first to her mother-in-law. Since she and her husband moved into a flat of their own, Fadime has borrowed money for a trip to Kulu not only to visit an *ocak* on behalf of her son but also to get a "blood injection"[18] for herself from a private practitioner in Konya. She has not yet found any indication that Swedish doctors are any better than the healers on whom she relies. Should anything happen to her or the children, she would try to return to Kulu.

Fadime's Son: The View of the Kulu Women

For Fadime the first sign of her baby's ill-health is that he will not eat. As long as a person copes with normal functions and meets the sex- and age-related expectations of those around him, he is regarded as healthy. For the Kulu women, illness is equivalent to being incapable of performing daily tasks, which consist in Kulu of keeping the house clean, sewing clothes, carrying water, preparing food, minding young children, and so on.

Illness interferes above all with everyday actions and functions, and it is such deficiencies that reveal its presence to other people. At no time during my field work in Kulu and Tensta did I hear a Kulu woman describe illness in terms of a changed appearance. Phrases that are common among towndwellers in Sweden—"How pale you are, are you sick?", "I can see you're not well, your eyes are glazed", "You do look tired!", "You don't look well, what's the matter, are you ill?"—do not occur among the Kulu women.

The point at which an adult gives in to pain and discomfort varies, individually as well as culturally. In the case of infants, the point is discerned by the group around the child in the light of symptoms as a kind of language. It is in early childhood that cultural expressions are acquired for perceptions of the body and its reactions. This occurs via reactions in the adult world [12:159–184].

In our case, several members of the family as well as relatives and friends from Kulu considered that the baby boy was too skinny. In Kulu a thin person is said to have less chance of surviving. A plump child is a healthy child, besides indicating that one is capable of feeding it properly. It is for this reason that formula feeds are all the rage for infants from Kulu—unlike breast-feeding, the women can see how much a baby eats. The Swedish doctor holds that the women often overdo formula feeds because he considers that too much fat is just as harmful for an infant as too little. This makes no impression on the Kulu women, who proudly show off their fat babies to each other and to doctors and nurses. Weighing children has become a popular pastime.

The symptoms of the skinny baby are interpreted by the Kulu women as an illness. Fadime and her mother-in-law identify the illness as *kurbağacık* but this does not meet with general agreement. Some women are more inclined to see the symptoms as evidence that Fadime, like her own parent, is no good as a mother and lacks the ability to protect her child.

Knowing what is wrong with her son, Fadime is unmoved by this slander. No blame attaches to her since she attributes the cause to powers over which she has no control. One woman believes that the baby has been bewitched out of envy by the sonless sister-in-law. Others are convinced that the illness is in fact *kurbağacık* and advise the family to have the boy treated in Kulu.

Most of the Kulu women who visit Fadime at this time are quite sure that the boy has been exposed to *nazar* and their comments are interlaced with *maşallahs*. They are most upset that Fadime left her newborn baby unprotected at the Swedish hospital; this was dangerous because people there do and say things without thinking. The women also criticize Fadime's family for not compelling the hospital staff to hand over her baby. The infant is hers, not theirs. How can they hold on to other's people's children at a hospital for no reason?

> In Sweden they decide far too much about other people's children. If we from Kulu couldn't take care of our children, we wouldn't get any, We get children because we should and want to have them. God sees to it that we get them.

The older women consider that they know better than Swedes how to take care of children. It is mostly the danger of *nazar* that some of them have in mind.

At the hospital they harm the children with their admiring looks and words. They are forever saying out loud that the children are so splendid and grand without knowing how to protect them from *nazar*.

Fadime said on one occasion:

The Swedish doctor at the hospital is not what a doctor should be. He asks about so much that he ought to know already; he's the doctor, not me. When he believes children are ill he doesn't help but thinks that other doctors elsewhere should take of them. When one then goes to other doctors, they just take blood, urine samples, and photographs of the child. After that you still have to wait a long time before they can tell which medicine to take. Sometimes they even say that the illness will dissapear by itself. If *ocak* and other doctors in Kulu were not prepared to treat sick children and did not provide medicine, many more children would die in winter. Treatment is the only thing that helps against illness. *Muska* and medicine.

Some Kulu women see the illness as something that children get in Sweden. They believe it to be Sweden's fault that children are sick from birth. They come across children with evident defects such as the lack of an arm or leg, and children who are blind or dumb. One woman points out that such children are not to be seen in Kulu.

Children born in Sweden are of a poorer quality than those born in Kulu. There God takes those that cannot live like ordinary children. In Sweden children are not allowed to die. They even oppose God.

Other women believe that the boy got worse in Kulu. According to them, it is normal to be ill in Turkey when one lives in Sweden.

Young children get ill in Kulu because it's so hot there. The sun is strong in summer and the smoke from the fire makes them ill in winter. It suffocates small children that are not used to smoke.

In Sweden they use medicine to make fruit and grain grow well. This can be dangerous for children who are used to food made from plants that have had a lot of sunshine. When children come to Sweden they get used to weaker food; that is not good. Then the food in Kulu makes them ill. In Sweden they say that we are ill because it is dirty in Turkey. That's not true. It's Sweden that is no good for women like us. We get ill here.

Swedish doctors believe that *kurbağacık* is due to diarrhea. They are wrong. You can tell when they treat diarrhea in their way; *kurbağacık* does not go away.

A child never gets over *kubağacık;* it will be ill for the rest of its life. We don't know what it comes from except that *nazar* may be involved.

Most of the people in the personal sector of Fadime's health care system consider that the boy ought to be taken to an *ocak* in Kulu. Although opinions differ about the exact nature of the illness and its cause, they are unanimous that this is a case for *ocak*.

Certain factors tend to reinforce Fadime's perceptions in these respects. Signs that the illness *kurbağacık* is being cured materialize as expected, while other symptoms such as diarrhea are taken to indicate that, under the influence of *nazar,* the child has been struck by a different illness.

Fadime is never at a loss to explain failures on the part of her health care system that she has been familiar with since childhood. With the combination of explanations employed by her, unexpected effects of a folk treatment are attributed not only to difficulties in repelling *nazar* but also to the ultimate outcome of an illness being in the hands of God. It is not the case that her actions invariably produce the intended result but that she feels she has done the right thing, even though it does not always work. Unforseen consequences can be explained when they occur. When it comes to health care in the Swedish system, Fadime has no such explanations.

The illness *kurbağacık* confirms for Fadime that she and her family are pursued by evil powers. She uses the illness to account for several features of her life. The illness process of her son involves something of a breach with the social network and her normal roles in the community. At the same time it helps to organize her life in such a way that she can explain—to herself and others—why she has not managed to achieve what she expected to do in Sweden.

Fadime's Son: The View of the Swedish Doctors

The doctor believes at first that the baby has meningitis and is therefore insistent about hospital care without delay. He also notes that the baby had diarrhea and is very weak. The symptoms may represent some dehydration but the doctor cannot tell for certain. Nothing can be established definitely until the examinations that are necessary for a diagnosis have been made at a hospital. The doctor never doubts that the boy has a disease.

According to the doctor, it is chiefly the mother who is responsible for her son's condition.

> She is too young and immature and has to look after too many children during the day. She is, quite simply, unsuited to look after small children; she is just a child herself. She never takes the children out and somehow lets them get on as best they can. She has come to the child health center several times with various children and has always seemed inaccessible and uninterested, almost timid.

The nurse who calls on Fadime provides the doctor with further information. His opinion about the causes of the boy's condition is strengthened by her reports. During her visits Fadime had smoked and read magazines while the children ran about and carried the baby. The other children had been allowed to hug and kiss the little boy even when they had a cold and appeared diseased. It seemed to the nurse that Fadime had a poor social situation. Her children received no stimulation and were left on their own too much. The nurse noted that the children were not undressed at night and had no toys, while the baby had no bath or bed of its own. She describes the situation as "real destitution."

From the medical angle the doctor and his colleague at the hospital consider that the boy is not getting the care he needs, particularly for infections. He needs to be fed a more varied diet to suit a child of that age, and be treated very patiently. Regulated mealtimes would also be desirable. The doctors believe that medically there is nothing fundamentally wrong, it is simply that the boy never recovers properly from one infection before he contracts a new one. All that is really wrong is the boy's management. Steps should be taken to get him into a Swedish day nursery, where he would receive the care he needs.

The doctors are very dubious about the trips to Kulu. A child born in Tensta is less able to stand up to the bacterial flora, the infectious diseases, and the parasites there. A child that is in poor condition should definitely not make the trip. Infant mortality is high in the Kulu district and the doctors in Tensta are in favor of recommending that some mothers leave their infants in Sweden while they holiday in Kulu. It has happened that children who accompanied their parents to Kulu died there.

The doctors do not believe that the magicians and healers in Kulu can do anything in a case like Fadime's son. At most it would be a matter of suggestion—Fadime feels better herself because she believes the treatment has helped the boy; this gives her a more positive attitude to the boy and she perceives him as better. Methods such as those employed by the healer in this case can only cause the skin around the fontanel to swell, giving it a flatter appearance.

Some of the methods employed by the women are harmless, according to the doctors, but others are dangerous and must be stopped as far as possible by informing and educating those concerned. It is quite in order that the women should return to their native country and obtain talismans if they believe in these. One has to intervene, however, when they are told not to give children with diarrhea liquid food because what comes out is already runny.

Hygiene is also a problem according to the doctors. Many cases of disease could no doubt be avoided if only the women would try to be meticulously hygienic, boiling water for formula feeds and peeling fruit and vegetables for the children.

C. Illness Beliefs in Continuity and Change

The Kulu women's stock of medical knowledge is founded, as I mentioned earlier, on a conviction that illness in various guises will enter the body like wind or smoke if a person lacks the power to resist. An illness cannot arise inside the body or exist there from the start; it comes from outside and is expelled with the aid of medicines and treatments. A person cannot be responsible for being struck but may be to blame when others succumb.

The women believe that all illness can be cured, provided one gets the right medicines and uses specialists and the correct methods. An illness may be difficult to eliminate not so much on account of faulty treatments as because the evil power makes the patient so weak that the medicine is not effective. The struggle between these powers determines how soon an illness can be driven out of the body. It is partly for this reason that the effectiveness of their treatments is confirmed, since unsuccessful as well as successful cures can be related to the persistence or otherwise of evil powers. Similarly the effectiveness of Swedish health care can be disregarded and explained away.

Treatment that is purely technical is regarded as most effective when one can see what happens to the symptom, i.e., the illness. When the *ocak* performs *kurbağacık* on the boy with a depressed fontarel, Fadime can see that the illness is removed. The treatment provided by Swedish doctors is not always as direct and visible. Two kind of effectiveness are involved here [cf. 49]. One refers to the removal of an observable illness/symptom while a treatment that is biomedically effective may have no direct visible impact on the illness but produce such a reaction after a time by affecting the disease.

The treatment that Kulu women opt for depends to a large extent on a variety of circumstances, not least when they travel between Tensta and Kulu. Several women have begun to wonder why their children are so ill in Kulu during the summer; when they return to Tensta, the children are sometimes taken to a hospital in Stockholm for treatment. Some women have even started to ask themselves why the children get well after a time at the Swedish hospital, whereas treatments in Kulu failed to cure them while they were there. There must be some effective method or medicine that exists in Sweden but not in Turkey.

At the same time there are women who say that the young children are struck by *nazar* when they arrive in Kulu. This exposes them to illnesses such as diarrhea, vomiting, and rashes, or a running nose and ears with a high temperature. In Kulu there are many relatives who have not seen the youngsters for a year; they admire them and show how proud they are, whereupon *nazar* strikes. The children get a *muska* but this may not act at once and perhaps not until they have returned to Sweden. By the time they are admitted to the Swedish hospital the *muska* has removed the evil power and the medicine can then do its work. At that stage Turkish medicines might have been equally effective.

Fadime does not feel that her boy gets worse in Kulu and better in Sweden. Other women point out that he was worse when he got back from Kulu and that after a while he became so ill that he had to be taken to hospital. These women are uncertain, however, whether Swedish doctors can in fact cure children who have fallen ill in Kulu. Some women are becoming reluctant to take their children to Kulu in the summer because they get so ill there.

As confidence grows in the methods and medicines provided by the Swedish doctor, he tries to teach ways of keeping the children healthy in Kulu. This, however, does not always help. His advice does not appear credible to women whose children still fall ill after their bottle has been filled with boiled water (but then dropped onto the ground) or after they have eaten peeled fruit (on which flies have roamed). Neither can they believe what he says about a cold clearing up by itself in a day or two when they travel to Kulu the next day and the child becomes much worse there.

In this process of change, involving an alternation between two very different environments, the perceived effectiveness of health care treatments is a relative, situational matter. New ways of explaining specific events are tested continuously. The ongoing adjustment of the Kulu women does not necessarily cause them to reject beliefs in customary treatments in order to strengthen a belief in other treatments. They use both and perhaps gradually favor the new treatment more and more until they forget the earlier method. But this presupposes that they believe they are doing the right thing. For people in general the causes of sickness as perceived by the Kulu women and the Swedish doctor respectively are a matter of belief. The bacteria theory and the *nazar* theory are both constructed on a phenomenon that is invisible to ordinary people, but they help those who believe in them organize their specific experiences of sickness.[19]

If the Kulu women are to alter their appraisal of Swedish health care and Swedish doctors, they must experience their treatments as effective. Reality, however, not least the trips to Kulu, often suggests that the treatments are ineffective. One woman expresses her conception as follows:

> Microbes (the word that these women use when referring, among other things, to bacteria) get onto people and give diarrhea. You have to get medicine against microbes. One cannot protect oneself against microbes. One cannot protect oneself against microbes as one can against *nazar*. But microbes are easier to cure than *nazar*. You can get rid of microbes as long as get the right medicine. Injections are good, too. But it depends on the doctor. You need a good doctor who knows that medicine is needed against all kinds of microbes.
>
> When our children return from Kulu and are ill I believe it may be microbes but t is also *nazar* and a doctor at a Swedish hospital can never cure that He talks only about microbes, never about *nazar*. He knows nothing about *nazar*.

This illustrates the change that has occurred among the Kulu women. They have started to regard bacteria in the same way as, for instance, cold and heat. There is a phenomenon of which this woman was previously unaware that can make people ill and which may be difficult to ward off in, for instance, Kulu. She believes Swedish doctors are able to cure microbes and therefore can help the children when they return to Tensta. But she knows that *nazar* is involved, too, and can therefore explain why a child may fail to get well after treatment at a Swedish hospital. Even though microbes are a specialty for Swedish health care, the treatment may be unsuccessful on account of *nazar*. In this case she does not conclude that the Swedish doctor is a failure—the process of adjustment has already started in that this woman has transferred some of her loyalty to the potential of Swedish health care. As far as microbes are concerned, she believes in the methods practiced by the Swedish doctor.

As a consequence of her explanations, the woman has also started to distinguish between types of illness that can be cured by the folk and scientific sectors in Kulu and those that can be cured in Sweden. She is still convinced that Swedish doctors cannot eliminate *nazar* or cure specific illnesses that are caused directly by *cins* or *büyü*.

V. CONCLUSION

This brings us finally to the question of which particular factors are of importance for an adjustment between the Kulu women and Swedish health care. As a prelude to summarizing the principal theme of this study I should like to recount a specific experience.

While staying with a family in Kulu, I had an acute illness. The symptoms— watery feces and a high temperature—suggested types of disease in these parts of the world that could have serious consequences: salmonella, cholera, dysentery. My spontaneous reaction was to stay in bed, drink boiled water, eat boiled rice, and if possible get in touch with a doctor.

I told my hosts that I was ill, mentioning the temperature and diarrhea. The oldest woman in the family took my hands in hers, brought them to her mouth, brushed my forehead with her mouth and then said with a smile that I was not particularly hot. As to my watery feces, they all had that quite often in the heat of summer. She asked her daughter-in-law to prepare me some *ayran*, i.e. yogurt diluted with water and salted.

That day we were to visit a relative who lives in a village twenty to thirty miles away. The older woman had clearly indicated that she did not perceive my illness—my experience of and expressions for bodily discomfort—as illness as she knew it, at least not a serious form. Meanwhile, I was on the verge of panicking. I had little chance of finding a doctor without the family's help. I had no telephone, form of transport, or information about who to ask for. What I did was to lie down on the mattress that served as my bed at night and await further reactions.

It upset the women that I would not get up. A woman remains in bed during the day only when she has just given birth or is about to die. The elder woman came and sat beside me on the floor, while her grandchildren crawled around, hugging me and playing. She presented me with a small object that I did not recognize at first. So she fetched a garlic and pulled off all the cloves until only the innermost one was left in her hand; that was what she had given me. She said I should wear it, somewhere under my clothes, against *nazar*.

Not knowing whether my disorder was infectious, I was uneasy about having the children so close. The only way of resolving the situation was to get up, dress and accompany this enthusiastic family to their relatives in the distant village. No one mentioned my condition in my presence, even through I had to withdraw time and again to use the privy in a corner of the garden.

When we got back that evening I was at the end of my tether. The fever had risen to 40°C and my mouth was so dry I could hardly speak. Before I could fall asleep the young woman came in with a dish of rice, over which a large lump of butter had started to melt.

After some days like this with no real improvement, except that the fever was on the way down, I decided to return home. Having my sick role ignored was more than I could cope with.

I talked to the young man of the house and he contacted a relative who owned a taxi. The two of them took me to Ankara after I had said good-bye to the women, who could not understand why I had to leave. They wondered what was wrong: perhaps I did not like the district, did not get on with them, and so on.

Safely back in Stockholm, I got in touch with a doctor, who recommended specialist care and various tests. Until the results were known, no doctors could identify the disorder. After a while I began to feel better and things slowly returned to normal. I was informed that I had a parasitic infection known as guardiasis. The intestinal parasite in question is very common among children and adults in Kulu. People can carry it all their lives without developing symptoms. Only the acute condition is associated with discomfort. Everyone in Kulu is no doubt a carrier without even being aware of it.

Just when I was beginning to feel better, the time came to start a course of medicine to get rid of the parasites. This cure, which lasted around ten days, produced adverse reactions and was most unpleasant. Nausea, giddiness, and disturbed sleep were what I associated with the treatment of my disease. My illness had already disappeared, while the medication generated new symptoms. Having complete faith in both the diagnosis and the medical treatment, I readily put up with the discomfort.

This example illustrates the difficulty of changing ideas about illness. It also indicates, that, provided one waits long enough, almost any method will "cure" an illness such as mine. The example shows, moreover, that people base their actions on what they believe in, whether this happens to be the evil eye, bacteria, or, as in this case, parasites. The person who is ill cannot know, in the sense of being able to see, that it is one cause rather than the other. One has to have confidence in the specialist. Given this confidence, faith in the specialist will be reinforced in that he does something. If this something has unpleasant consequences, these are explained in the context of the specialist's therapeutic logic.

Getting the feeling of being ill confirmed makes one favorably disposed to treatment, regardless of any discomfort that ensues from this. Without such confirmation from those around one, the situation becomes intolerable.

When we are ill, the women from Kulu and I react in the same way—we look for understanding and assistance. Without confirmation and forms of help in which we believe, we cannot cope. We are prepared to go to almost any length to obtain them. In neither case is it a question of insufficient knowledge or the force of habit. When threatened with chaos, we think and act with a view to making life predictable and orderly. When subjected to unaccustomed methods, we need to have tangible evidence of their effectiveness to regard them as an alternative next time we are ill with the same symptoms.

If we employ several different treatments, we have no means of distinguishing the one that is effective. We tend to favor the ones with which we are familiar. This is where the stock of knowledge and the stock of ideas in a culture help people to act "as they should." Numerous individual experiences provide support for certain theories in each health care system and turn them into general truths. In this way, personal experience that "this cured me" is converted in to the cultural thesis that "this can cure everyone."

It is by no means easy to exchange one belief for another, particularly when the general situation contains much that is new and unfamiliar. When people in this situation resort to what is familiar, clear evidence that this was inadvisable is seldom forthcoming. In the cases presented here, just as many women consider that they benefited from folk healers as from scientific medicine. On what grounds can one claim that scientific medicine is better for them?

Even if I had stayed on in Kulu, there is no reason to suppose that I would not have felt better after a time. This might have encouraged me to believe in *ayran* as a remedy for diarrhea. Recurrent experience of this process, personal as well as observed in others, might have led me to adopt this method. That is what happens with some of the Kulu women in Tensta. They stay on and resort to methods practiced by Swedish doctors. When they feel better in connection with these methods, they start believing in them.

There is no denying, moreover, that some of the methods of Swedish doctors are more effective than those used by the women. The children with grave hereditary disease would not have survived without the help of scientific specialists in Sweden. But as we have seen, the process of accepting a completely new way of interpreting illness takes a long time and can be trying. The chief reason for this is that the effectiveness of unfamiliar methods is something that has to be experienced. When this has been done, the new methods can be integrated in the common stock of knowledge. This does not imply that the methods in question are in fact effective in the scientific sense. As we have seen, it is a question of whether the person who is ill feels better. Such a feeling may be due instead to a healing process that the body achieves unaided. The healing process, moreover, may be influenced by a strong faith in the external help that is administered. Extensive research into placebo effects has provided evidence of this.

Consequently, Swedish health care practitioners must be aware that each one of us is dependent on what we believe to be the right thing to do in connection with illness. Until Swedish health care manages to convince the Kulu women that its methods are superior to those of other specialists whom these women employ, there will be no transfer of loyalty or belief. One can also ask whether such a transfer of loyalty is always necessary. Perhaps the evil-eye theory can exist in a complementary relationship with the bacteria theory. In any event, as it is hardly possible to present clear, convincing evidence that will quickly modify the Kulu women's ideas about illness, and as their morbidity is not particularly high, a slower transition generated by their day-to-day experiences would seem to be acceptable from the viewpoint of care. Meanwhile the evil-eye theory and the bacteria theory can coexist, though there will of course be cases where this coexistence is to be deplored.

As long as people strive for survival and health, they will always look for a cure that is effective in the context of their situation. As the incidence of disease among children and women from Kulu does not differ dramatically compared with Swedish women and children, it seems reasonable to presume that they are sufficiently competent to conduct their own search for this cure.

NOTES

1.   Sickness is used in this study as a comprehensive term, comprising illness as well as disease; illness refers to experiences expressed in a cultural form, disease to objective expressions whose form is necessarily scientific.

2.   Illness process refers here to the history and course of the perceived illness, not—as may be natural in a medical context—to the pathological process.

3.   The three sectors are seen here as separate cultures, each of which forms and influences the perception of sickness and health care. Kleinman [30:53] writes that, ''There are different interpretations of clinical reality reflecting different systems of meanings, norms, and power. In this sense, each of the health care system's sectors can be supposed a separate 'culture'.'' These terms have been discussed and elaborated by Kleinman [30:45–58].

4.   In particular there are the ethnographic accounts by two Turkish anthropologists: Yasa has described the villages of Hasanoğlan [46] and Sindel [47], and Kıray the community of Ereğli [27]. Apart from these studies, the best known are Stirling's reports on the villages of Sakaltutan and Elbaşi [41], which he revisited later [42]. Other ethnographic works from this period and later have been written by e.g. Makal [32], Beeley [7], Benedict [8], Magnarella [31], and Engelbrektsson [15].

5.   *Gelin* is used in the sense of bride, wife, and daughter-in-law, which indicates her divided loyalties and the demands that are placed upon her.

6.   I have experienced instance of this in Sweden, i.e., women who give birth in an ambulance on the way to hospital, or at home assisted by neighbors, because they could not bring themselves to tell a man who was at home that their time was approaching.

7.   A summary account will be found in *Paediatricus* [34:3–6].

8.   Turkish law prohibits the sale of medicines of the type which shops supply without a prescription. It is not an easy market to control, however, and the supply is governed by people's needs and demands. There are strong commercial interests behind the distribution of pharmaceuticals in general in countries like Turkey.

9.   The Koran warns one to beware of those that ''blow on knots,'' which is interpreted to signify persons who practice magic.

10.   The power of a *muska* is considered to come from contact with words from the Koran. It can be placed in water that the afflicted person then drinks, burnt so that he breathes in the smoke, and sewn into a holder that is attached inside his garments.

11.   The literal meaning of *ocak* is fireplace.

12.   When controlled immigration was introduced in 1967, it meant that persons wishing to immigrate to Sweden had to obtain a labor permit first. The controls were tightened later in the '70s

so that immigration was restricted chiefly to the children, husband/wife, and parents of persons who already resided in Sweden.

13.   Cf. the description of a bride's price, *başlık,* in Engelbrektsson [15:176–177].

14.   The goals for Swedish policy on immigrants and minorities are formulated in Bill no. 1975:26 as "equality, freedom of choice, collaboration." Treating everyone alike does not lead to the goal of equality, which often presupposes special measures to enable immigrants to utilize their rights and fulfill their obligations. Freedom of choice implies that immigrants are to have real possibilities of choosing to what extent they wish to "become Swedish" as opposed to preserving their own linguistic and cultural identity. Collaboration implies that, besides being the object of presumably well-intentioned measures by the Swedish community, immigrants are to be in a position to influence the society in which they live.

15.   In the period 1975–78, a total of 33 children in Tensta were taken into custody under regulations in the Child Welfare Act (§25a, §29) concerning maltreatment and suspected maltreatment of children. Of these children, 15 were Turkish. Of the population groups in Tensta from which children were taken into custody, the Turkish was the largest. Certain cultural differences between Turkey and Sweden should also be mentioned. In a Turkish upbringing, limits to a child's behavior tend to be indicated physically rather than verbally. The age at which childhood is considered to end also differs between rural Turkey and Sweden.

Swedish authorities consider that a girl who has been married off at the age of 14 has been "maltreated" by being forced into a "child marriage." Compulsory education in Sweden lasts until the age of 16 for girls as well as boys. Below this age Swedish authorities regard any work as "child labor." Instead of attending school, many young Turkish girls spend the time at home, e.g., looking after younger brothers and sisters.

16.   The health insurance system in Sweden entitles people to be absent from work for one week without a doctor's certificate. During this week the insurance office pays them a sickness benefit to cover most of the loss of earnings. After the first week, benefits continue only if a doctor's certificate is submitted. Sickness benefits are treated as taxable income.

17.   All the names given here to Kulu women and their children are fictitious.

18.   The women are often given an injection of a red solution of vitamin B; it makes them feel well and they perceive it as a shot of blood.

19.   A similar idea is expressed by Djurfeldt and Lindberg [14:158] in their analysis of Western medicine in India: "One could say that spirits and Gods are the germs of the ordinary Indian, and that germs are the spirits and Gods of the ordinary Westerner." The discussion by Horton [24:50–71] of the relationship between traditional thought and Western science is relevant here, too.

REFERENCES

1. Abadan-Unat, N. *Turkish Workers in Europe 1960–1975: A Socio-Economic Reappraisal.* Social, Economic and Political Studies of the Middle East, 19. Seiden:Brill., 1976.
2. Acipayamli, O. "*Anadolu' da nazarla iligili bazi âdet ve Inanmalar.*" (Certain beliefs and practices regarding the evil eye in Anatolia). Ankara Universitesi Dil ve Tarih-Cografya Fakültesi Dergisi 20:1–42, 1962.
3. _____ *Turkiye' de dogumla ilgili ve âdet inanmalarin etonolojik etüdü.* (An ethnologic study of beliefs and practices regarding birth in Turkey). Atatürk Universitesi Yayinlari 15, 1974.
4. Alpay, S. *Turkar i Stockholm.* (Turks in Stockholm). Stockholm: Liber., 1980.
5. Arberry, A.I. *The Koran Interpreted.* London: Allen and Unwin, 1956.
6. Baysal, A. "Nutritional Problems of Turkish women." In *Women in Turkish Society.* N. Abadan-Unat, ed. Leiden: Brill., 1981.
   ⁊ W. *Rural Turkey: A Bibliographic introduction.* Ankara: Hacettepe University Pub-

8. Benedict, P. "Aspects of the domestic cycle in a Turkish Provincial Town." In *Mediterranean Family Structures*, J.G. Peristiani, ed. pp. 219–241. Cambridge: Cambridge University Press, 1976.

9. Björklund, U. *North to Another Country: The Formation of a Suryoyo Community in Sweden*. Stockholm Studies in Social Anthropology, 9. Stockholm: Department of Social Anthropology, University of Stockholm, 1981.

10. Boratav, N.P. "*100 Sonda Türk Folklory*." (100 questions on Turkish Folklore). Istanbul: Gerçek Yayınevi, 1973.

11. Caudill, W. "Applied Anthropology in Medicine." In *Anthropology Today*. A.L. Kroeber, ed. pp. 771–806. Chicago: University of Chicago Press, 1953.

12.d _____ "The Cultural and Interpersonal Context of Everyday Health and Illness in Japan and America." In *Asian Medical Systems*. C. Leslie, ed. pp. 159–177. Berkeley: University of California Press, 1976.

13. Cohen, P. 350 Theories of Myth. *Man* 4:337–353, 1969.

14. Djurfeldt, G. and S. Lindberg. *Pills against Poverty: A Study of the Introduction of Western Medicine in Tamil Village*. Scandinavian Institute of Asian Studies Monograph Series, No. 23. Lund: Student Litteratur and Curzon Press, 1975.

15. Engelbrektsson, U-B. *The Force of Tradition :Turkish Migrants at Home and Abroad*. Göteborg: Acta Universitatis Gothoburgensis Gothenburg Studies in Social Anthropology, 1978.

16. Evans-Pritchard, E.E. *Witchcraft, Oracles and Magic among the Azande*. London: Oxford University Press, 1937.

17. Eyuboglu, J.Z. *Anadolu Büyüleri* (Magic in Anatolia). Istanbul: Seçme Kitaplar P.K. 713, 1978.

18. Fabrega, H. and P.K. Manning. Disease, Illness and Deviant Careers. In *Theoretical Perspectives on Deviance*. R.A. Scott and J.D. Douglas, eds. New York: Basic Books, 1972.

19. Fabrega, H. "Medical Anthropology." *Biennial Review in Medical Anthropology*, 1971. B. Siegel, ed. pp. 167–229. Stanford: Stanford University Press, 1972.

20. Fabrega, H. *Disease and Social Behavior: An Interdisciplinary Perspective. Cambridge, Mass.: MIT Press, 1974.*

21. Fallers, M.C. and L.A. Fallers. "*Sex Roles in Edremit.*" In *Mediterranean Family Structures*. J.G. Peristiani, ed. Cambridge: Cambridge University Press, 1976.

22. Flores-Meiser, E. "The Hot Mouth and Evil Eye." In *The Evil Eye*. C. Maloney, ed. New York: Columbia University Press, 1976.

23. Foster, G. "The Anatomy of Envy: a Study in Symbolic Behavior." Current Anthropology, No. 13, pp. 165–202, 1972.

24. Horton, R. "African Traditional Thought and Western Science." *Africa*, Vol. 37. pp. 50–71, 1967.

25. Kagitçibaşi, C. *Women and Development in Turkey*. Istanbul: Seminar Bogaziçi University, 1980.

26. Kandiyoti, D. "*Major Issues on the Status of Women in Turkey: Approaches and Priorities.*" Seminar report, Istanbul: Bogaziçi University, 1980.

27. Kiray, M. *Eregli: Ağır Sanayiden Önce Bir Sahil Kasabasi.* (Eregli: A Preindustrial Coastal Town). Ankara: State Planning Organization, 1964.

28. _____ "The new role of mothers: changing intrafamilial relationships in a small town in Turkey." In *Mediterranean Family Structures*. J.G. Peristiani ed. Cambridge: Cambridge University Press, 1976.

29. Kleinman, A., L. Eisenberg and B. Good, "Culture, Illness and Care: Clinical lessons from anthropological and cross-cultural research." *Annals of Internal Medicine*, 88:251–258, 1978.

30. Kleinman, A. "*Patients and Healers in the Context of Culture.*" Berkeley: Univ California Press, 1980.

31. Magnarella, P.J. *Tradition and Change in a Turkish Town*. New York: Wiley, 1974.
32. Makal, M. *A Village in Anatolia*. (Bizim Köy). Wyndham Deedes, trans.) London: Vallentine, Mitchell and Co, (1950) 1954.
33. Merdol, T. Nutritional Traditions in Turkey. *Journal of Tropical Pediatrics* Vol. 27. Nr. 6, pp. 273–278, 1981.
34. Mjönes, S. and T.O. Merdol. "Förändringar i näringstillstånd och kostvanor vid migration" (Change in Nutritional status and Food habits during migration) Stockholm: *Paediatricus*, pp. 3–6, No. 1, Vol 10, 1980.
35. Pickthall, M.M. *The Meaning of the Glorious Koran: an explanatory translation*. New York: Mentor Book, New American Library of World Literature Inc., 1953.
36. *Population in Turkey*. Ankara: Hacettepe University Institute of Population Studies, 1975, 1979.
37. Reminick, R.A. "The Evil Eye Belief among the Amhara." *Ethnology* 8 No. 3, 1974.
38. Rubel, A. "The epidemiology of a folk illness: Susto in Hispanic America" *Ethnology*, 3:268–283, 1964.
39. Spooner, B. "The Evil Eye in the Middle East." In *Witchcraft Confessions and Accusations*. M. Douglas, ed. London: A.S.A. Monograph 9, 1970.
40. Stein. "Envy and the Evil Eye: An essay in the Psychological Ontogeny of Belief and Ritual." In *The Evil Eye*. C. Maloney, ed. New York: Columbia University Press, 1976.
41. Stirling, P. *Turkish Village*. London: Widenfeld and Nicolson, 1965
42. ———— "Turkish Village revisited." In *Choice and Change: Essays in Honour of Lucy Mair*. J. Cavis ed. London: LSE Monographs in Social Anthroplogy. Athlone, 1974.
43. Taşkiran, T. *Women in Turkey*. Istanbul: Redhouse Yayinevi, 1976.
44. Terris, M. Approaches to an Epidemiology of Health. *The American Journal of Public Health*, Vol. 65, No. 10, 1975.
45. Turner, V. *The Forest of Symbols*. Ithaca, New York: Cornell University Press, 1967.
46. Yasa, I. *Hasanoglan: Socioeconomic Structure of a Turkish Village*. Ankara: Yeni Matbaa. Public Administration Inst., 1957.
47. ———— *Sindel Köyünün Toplumsal ve Ekonomik Yapısı*. (The Social and Economic Structure of the Village of Sindel). Ankara: Balkanogli Mathaacılik Ltd. Sti. Public Administration Inst., 1960.
48. Yerasimos, S. *Asgelişnuşlik Sürecinde Türkiye*. (Turkey in the Process of Underdevelopment). Gözlem Yay. Books II and III., 1977.
49. Young, A. "Some Implications of Medical Beliefs and Practices for Social Anthropology." pp. 5–24. *American Anthropologist*, 78: No. 1, 1976.
50. Örnek, S.V. *Türk Halkbilimi* (Turkish Folklore) Ankara: Iş Bankası Kültür Yayınları: 181, 1977.